AMSC

266821

CW01653450

P12 £5

MF

—

-

БМ

Theory of Microeconomics

THEORY OF MICROECONOMICS

TROUT RADER

Washington University

WITHDRAWN
CITY OF LONDON LIBRARIES

ACADEMIC PRESS New York and London

WITHDRAWN
266821 A MSC
Class 330
RAD

COPYRIGHT © 1972, BY ACADEMIC PRESS, INC.
ALL RIGHTS RESERVED
NO PART OF THIS BOOK MAY BE REPRODUCED IN ANY FORM,
BY PHOTOSTAT, MICROFILM, RETRIEVAL SYSTEM, OR ANY
OTHER MEANS, WITHOUT WRITTEN PERMISSION FROM
THE PUBLISHERS.

ACADEMIC PRESS, INC.
111 Fifth Avenue, New York, New York 10003

United Kingdom Edition published by
ACADEMIC PRESS, INC. (LONDON) LTD.
24/28 Oval Road, London NW1 7DD

LIBRARY OF CONGRESS CATALOG CARD NUMBER: 78-117637

PRINTED IN THE UNITED STATES OF AMERICA

To my beautiful wife, Deanna

Contents

Preface

This book is designed to give a modern approach to traditional topics in first-year graduate microtheory. It is written with the conviction that microeconomics should be closely tied with welfare economics and theories of choice and behavior.

Whereas graduate microtheory is often a one-semester course, the present volume contains enough for two semesters, especially if the problems and exercises are carefully worked out. Hence, the book would also be useful for the study of mathematical economics, possibly in combination with material from *Theory of General Economic Equilibrium*, hereafter referred to as the companion volume.

Prerequisites are calculus, linear algebra, and intermediate economic theory. Problems are included to strengthen the reader's grasp of the economic material presented. There are exercises mainly on the mathematics of the book. Should the reader fail to solve them, he might consult a standard textbook on mathematical analysis and/or general topology.

The book is organized into four major parts: Introduction, Production, Consumption, and Trade. This is according to the traditional approach to microeconomic theory. An alternative organization of the material would be to exclude Chapter 8 on "Consumer Demand" and merge Production and Consumption into a part called Foundations to which Chapter 9 on "Exchange" woud be added. Then Chapter 8 would be grouped with Chapters 10 and 11, to constitute a part called Markets. Still other sequences of presentation might be preferred by the reader.

Chapter 1 is written to motivate the student and is not essential to that which follows. The accompanying diagram illustrates the connections between the other chapters. Arrows point the direction in which the material should be read. Dotted lines indicate material related but not absolutely required.

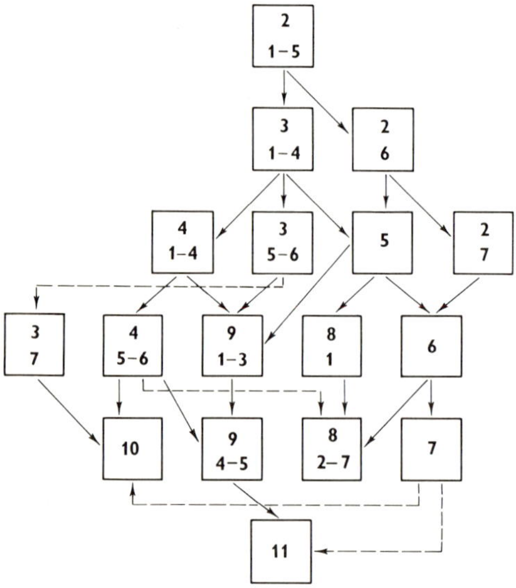

Although there are many references through the text, no pretense is made at completeness. The reader will find it advantageous to consult other books on economic theory, for example, Blaug's *Economic Theory in Retrospect*.

Acknowledgments

About half of the research for this volume and most of the preparation was supported by the National Science Foundation.

I am indebted to lectures and/or conversations with T. Bergstrom (Chapters 3–7), T. C. Koopmans (Chapters 1–7), G. Debreu (Chapters 1–6), J. Ochs (Chapters 1–5 and 8), P. van Moeseke (Chapters 1–5), W. Hildenbrand (Chapters 4 and 5), J. Chipman (Chapters 1–5), H. Sonnenschein (Chapters 4 and 5), M. Richter (Chapters 4 and 5), and L. Shapley (Chapters 5–7). I am also indebted to J. Kuhlman who suggested this project and to J. Harsanyi (Chapter 7), R. Muth (Chapter 7), H. Minsky (Chapter 8), R. Clower (Chapter 8), J. Tobin (Chapter 8), L. McKenzie (Chapter 6), H. Scarf (Chapter 4), J. Friedman (Chapters 3 and 7), L. Hurwicz (Chapter 4), T. N. Srinivasen (Chapters 3 and 4), D. McFadden (Chapter 2), J. F. Mertens (Chapter 4), J. Fei (Chapter 4), B. Grodal (Chapter 5), W. Leeman (Chapter 1), S. Kakutani (Chapter 3), J. Langier (Chapter 1), W. Hochwald (Chapter 1), and W. McMahon (Chapter 1).

Mrs. James Huddleston has contributed substantially to the manuscript by giving detailed criticism of style, organization, and content.

Several students have read parts of the manuscript and have made comments, of which J. Yawitz and L. Cardwell deserve special note.

My wife greatly helped in criticizing exposition, typing, and giving encouragement. Also, credit for typing should be given Mrs. Sharon Farley, Miss Elaine Frankel, Mrs. Sally Drda, Mrs. Vicki Ibera, Miss Heather MacKenzie, Mrs. Emma Williams, Mrs. Bess Erlich, Mrs. Pat Denault, Mrs. Linda Miskel, Miss Barbara Silverman, Miss Cathy Todd, and Mrs. Adele Reilly.

List of Notational Conventions and Basic Symbols

Capital script letters	Sets, e.g., $\mathscr{A}$
Lower case script letters	Traditional economic notations, e.g., $\mathscr{mc}$
Capital Latin letters	Matrices
Lower case Latin letters	Points, vectors, and numbers
Lower case Greek letters	Numbers

$x \in \mathscr{A}$	x is a member of $\mathscr{A}$
$x \notin \mathscr{A}$	x is not a member of $\mathscr{A}$
$\mathscr{A} \subset \mathscr{B}$	$\mathscr{A}$ is contained in $\mathscr{B}$
$\mathscr{A} \subsetneqq \mathscr{B}$	$\mathscr{A}$ is contained in but not equal to $\mathscr{B}$
$\{x \mid P\}$	The set of x satisfying proposition P
$\mathscr{A} \cup \mathscr{B}$	The set union of $\mathscr{A}$ and $\mathscr{B}$
$\mathscr{A} \cap \mathscr{B}$	The set intersection of $\mathscr{A}$ and $\mathscr{B}$
$\mathscr{B} {\sim} \mathscr{A}$	The set of points in $\mathscr{B}$ but not in $\mathscr{A}$
${\sim}\mathscr{A}$	The set of points not in $\mathscr{A}$
$\varnothing$	The empty set
$\{x\}$	The singleton set of x
$\mathscr{A} \times \mathscr{B}$	The cartesian product of $\mathscr{A}$ and $\mathscr{B}$
$P_{\mathscr{S}}(\mathscr{A})$	The projection of $\mathscr{A}$ on $\mathscr{S}$
$\bigcup_{\alpha \in \mathscr{A}} \mathscr{B}_\alpha$	The set union of $\mathscr{B}_\alpha$, α in $\mathscr{A}$

$\bigcap_{\alpha \in \mathscr{A}} \mathscr{B}_\alpha$	The set intersection of $\mathscr{B}_\alpha$, α in $\mathscr{A}$
$\bigtimes_{\alpha \in \mathscr{A}} \mathscr{B}_\alpha$	The cartesian product of $\mathscr{B}_\alpha$, α in $\mathscr{A}$
$\mathscr{R}$	A reflexive, binary relation
$\mathscr{P}$	An irreflexive binary relation
$\mathscr{I}$	An equivalence relation
$2^{\mathscr{S}}$	The set of subsets of $\mathscr{S}$
$\lim x_n$	The limit of x_n
$x_n \to x$	The limit of x_n is x
$\bar{\mathscr{A}}$	The closure of $\mathscr{A}$
Bnd $\mathscr{A}$	The boundary of $\mathscr{A}$
Int $\mathscr{A}$	The set of internal points of $\mathscr{A}$
$f(x)$	The function f evaluated at x
$f: \mathscr{X} \to \mathscr{Y}$	The function f mapping $\mathscr{X}$ into $\mathscr{Y}$
f^{-1}	The inverse correspondence for the function f
$d(x, y)$	The distance between x and y
$N_\epsilon(x)$	The ϵ neighborhood of x
$x = (x_1, \ldots, x_n)$	A row vector
x'	A column vector
$x \geqslant y$	$x_i \geqslant y_i$ for all i
$x > y$	$x_i \geqslant y_i$ for all i and for some j, $x_j > y_j$
$x \gg y$	$x_i > y_i$ for all i
(x, y)	The set of points between x and y according to the (partial) ordering $\gg$
$\langle x, y \rangle$	The line segment between and including x and y
Ω	The nonnegative orthant
$(x_\alpha, \alpha \in \mathscr{A})$	The abstract vector with coordinate index set, $\mathscr{A}$
$x_{\mathscr{I}}$	The vector with coordinates only in $\mathscr{I}$
$\sum_{\alpha \in \mathscr{A}} x_\alpha$	The sum of vectors in $\mathscr{A}$
$\lvert x \rvert$	$(\sum x_i^2)^{1/2}$
$\mathscr{A} + \mathscr{B}$	The set of all sums of pairs of elements, one in $\mathscr{A}$ and one in $\mathscr{B}$
$-\mathscr{B}$	The set of elements whose negatives are in $\mathscr{B}$
$a\mathscr{B}$	The set of elements which when divided by a are in $\mathscr{B}$
Δx	The change in x
(a_{ij})	The matrix with typical elements, a_{ij}
$\int f(x)\, dx$	The integral of f over linear measure
$\int f(x)\, d\mu$	The integral of f over measure μ
df/dx	The derivative of f with respect to x
f'	The derivative of f with respect to x
$\partial f/\partial x_i$	The partial derivative of f with respect to x_i
$(\partial f/\partial x_i)$	The vector of partial derivatives of f
inf	The greatest lower bound
sup	The least upper bound
$E(x)$	The expected value of x

Theory of Microeconomics

1

Introduction

CITY OF LONDON LIBRARIES

1

Methodology

... economics is much more difficult, much less understood, and undoubtedly in a much earlier stage of its evolution as a science than physics . . . .

John von Neumann and Oskar Morgenstern
THEORY OF GAMES AND ECONOMIC BEHAVIOR, 1944

1. Economics and Related Disciplines

The nature of a science determines its methodology. In this section, we state the definition of economics and enumerate the basic fields upon which it draws. It will be seen that economics depends on technology, psychology, physics, and even metaphysics. In the next section, several views of the importance of theory in economics are considered. Section 3 is concerned with the role of mathematics in economic theory.

To quote Adam Smith, economics is the study of the nature and causes of the wealth of nations. But the interpretation of this statement allows for much controversy. For instance, the very definitions of the phrases "nature and causes" and "wealth of nations" are open to question. In many cases, wealth can be thought of as something that brings benefit to society; such a description implies an ethical viewpoint or a value system. Although this definition is preferred by practicing economists, we will see in Section 2 that many economists want the science or the analysis of economics to be independent of value judgments.

Chapter 1 of Debreu's *Theory of Value* (1959) suggests, as a tentative definition (formalized in set theoretic terms in Section 2 of Chapter 3), that economics consists of:

(1) the specification of those states of the world that are possible (imaginable);
(2) the specification of a value system;
(3) the optimization of the value system among the various possible states of the world.

In optimization, two separate activities can be distinguished as (3a) the verification that an optimum exists, and (3b) the specification of procedures by which that optimum can be recognized, when obtained, and computed.

In the theory of the firm as presented in Chapters 4 and 10, all possible factor inputs and product outputs are surveyed for those that are technically feasible. Among these, the combination is chosen that maximizes profit.

In the theory of consumer demand, as developed in Chapters 5–8, preferences are optimized in choice among commodity bundles that satisfy a budget constraint.

The definition applies to the total economic system as well. First, information is given to consumers and firms—for example, market prices—that restricts their effective range of choice. Then consumers and firms optimize. Their choices define the range of choice for the economic system. Second, the social welfare system is specified. Third, information given to consumers and firms is adjusted to optimize with respect to that social welfare system.

Economists normally presume that the purpose of economic activities is to satisfy consumers, although some hold that military power is an important end of economic progress. In either case it follows that if there were no limitations on the available quantities of goods and services, there would be no particular social need for the study of economics. Of course, this abundance does not correspond to experience; rather, scarcity is the common element in economic affairs. The historical development of economics was based on the study of the allocation of scarce resources among alternative uses. (The relationship between the two subjects is discussed in Section 2 of Chapter 3.)

In order to establish our definition of economics, we must show, first, that all conceivable economic problems come under such a definition, and second, that any information about cases under it has some economic application. The former seems quite impossible; only a negative result would ever definitely settle the question, since ultimately we are always ignorant, in some respect or degree, about any empirical subject. For example, in physics, Einstein's reduction of mechanics to the study of invariants under certain coordinate transformations always remains a tentative characterization (subject to new experimental discoveries). So it is with economics. As to our second requirement, however, we could argue that anything known (at least in general) about problems (1), (2), and (3) should be of at least passing interest to the economic theorist. In effect, the variety among consumers, producers, and plausible economic systems is great enough that information about them is automatically of economic interest.

Parts of the definition of economics, such as the specification of a value system, help delineate the fields of enquiry on which economics draws. The determination of states of the world depends on physics and biology. For example, if the analysis of states of the world includes distinctions as to time and space, the analysis will differ according to whether the analyst is in a Cartesian universe or in a relativistic universe. If the analysis includes production processes, the existence and future possibility of engineering methods will affect the construction of the set of states in the world, as will the prospective efforts of scientists and engineers toward creating new knowledge and techniques.

It does not necessarily follow that the economist must know a great deal about technology. Economists ordinarily assume that the spectrum of techniques used in the production of different goods is so varied that it can be studied only for general properties. A few "self-evident" axioms that make only weak statements about the present and future state of technology are thought sufficient for a specific study. Although some examples of particular technologies will be considered in Chapter 4, no attempt is made to define precise technological bounds on the set of states of the world based on the present state of scientific knowledge. (Quite possibly, more explicit technical information could lead to significant economic results.)

In specifying the value judgments, we usually deal with microeconomic units such as producers and consumers. Their preferences, especially those of consumers, must turn on psychological factors. Again, the economist may develop a large body of knowledge without going into detailed psychological analysis, by making only the most obvious assumptions about behavior. Psychological behavior may be sufficiently varied that its more restrictive categories, which would be the subject of study in the science of psychology, would not give rise to universally applicable economic knowledge.

The optimization of values subject to constraints might be only a technical exercise in the mathematical theory and logical structure of general systems. *More often economists are interested in making judgments about an optimal system of economic organization, rather than in studying for study's sake or for the sake of understanding the empirical world.* In choosing these standards of optimality certain ethical judgments are made whose justification presumably lies in some kind of systematic metaphysics or ethical philosophy. Generally speaking the judgments made are versions of consumer sovereignty. On the one hand, the economist may adopt a highly deterministic system. Examples of two deterministic but opposing systems are the egalitarian ethic that all should be treated the same and the conservative ethic that all transactions should be based upon natural self-interest. On the other hand, the value judgments may be very weak ones on which most philosophies or ethical systems agree. For example, many economists use the criterion of Pareto optimality, discussed in Chapter 3 (Section 3) and Chapter 9. Only those courses of action are recommended that lead to a state of the world that cannot bettered for one consumer without hurting others; the economist requires social actions to be consumer efficient. The use of the Pareto criterion would seem to stand upon such metaphysical and/or ethical propositions as the independence of men from each other and the inviolability of that independence. It postulates first the existence of a certain separation of interests among individual consumers. Second, it accepts the desirability of this separation and judges economic alternatives by the benefits to these consumers. There is a contradiction, especially on the second point, between Pareto value and many philosphies, such as the philosophy of Hegel [1821] or possibly the Asian philosophies. On the other hand, most Western ethical systems are built on an atomistic system that places value with the individual (Kant [1788, 1791] and Bentham [1789]).

Adopting the Pareto optimal solutions involves the problem of deciding the true self-interest of the consumer. If it is taken to be his own opinion of what his interest is, there arises the psychological question whether his opinion is independent of that of his fellows. Actually total independence of opinion is not necessary for the idea of the Pareto ethic so long as a benevolence principle holds; that is, so long as the movement of one consumer from a worse to a better position does not distress the others. From the viewpoint of ethical considerations, however, should malevolence hold between individual consumers, it may not be clear that the consumer's opinion of his position should be respected. Indeed the same groups, especially religions, whose philosophy supports the Pareto ethic frequently disapprove of malevolent interrelations.

How to determine the true interest of the consumer is not clear. Many anthropologists argue that Western values are culture determined and are derived from social organization and behavior (Polanyi [1947] versus Cook [1960]). In particular, this viewpoint denies that the Pareto value judgment and similar Western values are valuable guides to social policy. A different metaphysics yields a different value system. Ethical considerations alone are not enough; generally, a broad metaphysical framework seems to be required in which both ethics and cosmology are integrated.

Hence the economic science as it is practiced draws on and systematizes various general ideas from the technological sciences, the psychological sciences, and metaphysics. A rough summary of this dependence can be given. The theory of the firm is usually stated in technological terms. The theory of consumer demand depends on psychology. Variants of these two theories may depend on both psychological and technological factors; examples are the theory of monopolistic firms and the theory of monopsonistic buyers, in which the capabilities and desires of other economic units are taken into account. Economists, however, are perhaps most famous for their recommendations for public policy, which usually amount to the imposition of ethical standards on a system that depends on both psychological and technological considerations.

It must be admitted that the typical economist feels more than a little regret when forced to recognize that his science is dependent on metaphysical conceptions. His misgivings arise primarily from standards that are imposed by the scientific community. The astonishingly successful logical and empirical development of physics, for example, is attributable both to the regularities inherent in the subject and to the intellectual prowess of its investigators. That modern developments in quantum mechanics have placed this most objective of sciences under the aegis of metaphysics should therefore console economists. Although it is not an ethical system that is needed, certain principles would appear beyond experimental verification. In other words, to presume experimention as the method for obtaining information about the universe is to presume a certain structure of the universe with regard to both its overall constituency and the role of the observer (Heisenberg [1958]).

2. The Purpose of Economic Theory

Modern views on the place of theory in economics differ partly with respect to the relative importance their proponents attribute to empirical or a priori phenomena and partly in their proponents' attitude toward the relative effectiveness of empirical and theoretical methodology. Four positions will be considered. Three are in the tradition of the logical positivist school of philosophy as set forth by Carnap, Ayer [1936], and others. This single tradition encompasses three contradictory doctrines: one esponses facts without theory; another considers theory for prediction only; and the third regards theory as the object of science. A fourth doctrine, normative economics, is in the idealist tradition as expounded by Berkeley [1710]. In economics, the idealist views theory as an instrument for the study of value judgments and their application to economic systems.

The dominant opinion found in recent work on economic methodology is that of logical positivism, which says that economics is an empirical science that must be analyzed by logical means to explain events (more properly, to coordinate simultaneous and sequential observations). Again, science should be judged by the extent to which it "fits the facts" and economics should become a "positive" science. Beyond this, there is little agreement among the three doctrines we will now consider.

The position of facts without theory was formerly associated with the National Bureau of Economic Research and especially with Wesley Mitchell (Vining [1949] versus Koopmans [1947, 1949]). Beyond the use of simple logic and analogy, no a priori views were entertained. Even long chains of logic and analogy were suspect, perhaps not without cause, since the way in which they were used often would not support very much beyond the "facts." The reason for adopting this extreme viewpoint is based on three points.

(1) There are too many variables in economics to be efficiently analyzed by a priori means.

(2) The variables are often discrete and not arranged in a continuum and therefore not easily placed in an a priori framework.

(3) There is not enough opportunity for collecting data to test empirically most important economic theories. Consequently, it is better to design new and simple theories that are appropriate to the data available.

Certainly, if these points are accepted, the empirical direction commands respect. For example, theoretical developments in science usually seize on a few fundamental relationships. Also, discrete variables give rise to many theoretical difficulties; witness the relative development of number theory as against classical analysis. Finally, the limitations of relevant data cestainly make a science more constrained by the data that are available. In effect, empirical and theoretical activities are to some degree substitutes in obtaining scientific results. To paraphrase Vining [1949], the bewildering detail of information relevant to economic decisions is belied by classical tradition and it is best to study now and deduce later. Nonetheless, the National Bureau seems to have overstated its case.

If a large number of variables make theoretical investigation difficult, empirical methods are even more difficult. Essentially, the lack of controlled experiments requires that empirical studies must be more or less content with historical data. For example, in the theory of consumer demand we may begin with the idea of consumer preferences. This idea must involve millions of consumers with a large variety of types of preferences. Preferences change over time and are influenced by such things as capital accumulation, experience, desire for variety, wars, and education. On the other hand, the years or months or weeks for which data about the demand for particular products are available always number in the hundreds, at most. From such data, we must derive the behavior of a diverse community at thousands of possible prices, many of which have not been experienced and are not likely to be experienced in the future. Hence the quantity of empirical knowledge is small relative to the number of principles available for use.

It is arbitrary to drop relevant information that is derived from one set of data about consumer behavior and is applicable to another set of data about the behavior of national markets simply because we cannot test all the steps in between. Yet this seems to be the thrust of point (3) against theory.

A main aim of the National Bureau was to chart and analyze the business cycle. Ironically, empirical investigation yielded great doubts as to the very existence of such a cycle as was originally postulated. So many cycles were found, one impressed on the other, that a student approaching the subject from the viewpoint of mathematical probability theory would dismiss it as random. (Perhaps the National Bureau was not cognizant of Fourier's theorem that any continuous function can be approximated by a sum of a finite number of periodic functions.) The strongest a priori consideration underlying the investigation was undermined. Far from verifying their position, the National Bureau investigations revealed the necessity for more careful specification of a priori considerations. For example, the desire to predict downturns in economic activity has led to the computation of economic indicators. These indicators do not move together, so that at any given time the future is not certain. Some method of evaluating the different indicators is necessary in order to predict the future. This is tantamount to using theory. The only choice left is whether the theory will be sophisticated or naive.

The inheritors of the National Bureau have turned to a more theoretical viewpoint, that of the Chicago school, which advocates theory for prediction. Economists such as Milton Friedman [1953, pp. 36–37] take the position that theory can be useful in analysis, although it is to be expected that any particular theory will have only a relatively narrow range of application. This is because sooner or later, and probably sooner, the facts will contradict the theory. Economic analysis, therefore, is a series of theories, each of which is designed to help classify certain economic phenomena. Essentially, knowledge is ultimately disordered and theory is useful only for temporary classification purposes. Any search for a true theory is vain. Originally, this point of view was stated in physics by Ernst Mach [1902].

The rationale for the Machian position is as follows. From the logical positivistic point of view, the purpose of economics is to predict economic phenomena. Therefore, a theory must be judged entirely by the extent to which its predictions are accurate. In particular, the postulates on which the theory is built are of no great consequence as long as a good prediction is obtained. The question as to what constitutes a good prediction is left as "econometric" and it is assumed that some criterion is in mind. Koopmans [1957] points out that the postulates do matter for the reason that the postulates are also the conclusions of any theory. Axioms themselves consist of trivial outcomes and, therefore, of trivial predictions; if they yield poor predictions, then by virtue of the positivits' (Friedman's) own standards they fail.

A more fundamental objection to this "disorder" school questions the basis on which we judge between a prediction of a business cycle or of the price of peanuts. To answer such a question we must order the things to be predicted and we must have some view of where the science should go. Of course, the word "should" indicates that some value judgments must be made. It might, therefore, be thought to constitute an objection to the whole positivistic viewpoint.

Other positivists argue that the purpose of a science is not only to predict but also to explain; that is, the purpose of a science is to explore the structure of the things being studied. This is the viewpoint, adopted by Karl Menger, Abraham Wald, and John von Neumann, that grew out of Karl Menger's seminar in Vienna. This group, sometimes referred to as the "Vienna circle" (Wien Kreis), paralleled Carnap's seminar in philosophy. For them theory is the structure of things. Its role is to coordinate different facts to show their relationship to one another The facts and their coordinating theory is all that passes under the name of "knowledge" or science. Exact prediction may result whenever there is pure causality, as in classical mechanics; probabilistic prediction may result if causality is imperfect, as in quantum mechanics. In all cases prediction is a manifestation of explanation, not an end in and of itself (Koopmans [1949, p. 89]).

To the Vienna circle, because theory is the relationship of facts and because facts are unlikely to change, a particular (valid) theory has a permanent life. It is never superseded in its own sphere, and is at best supported or amended by further investigation. For example, even though Einsteinian physics supersedes Newtonian physics as an explanation of structure of the universe, the Newtonian framework remains quite adequate at the level of application for which it was intended. It is not surprising that Newtonian physics is the limiting case of Einsteinian physics, where the speed of light is arbitrarily large. Theory is stable over time and space.

The Vienna circle considers theory very important for the development of science. Furthermore, since theory in economics tends to be complicated (because a large number of phenomena are coordinated), these positivists are in the forefront of the derivation of new economic theory and are especially enthusiastic over the role of mathematics in simplifying and analyzing economic axioms.

To an economist, disagreements over the fact–theory mix must be due to disagreement on the answers to the questions as to what science should do and what science can do. Even if we accept the aims of either the Chicago school or the Vienna circle, we may arrive at different positions because of disparate judgments about the possibilities of analysis. We must compare the "costs" of the empirical and the theoretical viewpoints. In particular, the transformation from the position of Wesley Mitchell to that of Milton Friedman was based on a judgment about these costs, not on a difference of opinion about what a science should accomplish. If empirical techniques are primitive, the cost of obtaining information by using facts is high. It is the comparison of the two that is relevant.

We have already pointed out some problems inherent in empirical methodology. A further complication in empirical economics is the absence of strong linear relationships. There are examples of approximate constants in economics, such as the relative labor share in national income, but these are fewer in number and less important than is the case in many natural sciences; for example, in physics the gravitational constant, Planck's constant, the charge of an electron, and the speed of light play important roles in Newtonian mechanics, quantum mechanics, and relativity theory, respectively. In contrast to physics, economics involves a diversity of the elements determining relationships and the determination is often nonlinear.

Nonlinear statistics requires a great deal more data than linear statistics. As a matter of practice nonlinear statistical methods are not widely used in economics and most empirical investigations are interpreted within a linear framework; hence, accuracy is sacrificed for simplicity and efficiency in empirical economics. Nonlinearities make a very precise science based mainly on empirical observations all the more difficult.

In summary, when history serves as the chief source for empirical study of economic systems, theory must play a large role. Great emphasis must be placed on the realism of the basic economic principles about which much is known and on the logical consistency of the theoretical structure built thereon. We must follow the rule that the nearer the underlying principles are to empirical reality, the nearer the theory will come to predicting the operation of the economic system. Implicit in such a rule are assumptions about the structure of scientific knowledge—namely, that its structure is amenable to logical methods and that relationships are continuous there; that is, the closer we approximate one part of the structure, the closer we come to approximating any other part that is derivable deductively, with possible temporary deviations. Although purely metaphysical, these principles seem to be acceptable throughout scientific enquiry.

In contrast to positive economics, normative economics is concerned with ethical judgments (J. Robinson [1962]). Before discussing the theoretical requirements of normative economics, we consider two objections by positivists against ethical sciences. The first, suggested earlier, is that economic rationality is culture determined; the second is that differences of opinion about value judgments are not important to economics.

Anthropological research has revealed that consumer choice in well-organized markets is a relatively recent phenomenon, beginning with the Greek city-states (Polanyi [1957]). Some anthropologists criticize economists as being too preoccupied with the market place and consumer values; since consumers in nonmarket economies do not display the "rationality" economists normally attribute to them, the anthropologists conclude that rationality is socially determined (Polanyi [1947] versus Cook [1960]). An idealistic reply to this is that rationality results from the necessity of choice (von Mises [1949, 1962]). It is not logically required by the mere act of choice and therefore it must be inherent in the self-interest and individuality of consumers. Hence the economist is correct in ascribing to it an a priori importance. That rationality is observable mainly in Western societies is a reflection of the fact that only in Western societies are economic affairs conducted in such a way as to determine whether or not consumers are rational. Consistency of choice is a priori, whereas the range of choice is subject to inquiry (Hochwald [1968]).

Contrary to the idealist, the logical positivist contends that even logical principles must be revised in response to empirical observations. He might point to the paradoxes of logic that result when views formerly held as self-evident seem to be in error. More specifically, the axioms of Aristotelean logic have been shown to be contradictory in their original form (Section 1 of Chapter 2). The choice of modified logical axioms that are valid is dependent on empirical experience. It can be argued equally well that today there is no clear way to reason all things from the axioms of logic. On idealistic grounds, therefore, we would expect that the axioms may be in contradiction; the search for and discovery of "true" logical principles will ultimately reveal all things. In platonic terms men are in a cave and only by thought can they find their way to the outside, that is, find the "true" axioms (*The Republic*, Chapter XXV).[1]

Friedman [1953] argues that most differences of opinion are on the basis of facts alone. Undoubtedly differences of opinion with regard to the facts are important. Nervertheless, economists have very great differences on ethical grounds and these differences lead to very different policy requirements. Consider the simple proposal that blacks should be granted income in perpetuity or compensation for the discrimination they have suffered from whites. There are, of course, possible differences on the facts. To what extent would a grant actually help blacks in the long run? To what extent have whites been responsible for the state of blacks? Most observers would agree that blacks would have had greater opportunities in the absence of discrimination. Even if subsidies were not helpful, some kind of aid, say state-financed education, could be imagined and such aid would help alleviate the wrong blacks have borne. The greatest differences on this pressing social question are due to ethical disagreements. On the one hand there is the egalitarian argument that different individuals should be treated similarly (by society). Many

[1] Attempts to resolve the realist and idealist differences have led to so-called dualist philosophies. There are two ways of knowing: the deductive method of logic and the inductive method based on facts commonly observed.

economists use this as grounds for favoring the state subsidy scheme. On the other hand, there is the argument that justice should be based on mutual self-interest and that discrimination is not a sufficient cause for retribution. If a man chooses not to deal with a particular person on such and such terms because of his own distaste for the other, it is this distaste that must be justified or denied. Once the motive of action or opinion or feeling is judged valid, then we can at best serve consumers as they are constituted. In effect, we can no more condemn discrimination than we can condemn the right of a man to choose his heir.

There may be many other positions differing from, and perhaps intermediate between, the egalitarian ethic and the mutual interest ethic. We might object to one or the other of these ethics, but it is clear that they lead to completely different social action even when there is agreement on the facts.

It often appears that the positivist economists actually adopt the Pareto ethic. They present society with a menu of actions that are consumer efficient and state that economics cannot cope with the question of the distribution of wealth. Political authorities may seize on this and distribute the wealth according to their own special interests, possibly ignoring the economist's admonitions about losses due to frequent changes in the rules of the game. It seems that too much is left undetermined and that the economist can say something against injustice even as an economist. To neglect normative economics is to pursue a dangerous course. To object that normative economics necessitates the introduction of noneconomic value judgments presumes that there is an important economic science that does not make such value judgments. It is argued here that no such economic science exists, nor is likely to, given the demands society makes of economists.

The importance of theory is partly dependent on the importance of value judgments in economics. So long as an ethical system, even Pareto optimality, is imposed on economics and economists are expected to make recommendations based on it, theory must play an important role. The value judgments are imposed from the outside and cannot be observed in economic affairs (although possibly they might be derived from observation elsewhere) and hence must be grafted onto the economic structure. If this is an accurate description of economic practice, then it constitutes an important argument for the use of theory.

The role of value judgments in economics is so great that economics might be said to be more a "prescriptive" or policy science than a descriptive or observational science. Some examples will suffice to show how these value judgments appear in economic investigations and how they introduce (inherently) a priori considerations.

Consider the economist who is hired by a business firm that follows the rule of maximizing profits. Within the framework of his analysis, this economist accepts profit maximization as the ethical system. No degree of observation of the actual activities of the firm can lead him unguided to the maximum income. Not only is the ethical system commanded by the firm's owners, it must be applied in an a priori or analytical way. An iterative process where the economist repeats a (finite) number of possible outputs over time may not lead to a good profit. Also, the firm's managers are not likely to welcome low-profit alternatives in the process of experimentation, even temporarily; the profit ethic itself restricts the possibility of experimental resolution. Hence the ethical system lies outside the set of testable alternatives; in principle the economist cannot discover the profit-maximizing point experimentally except by the extreme accident of hitting upon the one among an infinite number of possible modes of operation, and even then he will not know experimentally that he has discovered it; in practice he cannot even come close by pure trial and error because of the immediate losses that might be incurred en route to the solution. The economist of the firm cannot do his job until he has applied some theoretical tools, however simple they may be.

The case of the economist hired by the state for policy purposes is even more striking. He is confronted with the goals of the state, which fall into the two broad classes of national military and political power and the welfare of the state's consumers. Hence the value judgments are given from the outside. The economist must impose that ethical system upon the observed world and in doing so must follow some a priori formulations that amount to a theory. These may be very rough or even unsound, but they must be followed. Of course, the academic economist, himself, is usually imbued with certain notions of social welfare and may find himself in the role of a protagonist of society, calling upon one or more reforms on the basis of his view of the observable economic world, his value judgments, and the theoretical reasoning in between.

Finally, the economist who merely observes or is concerned only with relating experimental data finds that his reputation depends on the extent to which his work contributes to the solution of certain policy questions that are themselves stated from the viewpoint of a particular ethical system.

3. The Place of Mathematics in Economic Theory

It has been said that mathematics is a language. Just as language validates experiences, mathematical formulation validates science. It clarifies concepts and makes them easily subject to analysis. That which cannot be formalized cannot be valid, although formalization may or may not be advantageous.

Mathematics has at least three important roles in economic theory. First, the opus of mathematics is in part an accumulation from other sciences. Hence it represents ideas that have been successful elsewhere and that economists may likewise find useful. Second, mathematics is a valuable aid in long sequences of reasoning where it is easy to make mistakes. Third, mathematics makes possible a greater degree of generality than verbal or graphical methods of discourse.

Nevertheless there are economists who object to the use of mathematics. Their objections may be summarized in three statements. One, mathematical treatment implies quantification, which is impossible in economics: there are too many variables, variables are in many cases not observable, and variables are not arrayed in a continuum on which a formal theory can be developed, but rather are highly discrete. Two, the search for mathematical generality is a tedious enterprise that substitutes convoluted definitions and notational manipulations for new ideas. Three, even where mathematics does apply, the use of given mathematical results can lead to perverse orientation of economic theory because mathematical theory is devloped along lines not relevant to questions of economic interest. This is really an objection to the discretion used by those who apply mathematics. Hence, the major objections are the first two.

It is true that much of the mathematics applied to economics prior to 1950 was of the sort that assumed quantitative measurement. Since 1950, however, there has been an effort to escape from this restriction. The possibility of quantification of economic concepts is not necessarily implied; mathematical reasoning may deal with abstractions that are not at all quantifiable in a strict sense. In practice it may be that much of mathematical reasoning is oriented toward spaces in which quantity is definite and intuitively interpretable. The trend in modern mathematics, however, has been to break out of this bound and to extend greatly the scope of mathematical techniques.

It is not even necessary that the objects subjected to mathematical analysis be stated in a precise or fully determinant fashion. For example, topology is the study of spaces or sets for which only the logical possibility of precise statement exists; they are known only vaguely, according to some particular properties. The knowledge of the particular properties studied must be precise, although in extreme instances precision may mean only that a spectrum of possibly occurring properties can be assigned a probability density function.

The requirement for mathematical applications is that the analysis be applied to well-defined ideas that are capable of logical manipulation. In short, it must be clear from all possible logical approaches what a set of concepts denotes. This requirement has not always been met in sciences such as physics. However, since the analysis of economic systems depends on a priori reasoning and logical consistency, the requirement appears to be reasonable for usable economic concepts.

Establishment of the fact that a set of concepts may be subjected to formal mathematical analysis does not imply that such analysis is advantageous. To set up formal definitions of numbers and work them through logical exercises to verify axioms for one plus one equals two does little to clarify the discipline of accounting (although it may very well clarify other disciplines). For long sequences of reasoning, however, it is appropriate and often necessary to use a formal apparatus of one sort or another to preserve continuity and avoid error. In principle, the reasoning could be carried out without symbols and mathematical forms, but in practice these prove to be necessary. Much of economic theory must be expressed in propositions verified by long sequences of reasoning, and here mathematical methods become important.

To turn to the second objection, it must be admitted that a mathematical form can make an otherwise unimpressive presentation look important. A special variant of phony mathematical analysis is the proposition that is so general as to have every possible application but no important implication. To quote T. C. Koopmans, "with no assumptions there are no theorems." On the other hand we expect that there are minimal assumptions necessary to obtain a given result. How much effort should be expended to reduce assumptions to their minimum level?

For the Machian the conclusions are primary and the assumptions secondary; hence the rewards for finding new theorems exceed those for finding more general assumptions. Those scientists who are responsible for "new ideas" are highly regarded; others who study foundations are viewed as pedantic and unoriginal.

It is otherwise for the Vienna circle; since theory is the structure of things, the search for a more fundamental basis of current "knowledge" is at least as important as the search for new propositions. The further we trace a theory back to its most basic assumptions, the more we understand the subject being studied. The members of the Vienna circle preoccupied themselves with foundations, since prior to Karl Menger's seminar such analysis had been neglected in economics.

An example should suffice to show the importance of mathematical generality for normative economics. Here, an optimizing system is designed for a world with various kinds of consumers and producers. The more general the kinds of consumers and producers, the better the optimizing procedure. The uncertainty about the kind of producers or consumers makes the search for generality of special practical importance. One of the most spectacular advances along these lines is the welfare economics of Koopmans, Arrow, and Debreu, among others, which makes no mention of differentiability of utility, demand, and so forth (see Debreu [1959] and Chapter 9). To date, there are no known economic interpretations for many of the differentiability assumptions formerly used and certainly no assurance that consumers and producers display them.

2

Mathematical Prerequisites

The effort toward rigor substitutes correct reasonings and results for incorrect ones (and) it usually leads to a deeper understanding.

Gerard Debreu
THEORY OF VALUE, 1959
Reprinted by permission, Wiley, New York

1. Theory of Sets

The ideas of set theory are used throughout the remainder of the book. In set theory, a set is a collection of *elements* upon which certain operations can be performed, as described below. First, to state that element e belongs to the set $\mathscr{E}$ we write

$$e \in \mathscr{E},$$

or "e is in $\mathscr{E}$." There is the set consisting of the element e itself, denoted as $\{e\}$. In this section rules for construction of sets are given. One rather involved method is put off until the next section. In the rest of the chapter, set theory will be used to construct Euclidean n-space from the real line (Sections 3–5) and then to consider abstract spaces (Sections 6 and 7).

Given any set $\mathscr{Y}$ whose elements also appear in $\mathscr{X}$, it is said that $\mathscr{Y}$ is contained in $\mathscr{X}$ or is a subset of $\mathscr{X}$, and this is written as

$$\mathscr{Y} \subset \mathscr{X}.$$

(Equivalently, $\mathscr{X} \supset \mathscr{Y}$ or $\mathscr{X}$ contains $\mathscr{Y}$.)

The empty set, consisting of no elements whatever, is denoted by $\varnothing$. Thus, for example,

$$\varnothing \subset \{e\} \subset \mathscr{E}.$$

If $\mathscr{Y} \subset \mathscr{X}$ but $\mathscr{Y} \neq \mathscr{X}$, $\mathscr{Y}$ is a *proper* subset of $\mathscr{X}$. We write $\mathscr{Y} \subsetneqq \mathscr{X}$ or $\mathscr{X} \supsetneqq \mathscr{Y}$.

For any set $\mathscr{E}$, subsets can sometimes be defined according to properties as

$$\mathscr{X} = \{x \mid x \text{ has property } P, \quad x \in \mathscr{E}\}.$$

This is read "$\mathscr{X}$ is the set of elements x in $\mathscr{E}$ that have property P." An *index set* $\mathscr{A}$ is a set of objects such as integers used to name elements or sets, $\mathscr{X}_\alpha$, $\alpha \in \mathscr{A}$. We can construct sets from subsets $\mathscr{X}_\alpha$, $\alpha \in \mathscr{A}$, of $\mathscr{U}$ as follows:

(1) $\bigcup_{\alpha \in \mathscr{A}} \mathscr{X}_\alpha \equiv \{x \mid x \in \mathscr{X}_\alpha, \quad \alpha \in \mathscr{A}\}$

(if there are two sets, (1) is written $\mathscr{X} \cup \mathscr{Y}$). This is read "the *union* of $\mathscr{X}_\alpha$," defined as the set of elements that are in at least one $\mathscr{X}_\alpha$. (In general, $\bigcup_{\alpha \in \mathscr{A}} \mathscr{X} = \varnothing$ if and only if $\mathscr{X}_\alpha = \varnothing$ for all $\alpha \in \mathscr{A}$.)

(2) $\bigcap_{\alpha \in \mathscr{A}} \mathscr{X}_\alpha \equiv \{x \mid x \in \mathscr{X}_\alpha \quad \text{for all} \quad \alpha \in \mathscr{A}\}$

(or $\mathscr{X} \cap \mathscr{Y}$). This is read "the intersection of the $\mathscr{X}_\alpha$," defined as the set of elements that are in both $\mathscr{X}$ and $\mathscr{Y}$. (In general, $\mathscr{Y} \cap \mathscr{X}$ can be empty. Whenever this is true, $\mathscr{X}$ and $\mathscr{Y}$ are said to be disjoint.)

(3) $\sim\mathscr{X} \equiv \{x \mid x \notin \mathscr{X}, \quad x \in \mathscr{U}\}$.

This is read "the *complement* of $\mathscr{X}$ in $\mathscr{U}$," defined as the set of elements that are not in $\mathscr{U}$. For example, $\sim\varnothing = \mathscr{U}$, and $\sim(\sim\mathscr{X}) = \mathscr{X}$. Also, we can define the difference between two sets $\mathscr{X}$ and $\mathscr{Y}$ as follows:

(3)′ $\mathscr{X} \sim \mathscr{Y} \equiv \mathscr{X} \cap (\sim\mathscr{Y}) = \{x \mid x \in \mathscr{X}, \quad x \notin \mathscr{Y}\}$.

For example, the difference between $\mathscr{X}$ and x is the set $\mathscr{X}$ with x deleted:

$$\mathscr{X} \sim \{x\}.$$

1 Lemma[1] (De Morgan's Formulas)

(i) $\mathscr{Y} \sim \bigcup_{\alpha\in\mathscr{A}} \mathscr{X}_\alpha = \bigcap_{\alpha\in\mathscr{A}} (\mathscr{Y} - \mathscr{X}_\alpha)$.
(ii) $\mathscr{Y} \sim \bigcap_{\alpha\in\mathscr{A}} \mathscr{X}_\alpha = \bigcup_{\alpha\in\mathscr{A}} (\mathscr{Y} - \mathscr{X}_\alpha)$.

(The proof is left to the reader; Exercise 1.)

Throughout this book, sets that are not contained in a given set must be constructed. It might seem that this could be done quite freely; that is, any collection of items could be defined according to any particular property and treated as a set. This is not so, however, as many paradoxes have demonstrated (see Beth [1953] or Kleene [1952]). In the Russell paradox, a nonacceptable set is defined as

$$\mathscr{X} = \{x \mid x \notin x\}$$

where $\mathscr{X}$ is the (proposed) set of all sets that do not belong to themselves. A logical contradiction can easily be derived if it is assumed that $\mathscr{X}$ can be constructed. If $\mathscr{X}$ belongs to itself, then by definition it does not belong to itself. If $\mathscr{X}$ does not belong to itself, then by definition it does. Therefore, $\mathscr{X}$ belongs to itself if and only if $\mathscr{X}$ does not belong to itself. Such a conclusion is hardly acceptable under the rules of logic, whence it cannot be that $\mathscr{X}$ exists to be spoken of in such a fashion—that is, as having members. To avoid results not logically acceptable, we must be careful in constructing sets.

(4) $\mathscr{X} \times \mathscr{Y} = \{(x, y) \mid x \in \mathscr{X}, \quad y \in \mathscr{Y}\}$.

This is read "the *product* of $\mathscr{X}$ and $\mathscr{Y}$," defined as the set of ordered pairs with an element from $\mathscr{X}$ in the first component and an element from $\mathscr{Y}$ in the second component.

A *relation* $\mathscr{R}$ on $\mathscr{X} \times \mathscr{Y}$ is a subset where $(x, y) \in \mathscr{R}$ is denoted by $x \mathscr{R} y$; that is, x is "not inferior" to y. Thus

(5) $\mathscr{R}(x) \equiv \{y \mid (y, x) \in \mathscr{R}\}$.

This is read "*upper contour set* of $\mathscr{R}$." It represents the elements "not inferior to x." For the inverse relation, $\mathscr{R}^{-1} = \{(y, x) \mid (x, y) \in \mathscr{R}\}$, $\mathscr{R}^{-1}(x) = \{y \mid (y, x) \in \mathscr{R}^{-1}\}$, which is the "not superior to x" or *lower contour set.*

Let

$$\mathscr{R}(\mathscr{A}) = \bigcup_{y\in\mathscr{A}} \mathscr{R}(y).$$

[1] Throughout this chapter, results of purely mathematical interest are called lemmata, remarks, and corollaries.

2 Lemma

$$\mathscr{R}(\mathscr{A} \cup \mathscr{B}) = \mathscr{R}(\mathscr{A}) \cup \mathscr{R}(\mathscr{B}) \qquad \textit{and} \qquad \mathscr{R}(\mathscr{A} \cap \mathscr{B}) \subset \mathscr{R}(\mathscr{A}) \cap \mathscr{R}(\mathscr{B}).$$

The proof is left to the reader (Exercise 1).

If $\mathscr{R}$ is a relation in $\mathscr{X} \times \mathscr{Y}$,

(6) $P_{\mathscr{X}}(\mathscr{R}) \equiv \{x \mid (x, y) \in \mathscr{R} \text{ for some } y \in \mathscr{Y}\} = \bigcup_{y \in \mathscr{Y}} \mathscr{R}(y).$

This is read "the projection of $\mathscr{R}$ on $\mathscr{X}$," and is also denoted $P_1(\mathscr{R})$. For example,

$$P_1(\mathscr{X} \times \mathscr{Y}) = P_{\mathscr{X}}(\mathscr{X} \times \mathscr{Y}) = \mathscr{X},$$

$$P_2(\mathscr{X} \times \mathscr{Y}) = P_{\mathscr{Y}}(\mathscr{X} \times \mathscr{Y}) = \mathscr{Y}, \qquad P_{\mathscr{X}}(\varnothing) = \varnothing.$$

If a set has a finite number of elements n, the number of subsets is 2^n. The set of subsets is denoted

(7) $2^{\mathscr{X}} \equiv \{\mathscr{Y} \mid \mathscr{Y} \subset \mathscr{X}\}.$

Here $2^{\mathscr{X}}$ is the collection of all sets that are themselves contained in $\mathscr{X}$.

Exercise 1 Prove Lemmata 1 and 2.

Exercise 2 Suppose that every bounded set of integers $\{x_i \mid i = 1, 2, \ldots, n\}$ (x_i an integer) contains its *least upper bound* (lub)

$$\sup\{x_i \mid i = 1, 2, \ldots, n\}$$

defined as that y for which

$$y \geqslant x_i \qquad \text{for all} \quad i = 1, 2, \ldots, n$$

and there is no $\bar{y}$ such that $\bar{y} \geqslant x_i$ for all $i = 1, 2, \ldots, n$ and $\bar{y} < y$. Let $P(i)$ be sentences. Prove the induction result.

Lemma *If*

(i) $P(1)$ *is true,*
(ii) $P(i + 1)$ *is true whenever* $P(i)$ *is true,*

then

$$P(i) \textit{ is true for all } i = 1, 2, \ldots .$$

2. Relations

Relations are very important in mathematical analysis in general and in economic applications in particular. A formal presentation of various kinds of relations helps clarify many kinds of arguments.

If $P_{\mathscr{X}}(\mathscr{R}) = \mathscr{X}$, $\mathscr{R}$ is said to be a *correspondence* from $\mathscr{X}$ to $\mathscr{Y}$. We write

$$\mathscr{R} : \mathscr{X} \to \mathscr{Y}.$$

$\mathscr{X}$ is called the *domain*, $\mathscr{Y}$ the *range*. We say

$$y \in \mathscr{R}^{-1}(x) \qquad \text{for} \quad y \mathrel{\mathscr{R}} x.$$

The correspondence is *onto* if $P_2(\mathscr{R}) = \mathscr{Y}$. If also for every $x \in \mathscr{X}$,

$$\mathscr{R}^{-1}(x)$$

is a single element, then $\mathscr{R}$ is a *function* from $\mathscr{X}$ to $\mathscr{Y}$. We say $y = f(x)$ for $x \mathrel{\mathscr{R}} y$ and $f : \mathscr{X} \to \mathscr{Y}$. The function is *1–1* if $\mathscr{R}^{-1}$ is a function.

(8) The *composition* of two relations,

$$\mathscr{Q} \cdot \mathscr{R} = \{(x, z) \mid (x, y) \in \mathscr{R}, \quad (y, z) \in \mathscr{Q} \quad \text{for some} \quad y \in \mathscr{Y}\},$$

is a set.

For a function, $f \cdot g(x) = f(g(x))$.

We consider a relation $\mathscr{R}$ defined on $\mathscr{X} \times \mathscr{X}$. If $x \mathrel{\mathscr{R}} x$, $\mathscr{R}$ is *reflexive*. If never $x \mathrel{\mathscr{R}} x$, $\mathscr{R}$ is *irreflexive*. If $x \mathrel{\mathscr{R}} y$ and $y \mathrel{\mathscr{R}} z$ imply $x \mathrel{\mathscr{R}} z$, then $\mathscr{R}$ is *transitive*. If $x \mathrel{\mathscr{R}} y$ implies $y \mathrel{\mathscr{R}} x$, then $\mathscr{R}$ is *symmetric*. If either $x \mathrel{\mathscr{R}} y$ or $y \mathrel{\mathscr{R}} x$, then $\mathscr{R}$ is *complete*. If $\mathscr{R}$ is transitive and reflexive or irreflexive, $\mathscr{R}$ is called a partial ordering. If also $\mathscr{R}$ is complete, $\mathscr{R}$ is an *ordering*. If $\mathscr{R}$ is an ordering such that $x \mathrel{\mathscr{R}} y$, $y \mathrel{\mathscr{R}} x$ only if $x = y$, then $\mathscr{R}$ is said to be a *strict ordering*.

3 Remark (i) The only reflexive function is the identity $x = f(x)$.

(ii) If the relation is transitive, $\mathscr{R} \cdot \mathscr{R} \subset \mathscr{R}$. If also the domain has at least three elements, then the relation is not a function.

(iii) If the relation is symmetric and a function, $\mathscr{R} \cdot \mathscr{R}$ is the identity on $P_{\mathscr{X}}(\mathscr{R}) : \mathscr{R}^{-1} \cdot \mathscr{R}(x) = x$.

(iv) If $\mathscr{R}$ is complete and $\mathscr{X}$ has at least three elements, then it is not a function.

(v) If $\mathscr{R}$ is an ordering, $P_{\mathscr{X}}(\mathscr{R}) = \mathscr{X}$, $P_{\mathscr{Y}}(\mathscr{X}) = \mathscr{X}$ ($\mathscr{Y} = \mathscr{X}$) and either $\mathscr{R}^{-1}(x) \subset \mathscr{R}^{-1}(y)$ or $\mathscr{R}^{-1}(y) \subset \mathscr{R}^{-1}(x)$.

Proof is left to the reader (Exercise 3).

Often there will be an equivalence relation $\mathscr{R}$, and we wish to consider the set of *equivalence classes* $\mathscr{R}(x)$. These classes are subsets of $P_{\mathscr{X}}(\mathscr{R})$ and hence elements of $2^{\mathscr{X}}$. However, there is nothing in (1)–(8) that allows us to construct a set of equivalence classes. The following principle is sufficient.

(9) Let $\mathscr{R} \subset \mathscr{X} \times \mathscr{Y}$. Then the collection of elements of the form $(x, \mathscr{R}(x))$ is a subset of $\mathscr{X} \times 2^{\mathscr{Y}}$.

4 Remark The equivalence classes $\mathscr{R}(x)$ form subsets of $2^{\mathscr{X}}$.

Proof With some violence to terminology, consider $\mathscr{R}$ as subsets of $\mathscr{X} \times 2^{\mathscr{X}}$ ((9)). Then $P_{2^{\mathscr{X}}}(\mathscr{R})$ is the set of equivalence classes ((6)). q.e.d.

Orderings are discussed more fully in Section 3 of Chapter 3 and in Chapter 5.

3. Construction of the Real Line

Let m and n be positive integers $n > m$. Then $-m$ can be given the meaning the negative integer such that $(n + (-m)) + m = n$, $(n + (-m)) > 0$. This definition can be shown to be independent of n and thereby the negative integers are constructed. The number 0 is defined as the value of $n + (-n)$, whatever n, which closes the system under addition.

The *rational* number $r = m/n$ is defined by multiplication: $rn = m$. This forms a system of numbers closed under addition of numbers and closed under addition and multiplication.

Early, the Greeks posed problems whose solution required a sequence of rational numbers. An example was to find the number representing the area of a circle divided by its radius squared. Another example is the paradox due to Zeno. "Suppose a tortoise is moving forward toward the sleeping hare. In one-half hour the tortoise moves halfway to the hare. In one-fourth hour more the tortoise moves one-fourth the distance to the hare, and so forth. The conclusion must be that the tortoise never reaches the hare and thus never passes him."

Zeno's paradox is basically an illustration of the difficulties that arise from mixing assumptions of discreteness and continuity. The discrete movements of the tortoise are simply observations on a continuum of his movements and the paradox loses its sting; the paradox is solved by constructing a continuum of movement, namely, the real line. Unfortunately this solution is not completely satisfactory because it contradicts some observations at the subatomic level, but it is adequate in many contexts.

The line is constructed by filling in numbers as follows. Let $x_n \geqslant x_{n+1}$, $n = 1, 2, \ldots$, be a bounded sequence of rational numbers. If there is no rational number that is the limit of the sequence, then a limit is assigned. Identifications are made between limits of two sequences, x_n, $n = 1, 2, \ldots$, and y_n, $n = 1, 2, \ldots$, for which the sequence $x_n - y_n$ tends to zero: $(x_n, n = 1, 2, \ldots) \mathscr{I} (y_n, n = 1, 2, \ldots)$ if $x_n - y_n$ tends to zero (as defined in Exercise 3). Applying Remark 4, we define the *real line* as the set of equivalence classes under $\mathscr{I}$ in sequences of rational numbers. This ensures that the number system obeys the various addition and multiplication laws of rational numbers (Exercise 5). The line thus constructed is called Euclidean 1-space, $\mathscr{E}^1$.

Since the line is ordered by $\geqslant$, it is natural to define intervals. They are the *open interval*, $(x, y) = \{y \mid x > z > y\}$, the *half open intervals* $[x, y) = \{z \mid x \geqslant z > y\}$ and $(x, y] = \{z > z \geqslant y\}$, and the *closed interval* $[x, y] = \{z \mid x \geqslant z \geqslant y\}$. A set of numbers that is contained in an interval is called bounded.

Many functions are studied that have the real line as their range. Such functions are called *real valued.* A real-valued function is *continuous* if the $f(x^n)$ tends to $f(x)$ whenever x^n tends to x. Alternative definitions of continuity appear in Section 6.

Exercise 3 The sequence $\{x^n\}$ is said to *converge to limit* x, that is, $\lim x_n = x$, if and only if for any $\varepsilon > 0$ there exists $N(\varepsilon)$ such that

$$| x_n - x | < \varepsilon$$

whenever $n > N(\varepsilon)$. Show that

(i) $\lim x_n + y_n = \lim x_n + \lim y,$

(ii) $\lim - x_n = -\lim x_n ,$

(iii) $\lim x_n y_n = \lim x_n \lim y_n$

(iv) $\lim \dfrac{x_n}{y_n} = \dfrac{\lim x_n}{\lim y_n} .$

Exercise 4 Show that the real line as defined has operations of multiplication, addition, subtraction, and division by nonzero elements.

Exercise 5 Let two firms produce in the same industry with a demand curve given by $q = a - bp$, where p is price, a, b are positive. Assume that each firm takes the other firm's output as given and maximizes its profits. What are the outputs of the two firms over time? What are the limiting outputs?

4. Differentiable Functions in Euclidean n-Space

This section is concerned with the linear transformations of Euclidean n-space $\mathscr{E}^n$. We define $\mathscr{E}^n$ as the product of the real line n times: $\mathscr{E}^n \equiv \mathscr{E}^1 \times \mathscr{E}^1 \times \cdots \times \mathscr{E}^1$. This section and the next are sufficient mathematical bacground for the theory of production (Chapter 4). The methods are also used throughout the other chapters.

The elements of $\mathscr{E}^n$ are vectors $x = (x_1, x_2, \ldots, x_n)$. They are ordered by

$$x \geqslant y \quad \text{iff} \quad x_i \geqslant y_i \quad \text{for all } i,$$

$$x > y \quad \text{iff} \quad x \geqslant y \quad \text{and} \quad x_i > y_i \quad \text{for some } i,$$

and

$$x \gg y \quad \text{iff} \quad x_i > y_i \quad \text{for all } i.$$

The vectors can be added

$$x + y = (x_1 + y_1, x_2 + y_2, \ldots, x_n + y_n)$$

or multiplied by numbers a:

$$ax = (ax_1, ax_2, \ldots, ax_n).$$

A set $\mathscr{X}$ can be multiplied by a to give $a\mathscr{X} \equiv \{ax \mid x \in \mathscr{X}\}$. Also, $\mathscr{X} + \mathscr{Y} \equiv \{x + y \mid x \in \mathscr{X}, y \in \mathscr{Y}\}$.

A linear transformation T from $\mathscr{E}^m$ to $\mathscr{E}^n$ is a function such that

$$T(ax + by) = aT(x) + bT(y).$$

A matrix A is an array

$$A \equiv (a_{ij}) \equiv \begin{pmatrix} a_{11} & a_{12} & \cdots & a_{1n} \\ a_{21} & a_{22} & \cdots & a_{2n} \\ \vdots & \vdots & & \vdots \\ a_{m1} & a_{m2} & \cdots & a_{mm} \end{pmatrix}$$

For a vector x, $xA \equiv (\sum_{i=1}^{m} x_i a_{ij}, j = 1, \ldots, n)$.

5 Lemma (i) *A linear transformation T from $\mathscr{E}^n$ to $\mathscr{E}^m$ can be represented as a matrix transformation $T(x) = xA$.*

(ii) *Let S be a linear transformation from $\mathscr{E}^m$ to $\mathscr{E}^p$. The composition of T and S with respective matrices A and B is*

$$ST(x) = x, \qquad AB = \Big(\sum_{i=1}^{n} \sum_{j=1}^{m} x_i a_{ij} b_{jk}, \quad k = 1, \dots, p\Big).$$

(iii) *If $n = m$, T is* 1–1 *if and only if* det $A \neq 0$.

The lemma is a standard result of linear algebra and is not proved here, although the proof is easy.

If T is 1–1, A is said to be nonsingular and the matrix representing T^{-1} is denoted A^{-1}. Other results on linear transformation and matrices appear in Section 5 of Chapter 4.

If T maps into $\mathscr{E}^1$, then T is represented by a row vector

$$\begin{pmatrix} y_1 \\ \vdots \\ y_n \end{pmatrix}$$

which is denoted y'. When writing the *product* xy', the prime is often eliminated to read xy. In general, if A is defined as above,

$$A' \equiv \begin{pmatrix} a_{11} & a_{21} & \cdots & a_{m1} \\ a_{12} & a_{22} & \cdots & a_{m2} \\ \vdots & \vdots & & \vdots \\ a_{1n} & \cdot & \cdots & a_{mn} \end{pmatrix}.$$

Let the *norm of* x be $|x| \equiv (\sum x_i^2)^{1/2} = (xx')^{1/2}$. Note that $|x/|x|| = 1$. For a sequence $x^m = (x_1^m, \dots, x_n^m)$, $x^m \to x$ or $\lim x^m = x$ provided that each i, $\lim x_i^m = x_i$.

A correspondence is differentiable at x if near x it is nearly a linear transformation. A correspondence $\mathscr{F}$ is *differentiable* at x if (i) $\mathscr{F}(x)$ is a single point, and (ii) there is a linear transformation T (called the derivative of $\mathscr{F}$ at x), such that

$$0 = \lim_{x^m \to x} \left(\frac{\mathscr{F}(x^m) - \mathscr{F}(x)}{|x^m - x|} - T\left(\frac{x^m - x}{|x^m - x|}\right)\right).$$

Equivalently,

$$\lim_{x^m \to x} \frac{\mathscr{F}(x^m) - \mathscr{F}(x)}{|x^m - x|} = T\left(\lim \frac{x^m - x}{|x^m - x|}\right) = \lim \frac{x^m - x}{|x^m - x|} A$$

where A is the matrix representative of $\mathscr{F}$. If f is a function, A is the matrix of *partial derivatives*, defined when x_i only changes, $\partial f_j / \partial x_i = \lim_{\Delta x_i \to 0} \Delta f_j / \Delta x_i$ (Exercise 7).

Evidentally differentiability is applied to a *neighborhood*

$$\mathcal{N}_\varepsilon(x) = \{y \mid | x - y | < \varepsilon > 0\}.$$

Let $\mathcal{F} + \mathcal{G}$ be the correspondence with values $\mathcal{F}(x) + \mathcal{G}(x)$, and $a\mathcal{F}$ be the correspondence with values $a\mathcal{F}(x)$.

6 Remark Let $\mathcal{N}_\varepsilon(x) \subset \mathcal{E}^m$, $\mathcal{F} : \mathcal{N}_\varepsilon(x) \to \mathcal{E}^n$, $\mathcal{F}$ have derivative T at x, $\mathcal{G}$ have derivative S at x.

(i) If $\mathcal{G} : \mathcal{F}(\mathcal{N}_\varepsilon) \to \mathcal{E}^m$, then $\mathcal{G} \cdot \mathcal{F}$ has derivative $S \cdot T$.

(ii) *If* $\mathcal{G} : \mathcal{N}_\varepsilon(y) \subset \mathcal{E}^m \to \mathcal{E}^n$, then $\mathcal{F} + \mathcal{G} : \mathcal{N}_\varepsilon(y) + \mathcal{N}_\varepsilon(x) \to \mathcal{E}^n$ with derivative $T + S$.

(iii) $a\mathcal{F}$ has derivative aT.

(iv) If T is 1–1, and $\mathcal{F}^{-1}$ is a function, then it has derivative T^{-1}.

(v) If $\mathcal{F}$ is differentiable at every point of $\mathcal{N}_\varepsilon(x)$, then $\mathcal{F}$ is a function.

Proof Exercise 7.

7 Lemma (Mean Value Theorem for Differential Calculus) *If f is differentiable in $\mathcal{N}_\varepsilon(x)$ and real valued, then for some $\hat{x} = x + \theta(x - y)$, $0 < \theta < 1, f(x) - f(y) = A_{\hat{x}}(x - y)$ where $A_{\hat{x}}$ is the matrix representing the derivative of f at $\hat{x}$.*

Proof On the line segment from x to y, f is a real-valued function on the line. Application of the differential calculus mean value theorem and the formula in (i) of Remark 6 gives the lemma. q.e.d.

If f is everywhere differentiable and for all i, j, $\partial f_i/\partial x_i$ is continuous, f is *continuously differentiable.*

8 Lemma (Inverse Functions Theorem) *If f is continuously differentiable at every point of $\mathcal{N}_\varepsilon(x)$ and the derivative is everywhere nonsingular and everywhere continuous, then there is a $\delta > 0$ such that f is 1–1 on $\mathcal{N}_\delta(x)$ and the derivative of f^{-1} is T^{-1}.*

Proof Let $x^n, y^n \to x$, $x^n \neq y^n$. Let f_i have derivative b^i and let A^i be the ith column of A. Then

$$\frac{f_i(x^n) - f_i(y^n)}{| x^n - y^n |} = b^i_{\hat{x}^n} \frac{(x^n - y^n)}{| x^n - y^n |} \qquad \text{(Lemma 7)}$$

$$\to A^i \lim \frac{(x^n - y^n)}{| x^n - y^n |} \qquad \left(\text{continuity of } \frac{\partial f_i}{\partial x_j}\right).$$

Therefore,

$$\frac{f(x^n) - f(y^n)}{| x^n - y^n |} \to A \lim \frac{(x^n - y^n)}{| x^n - y^n |} \neq 0.$$

Hence, for large n, $f(x^n) - f(y^n) \neq 0$. This shows that if $\delta > 0$ is small enough, $f(y) \neq f(z)$, y, $z \in \mathcal{N}_\delta(x)$. Therefore, f is 1–1 on $\mathcal{N}_\delta(x)$. Applying (iv) of Remark 6 gives the lemma.

(The argument on $\lim(x^n - y^n)/| x^n - y^n |$ can be made tighter by noting that for a sequence of vectors with norm one there is a subsequence $x^{n_k} - x/| x^{n_k} \quad x |$ tending to some y, which is the Bolzano—Weierstrass theorem.) q.e.d.

9 Lemma *If $\partial f_i/\partial y_j$ is continuous for all i and j and for all y in $\mathcal{N}_\varepsilon(x)$, then f is differentiable everywhere in $\mathcal{N}_\varepsilon(x)$.*

Proof Exercise 8.

It does not necessarily follow that functions differentiable everywhere in $\mathcal{N}_\varepsilon(x)$ have continuous partial derivations.

A function f is *homogeneous of degree n* if $f(kx) = k^n f(x)$.

10 Lemma (Euler's Theorem) *If f is differentiable at x and homogeneous of degree n, then*

$$nf(x) = \sum_{i=1}^{n} \frac{\partial f}{\partial x_i} x_i .$$

Exercise 6 Show that ij element of A as defined above is $\partial f_i/\partial x_j$.

Exercise 7 Prove Remark 5.

Exercise 8 Prove Lemma 9. (Hint: Consider

$$\frac{f(x) - f(\bar{x})}{| x - \bar{x} |}.$$

Apply the mean value theorem for one variable, first changing x_1 to $\bar{x}_1$, other components of x_1 constant; then x_2 to $\bar{x}_2$, etc. Then take limits as $x \to \bar{x}$.)

Exercise 9 Prove Lemma 10 by differentiating f with respect to k on both sides and then setting k equal to one.

PROBLEM

A. Lagrange Multipliers

Let x in $\mathscr{E}^n$ maximize $f(x)$ subject to $g_i(x) = c_i$, $i = 1,\ldots, m$, g_i real valued, f and g_i having continuous partial derivatives, and show that if for the last m of the $\bar{x}_j$, $(\partial g_i/\partial x_j)$ has a nonzero determinant, then

$$\frac{\partial f}{\partial x_j} + \sum_i \lambda_i \frac{\partial g_i}{\partial x_j} = 0$$

where

$$\lambda_i = - \sum_{k=n-m+1}^{n} \frac{\partial f}{\partial x_k} \left(\frac{\partial g}{\partial x_j}\right)^{-1}_{ik}$$

and

$$\left(\frac{\partial g}{\partial x_j}\right)^{-1}_{ik} \quad \text{is the } (i, k)\text{th element of} \quad \left(\frac{\partial g}{\partial x_j}\right)^{-1}_{m\times m}.$$

(Hint: Use Lemma 8 to show that f can be expressed as

$$f(x_i, \ldots, x_{m-1}, h_1(x_1, \ldots, x_{m-1}), \ldots, h_m(x_1, \ldots, x_{m-1}))$$

and then maximize f.)

The problem is due to Lagrange [1787].

5. Geometry of $\mathscr{E}^n$

The theory of convex sets and functions underlies the economics of production functions (Chapter 4, Section 4) and resource allocation (Chapter 4, Section 6, and Chapter 9, Section 6). The theory of convex functions is relevant to the study of utility (Chapter 6, Section 6; Chapter 7, Section 8; and Chapter 8, Section 6). First we consider convex sets and then convex functions.

A subset $\mathscr{X}$ of $\mathscr{E}^n$ is *closed* if $x^m \to x$, $x^m \in \mathscr{X}$ implies that $x \in \mathscr{X}$. The *closure* of $\mathscr{X}$, denoted $\bar{\mathscr{X}}$, is the smallest closed set containing $\mathscr{X}$. In Figure 1, the set $\mathscr{B}$ is closed whereas the set $\mathscr{A}$ is not closed.

In $\mathscr{E}^n$, a *line segment* is a set

$$\langle x, y\rangle \equiv \{tx + (1 - t)y \mid 0 \leqslant t \leqslant 1\}.$$

A subset $\mathscr{X}$ of $\mathscr{E}^n$ is *convex* if for all $x, y \in \mathscr{X}$, $\langle x, y\rangle \subset \mathscr{X}$. For example, a disc in $\mathscr{E}^2$ is convex whereas the circle bounding the disc is not convex.

A point x is *internal* to $\mathscr{X}$ if for every y in $\mathscr{X}$ there is a $t > 0$ such that $x + ty \in \mathscr{X}$. The set of internal points of $\mathscr{X}$ is denoted Int $\mathscr{X}$.

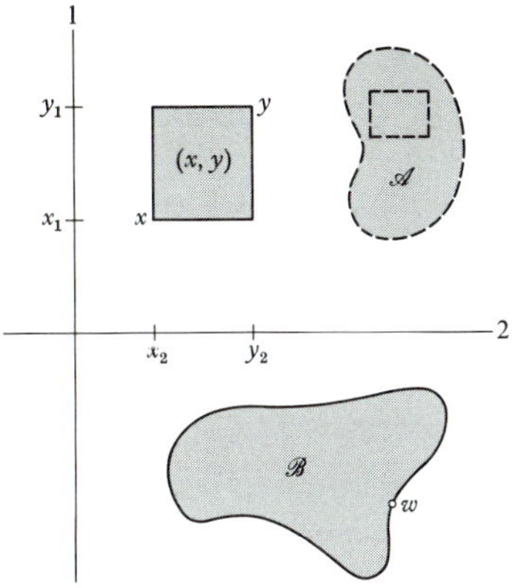

Figure 1

11 Remark If $\mathscr{X}$ is convex, Int $\bar{\mathscr{X}}$ = Int $\mathscr{X}$.

Points that are not internal to $\bar{\mathscr{X}}$ are *boundary* points. For example, the set of boundary points of a disc in $\mathscr{E}^2$ is the circle bounding the disc. The set of boundary points is denoted Bnd $\mathscr{X}$.

A *hyperplane* $\mathscr{H}(p)$ is a particular convex set, defined for a constant c and vector $p \neq 0$,

$$\mathscr{H}(p) = \{x \mid px - c\}.$$

In $\mathscr{E}^2$, a hyperplane is a line. In $\mathscr{E}^3$ a hyperplane is a plane.

12 Remark $\mathscr{H}(kp) = k\mathscr{H}(p)$ for $k \neq 0$.

As in Figure 2, a convex set is bounded by hyperplanes.

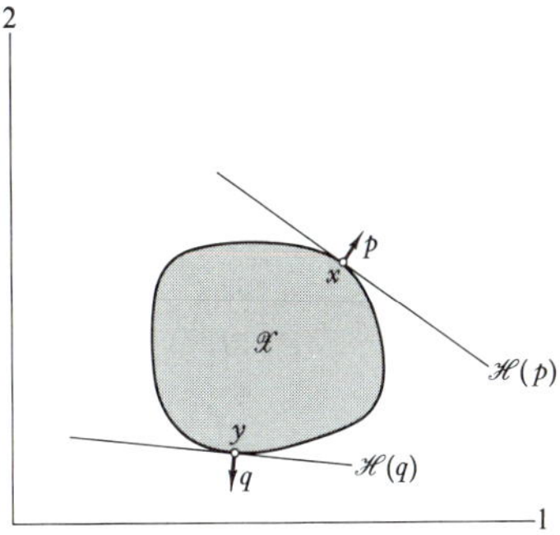

Figure 2

13 Lemma (Minkowski's Theorem) *If* $x \in \text{Bnd}\,\mathscr{X}$, *then there is a nonzero vector p such that*

$$px \geqslant py \qquad \textit{for all} \quad y \in \mathscr{X}.$$

Proof Hadley [1961, pp. 207–214].

A set $\mathscr{X}$ is a *cone* with origin x if for all $a > 0$ and $y \in \mathscr{X}$, $ay + x \in \mathscr{X}$. For example, a line through x is a cone with origin x.

A convex set $\mathscr{X}$ is *directional dense* at x, if either of the following equivalent conditions hold.

(a) There is at most one vector p, unique up to a multicative positive number, such that

$$p(\mathscr{X}) \geqslant px.$$

(b) For $\mathscr{Y}$ the smallest closed cone containing $\mathscr{X} - x$, $\mathscr{Y}$ has non-empty intersection with every line through the origin. (See Exercise 10.)

14 Remark If $\mathscr{X}$ is convex and directional dense at x, the smallest cone containing $\mathscr{X}$ contains the *half space* $\{y \mid py > px\}$.

Proof Exercise 11. The set $\mathscr{X}$ in Figure 2 is directional dense at all its points.

A real-valued function f is *convex* if

$$f(tx + (1-t)y) \leqslant tf(x) + (1-t)f(y) \qquad \text{for} \quad 0 \leqslant t \leqslant 1;$$

f is *strictly convex* if

$$f(tx + (1-t)y) < tf(x) + (1-t)f(y) \qquad \text{for} \quad 0 < t < 1;$$

f is *quasi convex* if

$$f(tx + (1-t)y) \leqslant \max(f(x), f(y)) \qquad \text{for} \quad 0 \leqslant t \leqslant 1;$$

f is *strictly quasi convex* if

$$f(tx + (1-t)y) < \max(f(x), f(y)) \qquad \text{for} \quad 0 < t < 1.$$

A real-valued function f is *(strictly) (quasi) concave* if $-f$ is *(strictly) (quasi)* convex.

In Figure 3, f is strictly concave and g is strictly convex.

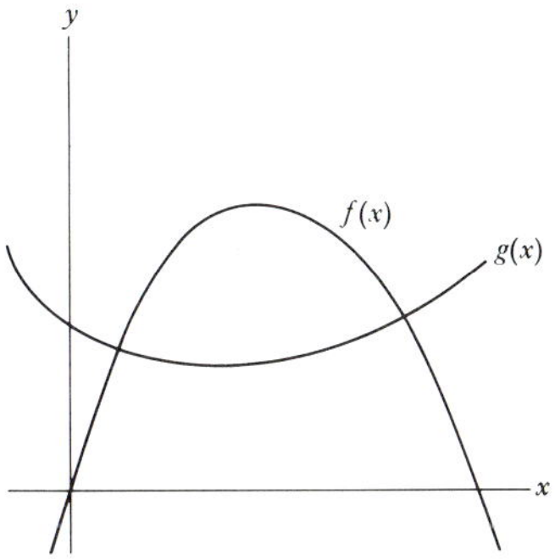

Figure 3

15 Remark (i) If f is strictly (quasi) convex, it is (quasi) convex.

(ii) If $f(x) \geqslant 0$ for all x, and f is (strictly) convex, it is (strictly) quasi convex.

(iii) On $\mathscr{E}^1$ any monotonic nondecreasing (increasing) function is (strictly) quasi concave. Any monotonic nonincreasing (decreasing) function is (strictly) quasi convex.

A set is *countable* if it is the union of points x_i, $i = 1, 2, \ldots$. For example, the set of rational numbers is countable. The real line is not countable.

16 Lemma *If f is convex or concave, f defined on $\mathscr{E}^1$, then excluding a countable set of points, f has a derivative df/dx that is continuous in x.*

Proof It suffices to consider the case of f convex. At a given x define the set

$$\lim_{\bar{x}\to x} \frac{\Delta f}{\Delta x} \equiv \left\{ y \mid \text{there is } x^n \to x \text{ such that } \frac{f(x^n) - f(x)}{(x^n - x)} \to y \right\}.$$

Then let

$$F^+(x) \equiv \lim_{\bar{x}\to x} \sup \frac{\Delta f}{\Delta x} \equiv \sup \left(\lim_{\bar{x}\to x} \frac{\Delta f}{\Delta x} \right).$$

Varying x, we have a function F^+ that for f convex can easily be shown to be monotonic nondecreasing. Also, monotonic functions are continuous except at a countable set of points (otherwise there would be so many gaps as to more than fill up the line).

Let $\inf g(x) \equiv -\sup(-g(x))$ be the greatest lower bound. Then by convexity of f,

$$F^-(x) \equiv \inf \left(\lim_{\bar{x}\to x} \frac{\Delta f}{\Delta x} \right)$$

is nondecreasing. Also, by convexity of f,

$$x \geqslant y, \qquad F^{-}(x) \geqslant F^{+}(y).$$

Except for a countable set, F^{-} and F^{+} are continuous and $F^{-} = F^{+}$. Therefore, at all but a countable set

$$\lim_{\bar{x}\to x} \frac{\Delta f}{\Delta x} = \lim_{\bar{x}\to x} \sup \frac{\Delta f}{\Delta x}$$

$$= \lim_{\bar{x}\to x} \inf \frac{\Delta f}{\Delta x} \qquad \text{and is continuous.} \qquad \text{q.e.d.}$$

Exercise 10 Show the equivalence of (a) and (b), in the definition of directional dense.

Exercise 11 Prove Remark 14.

Exercise 12 Prove Remark 15.

Exercise 13 Show that a strictly quasi-concave function takes a unique maximum (if any) on a convex set.

PROBLEMS

B. Concave Programming I

Consider the problem of maximizing $u(x)$, subject to

$$g^k(x) \leqslant p^k, \qquad k = 1,\ldots, n.$$

Let $f^k(x) = p^k - g^k(x)$, and $f(x) = (f^k(x))$.

Rewrite the problem: maximize $u(x)$ subject to $f(x) \geqslant 0$. This is the *primal problem.*

It is assumed that there is an x' for which $f^k(x') > 0$ for $k = 1,\ldots, m$. Suppose that u and f are concave functions. Consider the function

$$\phi(x, y) = u(x) + \sum_{k=1}^{m} y^k f^k(x)$$

$$= u(x) + \sum_{k=1}^{m} y^k p^k - \sum_{k=1}^{m} y^k g^k(x).$$

1. Show that ϕ has a saddle point whenever there is a solution to the primal problem by showing:

1a. If $\bar{x}$ solves the primal problem there are numbers v_k, $k = 0, 1, \ldots, m$, not all zero such that

$$v_0 u(\bar{x}) + \sum v_k f^k(\bar{x}) \geqslant v_0 u(x) + \sum v_k f^k(x)$$

for all x. (Hint: Use the concavity of the function and Minkowski's theorem: Lemma 13.)

1b. The v_k are nonnegative.

1c. $v_0 > 0$.

1d. Let $\bar{y}_k = v_k/v_0$, $k = 1, \ldots, m$. Then $\bar{x}$ is a maximizer of $\phi(x, \bar{y})$, that is,

$$u(\bar{x}) + \sum_{k=1}^{m} y^k f^k(\bar{x}) \geqslant u(x) + \sum_{k=1}^{m} y^k f^k(x).$$

1e. $\bar{y}$ defined in 1d is a minimizer of $\phi(x, y)$ given $y \geqslant 0$.

2. Show that a "saddle point" $(\bar{x}, \bar{y})$ of ϕ is such that x solves the primal problem.

This problem was solved by Karlin [1959, pp. 201–203]. The first solution was offered by Kuhn and Tucker [1951].

C. *Homogeneous Programming I*

Let u in Problem B be homogeneous of degree t_0. Let g^k in B be homogeneous of degree t_k. Then Euler's theorem gives

$$u(x) = t_0 \sum_{i=1}^{m} \frac{\partial u^k}{\partial x_i} x_i$$

$$g^k = t_k \sum_{i=1}^{m} \frac{\partial g^k}{\partial x_i} x_i, \qquad k = 1, \ldots, m.$$

(Assume that it is required that $x_i \geqslant 0$, $i = 1, \ldots, n$.) Hence,

$$\phi(x, y) = \sum_{i=1}^{n} \left(t_0 \frac{\partial u}{\partial x_i}\right) x_i - \sum_{k=1}^{n} \sum_{i=1}^{m} \left(t_k \frac{\partial g^k}{\partial x_i}\right) x_i + \sum_{k=1}^{n} p_k y_k.$$

1. Show that y minimizes

$$\sum_{k=1}^{m} p_k y_k$$

subject to

$$\sum_{k=1}^{m} \left(t_k \frac{\partial g^k}{\partial x_i}\right) y_k \geqslant t_0 \frac{\partial \phi}{\partial x_i}, \qquad i = 1,..., n,$$

$$y_k \geqslant 0, \qquad k= 1,..., n.$$

This is the *dual problem.*

2. Show that the "payoffs" from the dual and the primal are equal, that is,

$$u(\bar{x}) = \sum_{k=1}^{m} p_k \bar{y}_k .$$

3. Suppose the degree of homogeneity is 1, that is, $t_k = 1$ for $k = 0, 1,..., m$; show that if x and y satisfy the inequalities

$$g^k(x) \leqslant p_k, \qquad k = 1,..., m,$$

$$y^k \geqslant 0, \qquad k = 1,..., m,$$

$$\sum_{k=1}^{m} \frac{\partial g^k}{\partial x_i} y^k \geqslant \frac{\partial \phi}{\partial x_i}, \qquad i = 1,..., m$$

(for any $x_i \geqslant 0$, $i = 1,..., n$), then x and y are the solution of the primal and dual problem if, and only if, $u(x) = \sum_{i=1}^{m} p_k y_k$. (Hint: Concave functions satisfy the law

$$h(x) - h(x') \leqslant \sum_{i=1}^{n} \frac{\partial h}{\partial x_i} (x_i - x_i')$$

and homogeneous functions of degree 1 satisfy

$$h(x) = \frac{\partial h}{\partial x} x.)$$

The significance of 3 is that the dual may be solved independently of the primal, which is not generally true in concave programming. In fact, the solution of the dual is merely a linear programming program.

This problem was solved by van Moeseke [1964].

D. Linear Programming I

A linear programming problem is that of maximizing the linear form

$$u = \sum_{i=1}^{n} x_i c_i$$

subject to

$$\sum_{i=1}^{n} a_{ij} \leqslant b_j\,, \qquad j = 1,\ldots, m,$$

$$x \geqslant 0, \qquad i = 1,\ldots, n.$$

Use Problem B.1 to show that the foregoing primal problem has a solution if, and only if, there is a solution to the problem of minimizing

$$v = \sum_{j=1}^{m} y_i b_j$$

subject to

$$\sum_{j=1}^{m} a_{ij} \geqslant c_i\,, \qquad i = 1,\ldots, n,$$

$$y_j \geqslant 0, \qquad j = 1,\ldots, m.$$

(What condition is needed on the matrix (a_{ij}) ?) Show that for $\bar{x}$ solving the primal, $\bar{y}$ solving the dual,

$$v = \sum_{j=1}^{m} \bar{y}_j b_j = \sum_{i=1}^{n} a_{ij}\bar{x}_i = u.$$

Show that

$$\phi(x, y) - \sum_{i=1}^{n} c_i x_i - \sum_{i=1}^{n} \sum_{j=1}^{m} a_{ij} y_j + \sum_{j=1}^{m} b_j y_j$$

has a saddle point exactly at $(\bar{x}, \bar{y})$ solving the primal and dual problems; that is, ϕ has a maximum for $x \geqslant 0$ at $\bar{x}$, fixing $\bar{y}$, and a minimum for $y \geqslant 0$, at $\bar{y}$, fixing $\bar{x}$.

E. Linear Programming II

Consider the set

$$\mathscr{X} = \{x \mid Ax \leqslant b, \quad x \in \mathscr{E}^n\}.$$

1. Show that $\mathscr{X}$ is closed and convex.
2. Show that the boundary of $\mathscr{X}$ is contained in the union of hyperplanes of the form

$$\mathscr{A}_i = \left\{x \,\middle|\, \sum_{j=1}^{n} x_j a_{ij} = b_i\right\}.$$

(Hint: Show that Bnd $\bigcap \mathscr{A}_i \subset \bigcup_i$ Bnd $\mathscr{A}_i$ for $\mathscr{A}_i$ closed.)

3. An *extreme point* of $\mathscr{X}$ is a point that cannot be written as a convex combination of two other points in $\mathscr{X}$. Show that extreme points of $\mathscr{X}$ occur exactly at points where there is an intersection of n independent hyperplanes of the form

$$\sum_{j=1}^{n} x_j a_{ij} = b_i .$$

4. Show that $\mathscr{X}$ has a finite number of extreme points.
5. Suppose x maximizes $\sum_{i=1}^{n} c_i x_i$, all c_i not zero.
Show that if $\mathscr{X}$ has an extreme point, then there is at least one that has the same payoff as x. (Hint: Use the Krein–Millman theorem, that every point of a convex, compact set is the convex sum of extreme points (Kelly and Namioka [1963, p. 131]).)
6. A *search procedure* is a systematic consideration first of a point in the boundary of $\mathscr{X}$ and then of extreme points, one by one.
Show that a search procedure necessarily discovers the maximum payoff and maximizing x. (Hint: Show that if $\mathscr{X}$ has no extreme points, $z = \sum c_i z_i$ for maximizing the payoff and for any z in the boundary of $\mathscr{X}$, z_i extreme points.)

Much of the analysis here is contained in Hadley [1961, Chapter 6.]

F. Linear Programming III

An efficient search procedure is the *simplex* procedure. The equations $Ax \leqslant b$ are supplemented with slack variables to make up the difference between $\sum_{i=1}^{n} a_{ij} x_i$ and b_j. These are denoted x_{n+j} for the jth constraint. The new problem, equivalent to the old, becomes

$$b = ax^1 + x^2 = (A \mid I)\binom{x^1}{x^2}.$$

Now choose any m columns of $(A \mid I)$ that are linearly independent to form the matrix $A^{\mathscr{I}}$, $\mathscr{I}$ an m-element subset of $\{1, 2,..., m + n\}$. Solve $A^{\mathscr{I}} x^{\mathscr{I}} = b$, that is, $x^{\mathscr{I}} = (A^{\mathscr{I}})^{-1} b$.

1. Then estimate implicit prices $y^{\mathscr{I}}$ as

$$y^{\mathscr{I}} = (A^{\mathscr{I}})^{-1} c^{\mathscr{I}}$$

where $c^{\mathscr{I}}$ is the vector of payoff coefficients for the subset $\mathscr{I}$. Then, check to see if

$$Ay^{\mathscr{I}} \geqslant c.$$

If so, show that $x^{\mathscr{I}}$ is optimal. (Hint: Observe that by

$$\mathscr{I} = b(A^{\mathscr{I}})^{-1}c^{\mathscr{I}} = (x^1.)c^{\mathscr{I}}$$

and apply Problem K.)

A solution of this problem appears in Gale [1960]. It was first solved by George Danzig.

G. Concave Programming II

1. Show that if $\mathscr{A}$ is a closed convex set in $\mathscr{E}^n$, then $\mathscr{A}$ is the union of all points $\{x \mid \text{for every } p \text{ such that } p(\mathscr{A}) \geqslant c,\ px \geqslant c.\}$. (Hint: Use Minkowski's theorem, Lemma 28.)

2. Therefore, convex, closed, and bounded $\mathscr{A}$ can be approximated by the linear constraints

$$f_j(x) \leqslant f_j(y) = b_j\,, \qquad j = 1,..., n,$$

where the linear function bounds at grid points x^j in $\mathscr{A}$, $j = 1,..., m$. Show that the solution of the problem, maximize $u(x)$ subject to

$$f^k(x) \leqslant c^k, \qquad k = 1,..., m,$$

u and f concave, can be approximated by the simplex procedure. (Hint: Reduce the problem to maximize x_0 subject to

$$x_0 \leqslant u(x) + a, \qquad f^k(x) \leqslant c^k, \qquad k = 1,..., m,$$

where a is a constraint sufficiently large such that $x_0 \geqslant 0$. Then use linear constraints for $f^k(x)$ and solve the linear program. Let the number of linear constraints tend to infinity in such a way that the limit points of the solution satisfy the inequalities above.)

This problem was first solved in a modified form by Kelley [1960] and is known as the cutting plane technique. If the solution is stopped short of convergence, it may be that the estimated solution is not feasible. One procedure is simply to choose that grid point which is nearest the solution.

A modification appears in Hartley and Hocking [1963].

6. Open Sets and Topological Spaces

There are two reasons for moving to an abstract level of discussion as in Chapters 5, 6, and 7 on consumption. First, application can be made to space that are not $\mathscr{E}^n$, such as when there are an infinite number of coordinates. (This is especially important in the analysis of preferences over a infinite time horizon.) Second, certain properties of $\mathscr{E}^n$ are singled out for special attention and are more easily manipulated in proofs. The remainder of this chapter is necessary in order to follow Chapters 5, 6, and 7.

Closed subsets of $\mathscr{E}^n$ were defined in the previous section. Intuitively speaking, the limit points of a subset of a space are points in the set and on its boundary. *Closed* sets are sets that contain all their limit points. It is convenient to have a definition of *open* sets $\mathscr{O}$; namely, these are sets whose converse $\sim\mathscr{O}$ is closed. It should be emphasized that according to this rule once the open sets are specified, so are the closed sets, and vice versa. Therefore, the distinction between open and closed sets is an analytical convenience. Because it is not always obvious which sets are closed and which are open, formal definitions are needed.

A *topological space* is a set $\mathscr{U}$ for which certain subsets have been assigned the adjective *open* subject to the rules (a) arbitrary unions of open sets are open, (b) finite intersections of open sets are open, and (c) $\mathscr{U}$ is open, as is the empty set $\varnothing$.

A *closed* set $\mathscr{B}$ is a set such that $\sim\mathscr{B}$ is open. For example, the $\mathscr{B}$ in Figure 1 is such that any point not in $\mathscr{B}$ is contained in an open interval not in $\mathscr{B}$. Hence the set $\sim\mathscr{B}$ is open and $\mathscr{B}$ is closed. A set $\mathscr{A}$ is *dense* in $\mathscr{B}$ if every open set containing a point of $\mathscr{B}$ also contains a point of $\mathscr{A}$.

Example 1 In the Euclidean plane the open sets can be specified as all points or unions thereof. This space is called the *discrete* topology and it seems to be a rather trivial application of the definition.

Example 2 Common classification of open sets is the ordinary topology in the plane where open sets are defined to be any sets that are unions of open *intervals*, $(x, y) \equiv \{z \mid y \geqslant z \geqslant x\}$.

Such an open interval is illustrated in Figure 1. Also, the set $\mathscr{A}$ is open since it is the union of (possibly very small) intervals about each of its points.

Example 3 A metric space can be defined as follows. A distance function d is a metric if d is defined on $\mathscr{U} \times \mathscr{U}$ and

$$\begin{aligned}
&\text{(i)} \quad d(x, y) = d(y, x),\\
&\text{(ii)} \quad d(x, y) + d(y, z) \geqslant d(x, z) \qquad \text{(triangle inequality)},\\
&\text{(iii)} \quad d(x, y) = 0 \quad \text{iff} \quad x = y.
\end{aligned}$$

For example, in the plane, it can be verified that

$$d(x, y) = | x - y | = ((x_1 - y_1)^2 + (x_2 - y_2))^{1/2}$$

satisfies (i), (ii), and (iii).[1]

Equivalently, $\mathcal{O}$ is open if for each of its points x there exists an *ε-neighborhood*

$$\mathcal{N}_\varepsilon(x) = \{y : d(x, y) < \varepsilon\} \subset \mathcal{O}.$$

A set of open sets from which all open sets can be constructed by operations (a) and (b) is said to be a *base* for the topological space. For example, in the plane the open intervals of the form (x, y) make up a base. A subset of a base from which the base can be constructed is itself a base and hence is termed a *subbase*. For example, between any two real numbers there is a rational number—that is, a number of the form n/m, n and m integers. Let z be a point in an open set (such as $\mathcal{A}$ in Figure 1) and contained in an interval (z', z'') entirely in the open set. Then by taking a rational number between each of z_1 and z_1', z_2 and z_2', z_1 and z_1'', z_2 and z_2'' we can construct a new interval, whose end points have rational coordinates $(\bar{z}', \bar{z}'')$, that is entirely contained in the old interval and that contains z. Hence all open sets are the union of intervals with rational coordinates for the end points. When the base is such that its members can be counted out according to the positive integers, so that in the counting process every set in the base is counted, then the base is said to be *countable* and the topological space is said to be *completely separable*. For example, the rational numbers are countable, so points with rational coordinates are equivalent to pairs of rational numbers and hence countable; finally, intervals with "rational" end points are countable. The plane has a countable base and is therefore completely separable in the usual topology. The *closure* of a set $\mathcal{B}$ is the smallest closed set containing $\mathcal{B}$; $\mathcal{A}$ is dense in $\mathcal{B}$ if and only if the closure of $\mathcal{A}$ contains $\mathcal{B}$. If one point of $\mathcal{B}$ in Figure 1, say w, is eliminated, we have a set that is dense in the whole of $\mathcal{B}$. A space is *separable* if it has a countable subset dense in space. By choosing one point from each open set in the countable base (which is possible by the

[1] The class of metric spaces is very large. The theorem on metrization is due to Urysohn:

Lemma *Suppose the topology of a space is such that* (a) *every point of the space is closed,* (b) *for every open set $\mathcal{O}$ containing x, there is an open set $\mathcal{O}'$ containing x but whose closure is contained in $\mathcal{O}$, and* (c) *the space has a completely separable topology* (*defined below*). *Then there exists a distance function d such that the metric topology associated with this function is identical to the topology of the space.*

axiom of choice as stated in Chapter 3, Section 3), we have a dense countable set for completely separable spaces.

17 Remark A completely separable space is separable.

Proof Each open set contains at least one member of the countable base, provided the base includes all its finite intersections, which is possible without altering countability of the base. If $\mathscr{A}$ is a set of points with elements in each member of the countable base, then $\mathscr{A}$ has a point in each open set. The smallest closed set containing a set $\mathscr{A}$ is the complement of the largest open set not in the set $\mathscr{A}$. Hence, if $\mathscr{A}$ has a nonempty intersection with every open set, the largest open set not in $\mathscr{A}$ is the empty set, and its complement $\mathscr{U} \sim \varnothing$ is the whole space; that is, $\mathscr{A}$ is dense in $\mathscr{U}$. q.e.d.

An example of a space that is separable but not completely separable is the plane when it is assigned as open sets, sets that are complements of finite collections of points. In order to classify these open sets, we must be able to classify all possible finite collections of points,because arbitrary unions and finite intersections are applied to the complements of sets in the base of open sets to obtain all possible finite combinations of points. The points of the plane cannot be so derived from a countable set and hence a countable collection of sets cannot be a base for the open sets; the topology is not completely separable. On the other hand, the the only infinite closed set is the whole plane; so any nonfinite countable set has closure equal to the whole space—that is, is dense in the space—and hence the space is separable.

A set is *connected* provided it is not the union of two disjoint open sets. In Figure 1 the sets $\mathscr{B}$, $\mathscr{A}$, and (x, y) are, respectively, connected. The set $\mathscr{B} \cup \mathscr{A}$ in Figure 1 is not connected because it can be decomposed into two open disjoint sets $\mathscr{A}$ and $\mathscr{B}$ ($\mathscr{B}$ is open in $\mathscr{B} \cup \mathscr{A}$). In the separable but not completely separable space described above, every open set is connected.

Two applications of topological ideas are presented here for use in the theory of consumption.

The sets $\mathscr{X}_\alpha$, $\alpha \in \mathscr{A}$ *cover* $\mathscr{Y}$ if $\mathscr{Y} \subset \bigcup \mathscr{X}_\alpha$. The cover is *open* if the $\mathscr{X}_\alpha$ are open. A set $\mathscr{Y}$ is *compact* if for every open cover $\mathscr{X}_\alpha$, $\alpha \in \mathscr{A}$, there is an open cover consisting of only a finite number of the $\mathscr{X}_\alpha$.

18 Remark Arbitrary intersections and finite unions of compact sets are compact.

In $\mathscr{E}^n$ a set $\mathscr{X}$ is bounded if there is a k such that $k \geqslant |x|$ for all $x \in \mathscr{X}$.

19 Lemma (Heine–Borel Theorem) *In $\mathscr{E}^n$, a closed, bounded set is compact.*

20 Lemma (Finite Intersection Property) *If any finite intersection of compact $\mathscr{X}_\alpha$, $\alpha \in \mathscr{A}$, is nonempty, then*

$$\bigcap_{\alpha \in \mathscr{A}} \mathscr{X}_\alpha \neq \varnothing.$$

Proof Let $\mathscr{X} = \bigcup_{\alpha \in \mathscr{A}} \mathscr{X}_\alpha$, if to the contrary, $\bigcap_{\alpha \in \mathscr{A}} \mathscr{X}_\alpha = \varnothing$, then $\bigcup_{\alpha \in \mathscr{A}} \mathscr{X} \sim \mathscr{X}_\alpha = \mathscr{X} \sim \bigcap_{\alpha \in \mathscr{A}} \mathscr{X}_\alpha = \mathscr{X}$ covers all $\mathscr{X}_\beta$. Since $\mathscr{X}_\beta$ is compact, for some α_i, $i = 1,..., n$, $\mathscr{X}_\beta \subset \bigcup_{i=1}^n \mathscr{X} \sim \mathscr{X}_{\alpha_i} = \mathscr{X} \sim \bigcap_{i=1}^n \mathscr{X}_{\alpha_i}$. However by hypothesis, there is

$$x \in \left(\bigcap_{i=1} \mathscr{X}_{\alpha_i}\right) \cap \mathscr{X}_\beta .$$

Hence $x \in \mathscr{X}_\beta$ but not $x \in \mathscr{X} \sim \bigcap_{i=1}^n \mathscr{X}_{\alpha_i}$, contrary to $\mathscr{X}_\beta \subset \mathscr{X} \sim \bigcap_{i=1}^n \mathscr{X}_{\alpha_i}$.
q.e.d.

A function f is *continuous* if and only if f^{-1} takes open sets onto open sets; that is, $f^{-1}(\mathscr{O})$ is open whenever $\mathscr{O}$ is open. There is an equivalent definition in metric spaces where the metric topology is used: namely, f is *continuous* at x if and only if for $\varepsilon > 0$, there is a $\delta > 0$ such that

$$d(f(x), f(y)) < \varepsilon \qquad \text{whenever} \quad d(x, y) < \delta.$$

It is useful to show the equivalence of these two definitions. It is also useful to define a discontinuous function by denying the definition of a continuous function. Indeed anyone aspiring to do mathematical analysis must be able to handle the continuity definitions with skill and love; they form the very heart of mathematical analysis whence sprang both topology and modern functional analysis. In this regard it should be recognized that the work of such writers as Weierstrass and Bolzano in the first half of the nineteenth century on the continuous functions and their properties was literally the basis of modern mathematics.

Exercise 14 Show that $\mathscr{E}^n$ is a metric space for

$$d(x, y) = \left(\sum_{i=1}^{n} (x_i - y_i)^2\right)^{1/2}.$$

Exercise 15 Define a closed set to be one that contains its limit points. For a metric space, show that an arbitrary (or infinite) intersection of closed sets is closed and that a finite union of closed sets is closed.

Exercise 16 Define an *open* set to be a set whose converse is closed. Show that the arbitrary union of open sets is open and the finite intersection of open sets in open.

Exercise 17 Is the arbitary union of closed sets closed or the arbitarry intersection of open sets open?

Exercise 18 Show that a set is open if and only if it is the union of ε neighborhoods.

Exercise 19 Assume only (a) and (b) of the definition of a topological space. When are the universal set and the empty set both open and closed?

Exercise 20 Prove that $\mathscr{E}^n$ is completely separable.

Exercise 21 Prove that $\mathscr{E}^n$ is connected.

Exercise 22 Let f map a metric space $\mathscr{X}$ into a metric space $\mathscr{Y}$. f is *continuous* if $\lim f(x^n) = f(x)$ whenever $\lim x^n = x$. Show equivalence with two definitions in the text.

Exercise 23 For real numbers x and a constant c, show continuity of

(i) $f(x) = c$, (ii) $f(x) = x$,

(iii) $f(x) = x^n$, (iv) $f(x) = \dfrac{1}{x}$.

Exercise 24 Let f and g be continuous. Show continuity of

(i) $f + g$, (ii) fg,

(iii) $\dfrac{f}{g}$, (iv) f^k, k not necessarily an integer,

(v) $-f$.

Exercise 25 Suppose f is defined on the interval (x, y). Let f be continuous at one point z. Is it necessary that there be another point w at which f is continuous?

Exercise 26 Show that continuous functions take connected sets into connected sets.

Exercise 27 Show that the only connected sets in the line are intervals.

Exercise 28 Let f be real valued and continuous between x and y. Show that for any m for which $f(x) \leqslant m \leqslant f(y)$, there is an $x < z < y$ such that $f(z) = m$. (This is the intermediate value theorem.)

PROBLEM

H. International Prices and International Trade I

Let the world be denoted $\mathscr{X}$ and let each location have a goods price, $p(x)$. Suppose transport costs for x_i to y are $t(x, y)$, and assume

(a) $t(x, y) = t(y, x) \geqslant 0$,
(b) $t(x, y) = 0$ if and only if $x = y$,
(c) $t(x, y)$ is continuous in x and y,
(d) if $x \neq y$, there is an *arc* $f(s)$ from x to y (for which $f(0) = x$, $f(1) = y$, continuous and 1–1) such that $t(x, f(s)) + t(f(s)y) = t(x, y)$ for all $s \in [0, 1]$.

Suppose the good is produced at a finite number of locations x_i, $i = 1,\ldots, n$, for which $p(x_i) = p_i$. Let the trade areas $\mathscr{X}_i$ of each site be defined as regions over which goods from x_i are traded at the prices

$$p(x) = p(x) + t(x_i, x).$$

Presume the cheapest export plus transport price prevails. Show that

(a) $\mathscr{X}_i$ is closed.
(b) $\mathscr{X}_i \cap \mathscr{X}_j$ contains no open sets.
(c) $\mathscr{X}_i$ is connected.

7. Measure and Integration

In economics, measure theory is used in the analysis of continuum-type problems. In this book, the main application is to utility and probability in Chapters 6 and 7.

The *outer measure* of a set $\mathscr{X} \subset \mathscr{E}^n$, denoted $\mu(\mathscr{X})$, is the greatest lower bound of the sum of measures of intervals containing $\mathscr{X}$. Evidently, $\mu(\mathscr{X}) \geqslant 0$.

21 Remark A sequence of points x_i, $i = 1, 2,\ldots$, has outer measure equal to zero.

Proof

$$0 \leqslant \mu\left(\bigcup_{i=1}^{\infty} \{x_i\}\right) \leqslant \sum_{i=1}^{\infty} \mu(a_i, b_i), \qquad a_i > x_i > b_i .$$

Since (y_i, z_i) can be chosen such that

$$\mu(y_i, z_i) \leqslant (\tfrac{1}{2})^i\delta, \qquad \delta > 0,$$

$$0 \leqslant \mu\left(\bigcup_{i=1}^{\infty} \{x_i\}\right) \leqslant \sum_{i=1}^{\infty} (\tfrac{1}{2})^i\delta = \delta.$$

Since δ was arbitrary, $\mu(\bigcup_{i=1}^{\infty} \{x_i\}) = 0$. q.e.d.

There is a certain class $\mathcal{m}$ of subsets such that if $\mathscr{A}_i \in \mathcal{m}$ disjoint, $i = 1, 2, \ldots$, then $\mu(\bigcup_{i=1}^{\infty} \mathscr{A}_i) = \sum_{i=1}^{\infty} \mu(\mathscr{A}_i)$. Sets in the class $\mathcal{m}$ are called *measurable* with *measure* μ where μ is countably additive on $\mathcal{m}$.

The notion of a set of measure zero is a (strong) version of an insignificant set. If a property holds for all points except for a set of measure zero, it is said that the property holds *almost everywhere.*

22 Remark The class $\mathcal{m}$ is closed under the operations countable union, countable intersection, and set theoretic difference. Also, $\mathcal{m}$ has as elements the whole space and the empty set. Whenever a class of sets is closed under finite union, intersection, and set theoretic differences, it is said to be a *Boolean algebra.* Under the condition of the remark where countable operations are permissible, we have a *σ-Boolean algebra.* A *measure space* is a class of sets that are a σ-Boolean algebra together with a countably additive measure defined on the algebra.

The following definitions lead into the theory of integration. A *characteristic function* f on a set $\mathscr{M} \in \mathcal{m}$ is defined as

$$f(x) = 1 \quad \text{if} \quad x \in \mathscr{M}, \qquad f(x) = 0 \quad \text{if} \quad x \in {\sim}\mathscr{M}.$$

A *simple function* f is one of the form

$$f(x) = \sum_{i=1}^{n} c_i f_i(x)$$

where the f_i are characteristic function on $\mathscr{M}_i \in \mathcal{m}$. The *integral* of a simple function is defined as

$$\int f(x)\, d\mu = \sum_{i=1}^{n} c_i \mu(\mathscr{M}_i).$$

An integration theory for many other so-called integrable functions can be constructed by taking limits of simple functions (Halmos [1950, Chapter V]). Since the application of integration in this book is to only one topic, it would not be appropriate to develop the theory here. In the case of $\mathscr{E}^1$ the situation is much simpler than in the case of arbitrary measure spaces (Exercises 29–32).

Exercise 29 Let integrals on $[x, y]$ be defined as

$$\int_1 f = \lim_{\delta\to 0} \sum_{i=1}^{n} f(x_i)(x_{i+1} - x_i)$$

$$(x_1 = x, \quad x_n = y, \quad x_{i+1} - x_i < \delta) \qquad \text{(Riemann).}$$

$$\int_2 f = \lim_{\delta\to 0} \sum_{i=1}^{n} f(z_i)(x_{i+1} - x_i)$$

if

$$z_i \in [x_i\,,\, x_{i+1}] \qquad \text{(Riemann–Stieltjes).}$$

$$\int_3 f = \lim_{\delta\to 0} \sum_{i=1}^{n} (x_{i+1} - x_i) \sup_{z\in[x_i, x_{i+1}]} f(z) \qquad \text{(Darboux).}$$

(Recall that sup is the least upper bound and inf is the *greatest lower* bound.)

$$\int_4 f = \lim_{\delta\to 0} \sum_{i=1}^{n} (x_{i+1} - x_i) \inf_{z\in[x_i, x_{i+1}]} f(z)$$

$$= -\int_3 (-f) \qquad \text{(Darboux).}$$

Show that these integrals are defined and identical for continuous functions f. Show that in this case,

$$f = \frac{d}{dx}\left(\int f\right).$$

Exercise 30 Show that $\int_i$, $i = 1,\ldots, 4$, are *linear operators*:

$$\int_i (f + g) = \int_i f + \int_i g, \qquad \int_i cf = c \int_i f \qquad \text{for } c \text{ a constant.}$$

Exercise 31 Show that for f differentiable on $[x, y]$,

$$\int \frac{df}{dx} = f.$$

Exercise 32 Let $f(x)$ be bounded. Show that it can be changed on a set of measure zero without changing

$$\int_{x_0}^{x_1} f(x)\, dx$$

PROBLEMS

I. Calculus of Variations I

Suppose we wish to maximize

$$\int_0^T f(x, x')\, dt$$

subject to

$$x(0) = x_0\,, \qquad x(T) = x_1\,, \qquad g^k(x, x') = c_k\,, \qquad k = 1,\dots, m.$$

Then once $x'(t)$ is determined, $x(t)$ is immediately known. Let $\partial g_k/\partial x_j$ be the matrix of the last n partial derivatives of g_k and suppose

$$\det \frac{\partial g_k}{\partial x_j'} \neq 0$$

at the maximizer $x(t)$. Show that there are λ_k, $k = 1,\dots, m$, defined as in Problem A such that the Euler–Lagrange equations are satisfied:

$$\frac{\partial f}{\partial x} + \sum_{k=1}^{m} \lambda_k \frac{\partial g_k}{\partial x} = \frac{d}{dt}\left\{\frac{\partial f}{\partial x'} + \sum_{k=1}^{m} \lambda_k \frac{\partial g_k}{\partial x}\right\}.$$

(If there are no constraints, it is the Euler equation.) (Hint: 1. Write the last m components of x and m components of x' as functions of the first $n - m$ x_i and $n - m$ x_i', analogously to the case in Problem A. Then maximize freely

$$\int_0^T h\left(y, \frac{dy}{dt}\right),$$

y in $\mathscr{E}^{n-m}$, h derived from the inversion of the g^k's.

2. Let there be a change in dy/dt, $\delta(t)$, such that

$$\int_0^T \delta(t)\, dt = 0.$$

Then

$$0 \geqslant \int_0^T \left\{h\left(y + \int_0^t \delta(s), \frac{dy}{dt} + \delta(t)\right) - h\left(y, \frac{dy}{dt}\right)\right\} dt.$$

Apply the mean value theorem to show

$$0 = \int_0^T \left(\frac{\partial h}{\partial y} - \frac{d}{dt}\frac{\partial h}{\partial(dy/dt)}\right)\left(\int_0^t \delta(s)\, ds\right) dt.)$$

(Why does $(d/dt)(\partial h_i/\partial y_j)$ exist?)

The solution to the problem appears in Bliss [1945]. The problem was first solved by Lagrange [1787].

J. Calculus of Variations II

Maximize $\int_0^T f(x, x', t)\,dt$ subject to

$$x(0) = x_0\,, \qquad x(T) = x_1\,, \qquad g^k(x, x') = c_k\,, \quad k = 1,\ldots, m.$$

What additional conditions must be added to allow for variations in T?

K. International Prices and International Trade II

Let transportation costs per unit transported be $p_i e^{\rho T} \int_0^T g(x, x')\,dt$ where $-\rho$ is the rate of interest. What are the necessary conditions for maximization, and what is their interpretation?

UNSOLVED PROBLEM

L. International Prices and International Trade III

In Problem H what restrictions on g ensure that there is a cost-minimizing arc? (See Bliss [1945], Chapters II and IX.)

3

Economic Background

For a fruitful application of mathematics to economics, it is essential, *first*, that all assumptions on which the given mathematical representation of economic phenomena depends be enumerated completely and precisely; *second* that only those conclusions be drawn which are valid in the strictest sense.

Abraham Wald
"On Some Systems of Equations of Mathematical Economics"
Econometrica, 19 (1936), 368–369

1. Axiomatic Method

This section outlines the general method used through the book. In Section 2, the formal structure of economics as discussed in Chapter 1 is elaborated and compared with the theory of resource allocations and with classical mechanics. Details of this structure include orderings (Section 3) and the commodity space (Section 4). The case of market behavior pervades economic thinking and an introduction to its methods appears in Sections 5 and 6. The material presented in Sections 1–6 is of wide application in succeeding chapters. In Section 7, the treatment of noncooperative game theory is directly relevant, not so much to economics as to social science in general. Application of Section 7 to this book appears in Chapter 10 only.

Mathematical reasoning consists of the development of certain clearly defined propositions (remarks, lemmata, theorems) from certain equally clearly defined principles or assumptions (axioms). To carry out mathematical analysis, we must have some ground rules for the manipulation of axioms, as in Sections 1 and 2 of Chapter 2. In addition to the meta-axioms and the meta-theorems derived from them, we should note certain principles that mathematicians and scientific theorists have learned from experience. For example, a number of axioms, among them the ones defining the real number system (as in Section 3 of Chapter 2), are especially rich in consequences. Also, special variants of reasoning lead to especially rich results—many of these come up later in the text.

Requirements for an axiomatic mathematics are an important example for any science. David Hilbert set down such requirements in his *Grundlagen der Geometrie* [1899]. It cannot be said that his program was successful; nevertheless, the general outline of his approach has become a guideline for research into the meta-axiomatics of mathematics. The four main characteristics that axioms must fulfill are that they should be (a) logically consistent, (b) independent of each other—that is, one or more should not be implied by some combination of the others, (c) complete, at least in the sense that all known theorems or propositions of the science should be derivable from the axioms, and (d) general to the extent that no assumption is made unnecessary to deduce the conclusions in (c) (*Occam's razor*) (Popper [1959]).

Consistency is the most important requirement, since any proposition may be deduced from a collection of inconsistent propositions (Beth [1953]). That which makes no sense is not useful, although that which makes no apparent sense may prove to be useful. Independence of the axioms is achieved by tracing first causes, or in more common language "stating one's assumptions."

Hilbert originally suggested that completeness cover all possible theorems or propositions of the science but Gödel [1931] demonstrated that this was impossible in mathematics. Hence, we start with a given (finite) self-consistent collection of propositions, which are the foundations of the theory. Presumably there will be several independent subcollections of axioms, each subcollection implying the foundations. It is the practice of most mathematicians to isolate each of these systems with special emphasis on the simplest versions—that is, on those that can be stated in the most straightforward fashion or in the shortest amount of time. By consideration of each separate system, all possible applications of the theory can be ascertained as represented by all possible situations in which any of the axiom systems obtain.

There are certain principles with which scientific theorists alone are concerned. For example, the Aristotelean view of science is that the axioms should be obviously true. Such a stringent requirement is no longer regarded as a feasible basis for axiomatics in science, because many sciences are about phenomena of which there can be no direct experience, such as subatomic physics, and hence the theorist can expect no notion of self-evidence. Instead the main requirement is that every axiom used in an analysis should be capable of intuitive or empirical interpretation within the framework of the science being studied, whether or not it meets exact preconceptions of the obvious or even whether such preconceptions exist.

The axiomatic method in economics can be represented in the following sequence:

$$\begin{matrix}\text{Economic} \\ \text{assumptions}\end{matrix} \rightarrow \begin{matrix}\text{Mathematical} \\ \text{axioms}\end{matrix} \rightarrow \begin{matrix}\text{Mathematical} \\ \text{propositions}\end{matrix} \rightarrow \begin{matrix}\text{Economic} \\ \text{laws.}\end{matrix}$$

From economic assumptions, a precise formulation is made. This requires imagination and judgment. Then from known mathematical results or through skillful logical manipulation, propositions are proved. These must be intrepreted in economic terms before they are useful. Of course the actual theoretical investigation may begin anywhere in the sequence and work both backward and forward. In the final analysis, however, any weakness in the sequence weakens the overall effort of the theorist. For example, the theorist may be unable to interpret the mathematical axioms in terms of economics. Then the axioms are regarded as restrictions that may be made solely for logical and mathematical convenience. Propositions are proved about the subset of possibilities that satisfy certain mathematical properties, such as smoothness or regularity. Information gained by such proofs applies to a set of examples, possibly a very broad class. At some later date the theorist would hope to be able to establish this information for the nonregular systems of equal or possibly superior scientific interest. At worst, he would expect that some kind of approximation theory would apply whereby an upper bound on the margin of error could be specified for the variation between analysis for the nonregular cases and that for the regular cases used for approximation. Ideally, it would be shown that to any predetermined margin of error there corresponded a regular case suitable for use in approximation. Such procedures are especially important for applications or for empirical verifications; they are commonly employed in the physical sciences.

Through each chapter, there are propositions numbered consecutively. The term remark designates propositions that are important but not very difficult. Hereafter the word lemma refers to results without economic interpretation but leading to theorems with economic meaning. Theorems and their corollaries are those propositions which are economically important and relatively deep in proof. Generally speaking, axioms are not numbered but they are mentioned by name in the hypotheses of propositions. Simultaneously, there are numbered equations and inequalities that are especially useful in applications to business and government policy. Often these are approximations and hence less general than the numbered propositions.

2. The Definitions of Economics and Its Relationship to Resource Allocation and Classical Mechanics

The definition discussed in Section 4 of Chapter 1 can easily be stated in set theoretic terms.

Consider the notion of an (elementary) economic entity or element. Such an entity might be a nonliving substance, a human talent, an animal, a vegetable, a manufactured good, a movement from one place to another, information, a service, or a natural event; of course, some elements may exist in multiple form (for example, 1.00546 gallons of gasoline). Elements may be further distinguished as to time of occurrence, point of location, or consumer possession. At this stage it is desirable to keep the definition of any economic element as vague and as general as possible. In any case, we shall consider the set of all such imaginable quantities. *Events* are defined to be collections of such entities that represent an imaginable state of nature simultaneously containing each included entity. The set of all such possible events is denoted by $\mathscr{U}$, which may be relevant to the decisions of consumers, societies, or business firms.

A reflexive relation $\mathscr{R}$ will be defined on $\mathscr{U}$. It does not necessarily follow that all elements of $\mathscr{U}$ can be compared under $\mathscr{R}$, although in many applications this is so. Hence, in general, $\mathscr{R}$ is not complete, although it may be. It does not even follow that $\mathscr{R}$ is transitive—that is, that $u \mathscr{R} v$, $v \mathscr{R} w$, implies $u \mathscr{R} w$—although in application transitivity is usually a reasonable and desirable property for $\mathscr{R}$. For any subset $\mathscr{V}$ of $\mathscr{U}$, u is said to be *optimal* in $\mathscr{V}$ provided there does not exist a v in $\mathscr{V}$ such that $v \mathscr{R} u$ but not $u \mathscr{R} v$—that is, provided there is no better event v. In any application the discovery of the optimal u('s) in $\mathscr{V}$ is of paramount importance.

Finally, there is the set $\mathscr{E}$ of events physically possible under particular constraints, in contrast to the universal set of imaginable events $\mathscr{U}$.[1] For example, $\mathscr{E}$ is a subset of $\mathscr{U}$ derived from certain principles, such as the restriction of a budget constraint, the state of the arts, or the physical laws of the conservation of matter or of energy, or of both.

The science of economics can now be described more specifically as the study of three problems.

Definition I Economics consists of

(1) the specification of the set $\mathscr{E}$ in $\mathscr{U}$,
(2) the specification of the reflexive relation $\mathscr{R}$ on $\mathscr{U}$,
(3) the optimization of $\mathscr{R}$ on $\mathscr{E}$.

Problem (3) can be refined as requiring two activities: (3a) to show that an optimum $u \in \mathscr{E}$ exists and (3b) to adopt procedures by which the optimum u can be obtained. The procedures in (3b) could be further specified in terms of set theory.

The study of the allocation of scarce resources aims to discover methods by which the best feasible situation can be obtained even though the very best imaginable situation is impossible. It involves three steps.

Definition II Resource allocation theory consists of

(1) specification of the possible states of the world $\mathscr{U}$,
(2) classification of all pairs $(\mathscr{E}, \mathscr{R})$ for which $\mathscr{R}$ can be optimized in $\mathscr{E}$,
(3) optimization procedures for obtaining the optima.

Clearly, item (3) in Definition II is analogous to the specification of procedure (3b) in Definition I. On the other hand, item (2) in Definition II is more general than the specification that an optimum exists, (3a) in Definition I, since there the value system and the constrained set of events are stated to be determined separately.

An example of a subject whose study would *not* (directly) be the object of this discipline is the study of the "not less than" value on the open interval (0, 1); clearly there is no greatest element on this interval. On the other hand, there are many mathematical examples of the discipline defined by Definition II. For instance, in the linear transportation problem we are concerned with the allocation of goods from

[1] The specification of $\mathscr{U}$ is not trivial (see Hochwald [1968]).

plants to warehouses, given certain "costs" of movement; the value system is cost and the optimization procedure turns out to include informing plant managers of some decentralized prices that can be used as guides, although there are many other possible guides or methods of command. Here, specification of the constrained state of the world is obtained from the limitations imposed on the requirements or capacities of each warehouse and on the surplus from each of the plants. So long as cost minimization is the only value, the transportation problem can also be regarded as an economic problem.

More generally, a much larger set of possible goals in studied together with the guide or command sets $\mathscr{S}$ that will attain the possible events in $\mathscr{E}$. In fact, the study is so broad that only small parts of it have been specified under auspices of the mathematics of optimization such as Hancock's *Theory of Maximization*, Pontryagin's *Mathematical Theory of Optimal Controls*, or Bliss's *Calculus of Variations*. Economics may draw on these studies but even in the limited work now extant there are many systems that have no apparent application to economics.

Definition I reveals a similarity between economics and classical mechanics, where one specifies the space-time continuum, a field of forces, and then deduces the movement of particles along paths of least action. Samuelson [1947] has tried to establish a still closer connection between economics and classical mechanics. Statically, it is argued that economics like physics is just an application of the theory of resource allocation. Dynamically, it is argued that economics and physics are separate pieces of the same material. Samuelson further develops the latter argument in his 1938 article.

In classical mechanics, Euler suggested that Newton's laws were expressible as an optimization problem. Euler took this as evidence of an intelligent Creator. Modern physicists, however, appear to regard it as an analytical artifice or curiosity that has no special significance. The Newtonian method is one way of looking at classical mechanics, the Euler–Lagrange–Hamilton method is another. They are equally valid (Lindsay and Margenau [1936]). The maximand has no particular significance but is merely derived from observations. The situation appears to be quite different in economics; that which is maximized—social welfare or consumer preferences—has a meaning independent of the behavior of these units, or so it would seem.

Pursuing the analogy between physics and economics to its logical end, Samuelson [1938] and Houthakker [1950] and other members of the Revealed Preference School have offered the hypothesis that preferences can be derived from observation just as the maximand of physics can be. In particular, Samuelson and Houthakker refer to the competitive situation where the consumers choose according to a budget constraint. They consider that the existence of consumer preference requires that the choice of one commodity bundle over another implies that the second bundle will not be chosen in some other budget situation whenever the first can be had. This is the axiom of revealed preference. The conjecture was made that observation of the choices of the consumer would lead to deduction of the (consistent) preferences of the consumer, provided the axiom of revealed preference held. There are three possible interpretations of this statement.

(a) The underlying consumer preferences, if they exist, can be estimated by allowing the consumer to choose according to budget constraints at various prices.

(b) The behavior of the consumer under competitive conditions is as if he were optimizing his preferences.

(c) The behavior of the consumer under other noncompetitive conditions is as if he were optimizing his preferences.

Version (a) has been verified (Arrow [1959] and Afriat [1967]). Version (b) has also been shown to be true (Richter [1966]). Version (c) has been shown to be incorrect even with "regularity" restrictions on behavior in noncompetitive situations. Sonnenschein [1967a] has shown that there may be consumers whose behavior appears to reflect preferences but whose choices in noncompetitive situations would reveal that they were, in fact, making choices in an inconsistent fashion.

Even if a one-to-one reslationship between demand behavior and preference optimization had been discovered, the structure of economic problems is such that preference must have some meaning beyond the description of market behavior. If preferences are to be the basis of economic policy, they must represent the state of the consumer. Nevertheless, there is a striking formal similarity between physical problems and economic ones, and a great deal of the mathematics developed for physics is applicable to economics.

3. Some General Considerations on Orderings

In many cases, the relation in (2) of Definition I is further specified to be an ordering. Here orderings arising in situations of choice are considered. It is shown that relations are simply less specific partial orderings (Lemma 2). A powerful logical apparatus needed to show optimization is then discussed.

Two relations $\mathscr{P}$, $\mathscr{I}$ (read preferred to, indifferent to) are called a *decomposition* of $\mathscr{R}$ provided that

(i) $x \mathscr{P} x'$ or $x \mathscr{I} x'$ implies $x \mathscr{R} x'$,
(ii) $x \mathscr{R} x'$ implies $x \mathscr{P} x'$ or $x \mathscr{I} x'$, and
(iii) not both $x \mathscr{P} y$ and $x \mathscr{I} y$.

It is easy to derive the preferred to and indifferent to relations.

1 Remark For every reflexive partial ordering $\mathscr{R}$ there exists a decomposition $\mathscr{P}$, $\mathscr{I}$ such that $\mathscr{P}$ is an irreflexive partial ordering and $x \mathscr{P} x'$ implies not $x' \mathscr{R} x$ and such that $\mathscr{I}$ is an equivalence relation and $x \mathscr{I} x'$ implies both $x \mathscr{R} x'$ and $x' \mathscr{R} x$.

Several applications of Remark 1 are apparent. First, consider the experiment in which a consumer is offered alternative bundles of commodities. If he chooses bundle x over bundle x', it is said that $x \mathscr{P} x'$. If he refuses to make a choice, it is said that $x \mathscr{I} x'$. Then the complete reflexive relation $\mathscr{R}$ can be read, "is not rejected in favor of." On the other hand, we can begin with $\mathscr{R}$ and consider the case: x is not rejected in favor of x' but x' is not rejected in favor of x. It is then deduced that x is chosen over x' ($x \mathscr{P} x'$). If instead x' is not rejected in favor of x, then no choice is made between x and x' ($x \mathscr{I} x'$). This second derivation is the one described by the remark. Provided $\mathscr{R}$ were an ordering, $\mathscr{P}$ and $\mathscr{I}$ would be partial orderings.

Another example is the case of the partial ordering: a social situation x is not *Pareto inferior* to y (Chapter 1 and Chapter 9, Section 3). This relationship would hold for individuals 1, 2,..., n, with orders $\mathscr{R}_1$, $\mathscr{R}_2$,..., $\mathscr{R}_n$, provided not $y \mathscr{R}_i x$ for each i. If also $y \mathscr{P}_j x$ for some particular individual j; then there is *Pareto superiority*. *Pareto indifference is* defined to be $x \mathscr{I}_i y$ for all i. In this example, Pareto indifference serves as the equivalence relation in the remark, whereas Pareto superiority is the irreflexive partial order in the remark.

The Pareto preference relation leads to the more general notion, a partial ordering in which the relation $\mathscr{R}$ is transitive and irreflexive but not complete. Some economists would argue that pairwise choice never occurs to the consumer, but only choice of a less demanding sort. For example, the Revealed Preference School requires consumers to choose only from sets upon which budgets are defined. Hence, to postulate completeness would not be justified by the "facts." This is in keeping with the position of the logical positivists. The idealist or dualist might reply that the consumer has the potentiality of making pairwise choice. In Lemma 2 we show that a partial ordering can be extended to a complete ordering. Optimization according to a partial ordering is just as if optimizing by ordering.

For example, the Pareto ordering can be completed by reordering indices as $j(i) = i_j$ and specifying $x \mathscr{R} y$ if and only if for some m, $x_{i_k} \mathscr{R}_{i_k} y_{i_k}$ for $k \leqslant m$, and $x_{i_m} \mathscr{P}_{i_k} y_{i_m}$. This is the so-called lexicographic ordering whereby we first optimize $\mathscr{R}_{i_1}$, then $\mathscr{R}_{i_2}$, and so forth. In fact, if $\mathscr{R}$, determined solely by the choices of $\mathscr{R}_i$, is sufficiently strong, the lexicographic ordering is the only admissible complete ordering (Problem A).

We will show that relations can be refined into partial orderings in a natural way. For example, there might be a choice relation in which many alternatives were not compared. Then transitivity might not be tested in the sense that $x \mathscr{R} y$, $y \mathscr{R} z$, but neither $z \mathscr{R} y$ nor $y \mathscr{R} z$. Nevertheless there might be some basis for saying that x is not inferior to z. We would say that x is indirectly preferred or indirectly indifferent to z. The indirect relation proves especially useful when indirect and direct indifference are the same thing, since then choice is consistent with preferences as reflected by the more detailed partial ordering. To assume that indirect and direct indifference are the same is to postulate the Strong Axiom of Revealed Preference. Although this axiom is not necessary to refine the relation, as in the lemma below, it is true that the main application occurs when the axiom holds.

2 Lemma *Every reflexive relation $\mathscr{R}$ is the subset of the reflexive partial ordering*

$$\hat{\mathscr{R}} = \bigcup_{n=1}^{\infty} \mathscr{R}^n.$$

Proof Clearly,

$$(\mathscr{R}^*)^n = \mathscr{R}^* \circ \mathscr{R}^* \circ \mathscr{R}^* \circ \cdots \circ \mathscr{R}^*$$

is a set by (8), as is

$$\hat{\mathscr{R}} = \bigcup_{n=1}^{\infty} (\mathscr{R}^*)^n$$

by (1) of Chapter 2. Also, it is easy to show transitivity of $\hat{\mathscr{R}}$. q.e.d.

Further considerations on orderings as applied to economics appear in Chapters 5 and 6. One matter remains: in optimization, it is necessary to analyze ever increasing levels of preference. A rather powerful logical construct will be required. It is mentioned here, rather than in Chapter 2 on mathematical prerequisites, first because so far as this book is concerned, this construct is applied only to orderings and second because it is itself about ordering. Formally, the idea is that there is a choice relation (actually a function) that attaches one element in $\mathscr{Y}$ to each subset $\mathscr{Y}$. In effect we choose a point out of each $\mathscr{Y}$.

Axiom of Choice There is a (choice) function $c \subset 2^{\mathscr{X}} \times \mathscr{X}$ such that for every $\mathscr{Y} \in 2^{\mathscr{X}}$,

(a) $(\mathscr{Y}, c(\mathscr{Y})) \in c,$

and

(b) $c(\mathscr{Y}) \in \mathscr{Y}.$

Let $\mathscr{s}$ be a collection of subsets of $\mathscr{X}$; that is, let $\mathscr{s}$ be a subset of $2^{\mathscr{X}}$. Then $\mathscr{n} \subset \mathscr{s}$ is said to be a *nest* in $\mathscr{s}$ provided that for all $\mathscr{Y}$, $\mathscr{Z} \in \mathscr{n}$, either $\mathscr{Y} \subset \mathscr{Z}$ or $\mathscr{Z} \subset \mathscr{V}$ (or both). A nest is a collection of ascending (or descending) sets. A (decreasing) nest of descending sets, namely, discs, $\mathscr{A}_i$ is illustrated in Figure 1. In the case of an ordering, there are sets $\mathscr{R}(x)$, $\mathscr{R}(y)$ always one contained in the other. Such upper contour sets form a nest. A nest $\mathscr{n}$ is said to be *maximal* in $\mathscr{s}$ if there does not exist a $\mathscr{Y} \in \mathscr{s}$ such that

(a) either $\mathscr{Y} \subset \mathscr{Z}$ or $\mathscr{Z} \subset \mathscr{Y}$ for all $\mathscr{Z} \in \mathscr{N}$,

and

(b) $\mathscr{Y} \neq \mathscr{Z}$ for all $\mathscr{Z} \in \mathscr{n}.$

In Figure 1 the nest, composed of a countable number of discs, is not maximal in the set of subsets of the plane since there are discs between

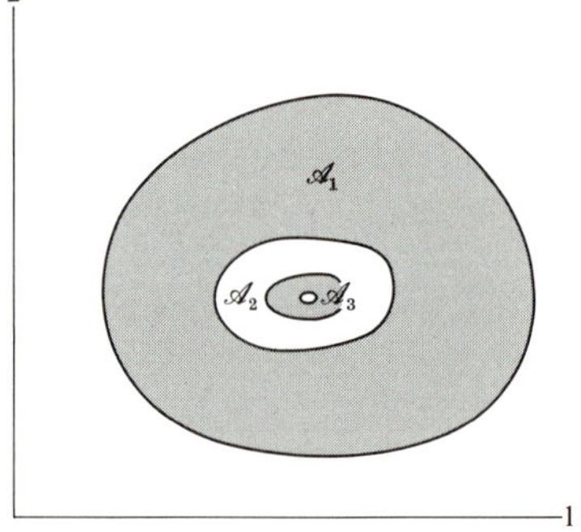

Figure 1

each $\mathscr{A}_i$ and $\mathscr{A}_{i+1}$ but not identical to either. The axiom of choice is equivalent to the Hausdorff maximal principle.

Maximal Principle For every nest in $\mathscr{n} \subset \mathscr{s}$, there is a maximal nest in $\mathscr{s}$ containing $\mathscr{n}$. (Since the maximal principle is perhaps not intuitive, it is of interest to know that it is equivalent to the axiom of choice.)

The idea of proving an optimum on a set $\mathscr{X}$ is to take a nest of subsets of $\mathscr{X}$ whose "minimum" level of preference is ever increasing. The intersection of a maximal nest of such sets will be the optimum. (For details, see Chapter 5.)

It is of some help in interpretation that the maximal principle is equivalent to the so-called well-ordering principle. A *well ordering* is a strict ordering such that for any subset $\mathscr{Y}$ of $\mathscr{X}$ there is an optimum point in $\mathscr{Y}$ under the ordering. The maximal principle is equivalent to the well-ordering principle.

Well-Ordering Principle Every set can be well ordered.

In effect, for each set we can list all the elements in the set. This listing would have to be a kind of supersequential listing, possible only for some infinite mind. The axiom of choice says that there is nothing in the nature of things to deny the existence of an infinite mind. For many determinists things ultimately possible must be ultimately true. For them the axiom of choice appears to be equivalent to the existence of an infinite mind. It is this equivalence that gives the axiom of choice its controversial nature and has brought the intuitionist school, led by L.E.J. Brouwer, to reject it as a legitimate tool of mathematical inquiry Unfortunately, much of modern mathematics seems to require the axiom of choice.

A recent study by Bishop [1967] has taken an even more radical stance. Following the intuitionist school of Brouwer, the whole principle of the excluded middle is rejected for sets with an infinite number of members on the grounds that men could not even verify such a conjecture in principle. A finite automaton cannot perform an infinite number of operations, so it is at best presumptuous for men to conjecture how an infinite mind can reason. Although Bishop has succeeded in establishing many theorems of mathematics on a constructionist basis, they are of radically altered form. A typical theorem of his states that we may approximate a maximum to any desired degree of accuracy although we cannot be assured that a maximum exists. Much of economic theory as constructed would be invalid under such constructivist scrutiny. There are good reasons why optimizing agents must be able to create an exact optimum.

PROBLEM

A. Construction of Orderings

Given a set of orderings $\mathscr{R}_1, \mathscr{R}_2, \ldots, \mathscr{R}_n$, the question arises as to whether there is a general procedure for combining them into a single ordering

$$\mathscr{R} = \mathscr{R}(\mathscr{R}_1, \mathscr{R}_2, \ldots, \mathscr{R}_n)$$

such that

(i) $x \mathscr{R} y$ whenever $x \mathscr{R}_i y$ for $i = 1, 2, \ldots, n$, x, y in $\mathscr{U}$ (Pareto optimality).

(ii) $\mathscr{R}$ is determined only by the pairwise orderings of the $\mathscr{R}_i$.

(iii) Variations in the $\mathscr{R}$ are allowed to the extent that for any u, x, y in $\mathscr{U}$, any possible order of u, x, y may occur.

Show:

(a) If the set of "individuals" $\mathscr{D}$ determines the relation $x \mathscr{R} y$ whenever $x \mathscr{R}_i y$ for each i in $\mathscr{D}$, $y \mathscr{P}_j x$ for j not in $\mathscr{D}$, then unanimity in $\mathscr{D}$ determines the relation of x and y to the alternative u in (iii). (Hint: Consider the possibilities:

$$x \mathscr{R}_i y \mathscr{R}_i u \quad \text{for} \quad i \text{ in } \mathscr{D}, \qquad y \mathscr{R}_j u \quad \text{for} \quad j \text{ not in } \mathscr{D},$$

$$u \mathscr{R}_i x \mathscr{R}_i y \quad \text{for} \quad i \text{ in } \mathscr{D}, \qquad u \mathscr{R}_j y \quad \text{for} \quad j \text{ not in } \mathscr{D}.$$

Use Pareto optimality to demonstrate that

$x \mathscr{R} u$ regardless of j's opinion on x and u

$u \mathscr{R} y$ regardless of j's opinion on x and u, respectively.)

(b) For any fourth element, unanimity of $\mathscr{D}$ determines the constructed ordering between u and any other of the elements x, y, and z Hence, unanimity in $\mathscr{D}$ always determines the constructed ordering.

(c) By Pareto optimality there is always at least one set upon which unanimity determines the constructed ordering, namely, the set of all i. Now consider any subset of individuals that determines the ordering. Show that a still smaller subset of individuals determines the ordering. (Hint: Consider proper (disjoint) subsets $\mathscr{A}$ and $\mathscr{B}$ of $\mathscr{D}$ and let the possibilities be

$$x \mathscr{P}_i y \mathscr{P}_i u \quad \text{for} \quad i \text{ in } \mathscr{A},$$

$$y \mathscr{P}_k x \quad \text{for} \quad k \text{ in } \mathscr{B}, \qquad \text{and}$$

$$u \mathscr{P}_j x \mathscr{P}_j y \quad \text{for} \quad j \text{ not in } \mathscr{A} \text{ or } \mathscr{B}.$$

Use (b) to show that $y \mathscr{P} u$. Then, if $y \mathscr{P} x \mathscr{P} u$ or $y \mathscr{P} u \mathscr{P} x$, $\mathscr{B}$ determines $y \mathscr{P} x$ in opposition to all others. If $x \mathscr{P} y \mathscr{P} u$, then $\mathscr{A}$ determines $y \mathscr{P} u$ in opposition to all others. Apply (b) again.)

(d) One ordering $\mathscr{P}_i$ determines $\mathscr{P}$.

(e) Repeat the foregoing to show that $x \mathscr{I}_{i_1} y$, then one ordering $\mathscr{P}_{i_2}$ determines $\mathscr{P}$.

(f) Hence, $x \mathscr{P} y$ if and only if there is some k for which $x \mathscr{P}_{i_k} y$ and $x \mathscr{I} i_j y$ for all $j < k$, $x \mathscr{I} y$ if and only if $x \mathscr{I}_i y$ for all i.

This problem was originally solved by Arrow [1951a]. The presentation here is due to Vickrey [1960].

4. Commodity Spaces

The commodity space is the domain in which production takes place and to which the preference relation is applied.

The very definition of commodity presents difficulties. Commodities are normally distinguished according to (1) physical type, (2) geographical location, and (3) time of existence. Commodities may even be made subject to a condition such as "a bushel of wheat if it rains in June." A commodity may be multiplicable—such that it can be increased arbitrarily in number (for example, one automobile, 15 automobiles, or a million automobiles). Often it is assumed that the commodity can also be divided into small parts (for example, $\frac{3}{4}$ pound of tea). Many commodities are merely a particular arrangement of molecules, and as such in a strict sense they cannot be divided indefinitely. On the other hand, if commodities are distinguished as to the point in space they occupy, neither can they be multiplied indefinitely. In fact, such commodities can be neither divided nor multiplied, since only one combination of molecules can occupy one point or small part of space. Commodities such as services are more complicated biophysical arrangements of molecules (and perhaps isolated elementary particles), but they also have the general characteristic of not being strictly multiplicable or divisible. Nevertheless, economic problems are not generally confined to small subdivisions of space and therefore the assumption of multiplication does not do too much violence to the facts. Divisibility may be a more damaging assumption with reference to a complex system, such as an automobile or an airplane. For some purposes, however, such as ascertaining the operation of an area densely populated with different types of commodities, the analysis based upon a divisibility assumption may be of some value. Whatever their validity, these are the terms in which economists normally think.

Given the concept of a commodity with the property of divisibility and multiplicability, we can denote the set of commodities as $\mathscr{A}$; the symbol y_α represents the qualities of the αth commodity in $\mathscr{A}$ as a vector in Euclidean space:

$$(y_\alpha, \alpha \in \mathscr{A}) \in \mathscr{E}^{\mathscr{A}}.$$

This vector is called a *commodity bundle.* Normally, the commodity space will be a proper subset of $\mathscr{E}^{\mathscr{A}}$, as when negative quantities have no meaning.

As mentioned, commodities can be distinguished according to the time period in which they appear. It must be decided whether time is understood to be continuous or discrete. Following traditional physical analysis, we commonly view time as continuous. Needless to say, the physicist's word stands undisputed. Nevertheless, use of a simpler form, discrete time, perhaps will not overly distort the facts, since discrete processes may be good approximation of continuous ones. Whenever we adopt discrete time, we can apply most of the production analysis that has been made up to the present time without further work. This is a great advantage, but the practice cannot be recommended without constant reminder that the discrete system is derived from a continuous one. In Section 6, it is seen that the discrete view of time without qualification has led to theorems unsatisfactory as approximations of the true theorems under a scheme of continuous time. Hence, we must always keep in mind that events in discrete time as presented are a sequence of photographs of an underlying continuous system.

Let y_{ij} be the quantity of the jth commodity at time i. If $\mathscr{A}$ is discrete, the commodity bundle has a countable listing

$$(y_{1,1}, \ldots, y_{1,n}, y_{2,1}, \ldots, y_{2,n}, \ldots)$$

whereas no such listing is possible if $\mathscr{A}$ is continuously graded. The difficulties that will arise from the use of continuous time should not be underestimated. To handle commodity bundles in such cases requires all the vast analytical apparatus designed to analyze functions measurable on the real line.

Exercise 1 Let the world be a sphere and let there be one commodity and one time period. What is the index set for commodities?

What if there are two commodities? A continuous time period? A time–space continuum requiring that

$$x_1^2 + x^2 + x^2 = c^2t^2$$

where x is the change from the time zero position in $\mathscr{E}^3$ and t is time? (The latter space is Einstein–Minkowski space.)

5. Statical Analysis under Parametric Behavior

One of the most fruitful concepts in economics has been pure competition where firms or consumers make decisions under the assumption that they cannot influence prices at which sales and purchases are made. This kind of behavior will be shown in Chapters 4 and 9 to lead to efficient allocation of resources. In Chapters 8 and 10 it will be used to derive theorems about the reponse of consumers and producers to price changes.

Even in the cases where sellers or buyers will not regard prices as parameters, other data may be taken as not subject to the agents' control. For example, the classical monopolist accepts his demand curve as parametric. The main directions of analysis under parametric behavior can be indicated with reference to competition only.

Let $e^i(p)$ be the function relating price to the excess of demand over supply of the ith agent. The range of $e^i(p)$ is the commodity space. Positive components indicate demand; negative components, supply. The community excess demand function is $e(p) = \sum_i e^i(p)$. Evidently, equilibrium is equivalent to

$$0 = e(p), \tag{1}$$

that is, supply equals demand. Changes in demand $\Delta e(p)$ lead to changes in equilibrium price. These can be evaluated by finding $\bar{p}$ that solves $\bar{e}(p) = e(p) + \varepsilon\, \Delta e(p) = 0$ as ε varies from zero to one. For $\varepsilon = 0$, there is the price without a change in demand. For $\varepsilon = 1$, there is the price in the new situation. Evidently,

$$\frac{\partial \bar{e}}{\partial p} \frac{dp}{d\varepsilon} = -\Delta e(p), \tag{2}$$

$$\frac{dp}{d\varepsilon} = -\left(\frac{\partial \bar{e}}{\partial p}\right)^{-1} \Delta e(p), \tag{2a}$$

whenever the inverse exists. Also,

$$p(1) - p(0) = \int_0^1 \frac{dp}{d\varepsilon}\, d\varepsilon \tag{3}$$

whenever $(\partial \bar{e}/\partial p)^{-1}$ and $e(p)$ are continuous, since they form differential equations in ε for which the dynamic law is continuous (Coddington and

Levinson [1955]). Equation (2) is fundamental to analysis of comparative statics. Virtually all such problems can be reduced to that form.[1]

[1] Infinite numbers of commodities can be treated as follows: If the space of excess demands is closed under addition and has compact neighborhoods, then

$$\sum_{i=1}^{n} f(t_i)(t_i - t_{i-1})$$

is defined and the limit as $t_i \rightarrow_{n\rightarrow\infty} t_{i-1} \rightarrow 0$ is the integral $\int_{t_0}^{t} f(t)\, dt$. Hence, integration is defined. Furthermore, it can be shown that

$$\frac{dx}{dt} = f(x)$$

has a solution $x(t)$ exactly as in finite-dimensional spaces (Birkhoff and Rota [1962, pp. 124–127]), which is by successive approximation through integration over an interval of length $\varepsilon\mu$, where f is defined on y for which $\| x - y \| \leqslant \varepsilon$ and on this ε-neighborhood of x, $|f(x)| \leqslant \mu$.

An *infinite matrix* is schematically represented as

$$A = \begin{bmatrix} a_{11} & a_{12} & \cdots \\ \vdots & \vdots & \\ a_{21} & a_{22} & \cdots \\ \vdots & \vdots & \end{bmatrix}$$

with matrix and vector multiplication defined in the obvious way. If $xA = y$, then

$$x_{\mathscr{I}} A_{\mathscr{I}} = y(\mathscr{I})$$

(not necessarily equal to $y_{\mathscr{I}}$), $\mathscr{I}$ finite. Evidently, $y_{\mathscr{I}}(\mathscr{I}) \rightarrow y$, $x_{\mathscr{I}} \rightarrow x$, $A_{\mathscr{I}} \rightarrow A$. Hence, $y_{\mathscr{I}}(\mathscr{I})(A_{\mathscr{I}})^{-1} \rightarrow yA^{-1}$, provided A has an inverse. If A^{-1} is a matrix (it need not be), then

$$x = yA^{-1}, \qquad x_{\mathscr{I}} = y_{\mathscr{I}}(A_{\mathscr{I}})^{-1} \rightarrow x$$

only if

$$(A_{\mathscr{I}})^{-1} \rightarrow A^{-1}$$

(infinite matrices do not have redundant elements since the space over which A^{-1} is defined is sufficiently large that any matrix differing from it has different values).

The infinite-dimensional comparative statics case can be accommodated as follows: If

$$\mathscr{I} \subset \bigcup_{i=1}^{\infty} \{i\},$$

(i) $$\frac{\partial e_{\mathscr{I}}}{\partial p_{\mathscr{I}}} \xrightarrow[\mathscr{I} \rightarrow \bigcup_{i=1}^{\infty}\{1\}]{} \frac{\partial e}{p\partial},$$

(ii) $$\left[\frac{\partial e_{\mathscr{I}}}{\partial p_{\mathscr{I}}}\right]^{-1} \rightarrow \left[\frac{\partial e}{\partial p}\right]^{-1}$$

Evidently, total changes of a set of variables can be evaluated by the use of *ceteris paribus* information given about changes when all but one of the variables are fixed. This is often regarded as a paradox, and criticism is sometimes offered of analysis that it involves a method inappropriate to the problem. There is no validity to such a criticism. In one form or another, the *ceteris paribus* method is fundamental to the analysis of economic equilibrium.

It is interesting that the *ceteris paribus* technique can be extended to the case where e is only *differentiable almost everywhere* in the sense that, except for a set of measure zero, for points p and every e_i, there is a hyperplane $\mathscr{H}^i(p)$ tangent to the graph of $(e_i(p) = \text{constant})$, but not parallel with any axis. In this case, $dp/d\varepsilon$ is evaluated almost everywhere as in (2a), even though it may not be that $p(\varepsilon)$ is the integral of its derivative (for details see Saks [1937, Chapter IX]). Nevertheless, if $dp/d\varepsilon > 0$, then p is increasing in the sense that $p(\bar{\varepsilon}) > p(\varepsilon) > p(\bar{\bar{\varepsilon}})$ for $\bar{\varepsilon}$, $\bar{\bar{\varepsilon}}$ in a (sufficiently) small open interval containing ε, $\bar{\varepsilon} > \varepsilon > \bar{\bar{\varepsilon}}$.

As it happens, both the signs of $\partial e_i/\partial p_j$ and quantitative restrictions on $\partial \bar{e}_i/\partial p$ are of importance. In addition to the derivatives $\partial \bar{e}_i/\partial p_j$, economists look at *elasticities*. These are given as

$$\varepsilon_{jk}^{i} = \frac{\partial e_j^i}{\partial p_k} \frac{p^k}{e_j^i}$$

for excess demand e_j^i.

3 Remark

$$\varepsilon_{jk}^{i} = \frac{\partial \log e_j^i}{\partial \log p_k}.$$

4 Remark

$$\varepsilon_{jk} = \sum_i \varepsilon_{jk}^i t_j^i$$

(iii) $e(p)$ is continuous in pointwise convergence.

Therefore

$$p(1) - p(0) = \int_0^1 \lim_{\mathscr{I} \to \bigcup_{i=1}^{\infty} \{1\}} - \left[\frac{\partial e_{\mathscr{I}}}{\partial p_{\mathscr{I}}}\right]^{-1} e_{\mathscr{I}}\, d\epsilon$$

$$= -\int_0^1 \left[\frac{\partial e}{\partial p}\right]^{-1} e\, d\epsilon,$$

which is formulas (2a) and (3) combined.

where

$$t_j^i = \frac{e_j^i}{e_j}, \qquad \sum t_j^i = 1.$$

Since $e = 0$ implies an infinite elasticity, we often look at the sum of the positive excess demands d_j and compute the elasticity of demand:

$$\varepsilon_{jk} = \frac{\partial d_j}{\partial p_k}\frac{p_k}{d_j} = \sum_{e_{ij}>0} \varepsilon_{ij} t_j^i .$$

Similarly, the negative demands are summed to obtain supplies and the corresponding elasticity of supply. As will be seen in Chapter 10, elasticities are especially relevant to the study of monopoly.

Even though the slopes and elasticities of individual demand and supply functions are related in an additive fashion to those of the community demand and supply functions, it is not true that all relevant properties of the individual functions hold for the community function. There are cases where the community acts as though it were one Marshallian representative man, but it is not a trivial matter to find such cases (Gorman [1953]). It is for this reason that the study of individual excess demand functions is motivated by the search for properties of the community excess demand function. In effect, the micro theory is dependent on the macro theory as well as vice versa.

Occasionally, the exceptional cases where the derivatives do not exist are discussed. In particular, the reader should note that exceptional points are not necessarily exceptional after transformation. Hence differentiability must always be verified directly for the space under consideration.

Exercise 2 Let a competitive trader have differentiable and additive utility $\sum u_i(x_i)$. Show that

$$\frac{du_j/dx_j}{p_j} = \frac{du_i/dx_i}{p_i}.$$

Show that demand will be differentiable if there are second derivatives of utility with respect to quantity. At the price system where new products are just beginning to be consumed, can differentiability be expected?

6. A Caveat on Time in Economies

Much of the theory in this book applies at equilibrium. Ordinarily there are dynamic adjustment processes that equilibrate. Therefore, equilibrium theories represent central tendencies, not a detailed account of the actual state of affairs. Furthermore, a specification of the appropriate adjustment system is by no means trivial. It is the subject of several chapters in the companion volume. Especially, the choice of continuous or discrete time is critical.

Several economists (Ezekial [1938], Samuelson [1939], and Metzler [1941]) have derived conditions for fluctuations of a linear difference equation of the form

$$x(t+1) = ax(t) + b.$$

It can be shown that such an equation implies a very peculiar underlying differential equation.

An example of a linear difference equation system is the standard cobweb diagram in Figure 2. Price begins at p_0, where supply exceeds demand. Brokers then set prices so that demand equals supply, assuming the supply is fixed, but the supply also changes. In Figure 2a the cobweb is stable; in Figure 2b it is unstable. The relative elasticities of demand and supply, $(dd/dp)\, p/d$ and $(ds/dp)\, p/s$, can be seen to determine the stability of the cobweb. What is more, if the brokers were instead to clear the supply side of the market, assuming fixed demand, the relative stability of the examples in Figure 2 would be exactly reversed. This might be called the "cobweb paradox."

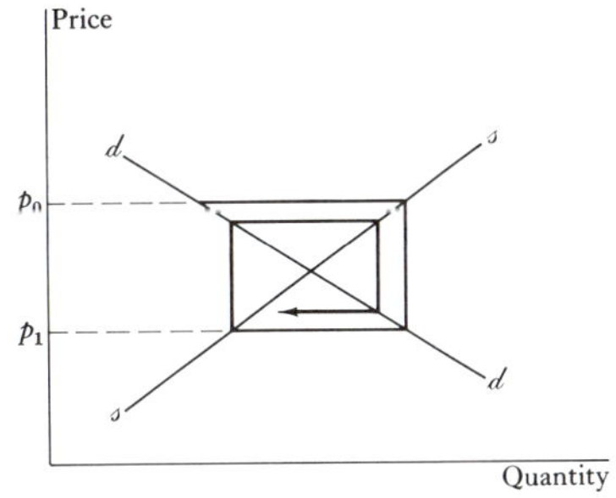

Figure 2a

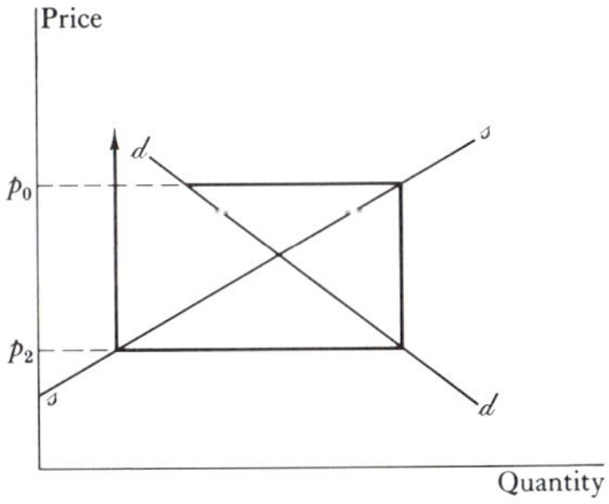

Figure 2b

For most markets the cobweb is not a convincing description of price adjustment, simply because price changes occur continuously and according to the laws of linear differential equations, which do not lead to linear difference equations. The cobweb theory is discredited as a general theory by the hypothesis of the continuum of time. In fact, provided that the demand curves are downward sloping and the supply curves are upward sloping, continuous adjustment is stable.

The cobweb would apply only if there were some natural lag that is not forecasted, so no effort is made to smooth the effect of supply or demand on the markets. Stability would then depend on which lagged, supply or demand, and on the relative elasticities. It is difficult to think of an empirical market resembling this outcome of the cobweb analysis.

PROBLEM

B. Multiplier–Accelerator Models

Let consumption today be linearly related to income yesterday. Let output today be equal to consumption yesterday. Describe the time behavior of this system. Change the difference equations into differential equations and solve.

This problem was first solved by Samuelson [1939].

7. Games and Conflict

In Chapter 10, market organization will be studied from the viewpoint of game theory. This section is a preparation and covers only those parts of game theory somewhat removed from a market situation. Here only noncooperative games are considered. Further developments relating to cooperative games appear in Section 2 of Chapter 10.

On the rare economic occasions in which a game can be reduced to one of pure conflict, where every gain of one player is a loss for the other, there is a natural outcome. Other cases are more controversial.

Consider two strategy spaces, $\mathscr{X}$ for player 1 and $\mathscr{Y}$ for player 2. There are resulting outcomes

$$(x, y) \in \mathscr{X} \times \mathscr{Y}$$

that lead to levels of preference for each. Preferences are defined on joint strategies $\mathscr{X} \times \mathscr{Y}$ with elements (x, y). For example, x might signify goods going from 1 to 2 and y goods going from 2 to 1. The vector x could be the output of 1 and y the output of 2 in a market shared by two firms. (These would probably not be games of pure conflict.)

There is *pure conflict* if for reflexive preference orderings $\mathscr{R}_i$, $\mathscr{R}_j$,

$$(x, y) \mathscr{P}_i (\bar{x}, \bar{y})$$

implies

$$(\bar{x}, \bar{y}) \mathscr{P}_j (x, y), \qquad j \neq i.$$

A strategy is *Pareto optimal* if it optimizes the Pareto relation.

5 Theorem *There is pure conflict if and only if all (x, y) in $\mathscr{X} \times \mathscr{Y}$ are Pareto optimal.*

A special case of pure conflict games are constant sum games where

$$u_1(x, y) + u_2(x, y)$$

is constant for all

$$(x, y) \in \mathscr{X} \times \mathscr{Y}.$$

The outcome (x, y) is an *equilibrium* if

$$(x, y) \mathscr{R}_1 (\bar{x}, y) \qquad \text{and} \qquad (x, y) \mathscr{R}_2 (x, \bar{y})$$

for all $\bar{x} \in \mathscr{X}$, $\bar{y} \in \mathscr{X}$. Evidently, an equilibrium is a pair of strategies to which no better replies exist by one player to the other.

6 Theorem *If there is pure conflict, equilibrium is unique except for the outcomes indifferent to each other for both parties.*

Proof Suppose there are two distinct equilibria of different levels of preference (x, y), $(\bar{x}, \bar{y})$. Without loss of generality, assume

$$(x, y) \mathscr{P}_2 (\bar{x}, \bar{y}).$$

Then also, by Pareto optimality,

$$(\bar{x}, \bar{y}) \mathscr{P}_1 (x, y).$$

Consider $(\bar{x}, y)$. Since (x, y) is an equilibrium point,

$$(x, y) \mathscr{R}_1 (\bar{x}, y)$$

which by Pareto optimality of $(\bar{x}, y)$ implies that

$$(\bar{x}, y) \mathscr{R}_2 (x, y)$$

whereupon

$$(\bar{x}, y) \mathscr{P}_2 (\bar{x}, \bar{y})$$

which contradicts the fact that $(\bar{x}, \bar{y})$ is an equilibrium point. q.e.d.

Of course, it is not proved that the equilibrium exists. For the existence of equilibrium, it is not sufficient for games to be pure conflict or even *zero sum games* (where $u_1(x, y) + u_2(x, y) = 0$ for all $(x, y) \in \mathscr{X} \times \mathscr{Y}$). This can be seen by reference to the game illustrated in Table 1, where the x's and y's refer to strategies in $\mathscr{X}$ and $\mathscr{Y}$ and the numbers (i, j)

are utilities of 1 and 2, respectively (clearly $i + j = 3$). Hence, we need only subtract 3 from 1's utilities, and Table 1 so modified represents a zero sum game without an equilibrium.

TABLE 1

	y	$\bar{y}$
x	(2, 1)	(1, 2)
$\bar{x}$	(1, 2)	(2, 1)

A *mixed* strategy occurs whenever one player plays x with probability t and $\bar{x}$ with probability $(1 - t)$. If $t = 0$ or $t = 1$, the strategy is *simple*. If mixed strategies are allowed, then an equilibrium point exists It is shown in Chapter 7 that utility can be defined linear in probabilities. Therefore, mixed strategies lead to a convex set of strategies $\mathscr{X} \times \mathscr{Y}$ upon which preferences are convex, indeed linear, by virtue of the expected utility result

$$u_i(tx + (1 - t)\bar{x}, y) = tu_i(x, y) + (1 - t)u_i(\bar{x}, y), \qquad i = 1, 2.$$

Incidentally, a pure conflict game before mixing may or may not be a pure conflict game afterward. In the game illustrated in Table 2,

$$\tfrac{1}{2}(3, 1) + \tfrac{1}{2}(1, 3)$$

is clearly superior for both 1 and 2 to (2, 1). Hence, the mixed game is not one of pure conflict.

TABLE 2

	y	$\bar{y}$
x	(2, 1)	(1, 3)
$\bar{x}$	(3, 1)	(2, 1)

Constant sum games ($\sum_i u_i(x, y) =$ constant) are pure conflict games even after mixing strategies.

To go on to the n-person game, and games not necessarily of pure conflict, the strategy of i, x^i, appears in the space $\mathscr{X}_i$. Evidently, preferences are defined on

$$\mathop{\times}_{i=1}^{n} \mathscr{X}_i$$

for each i.

In order to show that equilibrium exists, a fixed-point theorem is required. According to the intermediate value theorem of continuous functions, there is an x such that $f(x) = x$ for f taking the interval into the interval. The function f has a fixed point if $f(x) = x$. What is needed are general results of the same sort.

7 Lemma (Brouwer) *If f is a continuous function taking a compact, convex set into itself, then f has a fixed point.* A correspondence is *upper semicontinuous* if its graph is closed, that is, if $y^n \in \phi(x^n)$, $x^n \to x$, $y^n \to y$ $y \in \phi(x)$.

8 Lemma (Kakutani) *If ϕ is an upper semicontinuous correspondence taking a compact, convex set into itself and if $\phi(x)$ is convex, then ϕ has a fixed point.*

Lemma 7 is illustrated for the case of a continuous function f on the convex set [0, 1] (Figure 3). At the 45° line in Figure 3, $f(x) = x$.

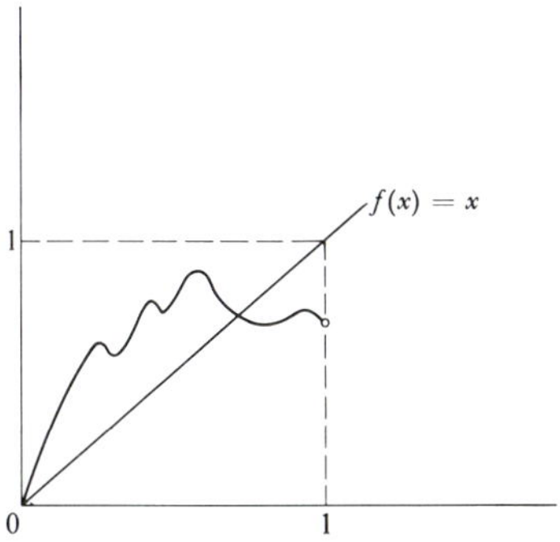

Figure 3

Proof (for Lemma 7) If f is a function and the domain of f is [0, 1], then

$$f(x) - x \quad \text{is continuous on} \quad [-1, 1].$$

Therefore, the set of points for which $f(x) - x \geqslant 0$ is closed, as is that for which $f(x) - x \leqslant 0$. Also, one or the other of the sets is empty, say, the set of points for which $f(x) - x \leqslant 0$. Now $f(x) - x \leqslant 0$ has a least upper bound y, and by compactness, $x^n \to \bar{x}$ for $f(x^n) \to y = f(\bar{x})$. In similar terms, f takes a maximum on the set of points for which $f(x) - x \leqslant 0$. If $f(\bar{x}) - \bar{x} = 0$, there is a fixed point. Otherwise, $f(\bar{x}) - \bar{x} < 0$. The set of x for which $f(x) - x > 0$ is empty, since otherwise $f(x) - x$ takes the connected set $[0, 1]$ into the disconnected sets $\{y \mid y \leqslant f(\bar{x}) - \bar{x} < 0\}$ and $\{y \mid y \geqslant f(x) - x \geqslant 0\}$ (continuous functions take connected sets into connected sets). Now $f(x) < x$ for x in $[0, 1]$ implies $f(0) < 0$, which is impossible. q.e.d.

In the n-dimensional case or in the case of a correspondence, the proof is much more difficult.

There is an *equilibrium* point x if for all i

$$x \mathscr{R}_i (y^i, x^{\sim i}) \qquad \text{for all} \quad y^i \in \mathscr{X}_i .$$

The main theorem is a generalization of a result due to Nash [1950].

9 Theorem (Nash) *If $\mathscr{X}_i$ is convex and compact and if $\mathscr{R}_i(x^i)$ is convex (where the strategies for all $j \neq i$ are fixed) and both $\mathscr{R}_i(x)$ and $\mathscr{R}_i^{-1}(x)$ are closed, then there is an equilibrium point.*

Proof Define

$$\phi_i(x) = \{y^i \mid (x^{\sim i}, y^i) \mathscr{R}_i (x^{\sim i}, \bar{y}^i) \qquad \text{for all} \quad \bar{y}^i \in \mathscr{Y}_i\}.$$

Clearly, ϕ_i is upper semicontinuous and $\phi_i(x)$ is convex. Therefore, $\phi = (\phi_i)$ has a fixed point (Lemma 7); that is, for some x,

$$x_i \in \phi_i(x) \qquad \text{for all } i.$$

Evidently, x is an equilibrium. q.e.d.

The following result due to von Neumann [1928] was the basis of game theory.

10 Corollary *If there are a finite number of simple strategies, then there is an equilibrium whenever mixed strategies are included.*

Proof $\mathscr{X}_i$ is the convex combination of a finite number of points that is compact. Utility is linear and therefore continuous. q.e.d.

One difficulty with this Nash theorem is that in the case of games that do not involve pure conflict, equilibrium may not be unique. One person may be favored by one equilibrium and not by another. It is then doubtful that the theory is adequate, since certainly there would be further interaction. Short of this, the actual outcome of the game is left in extreme doubt. Furthermore, even if equilibrium is unique, it is often not Pareto optimal and it would be to the advantage of both parties to collude to obtain another solution. Nash's cooperative theory is presented in Section 2 of Chapter 10.

PROBLEM

C. Prisoner's Dilemma

Let payoff be given by

	y	$\bar{y}$
x	(0, 0)	(2, 0)
$\bar{x}$	(0, 2)	(1, 1)

Is there an equilibrium? What is the outcome of the game?

II

Production

4

Production

Labour . . . is the real measure of the exchangeable value of all commodities. The real price of every thing is the toil and trouble of acquiring it.

Adam Smith
THE WEALTH OF NATIONS

1. The Production Correspondence

The meanness of nature is obvious. The exact limitations imposed on individuals in society are less obvious. To specify these limitations is to specify the set of possible alternatives in Definition I (Chapter 3).

Physical limitations appear in man's environment and in man himself. The former is the picture of the inhabited universe. The latter is the psychological complexion of man, economically manifested as various kinds of labor. It is the action of goal-pursuing persons on an inanimate universe that is of interest in production theory. For the moment, we will leave the particular goals unspecified.

In preparation for a study of properties of production (Sections 2 and 3), the neoclassical model of production (Sections 4 and 5), and the problem of producer efficiency (Section 6), this section specifies the definition and physical interpretation of production transformation.

A *production path* is a commodity bundle

$$(y_{i,t}, i \in \mathscr{A}_t, t \in \mathscr{T})$$

whose components are governed by physical laws.

In economics, it is usually assumed that the bundle

$$(y_i(t), i \in \mathscr{A}_t)$$

is dependent only on the bundle

$$(y_i(t-1), i \in \mathscr{A}_{t-1}).$$

This is the concept of *input–output*, and it is the simplest and most natural assumption of cause and effect. Strictly speaking, it is false. Whether a building is being built or dismantled depends not only on the parts of the building standing, but on whether they are fixed or falling. Not only the past quantities but their accelerations determine the present. This principle extends to all molecular configurations, since molecular changes require the movement of particles. Normally, however, a physical reaction tends to an equilibrium value, where acceleration is zero. If all processes obtained the equilibrium state sufficiently quickly (for purposes of economic theory), it would then be possible to minimize the loss involved in reversing or redirecting processes.

Further specifications of the input–output relationship can be made. The production of economic goods proceeds from primary factors of production and from intermediate goods. For example, steel may be produced from labor, capital, and coal. Labor and capital are generally regarded as factors, since to some degree they can be substituted one for the other. On the other hand, the quantity of coal needed per unit of steel is less subject to variation. The distinction between factors of production and intermediate goods is more of degree than of kind, and the more general term "inputs" is used for both.

Among other things, production involves

(1) the processing of materials into final products, at any given time,
(2) the use of factors as instruments of production,
(3) the physical deterioration of those factors with use and age, and
(4) the growth of factor quantities and services directly through the accumulation of the factor and indirectly through the accumulation of knowledge.

Production normally proceeds on the basis of techniques and subject to the "capital" constraint imposed by the quantity of goods available $y(t)$. There are both capital and current factors of production. These are governed by physical laws that limit economic opportunities.

Given a certain commodity bundle $y(t)$ with coordinates in $\mathscr{A}_t$, there are certain bundles available in time $t + 1$, with coordinates in $\mathscr{A}_{t+1}$. The set of these pairs $(y(t), y(t + 1))$ is denoted

$$_t\mathscr{Y}_{t+1} \subset \mathscr{E}^{\mathscr{A}_t} \times \mathscr{E}^{\mathscr{A}_{t+1}}.$$

Evaluating for one element in the first coordinate gives

$$_t\mathscr{Y}_{t+1}(y(t)) \subset \mathscr{E}^{\mathscr{A}_{t+1}}.$$

In obvious generalization, $_s\mathscr{Y}_t$ denotes the *production transformation correspondence* of possible paths beginning at time s and ending at time t. It is the graph of the *input-output* correspondence

$$_s\mathscr{Y}_t(y(s))$$

which gives the paths starting at $y(s)$ and proceeding until $y(t)$. Because there is nothing in the economic assumptions to prevent $y(t)$ from changing abruptly, acceleration—of capital stock or of changes in molecular form—is assumed to be an unimportant factor. This simplification could no doubt be avoided by merely assuming $_t\mathscr{Y}_{t+1}$ to be determined by summation (twice) of an acceleration factor, which would yield smoother production paths and perhaps more realistic ones. However, the form dependent on a single summation is used, for two reasons—because we need not specify an initial velocity in addition to an initial stock of the commodity and because this is traditional in economic theory (as opposed to physics).

In Figure 1a, there are two commodities and a set of possible capital stocks in time $t + 1$, $_t\mathscr{Y}_{t+1}(y(t))$, which is the area delimited by the shaded area. That $y(t)$ belongs to $_t\mathscr{Y}_{t+1}(y(t))$ indicates that commodities 1 and 2 are durable, that is, $y(t)$ can be preserved over time without deterioration. In fact, $y(t)$ may actually be increased in both components Also, commodity i can be greatly increased at the expense of 2 and vice versa. The influence of $y(t)$ on $_t\mathscr{Y}_{t+1}(y(t))$ is illustrated in Figure 1b. There, $y(t)$ is decreased to $\bar{y}(t)$ as in the production set. Apparently at $\bar{y}(t)$, no simultaneous increase in both commodities is possible. However, the $\bar{y}(t)$ is still in $_t\mathscr{Y}_{t+1}(y(t))$ and hence the system can remain stationary.

In Figure 1c, time paths of output are indicated, assuming that

$$_t\mathscr{Y}_{t+1}(y(t)) = {_0\mathscr{Y}_1}(\bar{y}(t)) + \{y(t) - y\}.$$

(Of course, this is a very simple law and is not the general case.) We may arbitrarily choose $y(t+1)$ to be that point in ${}_t\mathscr{Y}_{t+1}(y)$ which is closest to y along the line segment $\langle y, y(t+2)\rangle$. This gives the path $y(t)$. If we started at the $\bar{y}(t)$ in Figure 1b instead of at y, the stock of goods would be stationary over time. At lower stocks, it would deteriorate, presumably to the origin. Of course, from $y(0)$ many other paths could be chosen. The set of all such paths is the set ${}_0\mathscr{Y}_\infty(y\,(0))$.

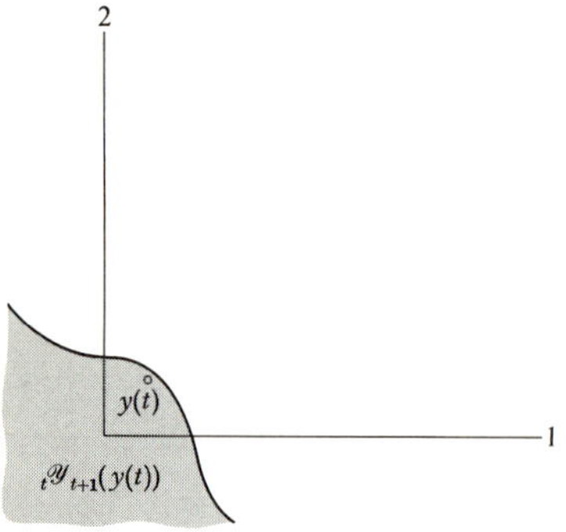

Figure 1a

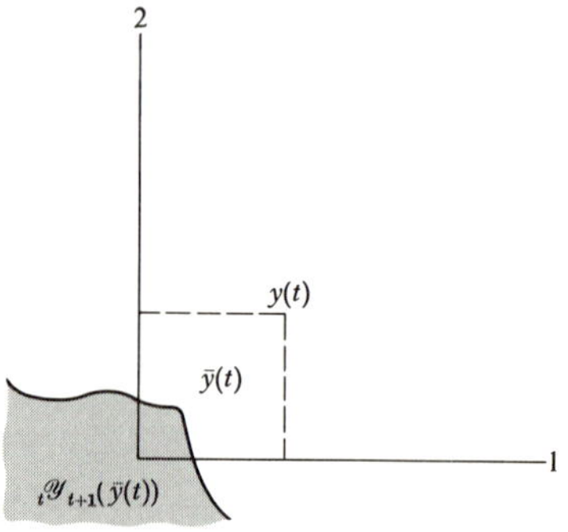

Figure 1b

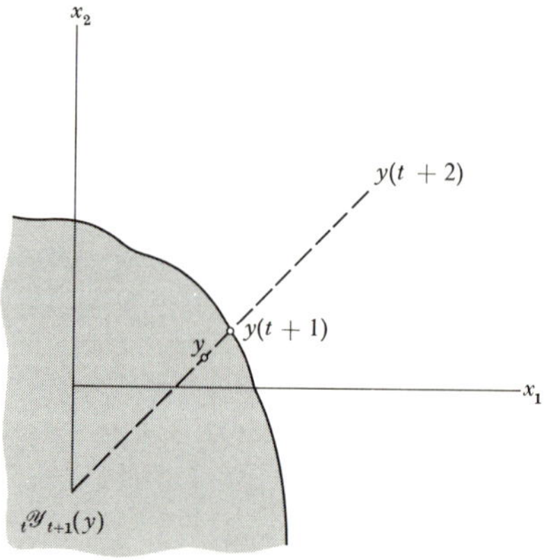

Figure 1c

An important point can be made at this rather general level of analysis. It should be observed that in order to transport or change a molecular configuration, at least some elementary particles must be made to travel a minimum distance, depending on the transformation. The rate of change is limited by the speed of light. Therefore, over a fixed time period there is a limit to the transformation of production from a given capital stock, whatever the outputs or inputs may be. That is, the ratios of production to capital are normally *bounded*. In some systems, mass may be entering from outside the system, so that there are outputs from seemingly zero inputs, but *this free output is limited by the quantity of entering mass*. Beyond such limitation, if there is also a limit on the output–capital input ratios, it is said that the output–input ratio is normally *bounded in the limit*, even if up to a certain level, there is free production and therefore an infinite output–input ratio. Another way of saying this is that there is *no free production in the limit* since if the output–input ratio did tend to infinity, in effect, we would be getting free production at infinitely large scales of operation. The limitation of the speed of light is important here, since the general formulation of energy output in other branches of physics, say thermodynamics, leads to a situation where it is possible that efficiency can be improved indefinitely at very high temperatures.

It is informative to apply the foregoing definitions to a simple technology. Let there be a finite number of commodities n and n independent production processes, each producing a single commodity. Let each commodity used in fixed proportions in the production of i be used in quantity x_{ji}, the amount of j used in the production of i. Let x_t be the *gross output* of i and

$$x_{ji} = a_{ji}\, x_i \,.$$

Therefore, x_{ji} is used up producing i, and net output is

$$\Delta y_j = x_j - \sum_{i=1}^{n} x_{ji} = x_j - \sum_{i=1}^{n} x_i a_{ji}$$

or

$$\Delta y = x - Ax = (I - A)x,$$

where x and Δy are column vectors and A is a square matrix.

Gross output is also subject to production capacity constraint

$$Bx \leqslant y(t),$$

which says that type i capital goods used in gross output of all commodities must be no greater than the available quantity. Therefore, if $(I - A)$ has an inverse,

$$B(I - A)^{-1}\, \Delta y \leqslant y(t)$$

is the constraint determining ${}_t\mathscr{Y}_{t+1}(y(t))$. If all output is accumulated,

$$B(I - A)^{-1}\, \Delta y \leqslant y(0) + \sum_{s=0}^{t-1} y(s).$$

The possibilities for Δy are illustrated in Figure 2 for a two-good case where

$$C = B(I - A)^{-1}.$$

Here $\mathscr{L}_1$ represents the line of y's just satisfying the first equation, and $\mathscr{L}_2$, those satisfying the second equation. Any of the y's below both lines satisfies the inequalities $\Delta y \leqslant Cy(t)$. For a consumer good, i, $b_{ji} = 0$ for all j. Otherwise, if all goods are used as capital goods, then C^{-1} may exist and all capital goods can be utilized to obtain

$$\Delta y = C^{-1}y(t),$$

which is a system of linear difference equations. This leads to the solutions

$$y(t) = C^{-t}y(0).$$

Therefore,

$$(C^{-t}y(0), t = 1, 2,\ldots)_0 \in \mathscr{Y}_\infty(y(0)).$$

(C^{-1} and C^{-t} may have negative values (Jorgenson [1961]). Then $y(t)$ might have negative components, which would not be sensible economically.)

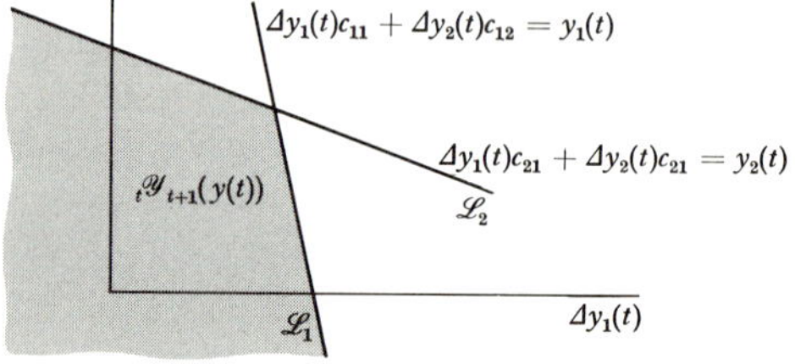

Figure 2

In the foregoing, we can replace the difference equations by differential equations whenever equality holds. Thus

$$C\frac{dy}{dt} \leqslant y(t)$$

solves (with equality) as

$$y = \exp(-C^{-1}t)\,y(0)$$

where

$$\exp(-C^{-1}t) = I - C^{-1}t + C^{-2}\frac{t_2}{2!} - \cdots.$$

Exercise 1 Let there be only two commodities, and let

$$B = \begin{pmatrix} b_{11} & b_{12} \\ 0 & 0 \end{pmatrix}.$$

Derive the efficient points in ${}_0\mathscr{Y}_\infty(y(0))$. How would negativity of b_{11} affect this and what would its economic interpretation be?

Exercise 2 Show that $e^{-At}e^{At} = I$ when

$$e^{At} = \frac{I}{0!} + \frac{A}{1!} + \frac{A^2}{2!} + \cdots.$$

2. Laws of Combination in Production Transformation

The geometric and topological properties of production transformation were first set forth by K. Menger [1936], J. von Neumann [1937], and T. C. Koopmans [1951]. There are a relatively large number of closely related properties which have resulted from the effort to keep assumptions as general as possible. Many geometric properties of the production set are matters of simple manipulation. They are considered here whereas the deeper topological properties are presented in the next section.

Production possibilities are said to be *divisible* whenever the possibility of the process y implies the possibility of any production on the line segment connecting y with zero. In particular, divisibility implies that $0 = \lim_{t\to 0} ty$, the point representing no outputs from inputs, is a possible production; this case of *inaction* is the limiting case of operation of y at a very small fractional level. The production set in Figure 3 is divisible. Production is *multiplicable* if the production process may be multiplied by an integer without loss of efficiency. This is illustrated in Figure 4, where y, $2y$,... are all possible productions.

The combination of divisibility and multiplicability implies *constant returns to scale*, where the production possibility can be multiplied by any constant greater than or equal to zero. Said differently, the scale of production may be adjusted to any level without loss of efficiency, as in Figure 5.

Under constant returns to scale, ${}_s\mathscr{Y}_t$ is a cone since ${}_s\mathscr{Y}_t$ is the union

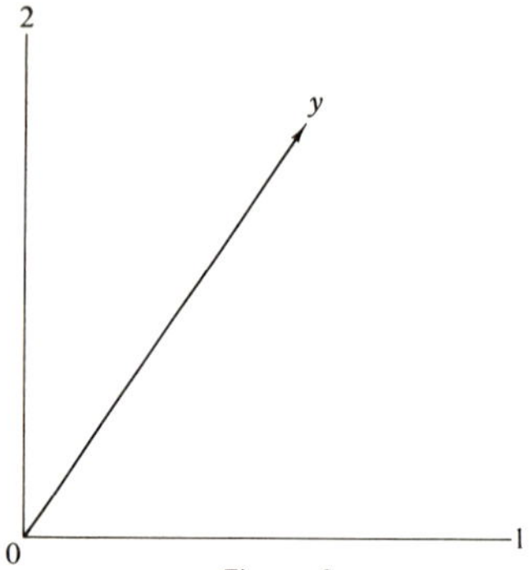

Figure 3

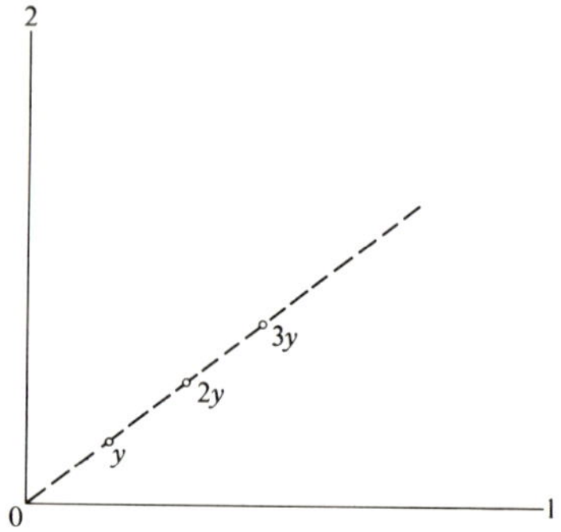

Figure 4

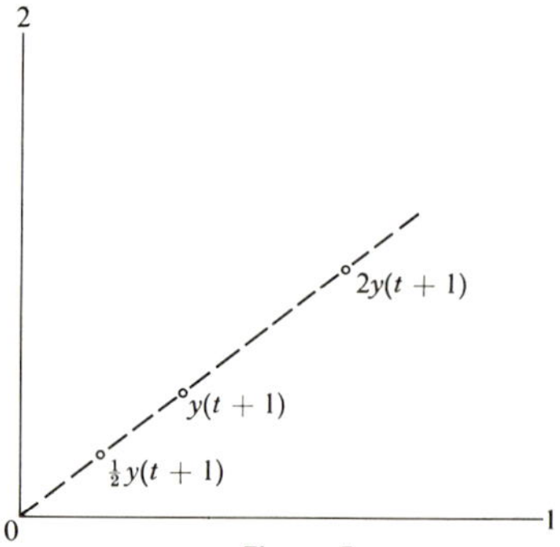

Figure 5

of rays, $\{\bar{y} \mid \bar{y} = ay\}$. On the other hand, the possible outputs from y may be subject to other scale effects. If

$$ {}_s\mathscr{Y}_t(ky) = (k^n)\,{}_s\mathscr{Y}_t(y), $$

it is said that the correspondence ${}_s\mathscr{Y}_t$ is *homogeneous of degree n*. If $n > 1$, there are *increasing returns* to scale. If $n < 1$, there are *decreasing returns* to scale. If $n = 1$, there are *constant returns* to scale. More generally, ${}_s\mathscr{Y}_t$ is *homothetic* if

$$ {}_s\mathscr{Y}_t(ky) = f(k, y)\,{}_s\mathscr{Y}_y(y). $$

In other words, production is homothetic if proportional increases in capital do not change the possible output–capital input vectors, but at most, change the level at which they can be operated. If for $k > 1$,

$$ \frac{f(k, y)}{k} < 1, $$

there are decreasing returns, whereas if

$$\frac{f(k, y)}{k} > 1,$$

there are increasing returns. If $f(k, y) = k$, there are constant returns to scale. Under additivity, if y and $\bar{y}$ are production possibilities, then their sum $\bar{\bar{y}}$ is also a production possibility. This is illustrated in Figure 6.

Production possibility sets are *convex* in Figures 3, 7, and 8. The rationale for convexity may be stated as follows. Consider that production takes place subject to some kinds of constraints, possibly limitations of space or entrepreneurship; then it may not be possible to combine $\bar{y}$ and y in an additive fashion. However, if $\bar{y}$ and y are appropriately reduced in scale, so that an adequate amount of the limiting factor is available, then it may be possible to combine them in a quasi additive manner. For example, the simultaneous operation of $\bar{y}$ at the level of $\frac{1}{2}$ and y at the level of $\frac{1}{2}$ may be possible without using more than the available space for production. Nevertheless, convexity is not a universal law since it does

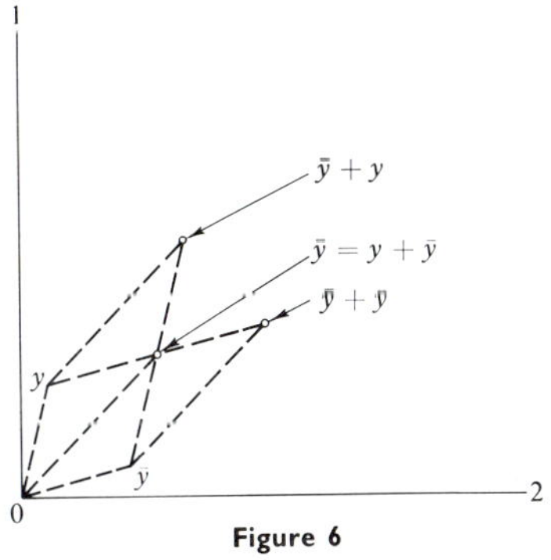

Figure 6

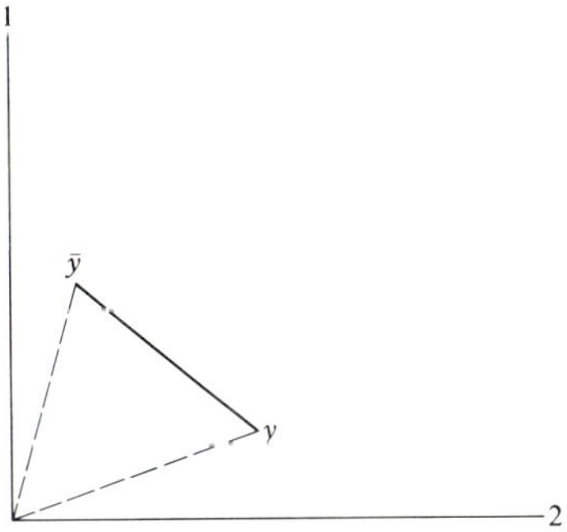

Figure 7

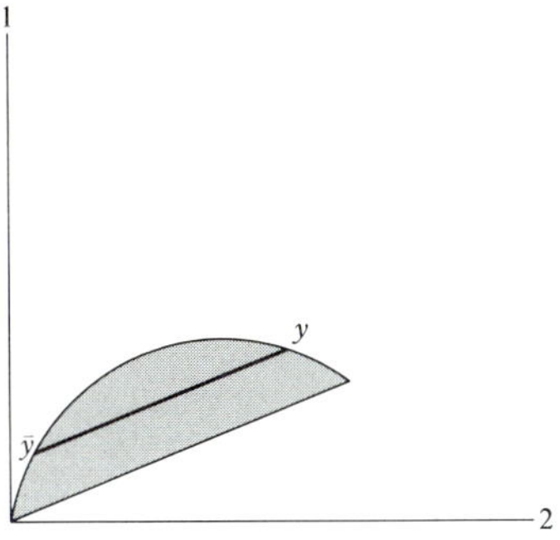

Figure 8

not apply to increasing returns industries. Results derived from convexity apply only to a subsector of the economy.

There are properties that apply only to the transformation set ${}_s\mathscr{Y}_t(y)$. There is *strong convexity* whenever (1) there is convexity, and (2) if $\bar{y}$ and y are not proportional to each other, then any vector near their convex combination can be obtained. In Figure 8, any points on the line segment between y and $\bar{y}$ are possible, but the producer can do better. By adding condition (2) to convexity to define strong convexity, we are saying that it is never efficient to use two processes simultaneously. We can always do better by finding another process. In effect, all production is joint. There is *strict convexity* if the qualification in strong convexity, "not proportional to each other," is eliminated. For example, a disc is strictly convex.

Production displays *weak superadditivity* if for any production possibilities y and $\bar{y}$, there is a production possibility $\bar{\bar{y}}$ at least as great as their sum, $\bar{\bar{y}} \geqslant y + \bar{y}$. Under *superadditivity*, $\bar{\bar{y}}$ is also greater than $y + \bar{y}$ in some components whenever y and $\bar{y}$ are not proportional. Under *strong superadditivity*, $\bar{\bar{y}}$ is also greater than $y + \bar{y}$ in all components whenever y and $\bar{y}$ are not proportional.

There is *free disposal* whenever the production can always be changed so as to provide less output and/or more input, as in Figure 9.

The relationship between these properties can be stated as follows:

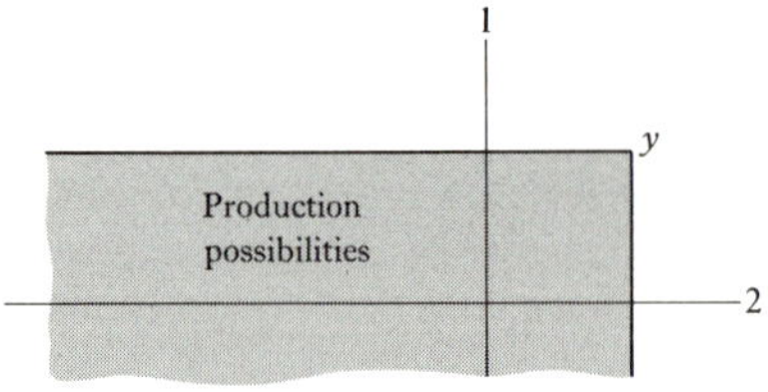

Figure 9

1 Theorem (i) *Additivity and constant returns to scale imply convexity.*

(ii) *Convexity and the possibility of inaction imply divisibility.*

(iii) *Divisibility and multiplicability imply constant returns to scale.*

(iv) *Superadditivity and free disposal imply additivity. If there are also constant returns to scale, then there is convexity.*

(v) *Strong convexity and additivity (or multiplicability) imply strong superadditivity.*

Proof (i) This is easy to see, since the production $ty + (1 - t)\bar{y}$ consists of simply reducing the scale of y to ty and the scale of $\bar{y}$ to $(1 - t)\bar{y}$, and then adding the two processes.

(ii) This is trivial, since given that y is a process, as is 0, clearly anything on the line segment between y and 0 can be produced, that is, y can be produced at any scale less than 1 (without loss of efficiency).

(iii) Trivial.

(iv) Use free disposal to reduce $\bar{\bar{y}}$ to $y + \bar{y}$ and apply (i).

(v) Simply chose $\bar{\bar{y}}$ greater than $\frac{1}{2}y + \frac{1}{2}\bar{y}$ and multiply by two. q.e.d.

Convexity does not necessarily imply additivity. This is the case in Figure 6 where production possibilities are convex but not additive. Even the addition of inaction to the production set does not imply that production is additive or multiplicative, although it does imply that production is divisible.

It is useful to state these definitions in terms of set theory. This provides a shorthand for otherwise lengthy proofs.

Divisibility $a\,{}_s\mathscr{Y}_t \subset {}_s\mathscr{Y}_t$ whenever $0 < a < 1$.
Inaction $0 \in {}_s\mathscr{Y}_t$.
Multiplicability $n\,{}_s\mathscr{Y}_t \subset {}_s\mathscr{Y}_t$ for $n = 0, 1, 2, \ldots$.
Constant Returns to Scale $a\,{}_s\mathscr{Y}_t \subset {}_s\mathscr{Y}_t$ whenever $a > 0$.
Additivity ${}_s\mathscr{Y}_t + {}_s\mathscr{Y}_t \subset {}_s\mathscr{Y}_t$.
Convexity $a\,{}_s\mathscr{Y}_t + (1 - a)\,{}_s\mathscr{Y}_t \subset {}_s\mathscr{Y}_t$ for $0 \leqslant a \leqslant 1$.
Free Disposal ${}_s\mathscr{Y}_{t(y)} - \Omega\ (= {}_s\mathscr{Y}_{t(y)} + (-\Omega)) \subset {}_s\mathscr{Y}_t(y)$, where

$$\Omega = \{x \mid x \geqslant 0\}.$$

Theorem 1 can be stated in these terms as well.

Exercise 3 Show that if $\mathscr{Y}$ is convex, additive, and inactivity is possible, then $\mathscr{Y}$ is a convex cone.

3. Laws of Returns in Production Transformations

In general terms, the change in the ratio of outputs to inputs from a change in inputs is regarded as returns to scale. In the limiting case of infinite returns, there is free production. If there is no change, the returns are precipitously decreasing. Between these two extremes there are several possibilities.

So far the returns to scale have been presented as assumptions (for example, constant returns to scale) or as simple consequences (for example, additivity and divisibility imply constant returns to scale). A deeper understanding of the relationship between returns to scale and the geometry of the production set is possible, but it requires the study of limiting processes. The same methods can be used to consider returns to nonproportional changes in factors of production.

The *returns to a change* in capital stock δ (normally, $\delta \leqslant y$) are said to be *constant* if

$$ {}_s\mathscr{Y}_t(y + \alpha\delta) = (1 + \alpha)\, {}_s\mathscr{Y}_t(y) $$

for all $\alpha > -1$. This is an extension of the notion of constant returns to scale, where $\delta = y$. It corresponds to the notion that proportional increases in some of the factors may give rise to proportional increases in outputs and current inputs. More generally, if

$$ {}_s\mathscr{Y}_t(y + \alpha\delta) = g(y + \alpha\delta, y)\, {}_s\mathscr{Y}_t(y), $$

production is homothetic in capital for changes δ from the initial stock y. If for $\alpha > 0$,

$$ g(y + \alpha\delta, y) < (1 + \alpha), $$

there are *decreasing returns*. If for $\alpha > 0$,

$$ g(y + \alpha\delta, y) > (1 + \alpha), $$

there are *increasing returns*. This is illustrated in Figure 10, where output increases with inputs according to constant returns when $\delta = y$, but if $\delta < y$, according to less than constant returns. Also, as we move along the constant y^2 line and increase y^1, $g(y^1, y^2)$ increases, but at a decreasing rate. However, as we move along a given ratio of y^2 to y^1, we move along a line in 3-space, so that $g(y^1, y^2)$ is increasing proportionately.

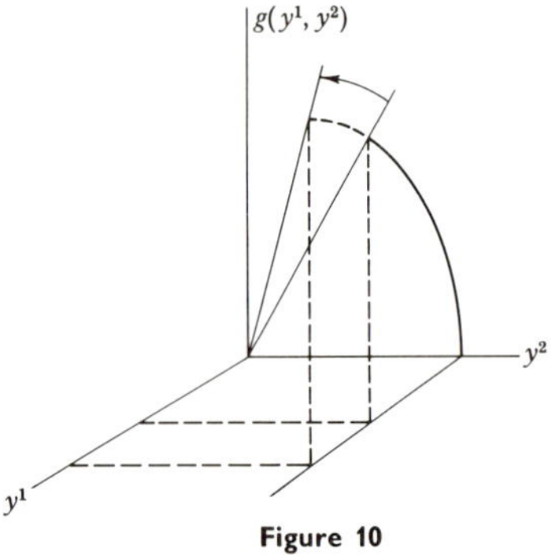

Figure 10

2 Theorem (i) *Let there be increasing returns to changes for $\delta < y$, there is free disposal and the possibility of inaction, ${}_s\mathscr{Y}_t(y)$ is convex and closed. Then ${}_s\mathscr{Y}_t(y)$ is a cone.*

(ii) *Let there be increasing returns to scale, the possibility of inaction, free disposal, and ${}_s\mathscr{Y}_t$ convex and closed. Then ${}_s\mathscr{Y}_t(y)$ is a cone.*

3 Corollary *If there is the possibility of inaction and* ${}_s\mathscr{Y}_{t(y)}$ *is bounded and closed, then there are not always increasing returns. If, also, all capital goods are productive, then there are not increasing returns when one factor is held constant while another is increased.*

As pointed out in Section 1, the boundedness of ${}_s\mathscr{Y}_t(y)$ is the consequence of the bounds on the speed of energy and matter.

Proof We first prove (ii). Consider x in ${}_s\mathscr{Y}_t(y)$. Then $\alpha x \in {}_s\mathscr{Y}_t(y)$ for all $0 < \alpha < 1$. More generally, if βx is in ${}_s\mathscr{Y}_t(y)$, then $\alpha x \in {}_s\mathscr{Y}_t(y)$ for all $0 < \alpha \leqslant \beta$. Let $\bar{\beta}$ be the least upper bound of $\beta x \in {}_s\mathscr{Y}_t(y)$. By virtue of the closedness of ${}_s\mathscr{Y}_t(y)$, $\bar{\beta}x \in {}_s\mathscr{Y}_t(y)$. Therefore, for $k > 0$, there is an $m > k + 1 > 1$ such that

$$(y + k\delta, m\bar{\beta}x) \in {}_s\mathscr{Y}_t \qquad \text{(increasing return to scale).}$$

Free disposal applies:

$$(y(1 + k), m\bar{\beta}x) \in {}_s\mathscr{Y}_t \,.$$

By virtue of convexity and inaction,

$$\frac{1}{k+1}(y(1 + k), m\bar{\beta}x)) = \left(y, \frac{m}{k+1}\bar{\beta}x\right) \in {}_s\mathscr{Y}_t\,, \qquad \frac{m}{k+1}\bar{\beta} > \bar{\beta},$$

which is impossible; $\bar{\beta}$ cannot be finite.

The proof of (i) is obtained by a straightforward modification of the argument above. q.e.d.

The production set allows no *free production in the limit* if the input–output ratios in ${}_s\mathscr{Y}_t$ are bounded outside of a bounded set. The production set in Figure 11 allows no free production outside the finite circle $\mathscr{C}$. Also, outside of $\mathscr{C}'$ the input–output ratios are bounded by the slope of $0d$ for the production of commodity 2 from commodity 1 and by the slope of $0f$ for the production of commodity 2 from commodity 1. Therefore, there is an upper bound on the returns to scale, in the limit. This is so even though there is the possibility of a limited amount of production that may be interpreted as free, thet is, where no inputs are required for outputs. On the other hand, in Figure 12, where inputs $y(t)$ are given negative coordinates, arbitrarily high returns to scale may be obtained by choosing y^n in ${}_s\mathscr{Y}_t$ which are also on the line $0d^n$. The returns to scale of such y^n, representing methods of producing commodity 2 from commodity 1, tend to plus infinity. Therefore, there is not an upperbound upon the returns to scale, in the limit.

In summary, not only is free production excluded outside a bounded set, but also there is no approximation to free production outside this

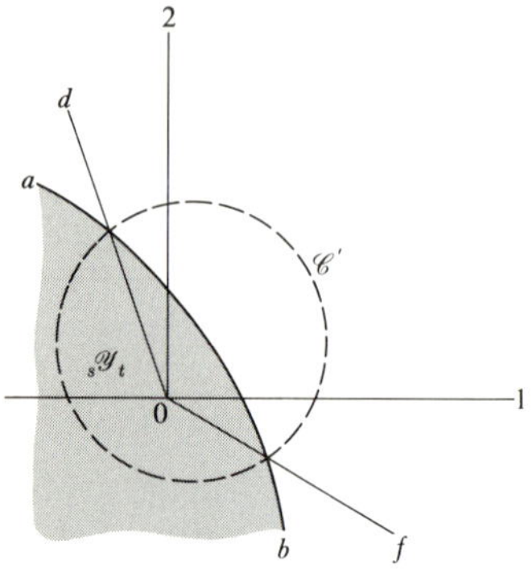

Figure 11

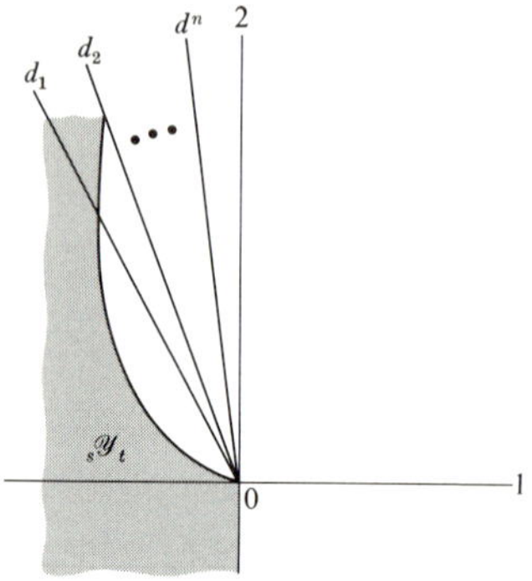

Figure 12

bounded set, even as scale increases to infinity. The definition of no free production in the limit can be applied to ${}_s\mathscr{Y}_t(y)$ only, simply by fixing y. Obviously, if ${}_s\mathscr{Y}_t$ allows no free production in the limit, then neither does ${}_s\mathscr{Y}_t(y)$.

${}_s\mathscr{Y}_t$ is *irreversible in the limit* if, outside a bounded set, the *input–output vector* $y(t)/|y| - \bar{y}(t)/|y|$ does not tend to zero, $y(t), \bar{y}(t) \in {}_s\mathscr{Y}_t(y)$. In many applications, this is equivalent to assuming the nonexistence of reversible cycles in the limit, since combining $y(t)$ and $-y(t)$ puts us back where we start, namely, at zero. Examples of reversible cycles appear in thermodynamics.

In Figure 13a, ${}_s\mathscr{Y}_t$ is irreversible in the limit, since no points both below $0e$ and to the left of $0d$ are the negative one of the other. Therefore, none of the limiting $y^n(t)/|y(t)|$ can be the negative one of the other. On the other hand, in Figure 13b (as in Figure 12), $0e$ and $0d$ do not have this property. In fact, there are points $y^n(t)$ in ${}_s\mathscr{Y}_t(y)$ and also in $0e^n$ such that $y^n(t)/|y|$ tends to limiting input–output vectors in $0e$; also vectors in $0d^n$ tend to vectors in $-0e$. Therefore, ${}_s\mathscr{Y}_t(y)$ in Figure 13b is not irreversible in the limit, that is, it is reversible in the limit.

Of course, there is *free disposal* if ${}_s\mathscr{Y}_t(y)$ contains ${}_s\mathscr{Y}_t(y) - \Omega$. There is *free disposal to* $\bar{y}$ if for y in $\mathscr{Y}$, $y \leqslant \bar{y}$, then for any y^1 such that

$$y \geqslant y^1 \geqslant \bar{y},$$

y^1 is in $\mathscr{Y}$. In Figures 11 and 12, viewing the shaded areas as ${}_s\mathscr{Y}_t(y)$, there is free disposal. In Figure 14, there is not free disposal to $(-1, 1)$ since since in particular

$$(0, 0) \geqslant (-\tfrac{1}{2}, -\tfrac{1}{4}) \geqslant (-1, 1),$$

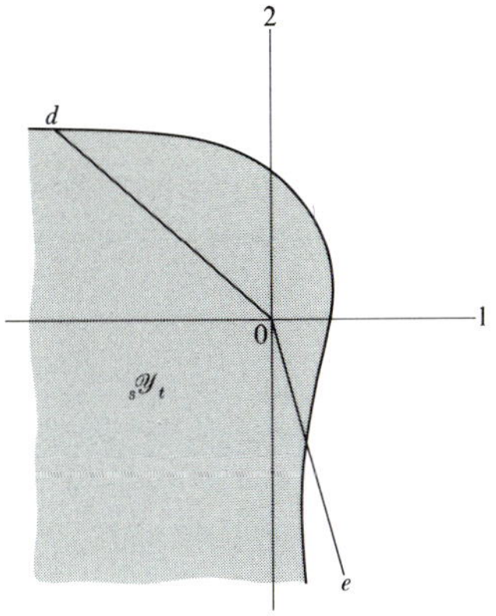

Figure 13a

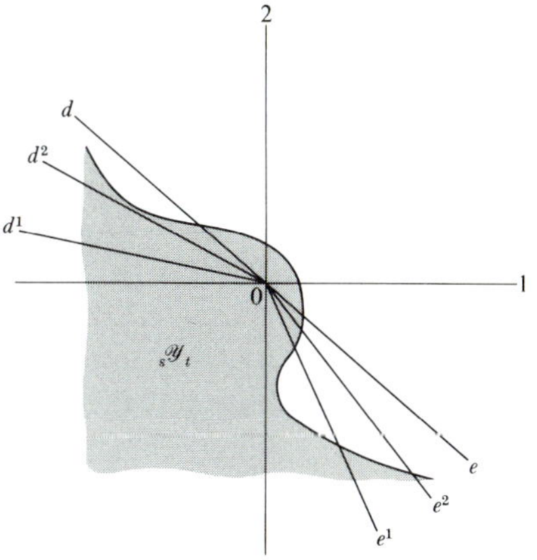

Figure 13b

but $(-\frac{1}{2}, -\frac{1}{4})$ is not in ${}_s\mathscr{Y}_t(y)$. There is free disposal if for all $y \in \mathscr{Y}$, there is free disposal to y, and if there are arbitrarily small y in $\mathscr{Y}$.

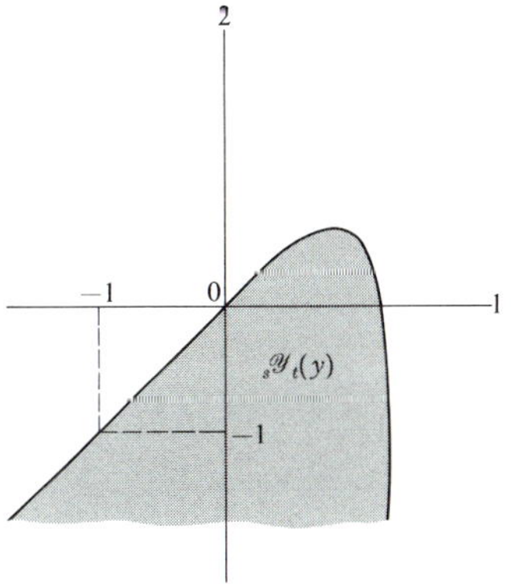

Figure 14

4 Theorem *If there is free disposal in ${}_s\mathscr{Y}_t(y)$ and if ${}_s\mathscr{Y}_t(y)$ is irreversible in the limit, then ${}_s\mathscr{Y}_t(y)$ allows no free production in the limit.*

The argument is simple if the origin is in ${}_s\mathscr{Y}_t(y)$ as in Figures 12–14. In this case where inaction is possible, the argument for Theorem 4 is is illustrated in Figure 13. Clearly for x^n in $\mathscr{Y}$ and on $0d^n$, $x^n/|x^n|$ tends to a point w in Ω whose negative is in ${}_s\mathscr{Y}_t(y)$.

Proof Suppose there is free production in the limit. Then, $x^n/|x^n|$

tends to a nonzero value in the nonnegative orthant $\Omega = \{x \mid x \geqslant 0\}$, as in Figure 12. Now choose any x in ${}_s\mathscr{Y}_t(y)$. Then,

$$\{x\} - \Omega \subset {}_s\mathscr{Y}_t(y),$$

since there is free disposal. But for $-w$ in $-\Omega$,

$$\frac{-kw + x}{|-kw - w|} = \frac{-kw}{|kw|} \frac{|kw|}{|x - kw|} + \frac{x}{|-kw + x|}$$

tends to $-w/|w|$. Therefore, if $x^n/|x^n|$ tends to w in Ω, there is $x - kw$ in ${}_s\mathscr{Y}_t(y)$. Also, $-kw + x/|-kw + x|$ tends to $-w$ and there is reversibility in the limit. q.e.d.

PROBLEMS

A. Production Continuity I

A correspondence $\mathscr{F}$ is *lower semicontinuous* if $x_n \to x$, $y \in \mathscr{F}(x)$ implies there exists $y^n \in \mathscr{F}(x^n)$ such that $y^n \to y$. Let ${}_t\mathscr{Y}_{t+1}$ be convex.

Show that on a line segment, ${}_t\mathscr{Y}_{t+1}(y)$ is lower semicontinuous (Hint: Observe

$${}_t\mathscr{Y}_{t+1}(sy + (1 - s)y) \supset s\, {}_t\mathscr{Y}_{t+1}(y) + (1 - s)\, {}_t\mathscr{Y}_{t+1}(y).)$$

B. Production Continuity II

$\mathscr{F}(x)$ is $\geqslant$*-convex*, if $\bar{x} \geqslant x \geqslant \bar{\bar{x}}$, $\bar{y} \in \mathscr{F}(\bar{x})$, $\bar{\bar{y}} \in \mathscr{F}(\bar{\bar{x}})$, $\bar{y} \geqslant \bar{\bar{y}}$ implies there is a $y \in \mathscr{F}(x)$ such that $\bar{y} \geqslant y \geqslant \bar{\bar{y}}$.

Show that if there is $\geqslant$-convexity, ${}_t\mathscr{Y}_{t+1}(y)$ is lower semicontinuous in the convergence $y^n \to y$ if, and only if, there are k^n, y^n for which

$$k^n y \geqslant y^n \geqslant t^n y; \qquad k^n, t^n \to 1.$$

4. Production Functions

The older neoclassical theories of production of Walras, Wicksteed, Wicksell, and J. B. Clark begin with the concept of a production function. This section defines the main properties of production functions. In Sections 5 and 6 the full theory of neoclassical production will be set forth.

In the two-commodity case where there is one input and one output, the production function is defined to be the maximum output that can be obtained from a given input. The graph of this function is seen to be the upper frontier of the production set. In Figure 15, imputs are given negative coordinates and the production function is the twisted curve in the second quadrant bounding the production possibility set.

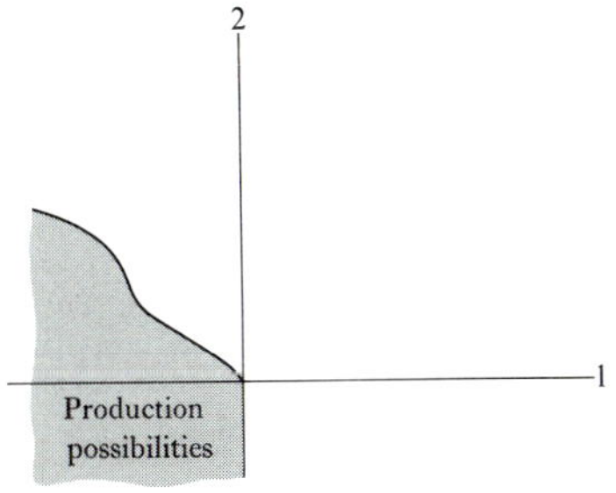

Figure 15

It is easily seen that if there is strong convexity but not constant returns to scale, production displays decreasing scale returns of outputs from inputs (Figure 16a). Let f be the production function. Then super-additivity (or strict convexity) of production implies

$$f(tx + (1 - t)\bar{y}) > tf(x) + (1 - t)f(y), \qquad 0 < t < 1.$$

This is shown in Figure 16b for the case $\frac{1}{2}x + \frac{1}{2}y$.

The case of two inputs and one output is similar. The production possibility set is now in three dimensions and the graph of the production function is no longer a curve in two-dimensional space, but rather a surface in three-dimensional space. This is often represented in terms of level curves in a two-dimensional space. The inputs are represented in two-dimensional spaces, as in Figure 17.

For concreteness, let the factors be capital and labor and indicate their quantities along the axes. A point in the factor space, as illustrated in Figure 17, has coordinates representing the inputs of the two factors. Isoproduct curves are drawn which indicate factor inputs giving equal production. Along the curve cc' inputs may differ, but output remains the same. For example, the points x and y represent different input combinations; nevertheless, they allow the same maximum outputs. Normally, isoquants upward and to the right in Figure 17 represent higher levels of output. This is the production map, where the isoquants represent points of equal elevation along the incline toward higher production. The strict concavity property can be shown to hold whenever x and y represent vectors of factor inputs, rather than merely single inputs. This is clear from the convexity properties. For example, if production is convex, then we can obtain at least the convex combination

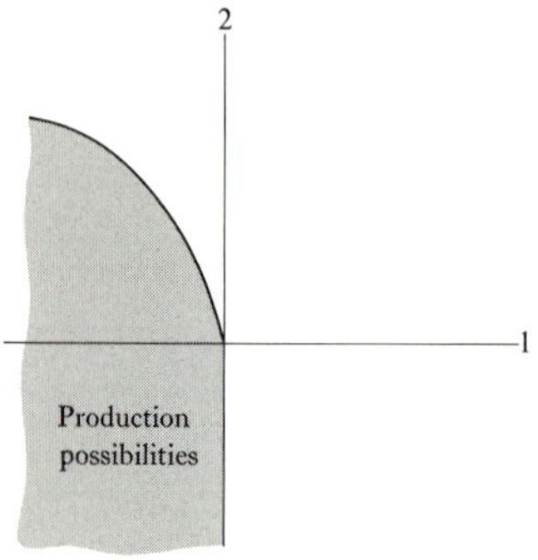

Figure 16a

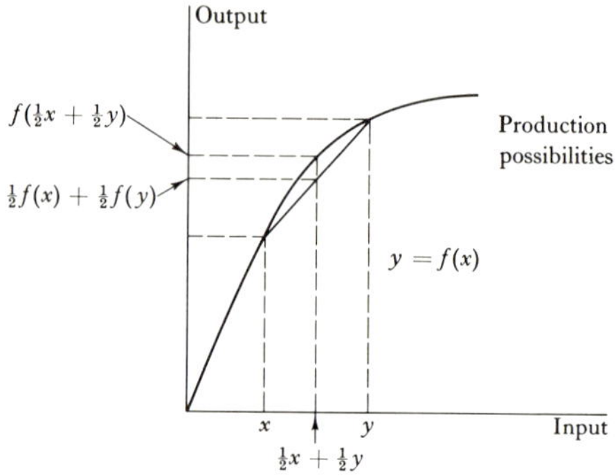

Figure 16b

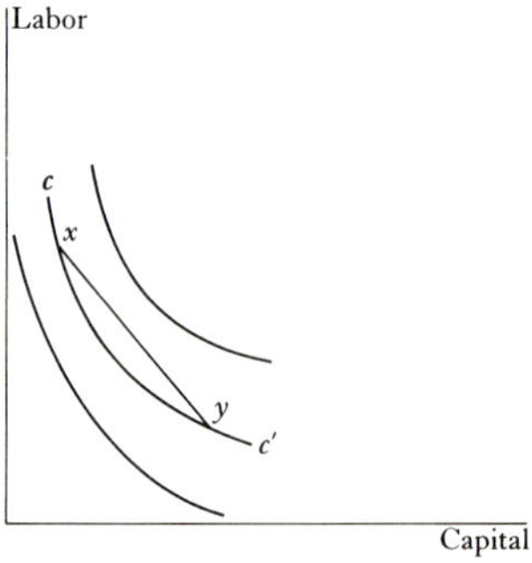

Figure 17

of outputs from the convex combination of inputs. This is merely in words the concavity property for production functions. In particular, the concavity of the production functions implies the convexity of the isoquants to the origin. For example, the convex combination of factor inputs between x and y in Figure 17 gives rise to higher production, as represented by the fact that the combination appears on the isoquants that are upward and to the right of cc'. In turn, the concavity of the production function can be used to show that there are diminishing returns to output from changing one input while holding the other constant. This follows immediately from the fact that concavity of f implies concavity of f in any one variable, while the other variable is held fixed.

Similarly, strict convexity of the production possibilities implies strict concavity of f in any single variable while the other is held fixed.

A line through the origin in the factor space, as in Figure 18, represents points at which the ratio of the factors applied is the same. For the production function to be concave, distance along the ray between isoquants representing equal increases in production must increase or stay the same. If the distance between such isoquants remains the same, there are constant returns to scale. If the distances increase as one moves out along the ray, then there are decreasing returns to scale.

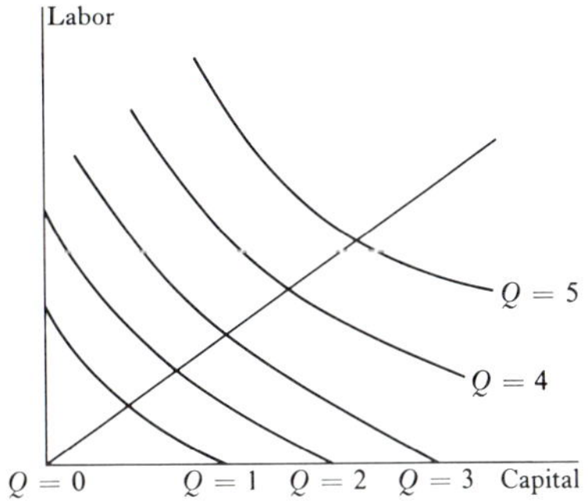

Figure 18

The slope of an isoquant at a given point is called a *marginal rate of substitution*:

$$\frac{\partial f/\partial L}{\partial f/\partial K} = mrs.$$

Usually, the marginal rate of substitution is negative and increasing in L (decreasing in absolute value). More generally, the set of factors giving more output is convex. Expressed mathematically,

$$f(tx + (1 - t)y) \geqslant \min(f(x), f(y))$$

or f is quasi concave.

The function f is *homothetic* if there is an increasing transformation T such that $T(f(x))$ is linear homogeneous. If the marginal rate of substitution is invariant along any given scale line, then it can be shown that the production function is homothetic.

If

$$f(tx) = t^k f(t, x)),$$

production is homogeneous of degree k. For $k = 1$ there are constant returns; $k < 1$, decreasing returns; $k > 1$, increasing returns.

5 Remark Every production function homogeneous of degree k is homothetic.

Proof Clearly,

$$Tf(x) = f(x)^{1/k}$$

is homogeneous of degree one. Therefore, there is an independence between the shape of the isoquants and the degree of homogeneity. In fact, given one isoquant for homothetic production f, all other isoquants can immediately be determined. The scale is then determined entirely by the speed of ascent in production as we move from one isoquant to another. q.e.d.

6 Theorem *If f is homogeneous of degree $0 < n \leqslant 1$, quasi concave, and continuous, then f is concave on the set*

$$\mathscr{X} = \{x \mid f(x) > 0\}.$$

Proof f is a concave function of $f^{1/n}$. Hence, it suffices to prove the theorem for $n = 1$. Consider the graph

$$\mathscr{F} = \{(w, x) \mid x \in \mathscr{X}, \quad w \leqslant f(x), \quad f(x) > 0\}.$$

Then, f is concave if and only if $\mathscr{F}$ is convex, since $\mathscr{X}$ is clearly convex.
Let

$$\mathscr{Y} = \{x \mid f(x) > 1\}.$$

Clearly, $\mathscr{Y} \subset \mathscr{X}$ is open (continuity of f). Also $\mathscr{Y}$ is convex (quasi concavity). If $f(x) = 1$, $x \in \operatorname{Bnd} \mathscr{Y}$ since $f(tx) = t < 1$ for $0 < t < 1$. Hence, Minkowski's theorem (Lemma 13 of Chapter 2) applies: there is a vector $p \neq 0$ such that $py > px$ for all $y \in \mathscr{Y}$. Also, for $k > 1$, $kpx \in \mathscr{Y}$, since $f(kx) > 1$. Hence,

$$pkx = kpx > px \qquad \text{or} \qquad px > 0.$$

Note that $-pxw + py > 0$ for $w < 1$, $f(y) > 1$. Hence, for any $(w, y) \in \mathscr{F}$,

$$\begin{aligned} -pxw + py &= f(y)\left(-px\frac{w}{f(y)} + p\frac{y}{f(y)}\right) \\ &= f(y)(-px\hat{w} + p\hat{y}) \\ &\geqslant 0 \end{aligned}$$

where $\hat{y} = y/f(y)$, $f(\hat{y}) = 1$, $\hat{w} = w/f(y)$, $\hat{w} \leqslant 1$ (since $w \leqslant f(y)$). Therefore, there is a hyperplane containing $(f(x), x)$ and bounding $\mathscr{F}$ for every $f(x) > 0$. Also, $-pxf(x) + px = 0$ and

$$-pxf(x) + px = pxkf(x) + pkx$$

for any $k > 0$. Hence, for any $(f(y), y) \in \text{Bnd}\,\mathscr{F}$, there is a bounding hyperplane through $(f(y), y)$ and the origin.

Let $\mathscr{S}_y$ be the half space containing $\mathscr{F}$ and the bounding hyperplane. Clearly, $\mathscr{F} \subset \bigcap_{y \in \text{Bnd}\mathscr{F}} \mathscr{S}_y$. Indeed, $\overline{\mathscr{F}} = \bigcap_{y \in \text{Bnd}\mathscr{F}} \mathscr{S}_y$, since otherwise there would be a bounding point z in Int $\bigcap_{y \in \text{Bnd}\mathscr{F}} \mathscr{S}_y$ contrary to the fact that $z \in \text{Bnd}\,\mathscr{S}_z$ and Bnd $\bigcap_{y \in \text{Bnd}\mathscr{F}} \mathscr{S}_y \subset \bigcup_{y \in \text{Bnd}\mathscr{F}} \text{Bnd}\,\mathscr{S}_y$. Also, $\mathscr{F} = \overline{\mathscr{F}}$ by the fact that $x^n \to x$, $w^n \leqslant f(x^n)$, $w^n \to w$ implies $f(x) \leqslant w$(continuity of f). As the intersection of convex sets, $\mathscr{F}$ is convex. q.e.d.

An important theorem of production is contained in Euler's theorem for homogeneous functions (Lemma 10 of Chapter 2).

If f is a homogeneous of degree k and is differentialble at x

$$kf(x_1, x_2) = \frac{\partial f}{\partial x_1} x_1 + \frac{\partial f}{\partial x_2} x_2 . \tag{1}$$

It is also easy to see that the partial derivatives of f with respect to the x_1 are homogeneous of degree $1 - k$. Application of Euler's theorem to such partial derivatives gives

$$(1 - k) \frac{\partial f}{\partial x_1} = \frac{\partial^2 f}{\partial x_1 \, \partial x_2} x_2 + \frac{\partial^2 f_2}{\partial x_1} x_1 . \tag{2}$$

7 Remark If f is homogeneous of degree 1 and is differentiable at x,

$$\frac{\partial^2 f}{\partial x_1 \, \partial x_2} = - \frac{\partial^2 f}{\partial x_1^2} \frac{x_1}{x_2} . \tag{3}$$

Therefore, whenever there are diminishing returns to one factor when the other is held constant, that is, whenever the second derivative of f with respect to x_1 is negative, then the cross partial is positive. This is *Wicksell's law*, which says that the marginal product of one factor increases when the other factor is increased. In the cases where f is not homogeneous of degree one, Wicksell's law is stated as an assumption, rather than a conclusion. (Note that no distinction is made between the two possible cross partials. By Young's theorem of differential calculus,

$$\frac{\partial^2 f}{\partial x_1 \, \partial x_2} = \frac{\partial^2 f}{\partial x_2 \, \partial x_1} . \tag{4}$$

Whenever all the partial derivatives are continuous, the order of differentiation is not important.)

A common measure of production is the so-called *elasticity of substitution* given by

$$\eta = \frac{\dfrac{\partial f}{\partial x_1}\dfrac{\partial f}{\partial x_2}}{\dfrac{\partial^2 f}{\partial x_1\,\partial x_2} f}. \tag{5}$$

In the case of constant returns to scale, this elasticity of substitution can be shown to be the percentage change in the marginal rate of transformation with respect to the percentage change in the capital labor ratio. In Chapter 10, it will be seen that η is important in the analysis of changes in factor shares.

In particular, if the elasticity of substitution is constant, not equal to one, and greater than zero, the CES[1] production function is of the form

$$f(k, l) = ((ak)^\rho + (bl)^{1/\rho} \tag{6}$$

derived by Arrow, Chenery, Minhas, and Solow [1961]. If $\eta = 1$, then the production function is the *Cobb–Douglas* function

$$f(k, l) = ck^\alpha l^{1-\alpha}.$$

Normally, the upper boundary of the production surface is of dimension one less than that of the production set. It can be represented as a solution of a real-valued equation

$$g(y) = c.$$

If there is a joint production of several goods, outputs may be variable in their ratios, which is the topic of the next section.

Exercise 4 Prove Young's theorem.

Exercise 5 Let $f(k, l) = a_0 + a_1k + b_1l + a_2k^2 + b_2l^2 + cke$. When is f concave? Strictly concave? When are factors always *productive*, in that an increase in one always leads to an increase in output? When are there decreasing returns to scale? Increasing returns to scale? Constant returns to scale?

Exercise 6 Let $f(k, l) = [(ak)^\rho + (bl)^\rho]^\sigma$ and answer the questions in Exercise 5.

Exercise 7 Let $f^i(k, l) = [(a_ik)^{\rho_i} + (b_il)^{\rho_i}]^{1/\rho_i}$, $i = 1, 2$. Suppose one agent produces capital using only consumer goods as intermediate

[1] Constant elasticity of substitution.

products and the other produces consumer goods, using both capital and consumer goods as intermediate products. Finally, let consumer goods be turned into labor services through consumption. Derive ${}_s\mathscr{Y}_t^i$, $i = 1, 2$, and ${}_s\mathscr{Y}_t$.

Exercise 8 Instead of using the CES functions, answer the questions in Exercise 7 with Cobb–Douglas production functions.

PROBLEMS

C. Constant Elasticity of Substitution I

1. Show that if η is constant

$$f(x_1, x_2) = (g_1(x_1) + g_2(x_2))^{\eta/(\eta-1)}.$$

(Hint: Solve

$$\eta \frac{\partial \ln \partial f/\partial x_i}{\partial x_j} = \frac{\partial \ln f(x_1, x_2)}{\partial x_j}, \qquad i = 1, 2, \quad j \neq i,$$

to obtain

$$\frac{\partial f}{\partial x_i}(f(x_1, x_2))^{-1/\eta} = h_j(x_j), \qquad i = 1, 2, \quad j = i.$$

Integrating, we get

$$f(x_1, x_2)^{(\eta-1)/\eta} = g_1(x_1) + g_2(x_2).)$$

2. Let $\eta = 1$. What is the production function?

This problem is due, essentially, to the article of Arrow *et al.* [1961]. The solution here is similar to that of Paroush [1964].

D. Constant Elasticity of Substitution II

1. Let $f(x_1, \ldots, x_3) = (\sum g_i(x_i))^{(\eta-1)/\eta}$.
Show that the elasticities of substitution,

$$\eta_{ij} = \frac{f_i f_j}{f_{ij} f}, \qquad i \neq j,$$

are equal to η, where

$$f_i = \frac{\partial f}{\partial x_i}, \qquad f_j = \frac{\partial f}{\partial x_j}, \qquad f_{ij} = \frac{\partial^2 f}{\partial x_i\, \partial x_j}.$$

2. Let the elasticities of substitution equal η. Show that f has the form given in 1.

3. Let

$$f(x_1, \ldots, x_n) = \prod_{s=1}^{k} \Big(\sum_{i=j(s-1)+1}^{j(s)} g_i(x_i) \Big)^{(\eta_s - 1)/\eta_s}$$

Show that η_{ij} is constant and equals 1 if for some s either $i \leqslant j(s) \leqslant j$, $i \neq j$, or $j \leqslant j(s) \leqslant i$, $i \neq j$, and is η_s otherwise.

4. Let η_{ij} be constant. Show that the production function has the form in 3.

A related problem was solved by Uzawa (1962].

5. Interindustry Production

The production set ${}_s\mathscr{Y}_t$ is *generated* by industries i, $i = 1, \ldots, k$, provided

$${}_s\mathscr{Y}_t = \sum_{i=1}^{k} {}_s\mathscr{Y}_t^i .$$

The y^i in ${}_s\mathscr{Y}_t^i$ may actually include inputs that have negative quantities, although $\sum y^i$ must be nonnegative.

The neoclassical description of production is that in which the production set ${}_s\mathscr{Y}_t$ is generated by (independent) industries whose efficient output is given by functions of the form

$$y(t+1) = f^i(y^i(t)), \qquad i = 1, \ldots, k.$$

This means that $(y(t), y(t+1)) = (\sum y^i, \sum f^i + y(t))$ and any convex combination of the $(y(t), y(t+1))$'s are in ${}_t\mathscr{Y}_{t+1}$. Industries can produce any output on the production function or any convex combination of outputs on the production function (by utilizing convex combinations of the inputs).

Here there appear some simple properties of interindustry production and then the theory of the complex of raw material requirements, first output, and industry.

8 Remark Suppose that f^i displays constant returns to scale and at least y^i, y^j are linearly independent and efficient. Then ${}_s\mathscr{Y}_t$ is not strictly convex.

Proof For any $\xi_i, \xi_j \geqslant 0$,

$$(\xi_i y^i + \xi_j y^j, \xi_i f^i, \xi_j f^j) \in {}_t\mathscr{Y}_{t+1} \qquad \text{where} \quad f^i = f^i(y^i), \quad f^j = f^j(y^j),$$

If y^i and y^j are independent, the ξ_i's and ξ_j's, $\xi_i + \xi_j = 1$, form a line segment between nonproportional input–output vectors. No greater output can be obtained so that such points are not internal to ${}_t\mathscr{Y}_{t+1}(y(t))$. q.e.d.

Production is *interindustry* if

(i) $\xi_i = f^i(y^i)$, f^i continuous, y^i productive in all nonzero components;
(ii) $\delta^i = g^i \xi_i$ is net output by industry i;
(iii) $x = \sum \delta^i$, and increases of all net outputs cannot be accomplished if any ξ decreases (therefore $| g^i_j |$ is monotonic in ξ_{ij});
(iv) $y = \sum y^i$.

In (ii), we may have positive components for those factors which endure the production process. Alternatively, we may ignore factors in the analysis of current output. An example is the *Leontief technology* where there are r industries with

$$\delta^i = x^i \xi^i,$$

x^i a vector of n constants, (x^i_j) is an $n \times r$ matrix, and the square matrix of the x^i for the first r goods is a nonsingular matrix. Note that the term Leontief system refers us to equation (ii) and not to the rest of the Leontief technology (i)–(iv). The interpretation is that all current inputs are actually intermediate products. In this case, the normalized matrix of outputs is denoted

$$X = (x^1, x^2, \ldots, x^k) \qquad \text{where} \quad x^i_i = 1, \quad i = 1, \ldots, k.$$

The factors producing X are denoted

$$Y = (y^1, y^2, \ldots, y^k).$$

9 Remark If

$$x^i_i > 0, \qquad x^i_j \leqslant 0, \qquad j \neq i,$$

and if it is possible for some input to produce a positive quantity of every commodity, then X^{-1} exists and is nonnegative. That is to say, if the economy under consideration is productive under autarchy, then the x^i are in fact linearly independent. Remark 9 is verified below.

The derivation of the properties of the Leontief system is useful as an explanation both of the structure of raw material requirement and of some basic facts about the class of matrices with the same signs for their off-diagonals, so-called Metzler–Mosak matrices.

Let a_{ij} be the quantity of j used to produce a unit of i. Then the total demand for j is

$$\xi_j = x_j + \sum_i a_{ij}\xi_i \tag{7}$$

or in matrix terms

$$\xi = x + A\xi. \tag{7a}$$

It will be assumed that variations in the intensity of operation of an industry do not change the ratio of gross output to raw material inputs. Of course, changes in price might lead to changes in A. If not, the technology is *Leontief*. That which follows draws upon Leontief [1941], Noble [1958], and Gale [1960].

From (7a), net output is given by $x = (I - A)\,\xi$. Such a system is called a *simple linear model*. A is *productive* if there exists a nonnegative vector $\bar{\xi}$ such that $\bar{\xi} \gg A\bar{\xi}$ that is, if an output can be attained that is at least as great as the total inputs of raw materials. It is also said that the matrix A itself is productive.

10 Lemma *If A is productive and $\xi \geqslant A\xi$, then $\xi \geqslant 0$.*

Proof By definition, there exists a vector $\bar{\xi} \gg A\bar{\xi}$. This means that in fact $\bar{\xi} \gg 0$. Hence, if ξ is any other vector that fits the hypothesis of the lemma, then

$$\xi' = \xi + \theta\bar{\xi} \gg (\xi + \theta\bar{\xi})A = \xi' A \qquad (\theta > 0).$$

Set

$$\theta = \max_i \left\{\frac{-\xi_i}{\bar{\xi}_i}\right\}$$

where ξ_i will be negative for some i whenever the conclusion of the lemma does not hold. One element of ξ' is equal to zero (namely, that for which $-\xi_i/\bar{\xi}_i$ takes a maximum), so that $\xi' \gg \xi' A$ cannot be. Denial of the conclusion of the lemma leads to a contradiction. q.e.d.

11 Corollary *If A is productive, then $I - A$ is nonsingular.*

Proof If $(I - A)\,\xi = 0$, then $\xi \geqslant 0$ (Lemma 10), or if $(I - A)\,\xi = 0$, then $-\xi \geqslant 0$ (Lemma 10), but then ξ must be zero. q.e.d.

12 Theorem *If the matrix A is productive, then for any $x > 0$ the equation $(I - A)\,\xi = x$ has a unique solution, $\xi > 0$.*

Proof By the corollary, $I - A$ is nonsingular, which gives the solution The lemma gives that x is greater or equal to zero in each of its components. Corollary 11 shows that $\xi \neq 0$. q.e.d.

13 Corollary *The matrix A is productive if and only if $(I - A)$ is nonnegative.*

Proof Let

$$e_i = (0, ..., 1, 0, ..., 0).$$

Thus, each element in the inverse must be nonnegative, as $\xi = (I - A)^{-1} e_i$ is nonnegative. q.e.d.

14 Lemma *If A is productive, then*

$$\lim_{n\to\infty} A^n = 0.$$

Proof There exists a $\xi \gg 0$ such that $\xi \gg A\xi$. In fact, $e\xi \gg A\xi$ for some $0 < e < 1$. Hence, $A^n\xi \ll e^n\xi$ and the theorem follows, for if $A^n \to \infty$, $A^n\xi$ would go to infinity for $\xi \gg 0$. q.e.d.

15 Theorem *Let x be any vector and let $\xi_n = (I + A + \cdots + A^n)\, x$ If A is productive, then $\lim(I - A)\, \xi_n = x$, that is,*

$$(I - A)^{-1} = (I + A + \cdots + A^n + \cdots).$$

Theorem 15 gives a method of computing x and the consequent intensity of industry operation.

Proof Since $\lim A^n$ is zero,

$$\lim I + A + \cdots + A^n = (I - A)^{-1}(I - A^{n+1})$$

exists and is equal to $(I - A)^{-1}$. q.e.d.

A *characteristic root* of a matrix A is a (complex) number for which there exists a (complex) characteristic vector x, such that $Ax = \lambda x$. Alternatively,

$$Ax - \lambda x = 0, \qquad \text{or} \qquad \det(A - \lambda I) = 0.$$

A mathematical curiosity that becomes of major importance in dynamical analysis is the fact that the roots of $I - A$ have positive real parts, but these parts are less than one in absolute value.

16 Lemma *If A is productive, then the roots of $I - A$ have positive real parts with absolute value less than one.*

Proof According to Lemma 14, for x a characteristic vector, λ a characteristic root,

$$A^n x = \lambda^n x \to 0.$$

Therefore,

$$\lambda = \lambda_1 + \lambda_2 i,$$

and

$$\lambda_1^2 + \lambda_2^2 < 1.$$

Also, the roots of $I - A$ are simply $1 - \lambda$, λ roots of A. Since $\lambda_1{}^2 < 1$, the real part of $1 - \lambda$, $1 - \lambda_1$, is greater than zero but less than one. q.e.d.

The matrix $I - A$ is *decomposable*, provided that a permutation of rows and columns gives the matrix

$$\begin{bmatrix} I - A_{\alpha\alpha} & 0 \\ -A_{\beta\alpha} & I - A_{\beta\beta} \end{bmatrix}.$$

On the other hand, we define an *ij chain* of A to be the product

$$a_{ie}a_{ef}a_{fg} \cdots a_{rs}a_{sj}$$

of components of A, where $i, e, f, g, \ldots, r, s, j$, are arbitrary, perhaps repetitive.

17 Lemma *For a productive A matrix, an element b_{ij} of the inverse matrix $(I - A)^{-1}$ equals the sum of the value of all chains ij of A (plus one when $i = j$).*

Proof By Theorem 15

$$b_{ij} = \sum_k a_{ik}a_{kj} + \sum_{kl} a_{ik}a_{kl}a_{lj} + \cdots,$$

whenever $i \neq j$; when $i = j$,

$$b_{ii} = 1 + \sum_k a_{ik}a_{ki} + \cdots. \qquad \text{q.e.d.}$$

18 Theorem *For $I - A$ nonsingular, "there is no nonzero ij chain" is equivalent to "the matrix can be decomposed with i in one sector and j in another."*

Proof Decompose $I - A$ so that i is in the first block and j is in the second. Then the inverse is given by

$$\begin{bmatrix} (I - A_{\alpha\alpha})^{-1} & 0 \\ X & (I - A_{\beta\beta}) - 1 \end{bmatrix} \tag{8}$$

where

$$X = (I - A_{\beta\beta})^{-1} A_{\beta\alpha} (I - A_{\alpha\alpha})^{-1}.$$

The ij element of the inverse is zero, which by Lemma 17 implies that there are no nonzero ij chains in A.

The proof that the condition no ij chains implies indecomposability is omitted. (See Noble [1958].) q.e.d.

Theorem 18 shows that the meaning of decomposability is that for i preceding j and decomposed from j, there must not be any use for j in the production of i, either directly or indirectly through the production of other commodities. One of the more stringent assumptions of the Austrian school was that production could be analyzed in terms of goods that were inputs into the production of more refined goods, but that did not use the refined goods in their production. This is the assumption that the matrix A can be completely triangularized, so that

$$I - A = \begin{bmatrix} 1 - a_{ii} & & 0 \\ & 1 - a_{jj} \ddots & \\ A & & 1 - a_{ss} \end{bmatrix}.$$

As a matter of empirical fact, interindustry matrices are never completely triangularized and show little triangularization in the intermediate stages of production, that is, in the production of consumer goods from producer goods.

19 Corollary *The inverse of an indecomposable block is positive in every element.*

Proof By Theorem 18 for every ij there is a nonzero chain, and hence by Lemma 17, $b_{ii} \neq 0$. Of course, $b_{ij} \geqslant 0$ by Lemma 17. q.e.d.

Define

$$c_k = \sum_{i=1}^{k-1} \sum_{j=1}^{k-1} a_{ki} b_{ij \cdot k-1} a_{jk}, \qquad c_1 = 0,$$

where $(b_{ij \cdot k})$ is the inverse of the matrix with, say, the first $n - k$ elements deleted. Define d_k to be the determinant of that k-order matrix.

20 Theorem *For a nonsingular $I - A$ submatrix of order k,*

$$\frac{1}{1 - a_{kk} - c_k} = b_{kk:k}$$

The theorem suggests one way of expressing a diagonal entry for the inverse of any submatrix.

Proof Let

$$g = a_{kk} + c_k = a_{kk} + \sum_{i=1}^{k-1} \sum_{j=1}^{k-1} a_{ki} b_{ij:k-1} a_{jk}$$

Consider the powers of g: $g + g^2 + \cdots$. Using Lemma 17, every $b_{ij:k-1}$ is a sum of chains, hence every term of a power of g is a sum of chains. Every term of each of these chains starts with a_{kk} or a_{ki} and ends with a_{kk} or a_{jk} ; thus every term is in the chain *kk*. Lemma 17 gives that the chains in $b_{ij:k-1}$ represent all possible chains in the matrix of order $k - 1$. The terms a_{kk} , a_{ki} , a_{jk} represent all possible ways to relate k to these chains, hence all possible chains *kk* are represented and summed. By the lemma, adding one to $g + g^2 + \cdots$ gives the inverse element $b_{kk:k}$. q.e.d.

21 Corollary

$$d_k = (1 - a_{kk} - c_k) d_{k-1} .$$

Proof By Cramer's rule,

$$b_{kk:k} = \frac{d_k}{d_{k-1}} . \qquad \text{q.e.d.}$$

22 Corollary

$$\frac{1}{d_n} = b_{nn:n} b_{n-1,n-1:n-1} \cdots b_{22:2} b_{11:1} .$$

Corollary 22 gives the Hawkins–Simon conditions of a positive determinant of principal minors when all $b_{nn:n}, \ldots, b_{11:1}$ are nonzero.

23 Theorem *For a productive A matrix where every a_{ij} is nonnegative, every i in the $k - 1$ submatrix of $I - A$ has the property that*

$$b_{ii:k} > b_{ii:k-1}$$

or else the submatrix can be decomposed with i in one sector and k in another.

Proof If every a_{ij} is nonnegative, then the value of every chain is positive. Either the *ki* chain and the *ik* chain are nonzero or they are not both nonzero. If they are both nonzero, then there is an *ii* chain that goes through k, and by Theorem 20, the first statement follows,

$$b_{ii:k} > b_{ii:k-1} \,.$$

If they are not both nonzero, then Theorem 18 gives the decomposability.

q.e.d.

A chain can be interpreted as feedback and $b_{ii:i}$ as the feedback introduced by adding industry i to an $i - 1$ order matrix. Likewise, $1/d_k$ is the measure of the total feedback.

24 Theorem *If every a_{ij} is nonnegative, and if the determinant of a productive A matrix equals the product of the diagonal elements, then the matrix can be put in a triangular form. If a productive A matrix can be put in a triangular form, then the determinant of the matrix $I - A$ equals the product of the diagonals.*

Proof Using Corollary 22, we have

$$d_n = (1 - a_{nn} - c_n)(1 - a_{n-1,n-1} - c_{n-1}) \cdots (1 - a_{22} - c_2)(1 - a_{11}).$$

The c_k are nonnegative, since $b_{kk:k}$ are nonnegative. If d_n equals the $\prod_{i=1}^{n}(1 - a_{ii})$, c_k is zero for all k, and thus the chain *kk* includes no industries except k. Therefore, there are for each i either no *ik* chains or no *ki* chains. By Theorem 23, k can be triangulated from each i.

Conversely, if we put the matrix in triangular form, every term of the determinant vanishes except the term that consists of the diagonals.

q.e.d.

According to Theorem 24, we might regard $(d_k - \prod_{i=1}^{n} (1 - a_{ii}))$ as the measure of the feedback since it is zero for the matrix when no true feedback exists, as in the Austrian case of waves of production.

Exercise 9 Let A be productive and triangularized. Compute $(I - A)^{-1}$.

Exercise 10 Let p and q be nonnegative row vectors, and let $A = p'q$ be productive. What is $(I - A)^{-1}$? What is the economic interpretation of $A = p'q$?

PROBLEMS

E. Leontief Production I

Consider the Leontief system described in Section 1. Show that in a productive Leontief system gross production can be solved by itereation from a desired net production

$$\xi^1 = x + Ax, \quad \xi^2 = x + A\xi^1, \quad \xi^3 = x + A\xi^2, \ldots .$$

This interpretation was suggested by Montias [1962].

F. Production Functions I

Suppose f is twice continuously differentiable and satisfies Wicksell's law.

Show that if f is homogeneous of degree $0 \leqslant k \leqslant 1$, then f is concave. (Hint: Use Lema 16 and the fact that a symmetric matrix $(a_{ij} = a_{ji})$ has negative quadratic form xAx if, and only if, A has negative characteristic roots.)

G. Production Functions II

Construct an example of a production function that is concave with decreasing returns, but does not satisfy Wicksell's law. (Hint: Observe that

$$\begin{pmatrix} -1 & \frac{1}{3} \\ \frac{1}{3} & -1 \end{pmatrix}$$

is negative definite.)

6. Producer Efficiency

For purposes of economic planning, we seek to find procedures for attaining the most outputs from inputs. In any given time period, there is available a fixed quantity of factors of production. A net output is *producer efficient* if there is no other feasible net output from the same initial inputs giving at least as much of all commodities and more of one.

This section is concerned with finding necessary and sufficient conditions for efficient outputs. It is assumed that there are n industries producing n goods from m factors. For concreteness, let factor quantities be denoted $y(t)$ in time t, $y(t)$ a vector with m components, and let net outputs be denoted $x(t)$, a vector with n components. In any given time period factors are fixed in quantity. Over time, they accumulate or deteriorate, or both, at rates that cannot be controlled except through production from other factors. Some of the coordinates of $x(t)$ refer to increments in factors. Other commodities may also accumulate and deteriorate. Their stocks can be denoted $z(t)$, a vector with $m - n$ components. Hence, both factors and nonfactors are referred to as *commodity stocks*, of which there are n, $(y(t), z(t))$. There is the law: $(y(t+1), z(t+1)) = (y(t), z(t) + x(t)$. One path of commodity stocks would be *producer superior* to another if in any time period it gave at least as much of all commodity stocks as the other and for some period, and for some commodity stock, it gave more. Formally, $\hat{c} = (\hat{y}(t), \hat{z}(t), t = 0, 1, \ldots)$ is producer superior to $c = (y(t), z(t)\ t = 0, 1, \ldots)$, if $c \geqslant \hat{c}$ but $c \neq \hat{c}$. It would then follow that whenever the two production paths started from the same initial quantities of commodity stocks, there would be a first time period such that one was superior, that is, a first time for which

$$(\hat{y}(t), \hat{z}(t)) \geqslant (y(x), z(x)),$$

but

$$(\hat{y}(t), \hat{z}(t)) \neq (y(t), z(t)).$$

In the preceding time period, both producers had the same factors (and other commodity stocks) and since only production can overcome the natural forces of deterioration, one must have produced more. The other utilizes its inputs inefficienctly at that time. Formally,

$$(\hat{y}(t), \hat{z}(t)) = (y(t-1), z(t-1)) + \hat{x}(t-1),$$
$$(y(t), z(t)) = (y(t-1), z(t-1)) + x(t-1),$$

and therefore,

$$(\hat{y}(t), \hat{z}(t) - (y(t), z(t)) = \hat{x}(t) - x(t) \geqslant 0.$$

25 Remark Producer efficiency over time results if, and only if, there is producer efficiency in each time period separately.

All results following will refer only to the given time period, although they are related to the case of factors variable over time. The time notation is dropped in favor of the variables, factor inputs y and net outputs x.

The output possibility set is ${}_t\mathscr{Y}_{t+1}(y) - \{y\} = \mathscr{X}$. Often there is a price system for goods p, and px is called *gnp*, gross national product.

26 Theorem *Maximizing gnp among the possible outputs gives an efficient output provided $p \gg 0$.*

Proof Clearly, if $\bar{x}$ is producer superior to x, $\bar{x} - x > 0$. Then, $0 < p(\bar{x} - x) = p\bar{x} - px$, or $px = gnp < p\bar{x}$. Hence, $\bar{x}$ cannot be in $\mathscr{X}$. q.e.d.

For $p > 0$, maximizing gnp is not necessarily sufficient for efficiency. In Figure 19, x maximizes gnp for $p > 0$, $p_1 = 0$ but is not efficient. Nevertheless, one gnp maximizer does provide a solution to the efficiency problem.

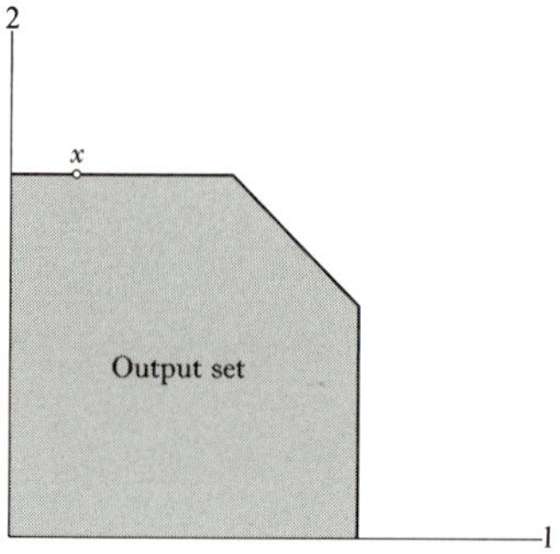

Figure 19

27 Theorem *If the output set is convex, output is efficient only if it maximizes gnp with respect to some nonnegative, nonzero price vector.*

Proof Let $\hat{\mathscr{X}} = \{y \mid y \leqslant x \text{ for some } x \in \mathscr{X}\}$. Then, $\hat{\mathscr{X}}$ is convex whenever $\mathscr{X}$ is.

An efficient point x must be in the boundary of $\mathscr{X}$. Minkowski's theorem, Lemma 13 of Chapter 2, applies: $px \geqslant p\bar{x}$ for all $\bar{x} \in \hat{\mathscr{X}}$.

Also, $p \geqslant 0$, since x can be decreased in any component and still be in $\hat{\mathscr{X}}$. q.e.d.

The maximization of gnp can be decentralized by allowing firms to maximize their contribution to gnp by trading factors of production. This point is elaborated in Chapter 9, where the connection between producers, consumers, and factors is made explicit.

The foregoing results are due to Koopmans [1951]. A particular application is where ${}_t\mathscr{Y}_{t+1}$ is convex. If instead there are increasing returns to scale, then convexity could be expected only in very special cases. The loss of scale from less intensive operation of increasing returns industries would have to be offset by economies achieved by rearranging the proportions in which factors were used. If there are two industries with increasing returns and only one factor of production, the output set has the form in Figure 20. It is not convex and maximization of *gnp* yields two outputs only.

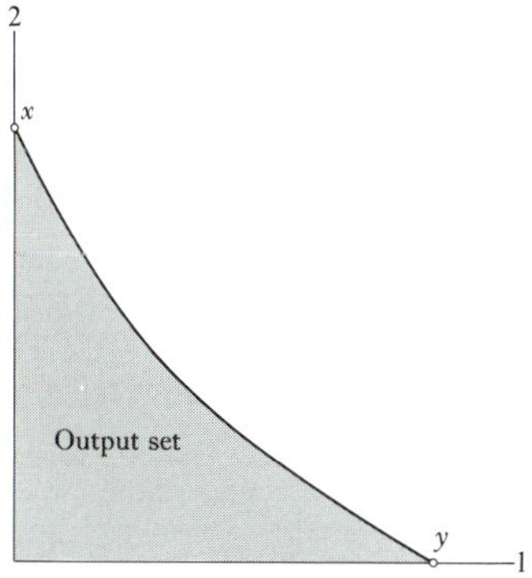

Figure 20

Hereafter, we follow Rader [1970] where output is interindustry.

Production is *quasi concave* provided the production functions are quasi concave. This does not exclude increasing, constant, or decreasing returns to scale since returns to scale are determined by the distance between the isoproduct curves (hypersurfaces). It does require, however, that the marginal rate at which one factor can be substituted for another not increase (in absolute value) as the one factor increases.

Factors are *productive* in an industry whenever their increase increases output in that industry. Production is *factor connected* if for any industries i and k, there are industries q_m, $m = 1,\ldots, p$, and factors $j(q_m)$ such that

$$q_1 = i, \qquad q_m = k,$$

and $j(q_{m-1})$ are utilized in positive quantities and are productive in the q_mth, q_{m-1}th industries. For example, every industry produces a positive (gross) output.

If labor is an indispensable factor in each industry and every industry is in operation, production is factor connected. On the contrary, if by changing the order of industries or factors we construct a matrix

$$(y_j^i) = \begin{pmatrix} A & 0 \\ 0 & B \end{pmatrix},$$

then production is not factor connected. Industries can be divided into two groups that use no factors in common. For example, there might be two industries, steel and coal, the one using only capital and the other only labor. Suppose there is idle capacity in steel because of an insufficient supply of coal, which goes into steel as an intermediate product. Then output of steel could be increased but only if less coal were available for other uses. A situation with idle steel capacity is efficient because more steel would mean less coal, net.

The following lemmata establish a close relationship between gross and net outputs in order to avoid the paradox above. Only then can we show conditions for efficiency under increasing returns to scale.

28 Lemma *If production is interindustry and factor connected, then whenever gross output can be increased in one industry without a decrease in others, gross output can be increased in all industries.*

Proof For some industry i we reduce gross output ξ_i^i and utilize the factors released in another industry j. Then we transfer appropriate resources out of j into another, k, without reducing the output of the one to its former level, etc. By factor connectivity, starting from any industry, we can find a chain leading to an increased output in any other industries. In this way, the output of any and hence all industries can be increased by small quantities. q.e.d.

29 Lemma *If production is interindustry and factor connected, a net output is efficient if, and only if, the corresponding gross output is efficient.*

The proof of the lemma would break down if more net outputs did not require more intermediate products.

Proof Clearly, in a given industry, a net output can be increased only if the gross output increases. Summation over industries proves that a larger gross output must accompany a larger net output.

On the other hand, we consider an increase in the gross output of one commodity. By Lemma 28, the gross output of all commodities can be increased. Producing only small amounts of one good and also enough of other goods to meet the intermediate product requirements of the one good, possibly leaving factors idle, makes attainable a net output with more of the one and no less of others. Repeated increases in net output from added factors allow all factors to be employed as required by (iv) of the definition of interindustry. Here continuity of f^i must be applied to an increasing sequence of factors employed to show that in the limit the net output is still larger than in transition.

Actually, there may be employed a maximal nest of factors that increase in quantity and whose limit will exhaust the factors available. The reader can consult any textbook on general topology, or the companion volume, for details on maximal nests. q.e.d.

30 Corollary *If production is interindustry and factor connected, the possibility of an increase in net output in one commodity with no decrease in others implies the possibility of an increase in the net output of all commodities.*

The proof is immediate from Lemmata 28 and 29.

31 Lemma *If production is interindustry and factor connected, a net output is efficient only if all factors are employed.*

The lemma might fail if production were not factor connected.

Proof As in the proof of sufficiency in Lemma 29, extra factors can be used to increase the gross output of one industry, freeing factors for use elsewhere. There is a collection of such transfers by which we can increase all gross outputs, and possibly by not employing some factors we can actually increase a single output. Indeed we can continue this process, using up all the factors and increasing outputs, just as in the proof of Lemma 29. Therefore, the original production was not efficient. q.e.d.

32 Lemma *If production is interindustry and factor connected, a decrease in one product can lead to an increase in one or more other products.*

According to Lemma 32, more desirable goods can always be substituted for less desirable ones.

Proof Use the factors freed to increase gross output in all industries, as in the proofs of the foregoing lemmata. For any industry other than the one in which the initial decrease in output took place, increase its net output by a small amount, leaving factors idle if necessary. This process can be continued until the factors are fully employed. q.e.d.

33 Theorem *If production is interindustry and factor connected, then a condition sufficient for producer efficientcy of a net output is that there is a strictly positive wage system w such that each industry i maximizes its gross output subject to wy constant. If also production is quasi concave, the condition is necessary.*

The implications of Theorem 34 for planned economies should be mentioned, since in Soviet-type economies factors are often assigned to industries instead of being allowed to circulate freely according to market laws. If the planning board arranges incentives to make firms or industries maximize output by allowing industries to trade factors among themselves, the board could bring about efficiency without going so far as to allowing factor owners to choose their industry of employment. Also, for planned economies, it would be useful to know that, whatever the initial factor holdings, there is an equilibrium system of factor wages. This follows from the Arrow–Debreu [1954] existence theorem, which appears in the companion volume. Existence of a wage system from any assignment of factors to industries is not proved here; hence, it is not listed as a theorem.

34 Lemma *If production is interindustry and factor connected, then in each industry, production is maximized with respect to a strictly positive wage system and a budget constraint on factors if and only if all factors are employed and factor costs are minimized with respect to a strictly positive wage system and a constant output constraint.*

Proof If greater output were possible with the same cost, a reduction in factors could take place for the industry and reduce costs without reducing output. Hence, production is maximized and factors are assigned to industries whenever costs are minimized and all factors are fully employed.

On the other hand, factors are fully employed whenever firms trade factors among themselves and maximize output, since in such a situation unemployed factors would be offered for sale. Also, were it possible to produce at lesser costs the same output, the difference could be used to obtain appropriate factors and increase output. Hence, maximizing production implies minimizing costs. q.e.d.

35 Theorem *If production is interindustry and quasiconcave, the following condition is sufficient for net output to be producer efficient. If, also, production is quasi concave, the condition is necessary.*

There is full employment of factors and the gross outputs minimize costs of each industry subject to a fixed output constraint with respect to a strictly positive wage system.

For example, competitive firms minimize costs at the given output.

Theorem 35 applies to private enterprise economics where there are monopolies. So long as the monopolies take factor wages as given, there is no producer inefficiency (although there may not be "consumer efficiency"). Contrariwise, collective bargaining with differential wages for the same factor leads to producer inefficiency.

In view of Lemma 34, Theorems 33 and 35 are logically equivalent. The proof of Theorem 35 is repeatedly used in classical welfare economics.

Proof **Sufficiency** If net output $\bar{x}$ exceeds x in one or more goods and is not less than x for any good, then the gross outputs for $\bar{x}$ bear the same relationship to those for x (Lemma 28). Hence, some industry is producing at a higher level, while others are producing at no lower level. However, should they utilize only the available factors y or less, then $\bar{y} \leqslant y$ and $w\bar{y} \leqslant wy$. Since $wy^i \neq 0$ for industry i having a greater output in $\bar{x}$ than in x, $w\bar{y}^i > wy^i$ (if not, cut down on factor inputs without reducing output to a level below that in x, which gives a lower cost of production than wy). In the same way, for all other industries, $w\bar{y}^j \geqslant wy^j$. By summation, $w\bar{y} = \sum w\bar{y}^j > \sum wy^i = wy$, a contradiction.

Necessity For good i, the set of factors producing more of i than the output in the efficient x is denoted $\mathscr{F}_i = \{\bar{y} \mid f^i(\bar{y}) > f^i(y^i)\}$. Clearly, $\mathscr{F}_i$ is a convex set, as is $\sum \mathscr{F}_i$. Also, $\sum \mathscr{F}_i$ cannot contain $y = \sum y^i$ since that would mean that y would be used to obtain more of all goods. Hence, apply Minkowski's theorem (Lemma 13 of Chapter 2): There is a vector w such that $w \sum \mathscr{F}_i \geqslant wy$. Since factors are productive, y^i is in the boundary of $\mathscr{F}_i$ and $w\mathscr{F}_i + \sum_{i \neq j} wy^j \geqslant wy$ or $w\mathscr{F}_i > wy^j$ for all j. Since small increases in a productive factor increase output, any input with the same output is in the boundary of $\mathscr{F}_j$, so that again it is no cheaper than y.

Since increases in factors increase production in some industry, w is nonnegative. It can easily be shown that a zero wage for one factor can lead to a lower cost of the same output. Simply substitute the factor with zero wage for one with positive wages. By factor connectivity, there will be some industry in which this is possible. q.e.d.

For quasi-concave production, marginal rates of substitution are defined almost everywhere in the factor space.

36 Theorem *If production is interindustry, factor connected, and quasi concave, and if marginal rates of substitution are defined with respect to all factors used, then a net output with strictly positive gross outputs is producer efficient if and only if*

(i) *all factors are employed,*
(ii) *all marginal rates of substitution of factors used are equal between industries, and*
(iii) *any marginal rate of substitution of used factors to unused factors is at least that in industries where both factors are used.*

Evidently, differential wages between industries in some but not all factors leads to inefficiency.

Proof The necessity is immediate from Theorem 35 and from the observation that cost minimization with respect to w leads to equality of w_j/w_k to the marginal rates of substitution of j for k whenever both factors are used. Otherwise, if j is not used, the marginal rate of substitution must not exceed w_j/w_k.

Sufficiency follows from the fact that a wage vector can be formed from the equality of marginal rates of substitution by letting $w_i = 1$ and then deducing the other wages as equal to the marginal rate of substitution of factors used in conjunction with i, etc. The values thus derived are all nonnegative, and for factors actually used the wages are positive. Hence, the wages define a hyperplane equal to the set of $\bar{y}$ for which $yw = \bar{y}w$, which is tangent to $\mathscr{F}_i$, and the industry minimized costs with respect to w. q.e.d.

Exercise 11 For two goods, two factors, use Cobb–Douglas production functions and characterize the efficient outputs. (If necessary, make simplifying assumptions about the coefficients.) Apply these results to Exercise 8.

Exercise 12 Suppose interindustry production with a limitation on factors. Show that the output set is bounded and closed whenever the production functions are continuous.

PROBLEMS

H. Production Functions III

Consider efficient points in the production set $\mathscr{Y}$, that is, the points $y \in \mathscr{Y}$ for which there does not exist $y' \in \mathscr{Y}$,

$$y' \geqslant y, \qquad y' \neq y.$$

Let $\mathscr{Y}$ be closed, convex, and have at least one interior point.

Show that there is a continuous h taking open sets onto open sets such that y is efficient only if $h(y) = 0$. (Hint: Let y^0 be the interior point of $\mathscr{Y}$ and define

$$g(y) = \sup\{k \mid ky + (1 - k)y^0 \in \mathscr{Y}\}$$

Define $h(y) = g(y) - 1$.)

I. Production Functions IV

Suppose $\mathscr{Y}$ is closed and strictly convex. Show that the efficient points of $\mathscr{Y}$ are solutions of

$$0 = y_n \quad f(y_1, \ldots, y_{n-1})$$

where

$$f(y_1, \ldots, y_{n-1}) = \max\{\bar{y}_n \mid (y_1, \ldots, y_{n-1}, \bar{y}_n) \in \mathscr{Y}\}.$$

UNSOLVED PROBLEMS

J. Generalized Commodity Index Sets

Formulate the theorems of this chapter to cover the case of arbitrary commodity and time index sets. (Information: The index set could be directed by time and form a measure space, as defined in Chapter 2, Section 7. Presumably integration theory would then play a role in deriving ${}_0\mathscr{Y}_\infty$ from laws of change.)

K. Efficiency under Increasing Returns

What are necessary and sufficient conditions for efficiency if raw material inputs are used in variable proportions?

III

Consumption

5

Preferences

The main postulate of the theory of value is that individuals can arrange their preferences in an order, and in fact do so.

Lionel Robbins
ESSAY ON THE NATURE AND SIGNIFICANCE OF ECONOMIC SCIENCE, 1935

1. Relationship and Choice

This chapter presents the general theory relating (2) of Definition I in Chapter 3: the determination of the reflexive relation $\mathscr{R}$ on $\mathscr{U}$. $\mathscr{U}$ is the set of imaginable states of the world; in many applications it is the commodity space (Chapter 3, Section 4). $\mathscr{R}$ is the value system determining consumer choice or economic optimality or the like (Chapter 3, Section 3).

In subsequent sections, various properties on preference and their interrelationships are shown. Some of these are shown to be sufficient to allow optimization of preferences. Other results on utility and on preferences over time, under uncertainty, or subject to competitive conditions are put off to later chapters.

It is assumed in this chapter that choice between pairs is reflected in choice among elements in a set in that the choice for the set is not inferior to another member of the set (in a pair). This presumes that

(i) the consumer can clearly envision the set in question, and
(ii) an optimizing choice exists in the set.

Requirement (i) is characterized as the dichotomy between preference and choice and is taken as axiomatic. Requirement (ii) is the result of more fundamental analysis and generally puts restrictions on both the preference relation and the sets over which choice can be made (Sections 3 and 4).

Historically, the concept of utility preceded and was thought to have determined that of preference. However, much of the theory can be developed without using utility (this chapter, Chapter 8, and Chapter 9).

The analysis of preferences originated with Jeremy Bentham [1789], who had in mind a physiological mechanism. The measurement of impulses in this mechanism led to a utility indicator u, which had the property that x was preferred to y if and only if

$$u(x) > u(y).$$

Similarly, x was indifferent to y if and only if

$$u(x) = u(y).$$

Development from Betham's analysis proceeded in two directions. Jevons [1871] and other neoclassicists (for example, Gossen [1854], Marshall [1890], and Walras [1874]) wrote utility as additive in commodities

$$u(x) = \sum_{i=1}^{n} u_i(x_i) \qquad \text{where} \quad x = (x_1, \dots, x_n).$$

On the other hand, Edgeworth [1881] recognized that more general utility functions could represent consumer preferences.

It was shown by Pareto [1906] and Hicks and Allen [1934] that economic theory is independent of a utility indicator. Economic behavior can be analyzed by using preferences alone.

Finally, various schemes were devised for deriving the utility function from preferences (for example Wold [1943–1944], von Neumann and Morgenstern [1944], Debreu [1954, 1964], Rader [1963a]). Preference, sufficiently regular, leads to utility. Demand theory can be based upon either utility or preferences.

The choice of approach is a matter of convenience. Occam's razor might require the use of preferences as a more basic concept. In many instances the use of preferences directly allows us to include in the theory partial orderings not representable by a utility function, but when we do this, there is still implied, under competitive conditions, a utility function, which the consumer "appears" to be maximizing (Section 3 and Problem L of Chapter 5).

The term rationality will be interpreted to be transitivity of the preference relation $\mathscr{R}$. Therefore, $\mathscr{R}$ is a partial ordering. A number of arguments for rationality are outlined in the problems at the end of Section 2 of Chapter 6. Briefly, it can be said that although transitivity of preferences may not be an inherent psychological characteristic, it is learned early in life. In a world in which people have contradictory interests between pairs of alternatives, the person whose choices reflect intransitivity can be "cheated." Hence, individuals learn to act according to a transitive preference relation. (Childhood trades of toys may be an experience by which the lesson is learned.) There may be a complication, however. Choice from a collection of alternatives may be inconsistent with choice between pairs in the collection. There can be transitivity for paired choice but not for choice from collections. This intransitivity may not subject the irrational person to possible cheating and therefore intransitivity may persist through life (Samuelson [1950]).

For social choice or for a system of ethics, transitivity would seem to be an elementary rationality requirement, and no further justification will be discussed.

Under restrictive assumptions, including convexity of preferences, the rationality axiom may be dropped from the theory of consumer choice under purely competitive conditions. However, whenever the consumer is faced with choices that are noncompetitive, no such relaxation seems possible. So long as the sets over which the consumer is maximizing are convex (as under competition), there is no need for the rationality postulate, but in the case of maximization over nonconvex sets, whether nonconvexity is due to production conditions or to the existence of noncompetition, the rationality assumption appears to be essential to the theory of consumer choice

In economics, it is postulated that there is consistent preference. Consequently, the process by which the consumer learns about his likes and dislikes is assumed to play no role in economic choice. This is the dichotomy of preferences and the process of choice that is commonly made in economics, but that has not gone completely unchallenged. There is an analogy here with the relationship of physics to production theory. Production theory is normally constructed as an input–output system, and hence, assumes dynamic physical equilibrium of all processes, ignoring the significance of velocities on the operation of processes; in the same way preference theory ignores the process of reaching opinion and only considers the equilibrium state after learning has taken place. Therefore, to an extent, economic theory abstracts from problems in psychology and neurobiology as well as those in physics.

2. Properties on Preferences

As will be seen in Chapters 8 and 9, theories of consumer behavior and welfare economics can be constructed upon axioms about preferences. These axioms express the various properties of preferences considered in this section from which the appropriate theorems can be proved.

Let $\mathscr{R}$ read "not inferior to," $\mathscr{I}$ read "indifferent to," and $\mathscr{P}$ read "preferred to":

$$\mathscr{R}(x) = \{y \mid y \mathscr{R} x\}.$$

This is illustrated in Figure 1 for a consumer choosing between two commodity bundles whose quantities are represented by coordinates of a point in the plane. The assumption here is that the consumer always prefers more of a good to less. Representative indifference curves $\mathscr{I}_1$, $\mathscr{I}_2$, $\mathscr{I}_3$, $\mathscr{I}_4$ are drawn so that the higher levels lie to the northeast of the commodity surface. For a point such as x, the indifference curve ($\mathscr{I}_3$) at x is identical with $\mathscr{I}(x)$. All points below this indifference curve (and greater than or equal to zero in their components) are identical with $\mathscr{P}^{-1}(x)$, the "worse than" set. If the indifference curve for x is included, then we have $\mathscr{R}^{-1}(x)$, the "no better than" set (or the lower contour set). All points above the indifference curve make up the set $\mathscr{P}(x)$, the "better than" set; with the indifference curve attached, we have $\mathscr{R}(x)$, the "no worse than" set (or the upper contour set).

For many commodities, people will prefer more to less, within limits, although one person may value some goods more than others do, and rank commodities according to these preferences. An individual's preferences may be represented by indifference curves, as in Figure 2a, where there are two goods. For example, the individual is indifferent between (x_a, y_a) and (x_b, y_b). These curves and their maps have certain properties.

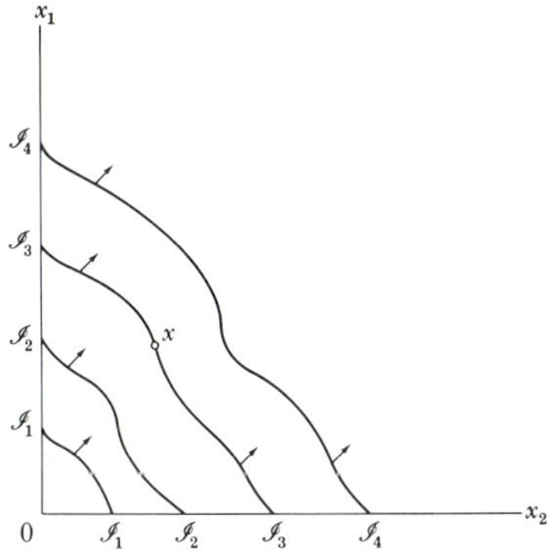

Figure 1

1. They are often locally *unsaturated*; that is, a higher degree of satisfaction can be attained by a small change in consumption of goods in some direction.

The locally unsaturated preference maps include, for example, the case in which there is a commodity always preferred in larger quantities, a so-called *Renior good*, and in which the larger quantities are always physically possible. It follows that for any open set in $\mathscr{C}$ containing c, the always preferred commodity can be increased by a certain (possibly very small) quantity and this preference point will still be within the open set, representing a commodity bundle c' preferred to c. Equivalently, if $\mathscr{R}$ is represented by a utility function that is monotically increasing in one or more components, then $\mathscr{R}$ is locally unsaturated.

2. They are *continuous*. That is, the indifference curves are continuous and closed and any two indifference curves are separated by an indifference curve of intermediate level of preference. Continuity can be stated in a more general manner to include cases where there are dense indifference classes, as in Figure 2a.

Two sets $\mathscr{A}$ and $\mathscr{B}$ are *separated* if $\mathscr{A}$ contains no limit points of $\mathscr{B}$, and if $\mathscr{B}$ contains no limit points of $\mathscr{A}$. Continuity requires that the indifference class $\mathscr{I}(x)$ be closed and that the indifference class separate the space into two parts, $\mathscr{P}(x)$ and $\mathscr{P}^{-1}(x)$. These other parts can have no points in common, and therefore, it can be shown that

$$\mathscr{R}(x) = \mathscr{P}(x) \cup \mathscr{I}(x)$$

is closed, as is

$$\mathscr{R}^{-1}(x) = \mathscr{P}^{-1}(x) \cup \mathscr{I}(x).$$

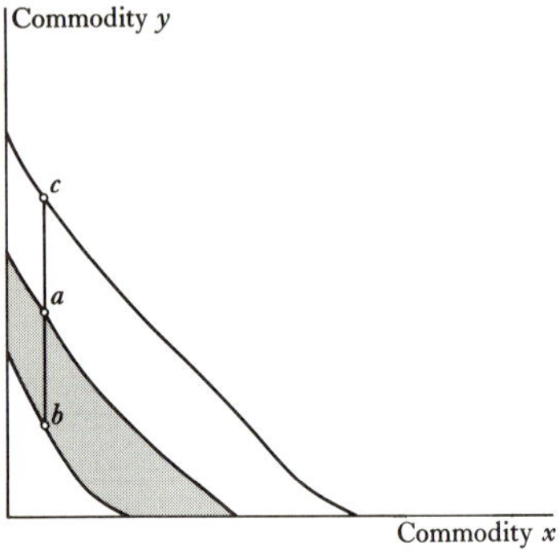

Figure 2a

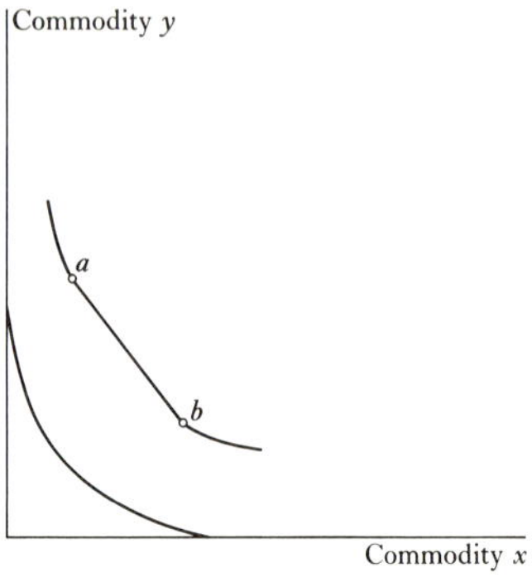

Figure 2b

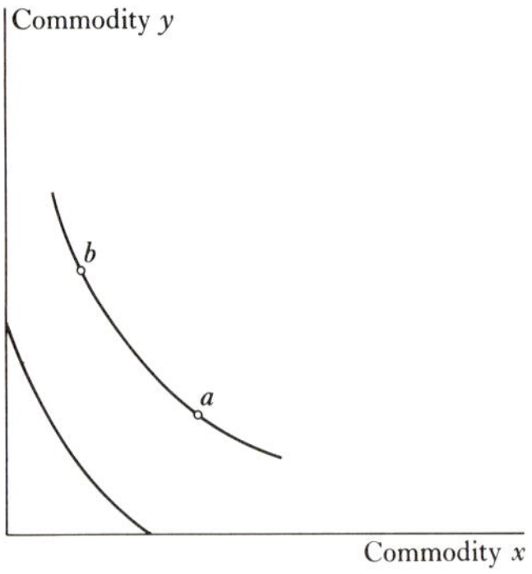

Figure 2c

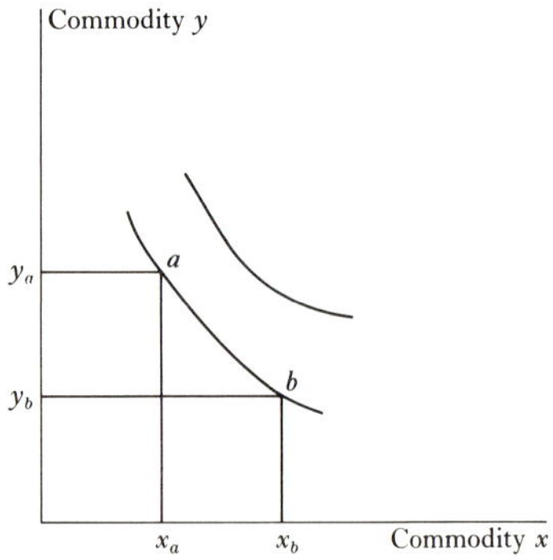

Figure 2d

On the other hand, if $\mathscr{R}(x)$ and $\mathscr{R}^{-1}(x)$ are closed, then $\mathscr{I}(x)$ is closed and $\mathscr{P}(x)$ and $\mathscr{P}^{-1}(x)$ are separated.

1 Remark $\mathscr{I}(x)$ is closed and $\mathscr{P}(x)$ and $\mathscr{P}^{-1}(x)$ are separated if and only if $\mathscr{R}(x)$ is closed and $\mathscr{R}^{-1}(x)$ is closed.

Proof If to the contrary $x_n \to x$, x_n in $\mathscr{R}(x)$, x not in $\mathscr{R}(x)$, then necessarily x is in $\mathscr{P}^{-1}(x)$. Let $\bar{\mathscr{A}}$ be the set $\mathscr{A}$ and all limit points of $\mathscr{A}$, called the *closure* of $\mathscr{A}$. Now if $\mathscr{P}(x)$ and $\mathscr{P}^{-1}(x)$ are to be separated, it must be true that

$$\overline{\mathscr{P}(x)} \cap \mathscr{P}^{-1}(x) = \varnothing,$$

and therefore, eventually, x^n is not in $\mathscr{P}(x)$, that is, x^n must be in $\mathscr{I}(x)$ for large n. But $\mathscr{I}(x)$ is closed, so that x is in $\mathscr{I}(x)$ and not in $\mathscr{P}^{-1}(x)$. Therefore, $x \in \mathscr{R}(x)$. Similarly, $\mathscr{R}^{-1}(x)$ contains its limit points. Since

$$\overline{\mathscr{P}(x)} \subset \mathscr{R}(x) \qquad \text{(closure of } \mathscr{R}(x)\text{)},$$

$$\mathscr{P}(x) \cap \mathscr{P}^{-1}(x) \subset \mathscr{R}(x) \cap \mathscr{P}^{-1}(x) = \varnothing.$$

Similarly,

$$\overline{\mathscr{P}^{-1}(x)} \cap \mathscr{P}(x) \subset \mathscr{R}^{-1}(x) \cap \mathscr{P}(x) = \varnothing. \qquad \text{q.e.d.}$$

Remark 1 leads to an alternative characterization of continuity and also suggests a weaker regularity condition on preferences. Preferences are *regular* if $\mathscr{R}(x)$ is closed for all x. In words, consumptions at leastas good as x tend to consumptions at least as good as x.

3. They show *directional density.* The indifference curves for goods that are not characterized by perfect nonsubstitutability may be *smooth.* This means that they are differentiable curves, or what is equivalent, they exhibit directional density—it is possible to increase preferences by a change in consumption in any direction (possibly negative) except along the tangent line itself. This is illustrated in Figure 3. The absolute value of the slope of the indifference curve is the *marginal rate of substitution* ($\mathscr{mrs}$) between goods, illustrated in Figure 4. This is the rate of substitution necessary to preserve preferences, that is, stay on the same indifference curve.

$$\mathscr{mrs} = \left| \lim_{\Delta x \to 0} \frac{\Delta y}{\Delta x} \right| = \left| \frac{dy}{dx} \right|.$$

2 Remark If preferences are locally unsaturated, convex, and directional dense at x, then $\mathscr{P}(x)$ contains all points on all lines through x, except for those in a hyperplane of the form $\{y \mid py = xp\}$. The proof is left to the reader (Exercise 1).

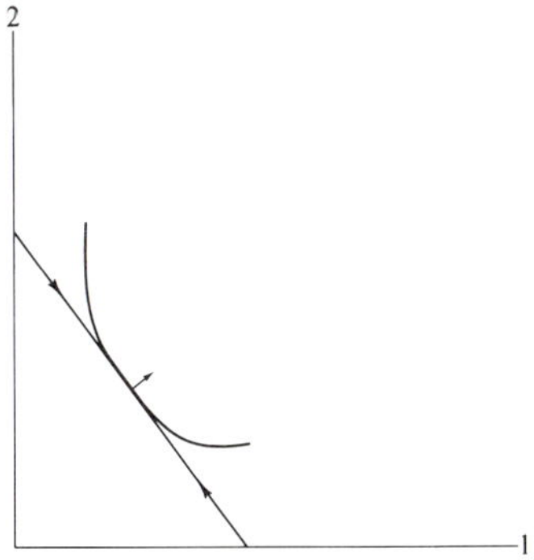

Figure 3

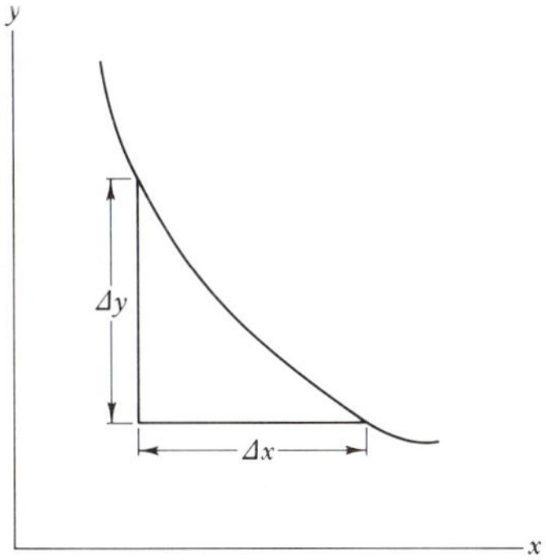

Figure 4

Any movement along an indifference curve reflects the substitution of one good for another. Goods can be *perfectly substitutable*, as in Figure 5a; *imperfectly substitutable*, as in Figure 5b, where no amount of the horizontal good can compensate for holding none of the vertical good; *nonsubstitutable* and nondirectional dense on a ray through the origin, as in Figure 5c; *partially nonsubstitutable*, as in Figure 5d; or *negatively substitutable*, as in Figure 5e.

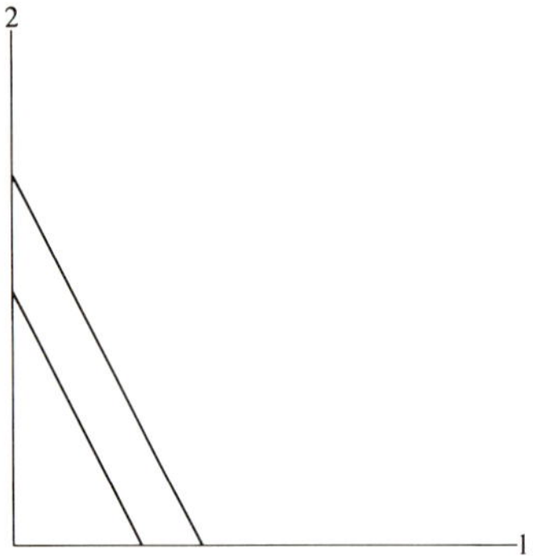

Figure 5a

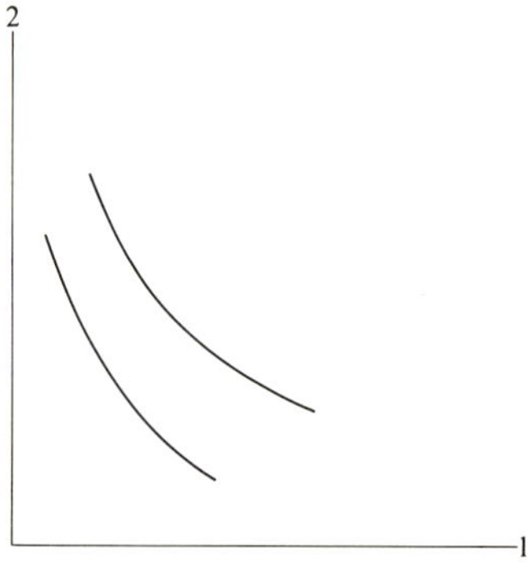

Figure 5b

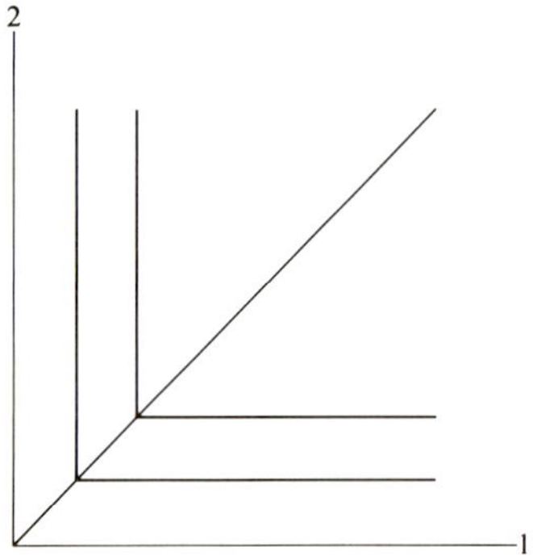

Figure 5c

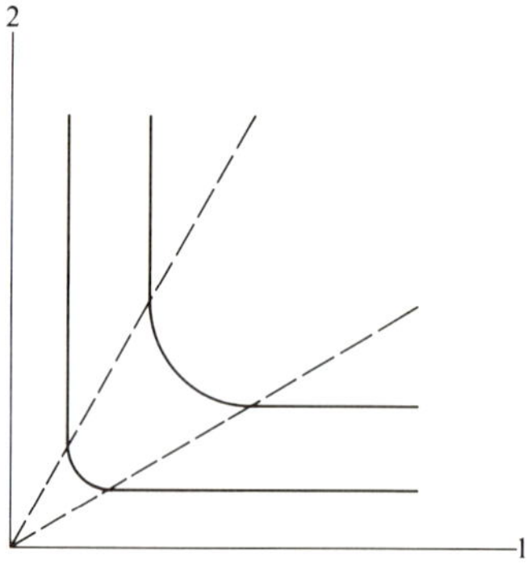

Figure 5d

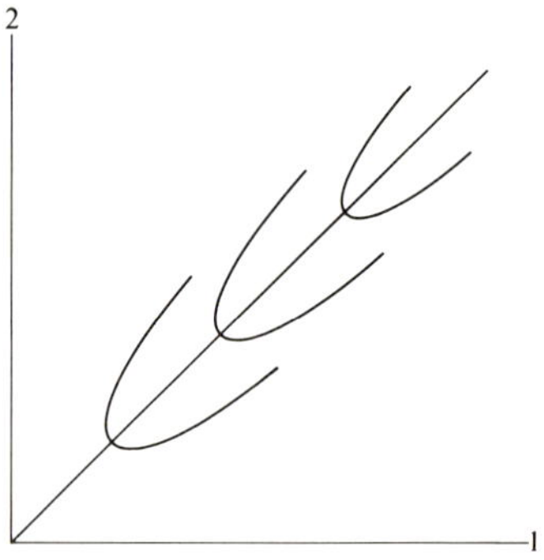

Figure 5e

4. They show *monotonicity*. As the amount of any good increases, preferences increase.

5. Preferences are convex if $x \mathscr{P} y$ implies $tx + (1 - t)y \mathscr{P} y$ for $0 < t < 1$. They are *strictly convex* if $x \mathscr{I} y$ implies $tx + (1 - t)y \mathscr{P} y$ for $0 < t < 1$.

These properties of preferences are not necessarily reasonable, nor are they equally restrictive. For example, if there is no preference for variety, the indifference curves may not be convex to the origin. An individual's preference map may assume the shape in Figure 6, if the two goods are, say, represented by the amount of time spent living in New York and Los Angeles with no allowance for transportation costs. If we were on the indifference curve through *a*, to spend more time living in Los Angeles and less in New York would require the establishment of more of the "comforts of home" in Los Angeles. (When the indifference curves are nonconvex, as here, there may be more than one point of tangency between a given indifference curve and the budget constraint line (*c* and *d* in Figure 6). When the indifference curve is concave, any point of tangency between the budget constraint line and the indifference curve is a point of minimum satisfaction (Figure 7). Movement along this tangent in either direction away from this point leads to a point where the consumer can derive greater utility with the same income.)

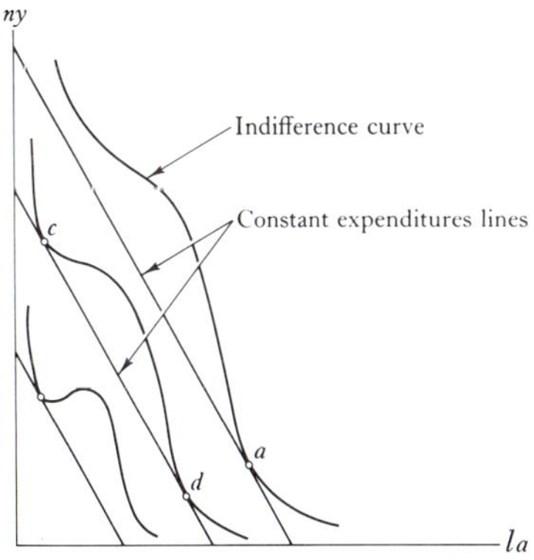

Figure 6

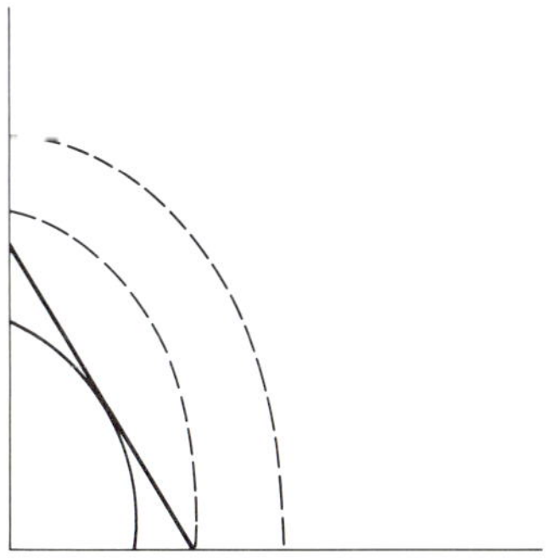
Figure 7

Note that preferences are defined on a possibility set $\mathscr{C}$.

3 Theorem (i) *If preferences are convex and c is not the preference-optimizing point in* $\mathscr{C}$, *then preferences are locally unsaturated at c.*

(ii) *If preferences are convex, everywhere locally unsaturated, and regular, then they are weakly convex. Consequently, if preferences are* *convex and regular and if there is no preference optimizing c in $\mathscr{C}$, then preferences are weakly convex.*

(iii) *If preferences are complete, convex, and strictly convex, they are weakly convex. If preferences are complete, strictly convex, and continuous, then they are convex. Consequently, if preferences are complete, strictly convex and continuous, then they are weakly convex.*

Most of the theorem was stated by Debreu [1959].

Proof (i) Consider any c in $\mathscr{C}$. There exists a still better c' in $\mathscr{C}$ and by convexity, $tc + (1 - t)\, c' \mathscr{P} c$ for $0 < t < 1$. Therefore, for any c, by choosing t near 1, we can obtain a better point near c.

(ii) Consider $c \mathscr{R} c'$. Near c, there is a $c^n \mathscr{P} c$. Let $c^n \to c$, $n \to \infty$. Then, by convexity and reflexitivity,

$$tc^n + (1 - t)c' \mathscr{R} c', \qquad 0 \leqslant t \leqslant 1.$$

Therefore, by the closedness of $\mathscr{R}(c)$,

$$tc + (1 - t)c' = \lim tc^n + (1 - t)c' \mathscr{R} c'.$$

(iii) Clearly, if $c \mathscr{R} c'$, then either $c \mathscr{I} c'$ or $c \mathscr{P} c'$, and therefore,

$$tc + (1 - t)c' \mathscr{P} c', \qquad 0 < t < 1.$$

Weak confexity follows immediately.

Let $c \mathscr{P} c'$. $\mathscr{I}(c')$ is closed (by continuity) and

$$\mathscr{R}^{-1}(c') \cap \langle c, c' \rangle$$

is closed and has a first element c''. Since

$$\mathscr{P}^{-1}(c') \subset \mathscr{R}^{-1}(c')$$

is open and c'' is in the boundary of

$$\mathscr{R}^{-1}(c') \cap \langle c, c' \rangle,$$

c'' is in the boundary of $\mathscr{R}^{-1}(c')$ and $c'' \notin \mathscr{P}^{-1}(c')$. Therefore,

$$c'' \notin \mathscr{R}^{-1}(c') \sim \mathscr{P}^{-1}(c') = \mathscr{I}(c'),$$

that is, $c'' \mathscr{I} c'$.Therefore,

$$\langle c'', c' \rangle \subset \mathscr{P}(c')$$

by strict convexity. By construction,

$$\langle c, c'' \rangle \subset \mathscr{P}(c').$$

Since $\mathscr{P}(c')$ is convex, there is the contradiction

$$c'' \in \mathscr{P}(c'),$$

unless

$$\langle c'', c' \rangle = \varnothing,$$

that is,

$$c'' = c'.$$

Therefore,

$$\langle c, c' \rangle \subset \mathscr{P}(c'), \qquad \text{q.e.d.}$$

Exercise 1 Prove Remark 2. (Hint: Use Minkowski's theorem, Lemma 13 of Chapter 2.)

3. Optimization: Some Formalisms and Extensions

Many economists are uneasy about the properties on preferences used in economic analysis. Hence, they (and others) have made inquiries into the foundations of preferences in order to find minimal conditions for optimization to be logically possible. For example, regularity is the weakest condition discussed in Section 2. The lexicographic ordering discussed in Section 3, Chapter 3, is not regular, even when the defining orderings $\mathscr{R}_i$ are regular. To see this, consider the lexicographic ordering of the numbers in the plane. The set of points not inferior to x are illustrated in Figure 8, and they do not form a closed set.

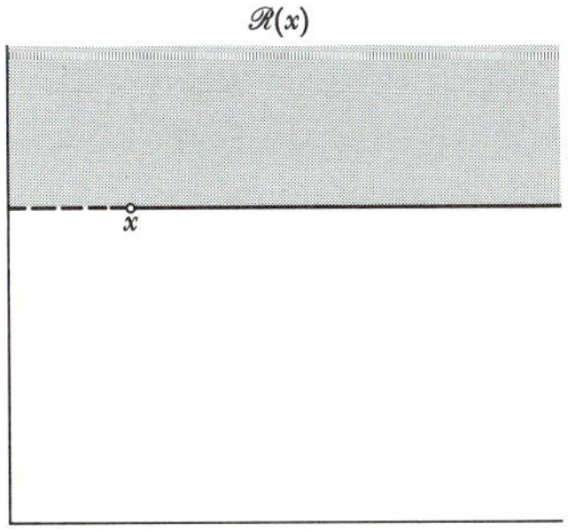

Figure 8

A more upsetting problem has occurred to the members of the Revealed Preference School. Suppose choice between pairs turns out to be irrational; is it possible for choice from competitive budgets to take place in a transitive manner? If so, is it possible that intransitivity exists in preferences even if it is not revealed in market choice?

Concern with kinds of sets over which optimization takes place leads to an existence theory for optimization on sets. Needless to say, this existence theory is of interest in its own right. Here it is presented to answer the particular question, how perverse can preferences be and and still be compatible with choice?

First, consider incomplete preferences.

4 Theorem *If $\mathcal{R}$ is transitive, irreflexive, and regular, then there is an optimum for $\mathcal{R}$ on compact sets. If instead of being regular, $\mathcal{R}$ has $\mathcal{P}^{-1}(x)$ open, then there is an optimum for $\mathcal{R}$ on compact sets.*

Proof In the collection of sets $\mathcal{R}(x)$, x in $\mathcal{U}$, $x \mathcal{R} \bar{x}$, there is a maximal collection by virtue of the Maximal Principle (equivalent to the Axiom of Choice), that is, there is a nest of $\mathcal{R}(y)$ such that

(i) either $\mathcal{R}(y) \subset \mathcal{R}(y')$ or else $\mathcal{R}(y') \subset \mathcal{R}(y)$, and

(ii) there does not exist a z for which $\mathcal{R}(y) \subsetneqq \mathcal{R}(z)$, $\mathcal{R}(y)$ in the maximal nest.

The maximal nest of (closed) sets is such that every finite intersection is nonempty, since for any finite collection there is one set that contains all the others. Applying the finite intersection property for compact sets (Lemma 20 of Chapter 2), we see that the maximal nest of closed sets has a nonempty intersection. This intersection gives the optimum x_0 under $\mathcal{R}$, for if there is a z for which $z \mathcal{P} x_0$, then $\mathcal{R}(x_0) \not\subseteq \mathcal{R}(z)$, contrary to (ii) in the definition of a maximal nest. Also, by construction, $x_0 \mathcal{R} \bar{x}$.

For the case of $\mathcal{P}^{-1}(x)$ open, we can simply consider $\sim\mathcal{P}^{-1}(x)$ closed in place of $\mathcal{R}(x)$. Evidently, if $z \mathcal{P} x_0$, then $\mathcal{P}^{-1}(z) \supsetneqq \mathcal{P}^{-1}(x)$ and $\sim\mathcal{P}^{-1}(z) \subsetneqq \sim\mathcal{P}^{-1}(x)$. q.e.d.

When $\mathcal{R}$ is a complete ordering, Theorem 4 gives the existence of a maximizing point for regular, real-valued utility on compact sets (Chapter 6, Section 1). An easy consequence of Theorem 4 is as follows.

5 Theorem *If $\mathcal{R}_i$ is regular (or $\mathcal{P}^{-1}(x)$ is open), transitive, and reflexive, $i = 1, \ldots, n$, then the lexicographic refinement gives an optimum on compact sets.*

If choice is restricted by compact convex sets, then the preference relation can be intransitive and the choice relation can still be well defined.

6 Theorem (Sonnenschein) *If $\mathcal{P}(x)$ is convex, $\mathcal{R}$ complete, reflexive, and continuous, then there is an optimum on compact, convex sets.*

Proof Problem A.

To my knowledge, this is the only known result for optimization of intransitive relations.

PROBLEMS

A. Nontransitive Relations I

Let

$$\mathscr{G}(\{a_i\} \mid i \in \mathscr{I}) = \left\{ \sum_{i \in \mathscr{I}} t_i a_i \,\middle|\, \sum t_i = 1, \quad t_i \geqslant 0 \right\}^{\sim}.$$

Prove Theorem 7 with the use of the lemma.

Lemma (Knaster, Kuratowski, and Mazukiewicz [1931]) *Let* $\mathscr{A} = \{a_0, a_1, \ldots, a_n\}$ *be a collection of* $n+1$ *points in* $\mathscr{E}^n$, *and* $\{\mathscr{S}_0, \mathscr{S}_1, \ldots, \mathscr{S}_n\}$ *be a collection of closed sets. Suppose that for any set of integers* $\mathscr{I}$ *that is a subset of* $\{0, 1, \ldots, m\}$,

$$\mathscr{G}(\{a_i\} \mid i \in \mathscr{I}) \subset \bigcup_{i \in \mathscr{I}} \mathscr{S}_i .$$

Then

$$\bigcap_{i=1}^{n} \mathscr{S}_i$$

is not empty. (Hint: Let $\mathscr{H}(p) = \{x \mid px = 0\}$. If $\mathscr{H}(p) \cap \mathscr{C}$ is compact, we can apply the finite intersection property to

$$\bigcap_{x \in \mathscr{H}(p) \cap \mathscr{C}} \mathscr{R}(x).$$

For any finite set of x_i, $i = 1, \ldots, m$, use the convexity of $\mathscr{R}(x_i)$, $\mathscr{H}(p) \cap \mathscr{C}$ and the completeness of $\mathscr{R}$ to show that

$$\mathscr{G}(\{x_i\} \mid i \in \mathscr{I}) \subset \bigcup_{i \in \mathscr{I}} \mathscr{R}(x_i).$$

Then apply the lemma.)

This problem was first solved by Sonnenschein [1967a].

B. Lexicographic Orderings

Show that the lexicographic ordering has upper contour sets that are neither closed nor open.

UNSOLVED PROBLEM

C. Nontransitive Relations II

What kinds of behavior can be subsumed under nontransitive relations satisfying the hypotheses of Theorem 6?

4. Construction of Partial Orderings from Orderings

It is common to define partial orderings from complete orderings, as in

$$\mathscr{R} = \bigcap_{\alpha \in \mathscr{A}} \mathscr{R}_\alpha .$$

For example, the Pareto ordering (Section 3 of Chapter 3) is $\bigcap \mathscr{R}_i$ for consumers $i = 1, 2, \ldots$. As another example, the relation "x more efficient than y" is equal to $\bigcap_i (\geqslant_i)$ where

$$x(\geqslant_i)y \quad \text{if, and only if,} \quad x_i \geqslant y_i .$$

The companion volume contains a consideration of final state efficiency, which is defined for m goods by

$$\bigcup_{n=1}^{\infty} \bigcap_{i=nm}^{n(m+1)} (\geqslant_i).$$

7 Remark If $\mathscr{R} = \bigcap_{\alpha \in \mathscr{A}} \mathscr{R}_\alpha$, then $\mathscr{R}^{-1} = \bigcap_{\alpha \in \mathscr{A}} \mathscr{R}_\alpha^{-1}$. If $\mathscr{R} = \bigcup_{\alpha \in \mathscr{A}} \mathscr{R}_\alpha$, then $\mathscr{R}^{-1} = \bigcap_{\alpha \in \mathscr{A}} \mathscr{R}_\alpha^{-1}$.

8 Remark If $\mathscr{R}_\alpha$ are transitive, then so is $\bigcap \mathscr{R}_\alpha$.

Unfortunately, unions of transitive relations are not always transitive.

9 Theorem *The intersection or finite union of regular relations is regular. The finite union and finite intersection of partial orderings with $\mathscr{P}^{-1}(x)$ open have $\mathscr{P}^{-1}(x)$ open.*

The intersection or finite union of continuous relations is continuous.

The intersection of (weakly, strictly) convex preferences is (weakly, strictly) convex.

10 Remark For transitive unions of regular orderings, $\mathscr{R}_\alpha$, the upper contour set $\bigcup \mathscr{R}_\alpha$ may not be closed. However, $\bigcup \mathscr{P}_\alpha^{-1}(x)$ will be open, and a weak optimum, y, exists on a compact set $\mathscr{Y}$ such that for every $x \in \mathscr{Y}$ for at least one α, $y \mathscr{R}_\alpha x$.

Remark 10 applies to preference for intertemporal efficiency and can be used to give an alternative proof for results in the companion volume. It remains to show transitivity, which follows from the fact that the factors are productive.

Exercise 2 Show that a regular function takes a maximum on compact sets, appealing only to sequences (see Section 1 of Chapter 6 for the definition of regularity).

6

Utility

By utility is meant that property in any object, whereby it tends to produce benefit, advantage, pleasure, good, or happiness (all this, in the present case, comes to the same thing), or (what comes again to the same thing) to prevent the happening of mischief, pain, evil, or unhappiness to the party whose interest is considered.

Jeremy Bentham
in PRINCIPLES OF MORALS AND LEGISLATION, 1789
as quoted by Jevons in THEORY OF POLITICAL ECONOMY

1. Regular Utility Functions

Utility is a powerful tool of economic analysis. Although some of economic theory can be stated without reference to utility, in other places, utility is still required. Even where the utility function can be discarded, it is not always easy to do so. The study of utility, while not the *sine qua non* it was thought to be, plays an important role in foundations of preferences (Problems A–E and Section 8), the theory of demand (Chapter 8), game theory (as applied in Chapter 10), and the analysis of intertemporal consumer choice (Chapters 1 and 6 of the companion volume).

The logical sequence of this chapter is from preferences to utility. This procedure is dictated by the fact that choice is the observable phenomenon, not utility. The first results along these lines were obtained by Wold [1934–1944] and von Neumann and Morgenstern [1944].

The present chapter moves from the weakest to the strongest forms of utility and through its varieties—ordinal, "cardinal," differential, concave, and additive. The presentation of utility linear in probabilities is connected with the theory of uncertainty and is treated in Chapter 7.

A reflexive ordering $\mathscr{R}$ is *representable* by a utility function if there exists a real-valued utility function u such that "$u(x) \geqslant u(y)$ if and only if $x \mathscr{R} y$ for all x, y in $\mathscr{C}$." The purpose of this section is to derive very general conditions under which such an ordering is representable by a utility function and to demonstrate a utility function and its mathematical properties.

To derive a utility function, we need only assume that $\mathscr{R}$ is a regular ordering, that is, the upper contour sets $\mathscr{R}(x)$ are closed. Before derivation, we show examples of regularity.

Example 1 The rather smooth indifference curves in Figure 1 of Chapter 5 are drawn such that the upper contour sets are closed in the usual topology for the plane.

Example 2 In Figure 1, goods 1 and 2 are useful to the individual i only in units. Any fractions of goods are merely discarded or laid aside: i is not forbidden from holding $1\frac{1}{2}$ automobiles, but the extra half gives him no service; he would not care if he had only one automobile instead. The individual i always prefers more (in units) of any commodity to less, and in the case of equal holdings, an extra unit of the second commodity to an extra unit of the first. The preference ordering is constructed as though only units of commodities were being compared, but it is not necessary to compare only units. In Figure 1, there is a natural extension to a set without indivisibilities of the preferences on a set with indivisibilities, in which the basic property of indivisibility of consumption is preserved. We can easily verify that the upper contour set for (x, y) is closed in the usual topology for the plane. For example, if (x, y) is taken as in Figure 1, then all points in the space that have nonnegative coordinates form the "as good as" set for (x, y), which is clearly a closed set. For $(\bar{x}, \bar{y})$ in Figure 1, the upper contour set for $(\bar{x}, \bar{y})$ is the set of points in the nonnegative quadrant (that is, with nonnegative coordinates) that are not also in the half open squares $\mathscr{I}_0, \mathscr{I}_1, \mathscr{I}_2, \mathscr{I}_3, \mathscr{I}_4$. This set is also closed.

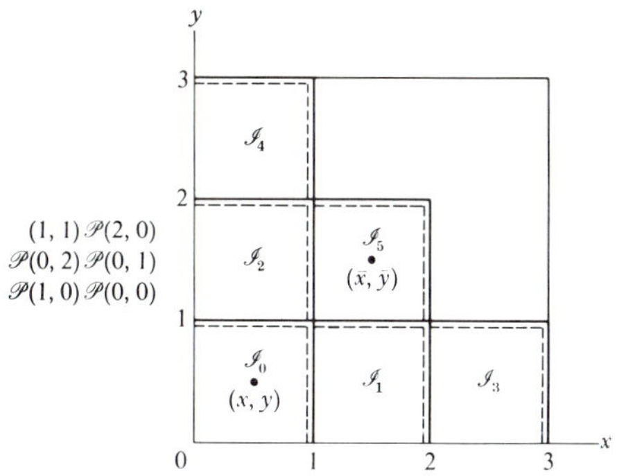

Figure 1

Example 3 Example 2 is a special case of a more general phenomenon called *aspiration*. An *aspiration set* is a finite set $\mathscr{A}$ of consumer "accomplishment," which is the sole concern of the consumer. If he obtains enough consumption to reach t he level of preference, any extra that is insufficient to obtain a better point in $\mathscr{A}$ is of no use to him. Formally, aspiration occurs whenever:

> There exists a finite set of points $\mathscr{A}$, called the aspiration set, such that $x \mathscr{R} y$ if and only if there is an x' in $\mathscr{A}$ such that $x \geqslant x'$ (that is, x accomplishes x') and $x' \mathscr{R} y'$ for all y' in $\mathscr{A}$ such that $y \geqslant y'$ (x' is superior to all points y' accomplished by y).

In general, $\geqslant$ in this definition may be any partial ordering, for example, the "greater than or equal to in each component" ordering of Euclidean space. Consider the order topology where $\geqslant(x)$ is closed for each x in $\mathscr{U}$. Then $\mathscr{R}(x)$ is equal to the union of all those $\geqslant(x')$ for which $x \geqslant x'$, which is a finite set. Hence, $\mathscr{R}(x)$ is the union of a finite set of closed sets and is closed.

The points of $\mathscr{A}$ might be coordinates of the plane representing the quality of automobile on one axis and quality of house on the other. Obtaining a certain quality automobile–house combination would allow the person to be invited to the parties of certain neighbors. The possibilities might be:

Invitations to parties of
- Physicians: Cadillac and large, new mansion
- Lawyers: Rolls Royce and small mansion
- Professors: Volkswagen and large, old mansion
- Skilled workers: Chevrolet and cottage
- Small businessmen: Cadillac and small mansion

Clergyman: Chevrolet and small mansion
Bum: Nothing

For example, with a Rolls and a large, new mansion, the consumer would be invited to all parties. With a Rolls and a large, old mansion, only the physicians would snub the consumer. With only a cottage, he would be invited only to parties of the bum.

Example 4 In Figures 2a, 2b, and 2c, there are indifference curves that define a preference ordering with closed upper contour sets. Some are reasonable, but many pathological cases are allowed, such as Figure 2c. Hence, this closedness property seems to be fairly general.

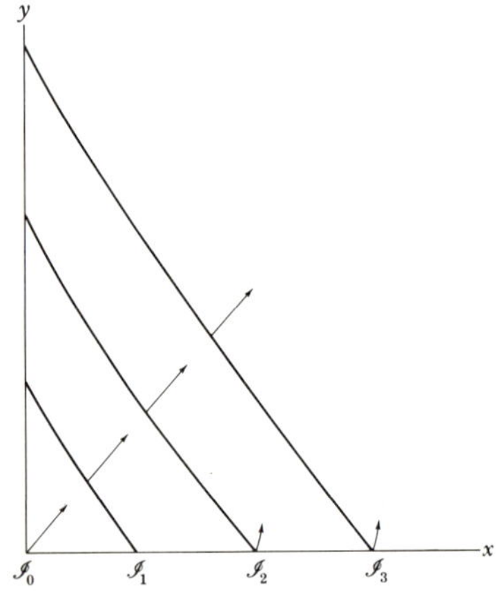

Figure 2a

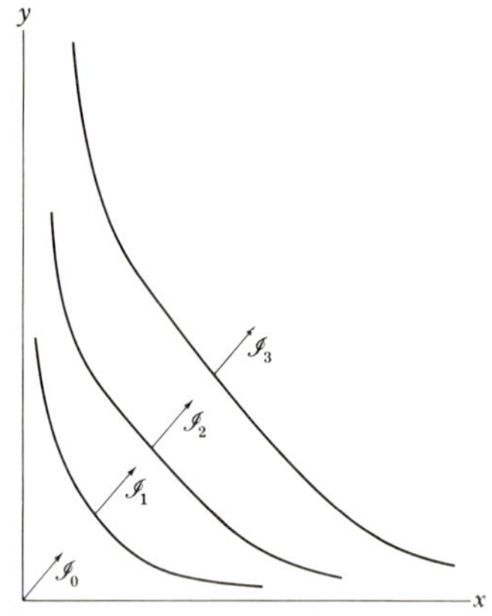

Figure 2b

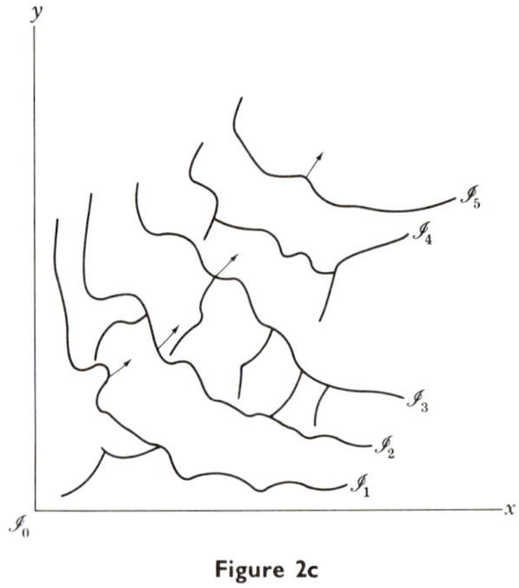

Figure 2c

Example 5 Combinations of the examples above may be made for three or more sets of commodities. For example, aspiration may characterize the relationship between two of the commodities, whereas their relation to a third may be characterized by the smooth indifference curves in Example 1.

In metric spaces, the closedness assumption has a very intuitive form. As we "march" down upon a point x from points x^n (that is, as the points x^n become arbitrarily close to the point x in the metric) such that x^n are as good as some reference point y, then x itself is as good as the reference point y. The idea is that there is no sudden discontinuity of preferences when an approach is made from a higher preference level. For example, we might have a starvation level below which preference levels are dropped. To be specific, consider the bundles (Cadillacs, bread). Then, if 1 is the biological minimum of bread, we have the condition $(0, 1)\ \mathscr{P}\ (1, t)$ for any $1 > t > 0$, while in limit as t tends to 1, the limit point $(1, 1)$ is clearly preferred to $(0, 1)$. This is allowable under the closedness assumption, for although there is a discontinuity in preferences, it occurs from an approach from an inferior level of preference. On the other hand, there cannot be the situation in which meeting the biological minimum causes starvation unless some arbitrarily small $\varepsilon > 0$ is added to one's bread rations.

A function u is *regular* if

$$\mathscr{S}^c = \{x \mid u(x) \geqslant c, \quad x \in \mathscr{C}\}$$

is closed. (Mathematicians commonly call such a function *upper semicontinuous*, but the word upper semicontinuity has a different meaning when applied to multivalued functions (correspondences) and hence it seems advisable to avoid the use of the same adjective for two different properties.)

1 Theorem *Suppose that $\mathscr{C}$ is a topological space with a countable base and that $\mathscr{R}$ is a reflexive, complete ordering on $\mathscr{C}$ such that $\mathscr{R}(x)$ is closed for all x in $\mathscr{C}$. Then there exists a real-valued regular utility function u such that $u(x) \geqslant u(x')$ if and only if $x\ \mathscr{R}\ x'$*

The theorem is due to Rader [1963a] and Debreu [1964]. Related theorems were proved by Birkoff [1948] and Milgram [1939]. Before proving the theorem, it is well to note that if the closedness of $\mathscr{R}(x)$ is replaced by the closedness of $\mathscr{R}^{-1}(x)$, we may derive u for $\mathscr{R}^{-1}$ and hence $-u$ for $\mathscr{R}$. Of course, $-u$ is not regular, but rather "negatively" regular or *lower semicontinuous*. If u is regular, this ensures that $\mathscr{R}$ will take an optimum on the kinds of sets normally met in economic theory; namely, on compact sets (closed, bounded sets in finite-dimensional Euclidean space), as discussed in Section 4 of Chapter 5. But, if $-u$ is regular, there is only the assurance that u takes a minimum on these sets and not necessarily a maximum.

As has been seen, lexicographic preferences may take optima on compact sets. However, they are not representable by a utility function (Problem A).

Proof (of Theorem 1) (i) Denote each member of the countable base by $\mathcal{O}_n$, $n = 1, 2, \ldots$. Consider $\mathcal{P}^{-1}(x)$; it is open for each x since it is the complement of the closed set $\mathcal{R}(x)$. Hence, $\mathcal{P}^{-1}(x)$ is exactly equal to the union of all members that it contains of the countable base. Let $\mathcal{N}(x)$ be the set of integers n such that

$$\mathcal{O}_n \subset \mathcal{P}^{-1}(x).$$

Set

$$u'(x) = \sum_{n \in \mathcal{N}(x)} (\tfrac{1}{2})^n.$$

To demonstrate that u' is a utility function representing $\mathcal{R}$, suppose $x \mathcal{R} x'$. By transitivity of $\mathcal{R}$,

$$\mathcal{P}^{-1}(x') \subset \mathcal{P}^{-1}(x),$$

so that

$$u'(x) \geqslant u'(x'),$$

by

$$\mathcal{N}(x') \subset \mathcal{N}(x).$$

On the other hand, suppose

$$u'(x) \geqslant u'(x').$$

Then, either $x \mathcal{R} x'$ or $x' \mathcal{R} x$, so that either

$$\mathcal{N}(x') \subset \mathcal{N}(x) \qquad \text{or} \qquad \mathcal{N}(x) \subsetneqq \mathcal{N}(x');$$

it must be the former, for otherwise

$$u'(x) < u'(x'),$$

contrary to the hypothesis. Hence, $x \mathcal{R} x'$. This gives a utility function.

(ii) To derive a utility function that is regular, note that $u'(x)$ varies solely in the interval [0, 1].

For c between zero and one, suppose $\mathscr{S}^c$ is not closed. Let a be the least upper bound of the $u'(x)$ for which

$$c \geqslant u'(x), \qquad a = u(x)$$

for some x in $\mathscr{S}$, for if a does not exist,

$$\mathscr{S}^c = \bigcap_{u'(x) \leqslant c} \mathscr{R}(x),$$

which is closed as the intersection of closed sets. Let b be the greatest lower bound of the $u'(x)$ for which

$$u'(x) \geqslant c, \qquad b \neq u'(x)$$

for any x in $\mathscr{C}$, for if b does not exist,

$$\mathscr{S}^c = \mathscr{R}(x),$$

which is closed, contrary to hypothesis. To conclude, for every $\mathscr{S}^c$ such that $\mathscr{S}^c$ is not closed, c must appear in a maximal *gap* in u' of the form a, b for which

$$(a, b] \cap u(\mathscr{C}) = \varnothing.$$

Take all intervals of the form $(a, b]$, where a and b are the greatest lower bound and least upper bound defined above for maximal gaps. These intervals are disjoint and countable in number and can be ordered according to length. (If they could not be so ordered, there would be an infinity of them with length greater than ε, which would give an infinite length to the union of disjoint subsets of an interval of finite length, which is impossible.)

Denote the intervals by $(a_i, b_i]$. Define

$$u(x) = \begin{cases} u'(x) & \text{if} \quad x \neq a_i \quad \text{for any } i \\ b_i & \text{if} \quad u'(x) = a_i \,. \end{cases}$$

The utility u represents $\mathscr{R}$, since $u(x) \geqslant u(y)$ if and only if $u'(x) \geqslant u'(y)$.

To show regularity of u, let $x^n \to x$, $u(x^n) \geqslant c$. If for any $nu(x) \geqslant u(x^n)$, then $u(x) \geqslant c$. Otherwise, $u(x^n) < u(x)$. Let $c' \equiv \inf\{u(y) \geqslant c\}$. If nonempty, (c, c') is a gap contained in a maximal gap $(a_i, b_i]$. Evidently, $c' = b_i$. There are $c_m \to a_i$, $u(y_m) = c_m \leqslant c$, $x \mathscr{R} y_m$. Hence $u(x) \geqslant \sup c_m = a_i$. Since $u(x) \neq a_i$, $u(x) \geqslant b_i = c' \geqslant c$. q.e.d.

There is a sense in which Theorem 1 is the best possible utility theorem for completely separable spaces in economic applications. Among usual properties of real-valued functions, only regular functions can be depended on to take a maximum upon the closed compact sets that are assumed in economic analysis. Any utility function that failed to have this property would be unsatisfactory for such analysis. On the other hand, it can easily be demonstrated that the upper contour sets of regular utility functions are closed. Hence, the closedness of the upper contour sets is necessary and sufficient for an "acceptable" utility function. In view of this, the program proposed by Chipman [1960] is fulfilled. It is interesting to note that the axiom of substitution suggested by Chipman is not necessary for a meaningful economic utility function. The role of substitution will be elaborated in the next section.

Exercise 1 Suppose that $\mathscr{R}$ in Theorem 1 is not complete. Show that there is a utility function u such that if $x \mathscr{R} y$, then $u(x) \geqslant u(y)$, and if $x \mathscr{P} y$, then $u(x) > u(y)$. Can u be made regular?

PROBLEMS

A. Utility for the Lexicographic Order

Two sets $\mathscr{A}$ and $\mathscr{B}$ are said to have the same *cardinal number* if there is a one-to-one function f taking $\mathscr{A}$ into $\mathscr{B}$. In addition to finite numbers, there are several classes of infinity. The set of positive integers define the notion of *countable* infinity. The set of points in a line are numbered as the set of subsets of the positive integers (Section 3 of Chapter 2). According to Kelly [1955, p. 276], the cardinal number of $\mathscr{A}$ is less than the cardinal number of $2^{\mathscr{A}}$. Hence, the cardinal number of the points in a line is greater than countable. Finally, the cardinal number of the set of subsets of the line is greater than the cardinal number of the line.

The question arises whether there is a real-valued utility function u such that $u(x) \geqslant u(y)$ if and only if $x \mathscr{R} y$. Consider this question for the lexicographic relation $\mathscr{R}$, as discussed in Chapter 3, Problem A.

Suppose a utility function exists for $\mathscr{R}$ lexicographic. Let

$$\mathscr{U}(x) = (\inf\{u(y) \mid y \mathscr{I}_1 x\}, \quad \sup\{u(y) \mid y \mathscr{I}_1 x\}),$$

where inf represents the greatest lower bound, and sup the least upper bound.

Show that

(a) $\mathscr{U}(x) \cap \mathscr{U}(x') = \varnothing$ for $x \sim\mathscr{I} x'$.

(b) The cardinal number of the set of indifference classes of 1 for which there is nonindifference for all $i > 1$ must be at most countable.

(Hint: Use (a) to construct a mapping from points to disjoint open intervals, which are at most countable in number.)

(c) Use induction to show that the cardinal number of the set of indifference classes of i for which there is nonindifference for all $j > i$ must be at most countable.

(d) Show that the lexicographic arrangement of the numerical relation $\geqslant$ cannot be represented by a continuous function in n-dimensional Euclidean space.

This problem is due to Hausdorff (Debreu [1959, pp. 72–73], gives a solution).

B. Necessary Conditions for Utility Functions I

Are there conditions on utility functions in some ways less restrictive than regularity that will ensure that they take maxima on convex, compact sets?

2. Continuous Utility Functions

In addition to the closure of the upper contour sets, the closure of the lower contour sets may be postulated, that is, continuity of preferences. It will be shown that continuous preferences may be represented by continuous utility.

As with regularity, it is desirable to elaborate on the meaning of continuity. Preferences in Figures 2a and 2b are continuous. In particular the sudden starvation aspect of preferences is forbidden. This is demonstrated in Figure 3. The two axes indicate consumption in two periods of time. If the consumer drops below the starvation level for the first period s_1, then he is unconcerned with what consumption is in the second period. For $(\bar{x}_1, \bar{x}_2)$ illustrated, we can ascertain that the lower contour set is not closed.

In general, if there is a finite aspiration set, the lower contour sets are not always closed. To see this, suppose that x is the best element under $\mathscr{R}$ in $\mathscr{A}$. (There is a best element since $\mathscr{A}$ is a finite set and $\mathscr{R}$ is complete and transitive.) Let y be the best element such that $x \mathscr{P} y$. Now $\mathscr{R}^{-1}(y)$ equals $\mathscr{P}^{-1}(x)$, which is open by the proof of the closedness of the upper contour set for aspiration; hence, $\mathscr{R}^{-1}(y)$ is open. Under the usual (metric) topology on Euclidean space or in fact on any connected space, the only sets that are both open and closed are the whole space $\mathscr{C}$ and the empty set $\varnothing$. Clearly, $\mathscr{R}^{-1}(y)$ is not equal to $\mathscr{C}$, since it does not contain the particular point x, while $\mathscr{R}^{-1}(y)$ is not empty, since it contains

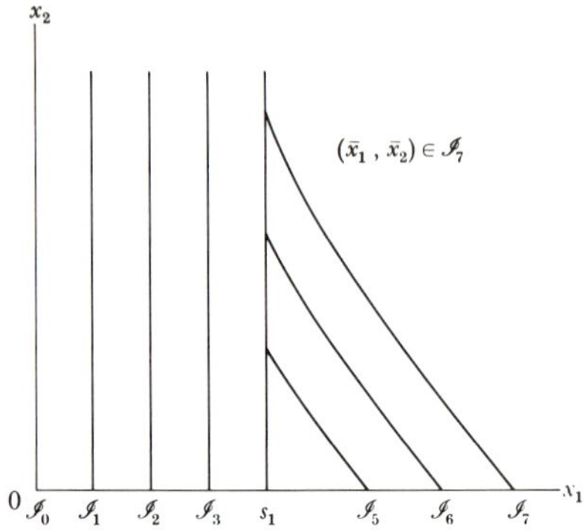

Figure 3

y. Hence, $\mathscr{R}^{-1}(y)$ is not closed and the order does not have closed lower contour sets. Similarly, it will be shown (Corollary 10) that in infinite time, the equal weight to equal generations generally excludes $\mathscr{R}^{-1}(y)$ as being open. This is because consumptions that are bad for everdistant generations are bad overall, even though they may tend to the "good" program, which is good for all generations.

Under the condition of continuity, for $y \mathscr{P} x$, the "between" sets $\mathscr{P}(x) \cap \mathscr{P}^{-1}(y)$ are open. If they are nonempty, then in metric spaces, small differences in distance make a difference in preferences, since x and y may be very close in distance and yet there are points z between x and y in terms of preferences. In the case where $\mathscr{C}$ is connected, $\mathscr{P}(x)$ cannot be disjoint from $\mathscr{P}^{-1}(y)$, for otherwise the space would be disconnected into two open disjoint subsets. Hence, in this case, further distinctions can be made between z and x and y and z, even though the distances involved may still be smaller. This process can be continued indefinitely as distinctions are made between elements that are arbitrarily close in distance.

The following result suggests finding u for which both u and $-u$ have no gaps.

2 Remark If f and $-f$ are regular, then f is continuous.

Proof An open set in the real line is the union of open intervals. For each open interval (a, b),

$$f^{-1}((a, b)) = (\mathscr{C} \sim \mathscr{S}^b) \cap (\mathscr{C} \sim \mathscr{S}_a)$$

where

$$\mathscr{S}^b = \{x \mid f(x) \geqslant b, \quad x \in \mathscr{S}\} \qquad \text{and} \qquad \mathscr{S}_a = \{x \mid -f(x) \geqslant -a, \quad x \in \mathscr{S}\}.$$

Hence, the inverse image of an open interval is the intersection of two open sets (by the regularity of f and $-f$), which is open. Finally, the inverse image of a union of sets is the union of the inverse images of the sets—in this case the union of open sets, which is open. q.e.d.

3 Theorem *If $\mathscr{C}$ is completely separable and $\mathscr{R}(x)$ and $\mathscr{R}^{-1}(x)$ are closed for all x in $\mathscr{C}$, then there exists a continous utility function representing the reflexive order $\mathscr{R}$.*

(The theorem was conjectured by Debreu [1954] and proven by Debreu [1964]).

Proof Use part (i) of the proof of Theorem 1 to derive a utility function u' for $\mathscr{R}$. As in the proof of Theorem 1, failure of regularity of u occurs for maximal intervals or gaps of the form $(a_i, b_i]$. Failure of regularity of $-u'$ occurs for maximal intervals or gaps in $u'(\mathscr{C})$ of the form $[a_i, b_i)$. Debreu [1964] has shown that there is an increasing function v from $u'(\mathscr{C})$ to [0, 1] such that maximal gaps are open, that is, $u = vu'$ is continuous. q.e.d.

A related proof is suggested in Exercise 4.

4 Theorem *If $\mathscr{C}$ is separable and connected and $\mathscr{R}(x)$ and $\mathscr{R}^{-1}(x)$ are closed for all x in $\mathscr{C}$, then there exists a continuous utility function representing the reflexive ordering $\mathscr{R}$.*

Theorem 4 is due to Debreu [1964]. The basic result needed for Theorem 4 was first set forth by Birkoff [1948, pp. 31–32].

5 Lemma *Let $\mathscr{R}$ be an ordering. If there is a countable set of points $\mathscr{X}$ such that $y \mathscr{P} z$ implies that there exists $x \in \mathscr{X}$ such that $v \mathscr{P} x \mathscr{R} z$, then $\mathscr{R}$ is representable by a (real-valued) utility function.*

By replacing $\mathscr{R}$ with $\mathscr{R}^{-1}$, we can obtain an alternative form of Lemma 5.

Proof Count the members of $\mathscr{X}$:

$$\mathscr{X} = \{x_n \mid n = 1, 2, \ldots\}.$$

Let $\mathscr{N}(x)$ be the set of integers n for which $x_n \mathscr{R} x$. Then set

$$u(x) = - \sum_{n \in \mathscr{N}(x)} (\tfrac{1}{2})^n.$$

To demonstrate that u is a utility function representing $\mathscr{R}$, suppose $x \mathscr{R} x'$. By completeness of $\mathscr{R}$, either $x \mathscr{P} x'$ or $x \mathscr{I} x'$. If $x \mathscr{I} x'$, then $u(x) = u(x')$. If $x \mathscr{P} x'$, by transitivity, $x_i \mathscr{P} x$ implies $x_i \mathscr{P} x'$. Also, there is an $x_i \in \mathscr{X}$ such that $x \mathscr{P} x_i \mathscr{R} x$, so that

$$\mathscr{N}(x') \supset \mathscr{N}(x), \qquad \mathscr{N}(x') \neq \mathscr{N}(x), \qquad \text{or} \qquad u(x') < u(x).$$

On the other hand, either

$$\mathscr{N}(x') \supset \mathscr{N}(x) \qquad \text{or} \qquad u(x') > u(x).$$

If

$$u(x') \leqslant u(x),$$

then clearly

$$\mathscr{N}(x') \supset \mathscr{N}(x) \qquad \text{and} \qquad x \mathscr{R} x'. \qquad \text{q.e.d.}$$

Proof (of Theorem 4) Denote the countable dense subset by x_n, $n = 1, 2, \ldots$. Consider that $\mathscr{P}^{-1}(y) \cap \mathscr{P}(z)$ is open. It is nonempty since otherwise

$$\mathscr{C} = \mathscr{P}^{-1}(y) \cup \mathscr{P}(z)$$

is made up of two disconnected components. Apply Lemma 5 to obtain a utility function u'.

The remarks at the end of the proof of Theorem 4 can be applied here. There is, however, an easy version of Debreu's method that yields the desired result. The reader may fill in details.

Note that for every pair of utilities not extremal in $u'(\mathscr{C})$, there is another between, and hence, an infinite number between (if not, $\mathscr{C}$ would be the union of $\mathscr{R}^{-1}(x)$, $\mathscr{R}(y)$, two closed sets). Such a set of numbers can be mapped into a dense subset of (0, 1) by identifying a countably dense subset with appropriate rational numbers and identifying others with the irrational numbers. Identify the first with $\frac{1}{2}$, the second with $\frac{1}{4}$ if it is greater than the first, and with $\frac{3}{4}$ if it is less than the first. Proceeding onward, there will always be numbers $n/2^m$ to choose and all will eventually be chosen. Also, any x in $u'(\mathscr{C})$ can be approximated by numbers from the countable subset, some larger and some smaller. Of course, there will be only one point in (0, 1) in which to "fit" x. The extrema in $u'(\mathscr{C})$ are identified with 0 and 1. Clearly, there are no gaps at all, and $v = uv'$ so constructed is continuous. q.e.d.

Exercise 2 Under what conditions can u in Exercise 1 be made continuous?

Exercise 3 Prove Theorem 3 by inserting artificial preference levels into gaps.

PROBLEMS

C. Necessary Conditions for Utility Functions II

(a) Show that the upper contour sets of a reflexive ordering $\mathscr{R}$ represented by a regular utility function u are necessarily closed.

(b) Show that the upper and lower contour sets of a reflexive ordering $\mathscr{R}$ represented by a continuous utility function u are necessarily closed.

D. Transitivity I

Suppose two individuals are to agree to decisions that affect them both. Suppose they have contrary interests to the extent that in comparing two indifference classes $\mathscr{I}(x)$ and $\mathscr{I}(y)$, if $x \mathscr{P}_1 y$, then there is an x' in $\mathscr{I}(x)$ and a y' in $\mathscr{I}(y)$ such that $y' \mathscr{P}_2 x'$. Presume that 2 is transitive in his preferences. Then demonstrate that by pairwise offers 2 can persuade 1 to any position 2 wishes in the set of intransitivities for 1. (Hint: Consider the set $\{x \mid \text{there exists } y, z \text{ such that } x \mathscr{R}_1 y, y \mathscr{R}_1 z, z \mathscr{R}_1 x\}$. Obtain the maximum in this set for 2. Show that from any other point in the set, 1 can proceed to the maximum.)

E. Transitivity II

Suppose that instead of the transitivity of $\mathscr{R}$, $x \mathscr{P} y$, $y \mathscr{I} z$, implies $x \mathscr{P} z$, that is, there are nonoverlapping indifference classes that are ranked, not necessarily consistently, by the relation $\mathscr{R}$.

(a) Show that $\mathscr{I}$ is transitive.

(b) Suppose that $\mathscr{C}$ is connected, $\mathscr{P}(x)$ and $\mathscr{P}^{-1}(x)$ are open for all x in $\mathscr{C}$.

(i) Show that $\mathscr{R}(y)$ cannot be divided into two components such that $\mathscr{I}(y)$ is contained in one of them.

(ii) Use the weak transitivity property to demonstrate that $\mathscr{R}(y)$ is contained in either $\mathscr{P}(z)$ or $\mathscr{P}^{-1}(z)$ for $z -\mathscr{I} y$.

(iii) Show that if $x \mathscr{P} y$, $y \mathscr{P} z$, then $x \mathscr{P} z$.

(c) Show that $\mathscr{R}$ is transitive,

(d) Use Theorem 4 to derive the existence of a continuous utility function.

This problem was solved for $\mathscr{R}(x)$ connected by Rader [1963a], using results of Eilenberg [1941]. The present form was suggested by Sonnenschein [1965].

F. Transitivity III

Under the conditions of Problem H, suppose that instead of the weak transitivity there, it is known only that $\mathscr{I}$ is transitive. Suppose that $\mathscr{I}(x)$ is connected for all x in $\mathscr{C}$. Show that the weak transitivity property of Problem E follows. (Hint: If $x \mathscr{P} y$, $y \mathscr{I} z$, but $z \mathscr{P} x$, then there are points of both $\mathscr{P}^{-1}(x)$ and $\mathscr{P}(x)$ in $\mathscr{I}(z)$; hence, $\mathscr{I}(z)$ can be decomposed into two nonempty components.) We can then use Problem E to derive transitivity of $\mathscr{R}$ and a continuous utility function.

This problem was solved by Sonnenschein [1965].

G. Transitivity IV

Every convex set $\mathscr{X}$ in Euclidean n-space has the Phragmen–Brouwer property that if $\mathscr{X} = \mathscr{A} \cup \mathscr{B}$, $\mathscr{A}$ and $\mathscr{B}$ closed and connected, then $\mathscr{A} \cap \mathscr{B}$ is connected (Wilder [1949]). Use this property to show that if $\mathscr{I}$ is transitive as in Problem F and $\mathscr{R}(x)$ and $\mathscr{R}^{-1}(x)$ are connected, then $\mathscr{R}$ is transitive (assuming conditions on $\mathscr{C}$ and $\mathscr{R}(x)$, $\mathscr{R}^{-1}(x)$ as in Problems E and F).

Again, we can derive a continuous utility function.

This problem was solved by Sonnenschein [1965], who actually proved the theorem for $\mathscr{R}(x)$ arcwise connectedness instead of $\mathscr{R}^{-1}(x)$ connected.

3. Utility for Partial Orderings

It has been pointed out by Richter [1966] that Lemma 5 gives a method for obtaining utility on incomplete relations.

$\mathscr{R}$ is *quasi representable* by a real-valued utility function u if $x \mathscr{P} y$ implies $u(x) > u(y)$, and $x \mathscr{I} y$ implies $u(x) = u(y)$. In effect, $\mathscr{R}$ is extendable to an ordering that is representable by a utility function.

6 Theorem (Richter) *Let $\mathscr{R}$ be a partial order. If there is a countable set of points $\mathscr{X}$ such that $y \mathscr{P} z$ implies that there exists $x \in \mathscr{X}$ such that $y \mathscr{P} x \mathscr{R} z$, then $\mathscr{R}$ is quasi representable by a (real-valued) utility function. More generally, if $\mathscr{R}$ is a reflective relation and the indifference classes of $\mathscr{R}$ are the same as those for $\mathscr{R}^* = \bigcup_{n-1}^{\infty} \mathscr{R}^n$, then $\mathscr{R}$ is quasi representable by a utility function.*

Proof Consider the set of equivalence classes, denoted $\{y\}$, under $\mathscr{I}$ ordered by: $\{y\} \mathscr{R} \{x\}$ if and only if $\bar{y} \mathscr{R} \bar{x}$ for some $\bar{y} \mathscr{I} y$, $\bar{x} \mathscr{I} x$. By Lemma 2 of Chapter 3, for $\mathscr{R}$ only a reflexive relation extend the induced relation to a partial ordering, $\mathscr{R}^* = \bigcup_{n=1}^{\infty} \mathscr{R}^n$. Next, "close" the partial ordering by defining $\mathscr{R}^{**}$:

$$\{y\} \mathscr{R}^{**} \{z\}$$

if $\{y\} \mathscr{R}^* \{z\}$ and also

$$\{y\} \mathscr{I}^{**} \{z\}$$

if there is no $x \in \mathscr{C}$ for which

$$\{y\} \mathscr{P}^* \{x\} \mathscr{R}^* \{z\}.$$

It is easy to verify that $\mathscr{R}^{**}$ is an ordering and is representable by a utility function u (Lemma 5). Also, if $y \mathscr{P} z$, then there is an $x \in \mathscr{X}$ such that $y \mathscr{P} x \mathscr{R} z$, or

$$\{y\} \mathscr{P}^* \{x\} \mathscr{R}^* \{z\}$$

so that

$$\{y\} \mathscr{P}^{**} \{z\}, \qquad \text{or} \qquad u(y) > u(z).$$

If

$$y \mathscr{I} z,$$

then

$$\{y\} \mathscr{I}^* \{z\} \qquad \text{and} \qquad \{y\} \mathscr{I}^{**} \{z\}$$

so that

$$u(y) = u(z). \qquad \text{q.e.d.}$$

PROBLEMS

H. Nontransitive Relations III

Suppose preferences are not sensitive to small differences but are to large ones, that is, $x \mathscr{P} y$, $y \mathscr{P} z$ implies $x \mathscr{P} z$, but $x \mathscr{I} y$, $y \mathscr{I} z$, does not necessarily imply $x \mathscr{I} z$ (Armstrong [1939] and Chipman [1965]).

(i) When can we find a utility U that quasi represents $\mathscr{P}$? (Hint: Let $x \mathscr{P}^* y$ if $\mathscr{R}(x) \subsetneqq \mathscr{R}(y)$.)

(ii) What conditions on $\mathscr{R}$ ensure the various properties of preference on U?

(iii) For what kinds of sets would maximizing U imply optimizing $\mathscr{R}$?

I. Revealed Preference I

Suppose $e(p, \theta)$ is such that

(a) $pe(p, \theta) \leqslant \theta$,
(b) $e(p, \theta)$ is closed,
(c) $p\bar{x} < \theta$ and $\bar{x} \in e(\bar{p}, \bar{\theta})$, $\bar{p}x \leqslant \bar{\theta}$, $x \in e(p, \theta)$ imply $x \in e(\bar{p}, \bar{\theta})$;

(c) is the weak axiom of revealed preference, p is price, and θ is interpreted as "income" in the Marshallian sense (see Chapter 8).

Show that $e(p)$ can be derived from (complete) preference ordering. (Hint: Use Theorem 6 to show that the set of points "revealed inferior" to x is closed.)

This question is due to Houthakker [1950] and Samuelson [1938] and solved by Richter [1966].

J. Revealed Preference II

In addition to (a), (b), (c) of Problem I, assume that

(d) e is defined on a closed, convex set of prices, $\mathscr{P}$, for which $e(\mathscr{P})$ is closed and convex,

(e) e is a (single-valued) function,

(f) $e(p, \theta) = e(p, \bar{\theta})$ implies $p = k\bar{p}, \theta, k \neq 0$.

Show that

(i) $pe(p, \theta) = \theta$. (Hint: Use (c) and (d).)

(ii) y revealed preferred to x implies $e^t = ty + (1 - t)x$ is revealed preferred to x and to all $\bar{x}$ nearby to x, $0 < t < 1$. (Hint: Use (i) and (c).)

(iii) Suppose y revealed preferred to x and let $y \in e(p, \theta)$, $e^t \in e(\bar{p}, \theta)$. Then

$$p^s \equiv s\bar{p} + (1 - s)p, \qquad \theta^s \equiv p^s(ty + (1 - t)x), \qquad py > pe^s$$

where $e^s \equiv e(p^s, \theta^s)$. (Hint: Assume $py \leqslant pe^s$ and show that $pe^s > pe^t$. Next, use $p^s e^s = p^s e^t$ to show that $\bar{p}e^s \geqslant pe^t$.)

(iv) If $p^k \to p$, $x^k \to x$, y revealed preferred to x, then $p^k x^k > p^k e^s$.

(v) e is continuous. (Hint: Use Problem I and (b) to establish $u(x^k) > u(e^s) > u(e^t) > u(x^k)$. Are there assumptions needed other than (a)–(f)?)

This problem was first solved by Sonnenschein [1967b]. He also gives examples to show that the theorems fail in the absence of any one of the of the assumptions.

4. Additive Utility

This section derives a utility function whose derivatives when they exist have meaning. Such utility functions are used when the laws of demand are stated in terms of marginal utility.

Applications are to preferences over time (Section 5), choice under uncertainty (Chapter 7), and consumer demand (Chapter 8).

The utility functions derived in the previous sections are "ordinal" utility functions u such that

$$u(x) \geqslant u(y)$$

if and only if x is not inferior to y. The values that an ordinal utility function associates with the various alternative commodity bundles serve only as an index of consumer preference. Thus, given an ordinal utility function, any monotonic transformation of the utility function yields the same ordering of preferences as the original utility function: For any increasing transformation t,

$$t(u(x, y)) \geqslant t(u(z, w)) \qquad \text{if} \qquad u(x, y) \geqslant u(z, w).$$

Therefore, $t(u)$ shows the same ordering of preferences as does u. However, when a monotonic transformation of the original utility function is effected, marginal utility is affected in a more or less arbitrary fashion. This can be shown as follows. Let

$$t(u) = cu^2 + bu, \qquad mu_x = \frac{dt}{du}\frac{\partial u}{\partial x},$$

and

$$\frac{\partial}{\partial x}\left[\frac{dt}{du}\frac{\partial u}{\partial x}\right]^2 = 2c\left[\frac{\partial u}{\partial x}\right]^2 + (2cu + b)\left[\frac{\partial^2 u}{\partial x^2}\right]$$

where

$$\frac{\partial u^2}{\partial x} > 0, \qquad \frac{dt}{du} > 0,$$

and by definition of the diminishing marginal utility of u,

$$\frac{\partial^2 u}{\partial x^2} < 0.$$

Evidently, d^2t/du^2 may be greater or less than zero.

Now u may be assumed to be any size. If it is small, and c is assumed positive and very large,

$$\frac{d^2t}{du^2}\left(\frac{\partial u}{\partial x}\right)^2 + \frac{dt}{du}\left(\frac{\partial^2 u}{\partial x^2}\right)$$

is greater than zero. $(\partial/\partial x)(dt/du)$ is positive, $t(u)$ may exhibit increasing marginal utility while u shows diminishing marginal utility. Thus, marginal utility has no meaning in an ordinal context. (As an example, the reader may verify these results for

$$u = x + y + x^{1/2}y^{1/2}, \qquad t(u) = c(x + y + x^{1/2}y^{1/2})^2.)$$

In the case of additive utility, utility is unique up to an increasing linear transformation. Therefore, marginal utility is unique up to a multiplicative positive constant. It is for this reason that additive utility has been called cardinal utility. Of course, it has none of the welfare content which that term originally implied. Nevertheless, additive utility leads to stronger results in the theory of demand (see Chapter 8). If the assumptions on consumer preferences that lead to an additive representation are reasonable for a particular consumer, the economic theorist can be more definite about the consumer's response to prices and wealth. In particular, should Bentham's view be confirmed by future biological investitations, and if additive utility functions are, after all, natural, then the theory will be greatly improved as a predictive device (Section 8).

Utility is *additive* on the decomposition of subscripts, $\mathscr{A}_i$ disjoint,

$$\mathscr{A} = \bigcup_{i=1}^{n} \mathscr{A}_i,$$

if preferences are representable by

$$u(x_\alpha, \alpha \in \mathscr{A}) = \sum_{i=1}^{n} u_i(x_\alpha, \alpha \in \mathscr{A}_i).$$

Conditions for additivity when $\mathscr{A}$ is a set of commodity types have beeen derived by Samuelson [1947, Chapter 7], Sono [1961], and Leontief [1947]. The approach adopted here is a later one due to Debreu [1960].

Consider first the case of only two $\mathscr{A}_i$, $i = 1, 2$.

7 Theorem *Suppose*

(i) $\mathscr{R}$ *is continuous,*

(ii) $\mathscr{C}$ *is connected and separable or else completely separable, and*

(iii) $(x_1, x_2) \mathscr{I} (y_1, y_2) \mathscr{I} (z_1, z_2)$ *implies that* $(x_1, y_2) \mathscr{I} (z_2, y_1)$, *where* (x_1, x_2) *is the vector* x_1 *on* $\mathscr{A}_1$ *and* x_2 *on* $\mathscr{A}_2$.

Then there exists a utility u such that

$$u(x) = u_1(x_\alpha, \alpha \in \mathscr{A}_1) + u_2(x_\alpha, \alpha \in \mathscr{A}_2).$$

Furthermore, u is unique up to an increasing linear transformation.

Figure 4 may be regarded as a schematic representation of (iii), applying to the particular example of two commodities.

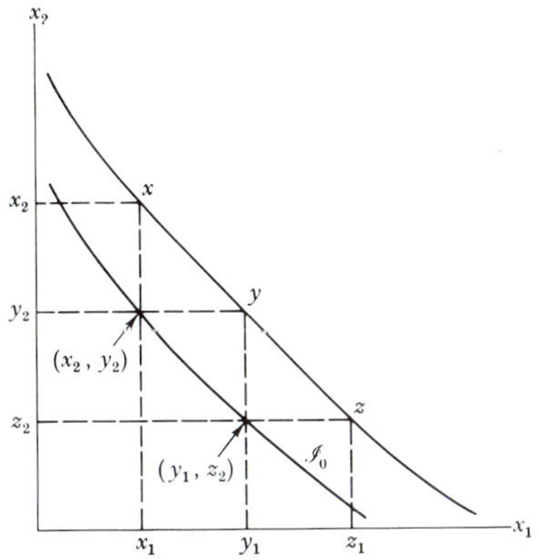

Figure 4

The proof of Theorem 7 appears in Debreu [1960] and Koopmans [1966]. It is omitted here, since it depends on a result from geometry that is outside the scope of this book.

To derive additive utility for $n > 2$, define $\mathscr{R}$ to be *separable* in $(\mathscr{A}_i, i = 1, 2, \ldots, n)$ if

(i) $n \geqslant 3$,
(ii) preference on $(x_{\mathscr{I}}, x_{\sim\mathscr{I}})$ varying $x_{\mathscr{I}}$ only is independent of $x_{\sim\mathscr{I}}$,
(iii) there is more than one level of preference for each $(x_{\mathscr{I}}, x_{\sim\mathscr{I}})$, $x_{\mathscr{I}}$ variable.

If hypothesis (i) is excluded, then preferences are *independent* between commodities. Therefore, preferences are separable if they are independent and $n \geqslant 3$.

8 Theorem *Suppose*

(i) $\mathscr{R}$ *is continuous,*
(ii) $\mathscr{C}$ *is connected and separable or else completely separable, and*
(iii) $\mathscr{R}$ *is separable on* $(\mathscr{A}_i, i = 1, \ldots, n)$.

Then there exists a u representing $\mathscr{R}$ *and additive on* $\mathscr{A}_i$. *Furthermore, this utility is unique up to an increasing linear transformation.*

Again, the reader is referred to Debreu [1960] for the proof. On a Boolean algebra a the function u is *set additive* if for

$$\mathscr{A}, \ \mathscr{B} \in a, \quad \mathscr{A} \cap \mathscr{B} = \varnothing, \qquad \text{if} \quad u(\mathscr{A} \cap \mathscr{B}) = u(\mathscr{A}) + u(\mathscr{B}).$$

The function u is *σ-additive* if for $(\mathscr{A}_i \in \mathscr{A}, i = 1, 2, \ldots)$, $\mathscr{A}_i \cap \mathscr{A}_j = \varnothing$, $i \neq j$,

$$u(\mathscr{A}_i, i = 1, 2, \ldots) = \sum_{i=1}^{\infty} u_i(\mathscr{A}_i).$$

The following definitions are stated for utility functions, but their application to $\mathscr{R}$ is made in the straightforward way of assuming upper and lower contour sets to be closed in the relevant convergence.

The utility u is *continuous for finite decompositions* if

$$u(x^n_{\mathscr{A}_i}, i = 1, 2, \ldots, n) \to u(x_{\mathscr{A}_i}, i = 1, 2, \ldots, n)$$

whenever $x^n_{\mathscr{A}_i} \to x_{\mathscr{A}_i}$. (Obviously, the definition applies only after convergence in $x_{\mathscr{A}_i}$ is defined.) Utility u is *σ-continuous* if

$$u(x_{\mathscr{A}_i}, i = 1, 2, \ldots, n, \bar{x}_{\mathscr{A}_i}, i = n + 1, \ldots) \to u(x_{\mathscr{A}_i}, i = 1, 2, \ldots).$$

(The σ-continuity is a weak variety of a strong notion of continuity; namely, continuity in *pointwise convergence*: $x^n \to x$ if $x^n_{\mathscr{A}_i} \to x_{\mathscr{A}_i}$ for all $i = 1, 2, \ldots.$)

9 Theorem *If*

(i) *$\mathscr{R}$ is continuous for finite decomposition,*

(ii) *$\mathscr{R}$ is separable on any decomposition into sets of a Boolean algebra of subsets of $\mathscr{A}$, denoted a,*

(iii) *$\mathscr{C}$ is separable and connected or completely separable,*

then there is a set-additive u representing $\mathscr{R}$, unique up to an increasing linear transformation. If, also,

(iv) *$\mathscr{R}$ is σ-continuous,*

then u is σ-additive.

Theorem 9 can be applied to the case of an infinite number of independent generations, $i = 1, 2, \ldots$. *Generations* have separable preferences, and they are *treated equally*, if $u_i = u_j$ for all i, j.

10 Corollary *If $\mathscr{R}$ is σ-continuous, an infinite number of generations cannot be treated equally.*

The corollary is due to Diamond [1965], who also treats the non-separable case. For example, preferences leading to the intertemporally efficient paths of capital must be discontinuous.

Proof For any x such that $c = (x_\alpha, \alpha \in \mathscr{A}_i)$ is constant for all i,

$$u(x) = \sum_{i=1}^{\infty} u_i(c).$$

Therefore, $u_i = u_j$ for all i, j implies that

$$u_i = u_j = 0,$$

contrary to condition (iii) of the definition of separability, which implies the nonconstancy of utility. q.e.d.

Proof (of Theorem 9) In what follows, fix $u(x_{\alpha_1})$, $u(x_{\alpha_2})$, which we can do with additive utility (since it is determined up to an increasing linear transformation).

Decompose $\mathscr{A}$ into n parts, $n \geqslant 3$. Then,

$$u^1(x_\alpha, \alpha \in \mathscr{A}) = \sum_{i=1}^{n} u_i^1(x_\alpha, \alpha \in \mathscr{A}_i).$$

For any further decomposition $(\mathscr{A}_{ij}, i, j)$, where

$$\bigcup_j \mathscr{A}_{ij} = \mathscr{A}_i,$$

there is a utility

$$u^2(x_\alpha, \alpha \in \mathscr{A}) = \sum_{i=1}^{n} u_{ij}^2(x_\alpha, \alpha \in \mathscr{A}_i).$$

Since u^2 agrees with u^1 and is identical in α_1 and α_2,

$$\sum_j u_{kj}^2 - u_k^1 \qquad \text{(plus a constant)}$$

for any other k. Therefore u^1 was already additive on the new decomposition. Any decomposition can be obtained from $(\mathscr{A}_i, i = 1,..., n)$ by a further decomposition of $\mathscr{A}_i$ and then set addition. Therefore, it is additive on any other subset of sets.

In particular, for an infinite decomposition $(\mathscr{A}_i, i = 1, 2,...)$,

$$u(x_\alpha, \alpha \in \mathscr{A}) = \sum_{i=1}^{n} u(x_\alpha, \alpha \in \mathscr{A}_i) + v_n(x_\alpha, \alpha \in \mathscr{A}_i, i = 1 + 1,...).$$

Now for any other $(\bar{x}_\alpha, \alpha \in \mathscr{A})$

$$\begin{aligned} &| u(x_\alpha, \alpha \in \mathscr{A}_i, i = 1, 2,...) \\ &\qquad - u(x_\alpha, \alpha \in \mathscr{A}_i, i = 1, 2,..., n, \bar{x}_\alpha, \alpha \in \mathscr{A}_i, i = n + 1,...)| \\ &= | v_n(x_\alpha, \alpha \in \mathscr{A}_i, i = n + 1,...) - v_n(\bar{x}_\alpha, \alpha \in \mathscr{A}_i, i = n + 1,...)| \to 0 \end{aligned}$$

(σ-continuity of u). Also, we can set

$$u(\bar{x}_\alpha, \alpha \in \mathscr{A}_i, i = 1, 2, \ldots) = 0,$$

whereupon

$$\begin{aligned} u(x_\alpha, \alpha \in \mathscr{A}_i, i = 1, 2, \ldots) \\ &= \sum_{i=1}^{n} u_i(x_\alpha, \alpha \in \mathscr{A}_i) + \sum_{i=1}^{n} u_i(\bar{x}_\alpha, \alpha \in \mathscr{A}_i) \\ &\quad + v_n(x_\alpha, \alpha \in \mathscr{A}_i, i = n+1, \ldots) - v_n(\bar{x}_\alpha . \alpha \in \mathscr{A}_i, i = n+1, \ldots) \end{aligned}$$

or

$$u(x_\alpha, \alpha \in \mathscr{A}_i, i = 1, 2, \ldots) = \sum_{i=1}^{\infty} [u_i(x_\alpha, \alpha \in \mathscr{A}_i) + u_i(\bar{x}_\alpha, \alpha \in \mathscr{A}_i)].$$

Evidently, the sum of utility functions in the brackets is an admissible utility for $(x_\alpha, \alpha \in \mathscr{A}_i)$. q.e.d.

If the Boolean algebra is a measure space and if preferences are not affected by a change of measure zero, then utility is an integral of conditional utilities.

11 Theorem *If*

(i) *$\mathscr{R}$ is continuous on finite decompositions and σ-continuous,*
(ii) *$\mathscr{C}$ is separable and connected or else completely separable,*
(iii) *$\mathscr{R}$ is separable on a measure space $\mathscr{A}$ with measure μ,*
(iv) *changes in $(x_\alpha, \alpha \in \mathscr{B})$, $\mathscr{B}$ a set of measure zero, lead to no change in preference,*

then there are conditional utilities v_α, $\alpha \in \mathscr{A}$ such that

$$u = \int_{\alpha \in \mathscr{A}} v_\alpha \, d\mu$$

represents $\mathscr{R}$.

Proof Utility u in Theorem 9 takes sets of measure zero into sets of measure zero. Therefore, for a given $x = (x_\alpha, \alpha \in \mathscr{A})$, the Radon–Nikodyn theorem applies (Halmos [1950, pp. 128–129]). There is an almost-everywhere derivative v_α such that

$$u(x_\alpha, \alpha \in \mathscr{A}) = \int_{\alpha \in \mathscr{A}} v_\alpha \, d\mu. \qquad \text{q.e.d.}$$

Exercise 4 Show that continuity in pointwise convergence in $\mathscr{E}^\infty$ implies continuity on finite decompositions and σ-continuity.

Exercise 5 Show that $\mathscr{E}^\infty$ is connected and completely separable in pointwise convergence.

5. Preferences over Time

Over time the commodity bundles evaluated by $\mathscr{R}_i$ are of the form $x^i = (x^{i,t}, t = 0, 1, \ldots)$, where the $x^{i,t}$ are vectors giving the quantities of goods in time t. $\mathscr{R}_i$ is τ-time *separable* if it is separable in any sequence of consumption vectors that differ by at least τ periods. The consumer can remember or anticipate no more than τ periods in judging the value of changes in consumption. As an example, consider a consumer with maximum life of τ years. Suppose that he considers the preference levels attained by his children and they in turn consider their children. A change in the father's consumption does not affect the preferences of his son or at least of some sufficiently distant descendant. Hence, the evaluation of the change can be made independently of events in the remote future (or past).

12 Theorem *If $\mathscr{R}_i$ is continuous and σ-continuous on a completely separable (or connected and separable) space, variable in preference level, reflexive, transitive, complete, and τ-time separable, then $\mathscr{R}_i$ is representable by a continuous and σ-continuous utility function*

$$\sum_{t=\tau}^{\infty} u_t({}^{t-\tau+1}x^t),$$

where ${}^s x^t = (x^s, x^{s+1}, \ldots, x^t)$.

Proof Preferences $\mathscr{R}_i$ are representable by a utility function u (Theorem 9). Let $t_i \to \infty$, $|t_i - t_j| > \tau$ for $i \neq j$, $t \geqslant \tau$. Let $x(s) = \bar{x}(s)$ for $s \neq u + t_i$, $-\tau \leqslant u \leqslant 0$. Then preferences are separable on $(x^{t_i-\tau+1}, \ldots, x^{t_i}) \equiv {}^{t_i-\tau+1}x^{t_i}$ and representable as

$$U^{t_1, t_2, \ldots} = \sum_i u_i^{t_1 t_2 \ldots}({}^{t_i-\tau+1}x^{t_i}).$$

The uniqueness of $u_i^{t_1, t_2, \ldots}$ up to an increasing linear transformation allows us to construct an additive representation. Let $t_i = \tau(i+1) - 1$. Then preferences are represented by

$$U = \sum_{k=0}^{\infty} u_k({}^{k\tau}x^{\tau(k+1)-1}).$$

Also, in the relevant variables, U is an increasing linear transformation of any $U^{t_1,t_2,\dots}$ such that $t_i = \tau k(2\tau + 1)$ for some k. Clearly, $U^{t_1,t_2,\dots}$ is also an increasing linear transformation of any $U^{s_1,s_2,\dots}$ such that $s_j = t_i$ for some j and i. Also, U is an increasing linear transformation of any $U^{s_1,s_2,\dots}$ (compositions of increasing linear transformation are linear transformations).

Note that for any t,

$$U(x^0,\dots, x^t, x^{t+1},\dots) = V_t(x^0,\dots, x^t) + \overline{V}_t(x^{t+1-\tau},\dots, x^t,\dots).$$

By induction,

$$V_t(x^0,\dots, x^{t+\tau}) = \sum_{\tau\leqslant s\leqslant t} u_s(x^{s-\tau+1},\dots, x^s)$$

where $u_\tau = V_\tau$. By σ-continuity, $U = \sum_{\tau\leqslant t} u.$ represents preferences. q.e.d.

Preferences are *stationary* if

$$(x^1, x^2,\dots, x^m,\dots)\, \mathscr{R}_i\, (x^1, y^2,\dots, y^m,\dots)$$

if, and only if,

$$(x^2,\dots, x^m,\dots)\, \mathscr{R}_i\, (y^2,\dots, y^m,\dots).$$

Preferences are *τ-stationary* if there exists a $y = (y^1,\dots, y^{\tau-1})$ such that $(z, y, x)\, \mathscr{R}\, (z, y, \bar{x})$ if and only if $x\, \mathscr{R}\, \bar{x}$. Memory extends back to y, and for all t, with memory y, preferences are the same from time t.

13 Theorem *If $\mathscr{R}_i$ is continuous and σ-continuous in a separable, connected (or completely separable) topological space, transitive, complete, reflexive, τ-stationary, and τ-time separable, then $\mathscr{R}_i$ is representable by a continuous utility function*

$$\sum_{t=1}^{\infty} u({}^{t-\tau+1}x^{t+\tau})\alpha^t + \sum_{s=0}^{\tau-1} u({}^1y^s, {}^0x^{\tau-1-s})\alpha^{s-\tau-1}.$$

Proof In the following, a utility function is τ-time separable if it is additive between consumptions at least τ periods apart. The proof is by induction on τ.

In the case for $\tau = 1$, the method of proof is due to Koopmans [1966]. From Theorem 9, preferences are represented by $\sum_t u_t$ and, since preferences are identical in $u_t + u_{t+1}$ and $u_1 + u_2$ (τ-stationarity), up to an increasing linear transformation, we have

$$u_t(x^t) = u_{t+1}(x^{t+1}) + A_t(u_1(x^t) + u_2(x^{t+1}) + b_t.$$

Identifying the functionally independent terms,

$$u_t = a_t u_1 + c_t .$$

From above,

$$u_t + u_{t+1} = a_t(u_1 + a_2 u_2) + b_t \qquad \text{or} \qquad u_{t+1} = a_t a_2 u_2 + b_t - c_t .$$

Hence,

$$a_{t+1} = a_t a_2 \qquad \text{or} \qquad a_t = a_2^{t-1} a_1 = a_2^{t-1},$$

which gives $U = \sum u_1 \alpha^t$, $\alpha = a_2$.

The general case is more complicated. Let

$$w_t = \sum_{s=-\tau}^{\tau} u_{t+s}(y^1,\ldots, y^s, x^{t-\tau+1},\ldots, x^t, y, y,\ldots).$$

Preferences on $(y,\ldots, y, y^1,\ldots, y^{\tau-1}, x^{t-\tau+1},\ldots, x^t, y,\ldots)$ are the same as on $(x^{t-\tau+1},\ldots, x^t, y,\ldots)$ (τ-stationarity). From Theorem 12 and uniqueness up to an increasing linear transformation,

$$w_t = a_{t,s} w_s + b_{t,s} ,$$

and

$$w_t = a_{t,s}(a_{s,r} w_r + b_{s,r}) + b_{t,s} ,$$

or

$$a_{t,r} = a_{t,s} a_{s,r} . \tag{I}$$

Also, preferences on

$$(y,\ldots, y, y^1,\ldots, y^{\tau-1}, x^{t-\tau+1},\ldots, x^t, y,\ldots, y, x^{t-\tau+1+s},\ldots, x^{t-\tau+s}, y,\ldots)$$

are the same as on $(x^{t-\tau+1},\ldots, x^t, y,\ldots, y, x^{t-\tau+1+s},\ldots, x^{t-s}, y,\ldots)$. For $s > \tau$, $w_t + w_{t+s}$ is an increasing linear transformation of $w_r + w_{r+s}$. Indeed,

$$\begin{aligned} w_t + w_{t+s} &= a_{t,r} w_r + a_{t+s,r+s} w_{r+s} + b_{t+s,r+s} \\ &= a_{t,r}\left(w_r + \left(\frac{a_{t+s,r+s}}{a_{t,r}}\right) w_{r+s}\right) + c, \end{aligned}$$

so that

$$a_{t+s,r+s} = a_{t,r} . \tag{II}$$

It can be shown that (I) and (II) imply $a_{t,s} = \alpha^{s-t}$. Define $\alpha_s = (a_{t,t+s})^{1/s}$ for $s > \tau$. Then for $r > \tau$,

$$\begin{aligned} a_{t+rs,t} &= a_{t+rs,t+(r-1)s} \cdots a_{t+s,t} && \text{(I')} \\ &= a_{t+s,t} \cdots a_{t+s,t} && \text{(II')} \\ &= (a_{t+s,t})^r = (\alpha_s)^{s\alpha}. \end{aligned}$$

Symmetrically, $a_{t+s\tau,t} = (\alpha_\tau)^{\tau s}$, and $\alpha_s = \alpha_\tau = \alpha$. For any t, s, say $t > s$,

$$a_{t,s} = a_{t,t+\tau+1}a_{t+\tau+1,s} = \frac{a_{t,t+\tau+1}}{a_{s,t+\tau+1}} \qquad [(\text{I}) \text{ and } a_{tt} = 1)]$$

$$= \alpha^{\tau+1}\alpha^{s-(t+\tau+1)} = \alpha^{s-t}.$$

In w_τ, only u_τ is not $\tau - 1$ time separable. Define $v = \alpha^{-\tau}u_\tau$. Then

$$V = \sum v\alpha^t + \sum_{s=0}^{\tau-1} v({}^1y^s, {}^0x^{\tau-1-s})\alpha^{\tau-1-s}$$

is τ time separable and τ-stationary, and $U - V$ is $\tau - 1$-stationary and $\tau - 1$ time separable. By the induction hypothesis there is a $\hat{u}$ such that

$$U - V = a\left(\sum_{t\geqslant\tau-1} \hat{u}({}^{t-(\tau-1)+1}x^t)\right)\beta^t + \sum_{s=0}^{\tau-1} u({}^1y^s, {}^0x^{\tau-1-s})\beta^{\tau-1-s} + b.$$

Hence,

$$U = \sum_{t>\tau} \{a\hat{u}({}^{t-(\tau-1)+1}x^t)\beta^t + v({}^{t-\tau+1}x^t)\alpha^t\}$$

$$+ \sum_{s=0}^{\tau} \{a\hat{u}({}^1y^s, {}^0x^{\tau-2-s})\beta^{\tau-2-s} + v({}^1y^s, {}^0x^{\tau-2-s})\alpha^{\tau-2-s}\},$$

which is τ-stationary and unique in each time period up to an increasing linear transformation only if $\alpha = \beta$.
Hence,

$$U = \sum u({}^{t-\tau+1}x^t)\alpha^t + \sum u({}^1y^s, {}^0x^{\tau-1-s})\alpha^{\tau-1-s}$$

where

$$u({}^{t-\tau+1}x^t) = \hat{u}({}^{t-\tau-2}x^t) + v({}^{t-\tau+1}x^t). \qquad \text{q.e.d.}$$

PROBLEMS

K. Utility over Time I

(i) Let there be a representation

$$U(y(t), t = 0, 1, 2,\ldots) = \sum_{t=0}^{\infty} u_t(y(t)).$$

Show that if there are two subcategories of goods upon which preferences are separable, both over time and between the two subcategories, and preferences restricted to one time period are the same as in another, then

$$U(y(t), t = 0, 1, 2,\ldots) = \sum_{t=0}^{\infty} u(y(t))\alpha_t , \qquad \alpha_t > 0.$$

(ii) When is the rate of time discount, defined as

$$\rho_{t,t+1} = \left[\frac{\partial u_t}{\partial x_i(t)} \Big/ \frac{\partial u_{t+1}}{\partial x_i(t+1)}\right] - 1,$$

constant?

L. Utility over Time II

Let

$$U(x) = \inf_{t \in (0,\infty)} u_t(x(t)).$$

Show that

(i) U is regular whenever u_t is regular.

(ii) U is continuous on line segments whenever both u_t is continuous on line segments and $| u_t(x) - u_t(y)| \leqslant M | x - y |$ for all t.

(iii) U is $\geqslant$-continuous whenever u_t is $\geqslant$-continuous.

M. Utility over Time III

Let $w(x) = \lim_{s\to\infty} \inf_{t>s} u(x(t))$.
Show that

(i) w is regular in uniform convergence whenever u_t is regular,

(ii) w is continuous on line segments whenever both u_t is continuous on line segments and $| u_t(x) - u_t(y)| \leqslant m | x - y |$ for all t.

N. Utility over Time IV

Suppose that preferences are given by maximizing first $w(x)$ in Problem M and then u continuous over time as in Problem L. Under what conditions would outcomes be identical with those under Problem M?

6. Concave Utility Functions

If preferences are weakly convex, the utility function representing them is quasi concave. If they are convex and strictly convex, the utility function is strictly quasi concave. Convexity of preferences says nothing about the possibility of representation by a concave utility function. In fact, convexity of preferences can exist with nonconcavity of utility for all possible representations (Arrow and Enthoven [1961]). As will be seen, separable preferences are representable by a concave and additive utility function if and only if every good is normal (that is, as income increases, the consumption of all goods simultaneously increases (under a competitive price system)).

A concave representation does exist whenever preferences are *homothetic*, that is, when along any line through the origin, marginal rates of substitution are constant.

14 Theorem *If preferences are homothetic, continuous, unsaturated along a ray through the origin, locally unsaturated, and weakly convex, there is exactly the collection of indifference surfaces determined by the marginal rates of substitution, and preferences are represented by a linear homogeneous utility function.*

15 Corollary *If preferences are homothetic, continuous, locally unsaturated, and weakly convex, they are represented by a concave utility function.*

Proof Apply Theorem 6 of Chapter 4. q.e.d.

Proof (of Theorem 14) The indifference surfaces can be derived by considering two goods only, since they can be traced out by several variations of pairs of variables. Hence, the case for two goods only is important.

The main idea of the proof is to consider polar coordinates:

$$y = r \sin \theta, \qquad x = r \cos \theta.$$

An indifference curve is a convex relationship $y = f(x)$ (weak convexity). In polar coordinates, $r = g(\theta)$. Also, convexity gives that df/dx exists almost everywhere, and it equals the marginal rate of substitution, which depends only upon θ (homotheticity):

$$\frac{dy}{dx} = p(\theta), \qquad p(\theta) \text{ nonincreasing.}$$

A function is absolutely continuous if it is the integral of its derivative. Since $y = f(x)$ and $x = f^{-1}(y)$ are convex,

$$r = R(x) = (x^2 + f(x)^2)^{1/2}, \qquad \theta = \Theta(x) = \frac{f(x)}{x}$$

are each 1–1 and absolutely continuous on the curve defined as $y = f(x)$, as are their inverses. (Indeed, they all satisfy a Lipschitz condition.) Hence $r = R\theta^{-1}(\theta)$ is absolutely continuous and the integral of its almost-everywhere derivatives. Also, an elementary computation shows that

$$\frac{dr}{d\theta} = \frac{dR}{dx}\frac{d\Theta^{-1}}{d\theta}$$

so long as $d\theta^{-1}/d\theta$ is defined and nonzero and $dr/d\theta$ is defined, which is true for almost all θ.

These derivatives can be evaluated whenever $dy/dx = p(\theta)$,

$$\frac{dr \sin\theta}{dr \cos\theta} = p(\theta).$$

Let $g = R\Theta^{-1}$. Then

$$\frac{dg(\theta)\sin\theta}{d\theta} = p(\theta)\frac{dg(\theta)\cos\theta}{d\theta}$$

or

$$g'\sin\theta + g\cos\theta = p(\theta)(g'\cos\theta - g\sin\theta),$$

$$g'(\sin\theta + \cos\theta\, p(\theta)) = g(p(\theta)\sin\theta - \cos\theta).$$

If $\sin\theta + \cos\theta\, p(\theta) = 0$, $-p(\theta) = \tan\theta = y/x$. Since $p(\theta)$ is nonincreasing, but $-\tan\theta$ is decreasing in θ, $\theta + \cos\theta\, p(\theta) = 0$ for at most one θ. Hence, for almost all x, by differentiability of θ in $y = f(x)$ and y, for almost all θ,

$$\frac{g'}{g} = \frac{p(\theta)\sin\theta - \cos\theta}{\sin\theta + \cos\theta\, p(\theta)},$$

which is uniquely solved for $\log g = \log r$ by ordinary integration.

Furthermore, starting from different (x, y) but along the same ray, the laws of change of $\log r$ are the same. Hence, for two indifference curves $r(\theta)$ and $r'(\theta)$, $r(\theta)/r'(\theta)$ is everywhere constant.

To return to the n-dimensional case, let $u(k\bar{x}) = k$ for $\bar{x}$ in the unsaturated ray. Also, let $u(x) = k$ if x is indifferent to $k\bar{x}$. This is possible by continuity and the fact that at low values of l, lx is indifferent to some kx, whereas as l increases, the appropriate k increases proportionately. The function u is continuous and represents preferences. Also, u is linear homogeneous, since for $x \neq \bar{x}$, x indifferent to $\bar{x}$, $u(kx) = k$ from above (in the two-dimensional space spanned by 0, x, and $\bar{x}$). q.e.d.

Another concavity result applies to additive utility.

16 Theorem *If $u(x) + u(y)$ is quasi convex and continuous in (x, y), then it is concave.*

Proof

$$2u(\tfrac{1}{2}x + \tfrac{1}{2}y) = u(\tfrac{1}{2}x + \tfrac{1}{2}y) + u(\tfrac{1}{2} + \tfrac{1}{2}x)$$
$$\geqslant \min(u(\tfrac{1}{2}x) + u(\tfrac{1}{2}y), u(\tfrac{1}{2}y) + u(\tfrac{1}{2}x))$$
$$= u(\tfrac{1}{2}x) + u(\tfrac{1}{2}y) \qquad \text{(quasi concavity).}$$

Hence,

$$u(\tfrac{1}{2}x + \tfrac{1}{2}y) \geqslant \tfrac{1}{2}u(\tfrac{1}{2}x) + \tfrac{1}{2}u(\tfrac{1}{2}y).$$

By repetition, it can be shown that

$$u\left(\frac{m}{2^n}x + \frac{2^n - m}{2^n}y\right) \geqslant \frac{m}{2^n}u(x) + \frac{2^n - m}{2^n}u(y).$$

By continuity, $u(tx + (1 - x)y) \geqslant tu(x) + (t - t)u(y)$. q.e.d.

17 Corollary *If $\sum_{t=0}^{\infty} u\alpha^t$ is quasi concave and continuous and $\alpha \geqslant \frac{1}{2}$, then u is concave.*

Proof There are $t_i \neq 0$, $i = 1, 2,\ldots$, such that $\sum \alpha^{t_i} = 1$. Fix $x^{t_i} = y$. Then $u(x) + \sum \alpha^{t_i}u(y) = u(x) + u(y)$ is quasi concave. q.e.d.

UNSOLVED PROBLEM

O. Concavity of Utility

Suppose $u(x) + \alpha u(y)$ is quasi concave, $\alpha > 0$. Is u concave? (See Theorem 16 and also Theorem 36 of Chapter 8.)

7. Differentiable Utility

One of the earliest developments in theoretical economics was the concept of marginal utility, due to Gossen [1854], Marchall [1890], Walras [1874], Menger [1871], and Jevons [1871]. This concept still plays an important role in economic instruction at both the graduate and undergraduate levels, and it is used widely as a tool for applied economics. However, the more abstract theoreticians have tended to avoid arguments based upon marginal utility, both because marginal utility was not solidly grounded on assumptions about consumer preferences and because other arguments seemed more efficient. The purpose of this section and the next is to alleviate the first problem by displaying economically meaningful assumptions under which preferences may be represented by differentiable utility functions.

18 Theorem *If preferences are separable and directional dense, and if for any i, du_i/dx_i exists for some x_i, then u_i, $i = 1, 2,\ldots$, are everywhere differentiable.*

A particular case of Theorem 18 is that in which one of the u_i's is increasing over at least some range of values of x_i.

Proof Consider the equation

$$u_i(\bar{x}_i) + u_j(x_j) = c.$$

Clearly,

$$\frac{du_i}{d\bar{x}_i}\frac{d\bar{x}_i}{dx_j} + \frac{du_j}{dx_j} = 0$$

solves for the derivative du_j/dx_j for different x_j. Similarly,

$$\frac{du_j}{dx_j}\frac{dx_j}{dx_i} + \frac{du_i}{dx_i} = 0$$

solves for du_i/dx_i for $x_i \neq \bar{x}_i$. q.e.d.

For more general preferences, there is no such simple solution. It was shown in Chapter 2 that concave functions of one real variable have continuous derivations almost everywhere.

19 Remark If utility is concave, it is continuously differentiable almost everywhere on any line segment $\langle x, y\rangle$.

An *arc* $\mathscr{A}$ is topological space such that this is a 1–1 function f from [0, 1] onto $\mathscr{A}$ such that both f and f^{-1} are continuous; the number $t \in [0, 1]$ is called a *parameter* of $\mathscr{A}$. Lemma 20 can be applied to such arcs as illustrated in Figure 5.

20 Lemma *If $u(f(t))$ is nondecreasing in t, then uf has derivatives almost everywhere.*

The lemma is due to Lebesgue (Riesz and Sz-Nagy [1955, p. 5]).

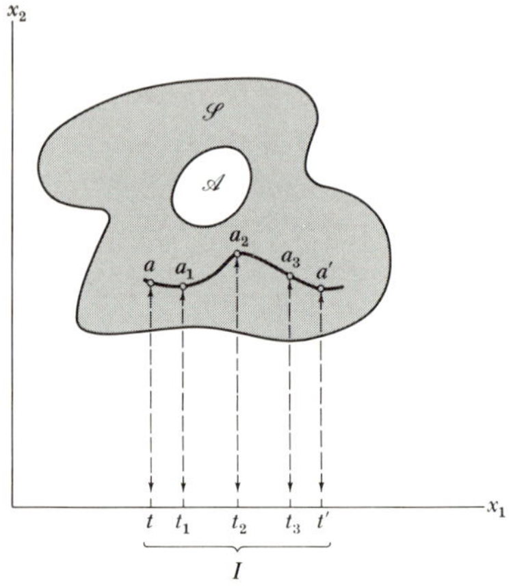

Figure 5

21 Remark If preferences are weakly convex, then utility is nondecreasing in the interval $\{y : y \neq tx + (1 - t)\, \bar{x}, \bar{x}$ maximizing u on set of convex combinations of x and x', $1 \geqslant t \geqslant 0\}$, and is nonincreasing elsewhere. Hence, u is almost everywhere differentiable.

Proof The set of exceptional points is the union of the set of measure zero for the interval of nondecreasing u and the set of measure zero for the interval of nondecreasing u quoted in Lemma 20, together with the point of maximization $\bar{x}$ whose union is the measure zero. q.e.d.

8. Utility Equal to the Integral of Its Derivative

For most purposes, it is not sufficient that the utility function be differentiable almost everywhere on the arc; we must also know that the utility function is the integral of its derivation on the arc. For example, we might argue that the marginal utility on the arc $\mathscr{A}$ with end points a and a' is always zero, and therfore that the difference between the utility levels along the arc is always zero. The argument will be valid only if the utility function is in fact the integral (say, starting from a) of its almost-everywhere derivative—plus the usual constant, namely, the value of the u at the point a. Hence, it is useful to know conditions that ensure that

$$u(f(t)) = u(f(t_0)) + \int_{t_0}^{t} \left(\frac{du}{dt}\right) dt$$

where du/dt is the almost-everywhere derivative.

The function f satisfies a *Lipschitz* condition if $d(f(x), f(y)) \leqslant Kd(x, y)$.

22 Remark If f and u satisfy a Lipschitz condition,

$$u(f(t)) = \int_{t_0}^{t} \frac{duf}{dt}\, ds + u(f(t_0))$$

(Riesz and Sz-Nagy [1955, pp. 50–54]).

The Lipschitz condition on f is a property of the arc chosen. The rest of this section is concerned with finding a utility representation satisfying a Lipschitz condition.

Consider the notion of distance between disjoint sets:

$$d(\mathscr{X}, \mathscr{X}') = \inf\{d(x, x') \mid x \in \mathscr{X},\quad x' \in \mathscr{X}'\}.$$

(If $\mathscr{X} = \{x\}$, $\{\ \}$ is eliminated to write $d(x, \mathscr{X}')$.) Preferences are *uniformly sensitive* if for x and y sufficiently close, there exists a t such that

$$d(x', y') \geqslant t\, d(x, \mathscr{I}(y))$$

for all $x' \in \mathscr{I}(x)$, $y' \in \mathscr{I}(y)$. The meaning of uniform sensitivity is as follows. Consider that a change from x to the preference level of y can be achieved with a certain minimum magnitude (in distance). Then a change from any other x' indifferent to y can be achieved only with movement at least some fraction of the minimum distance necessary from x. The important point is that the fraction does not depend on x and is not dependent on how close y is to x. However, the sensitivity of preferences to the magnitude of a change in position is always limited by the sensitivity of preferences at any given point on the indifference set $\mathscr{I}(x)$.

In Figure 6, preferences are continuous, but not uniformly sensitive. In Figure 6a, the distance between indifference curves $\mathscr{I}_0$, $\mathscr{I}_1$, $\mathscr{I}_2$, $\mathscr{I}_3$, $\mathscr{I}_4$ decreases arbitrarily as we proceed along them in a northwest direction. The ever-closer points along $\mathscr{I}_1$ and $\mathscr{I}_2$ in the northwest direction violate the inequality $d(x', y') > t\, d(y, \mathscr{I}(x))$. Notice that there is no lower bound on $\mathscr{C}$, since $\mathscr{C}$ is taken to be the whole plane. In general, this is not true in economics; what is more, the direction of increase in the preference levels is normally in reverse direction of these bounds. For example, for a consumer, there would be a lower bound on his consumptions, as in Figure 6b, where the consumer evaluates only nonnegative holdings of goods. In this case (Figure 6b), all bundles that do not have a positive amount of both goods are indifferent; as the consumer has more and more of a given good, it takes a smaller and smaller amount of the other good to effect a given increase in preferences. This seems plausible, since we would expect that the worst thing that would happen as a consumer accumulated more and more of a good would be that the function of another good would simply go unfilled, whereupon the additions of that good would lead to increases of preference levels similar to those at smaller amounts of the abundant good. Insofar as there was a substitution of the abundant good in the function normally performed by the other good, it would take *smaller* quantities of the other good to effect a new, higher level of preference.

In any case, the violations of uniform sensitivity illustrated in Figures 6a and 6b are not decisive whenever the consumer's environment makes only a bounded subset of commodity bundles relevant for practical purposes, so that we can restrict our attention to a bounded subset of the plane. A more serious violation of uniform sensitivity appears in Figure 6c, which is similar to Figure 6b except that the consumer need not hold both goods in order to obtain a given level of preference. Here the points $y_1, y_2, \ldots$ move closer to x' more rapidly than do the corresponding points $y^1, y^2, \ldots$ to x. The ratios $|y^i - x'|/|y^i - x|$ tend to zero. Hence, there does not exist a number t giving the inequality $d(x', y') > t\, d(y, \mathscr{I}(x))$, since a smaller and smaller one would be needed for $d(x', y'^n)$ as compared with $d(x, y^n)$, n tending to infinity. In effect, x' represents a commodity bundle of infinitely greater sensitivity of preference than x; again, this case appears pathological.

A set $\mathscr{S}$ is *convex* provided that

$$s_t = ts + (1 - t)s'$$

is in $\mathscr{S}$ whenever s and s' are $0 \leqslant t \leqslant 1$. If $\mathscr{S}$ is metric, then also

$$d(s, s') = d(s, s_t) + d(s_t, s').$$

23 Theorem *Suppose $\mathscr{C}$ is convex, separable, and metric. Then $\mathscr{R}$ is continuous and uniformly sensitive if and only if there exists a function v representing $\mathscr{R}$ such that v satisfies a Lipschitz condition.*

Proof **Sufficiency** Pick a point y and set

$$v(x) = d(\mathscr{R}(y), \mathscr{R}^{-1}(x)) - d(\mathscr{R}(x), \mathscr{R}^{-1}(y)).$$

For each x, at least one of the terms on the right side of the equality is zero. If x and y are fixed, by the continuity of preferences, and if x and z are sufficiently close, then either both x and z are not inferior to y or else both x and z are not superior to y. For definiteness, consider the former case, whereupon

$$|v(x) - v(z)| = |d(\mathscr{R}(x), \mathscr{R}^{-1}(y)) - d(\mathscr{R}(z), \mathscr{R}^{-1}(y))|.$$

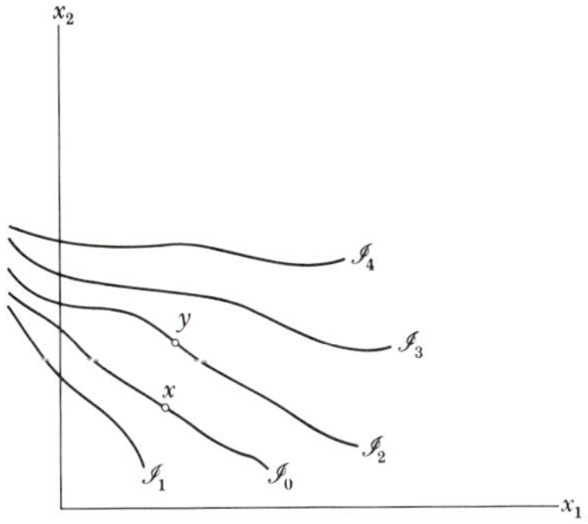

Figure 6a

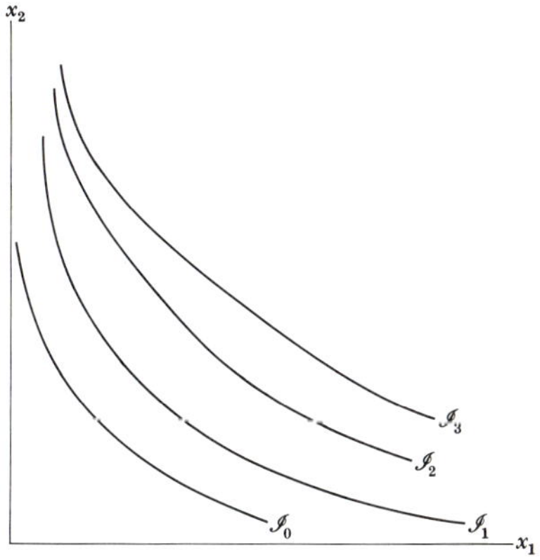

Figure 6b

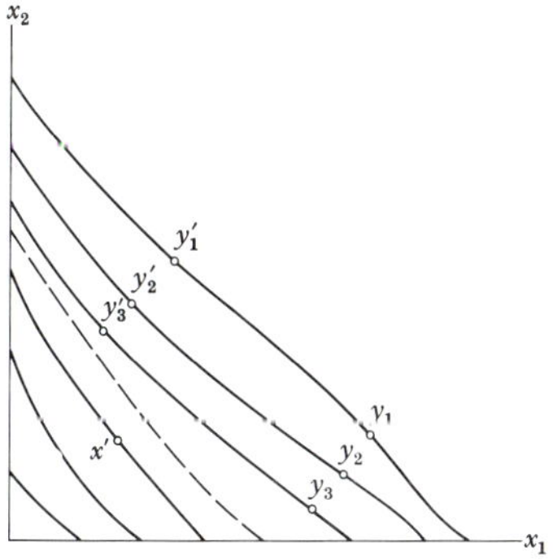

Figure 6c

It can be demonstrated from the continuity of $\mathscr{R}$ and the convexity of $\mathscr{C}$ that for any $x \mathscr{R} y$

$$d(\mathscr{R}(x), \mathscr{R}^{-1}(y)) = d(\mathscr{I}(x), \mathscr{I}(y)).$$

If $x' \in \mathscr{R}(x)$ and $y' \in \mathscr{R}^{-1}(y)$, there are points on the line segment,

$$\langle x', y' \rangle$$

that are in $\mathscr{I}(x)$ and also points that are in $\mathscr{I}(y)$. Since $\mathscr{C}$ is convex, it is connected. Hence, by Theorem 4, there is a utility function that is continuous; by the intermediate value theorem for continuous function, u takes all values between $u(x')$ and $u(y')$ on the line segment; in particular u takes the values $u(x)$ and $u(y)$ at points x'' and y'', respectively.

Now

$$d(x', y') = d(x', x'') + d(x'', y'') + d(y'', y'),$$

whereupon

$$d(x', y') \leqslant d(x'', y'').$$

Hence, $\mathscr{I}(x)$ is always at least as close to $\mathscr{I}(y)$ as is $\mathscr{R}(x)$ to $\mathscr{R}^{-1}(y)$; in fact, the respective pairs are equally close, since

$$\mathscr{I}(x) \subset \mathscr{R}(x) \qquad \text{and} \qquad \mathscr{I}(y) \subset \mathscr{R}^{-1}(y).$$

In conclusion,

$$|\, v(x) - v(z)| = |\, d(\mathscr{I}(x), \mathscr{I}(y)) - d(\mathscr{I}(z), \mathscr{I}(y))|.$$

For any $\varepsilon > 0$, there exists $x' \in \mathscr{I}(x)$, $z' \in \mathscr{I}(y)$ such that

$$|\, v(x) - v(z)| \leqslant d(x', \mathscr{I}(y)) - d(z', \mathscr{I}(y)) + \varepsilon,$$

$$d(x, y) \geqslant d(z', \mathscr{I}(y)) \qquad \text{and} \qquad d(x, y) \geqslant d(x', \mathscr{I}(y))$$

by definition of distance. On the other hand, by choosing $y' \in \mathscr{I}(y)$ appropriately, we get

$$d(z', \mathscr{I}(y)) + \varepsilon \geqslant d(z', y') \qquad \text{and} \qquad d(x, y) \geqslant d(z', y').$$

Of course,

$$d(x', \mathscr{I}(y)) \leqslant d(x', y').$$

Hence,

$$\begin{aligned} |\, v(x) - v(z)| &\leqslant d(x', \mathscr{I}(y)) - d(z', \mathscr{I}(y)) + \varepsilon \\ &\leqslant d(x', y') - d(z', y') + 2\varepsilon \\ &\leqslant d(x', z') + 2\varepsilon \leqslant \frac{1}{t}\, d(x, z) + 2\varepsilon; \end{aligned}$$

the last two inequalities are due to the triangle inequality for distance and uniform sensitivity, respectively. Since ε was arbitrary,

$$|\, v(x) - v(z)| \leqslant \frac{1}{t}\, d(x, z),$$

for x and z sufficiently close, which is the desired Lipschitz condition. Integrability on arcs of finite length (rectifiable arcs) follows from the theory of integration (see, for example, Reisz and Sz-Nagy [1955, pp. 50–54]). Hence, it remains only to prove that v represents $\mathscr{R}$.

If $x \mathscr{R} x'$, then

$$v(x) \geqslant v(x').$$

Suppose $v(x) \geqslant v(x')$. There are two possible cases of x' with respect to y. In the first case, $x' \mathscr{P} y$. By uniform sensitivity, indifference sets are finite distances apart. Therefore, $x \mathscr{P} y$ also, for otherwise, $v(x')$ would be positive and $v(x)$ nonpositive. Consider $\bar{x}$ in $\mathscr{I}(x)$ and $\bar{y}\, \mathscr{I}(y)$. If $x' \mathscr{P} x$, then there exists as t_0 such that

$$\bar{x}_0 = t_0 \bar{x}' + (1 - t_0)\, \bar{y}\, \mathscr{I}\, x.$$

Since there is an ε such that $\mathscr{I}(x)$ and $\mathscr{I}(x')$ are at least ε distance apart, it follows that

$$d(\bar{x}', x_0) > \varepsilon.$$

Also,

$$d(\bar{x}, \bar{y}) = d(\bar{x}, y) + d(\bar{x}, \bar{x}') > d(x, y) + \varepsilon.$$

Therefore, $\mathscr{I}(x')$ is greater in distance from $\mathscr{I}(y)$ than $\mathscr{I}(x)$ is from $\mathscr{I}(y)$ by at least ε. In view of the remarks above, $v(x')$ must exceed $v(x)$ by at least ε, contrary to $v(x) \geqslant u(x')$. In this case, $x \mathscr{R} x'$. In the second case, $y \mathscr{P} x'$ and $y \mathscr{P} x$ whenever $x' \mathscr{P} x$. An exactly parallel argument with that above can be given to demonstrate that $x \mathscr{R} x'$.

Necessity Clearly $\mathscr{R}$ is continuous. Also, if

$$d(v(x), v(y)) < \frac{1}{t}\, d(x, y) \qquad \text{for all} \quad |x - y| < \varepsilon,$$

indifference curves with utility difference $d(v(x), v(y))$ must be at least $td(v(x), v(y))$ apart. Hence, there is uniform sensitivity. q.e.d.

The derivation of v in Theorem 21 is illustrated in Figure 7 for particular x and $\bar{x}$, where

$$v(x) = \varepsilon, \qquad v(\bar{x}) = \varepsilon'.$$

9. A Digression on Utility and Biology

The question arises whether there is some fundamental mechanism by which utility maximization takes place.

Neural mechanisms by which commands of the central nervous system are implemented and influenced by outside factors are one of the

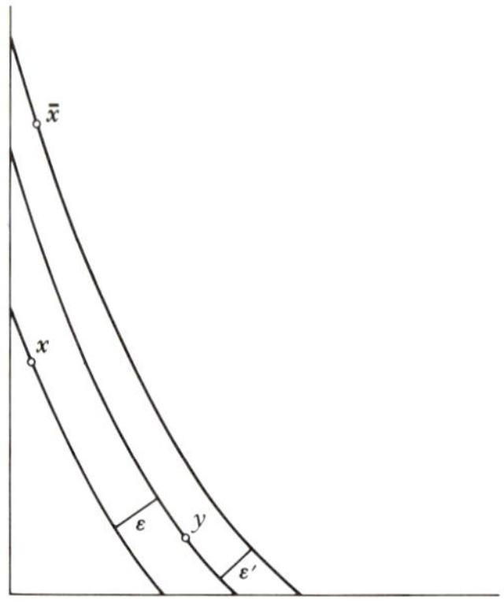

Figure 7

concerns of mathematical biology. Because hedonistic or personal maximizing behavior is strong, some mathematical biologists and psychometricians postulate the existence of a "pleasure center" that is activated by the neurons and is a basis for decisions by the "thinking center." It appears that there is no physiological evidence for the existence of this pleasure center. However, experimental work makes it clear that pleasure maximization, if it in fact exists, is not an automatic process, but rather that it takes place only after experimentation and learning. Hence, the scope of preferences is normally limited both by the range of past experience of the individual and by the individual's capacity to remember and relate. Among other things, this involves a complex of social interrelationships.

If there is a pleasure center then it may be that some sense can be made of cardinal utility as originally postulated by Bentham [1789]. Utility would be measured perhaps by the intensity of excitement of this pleasure center. Given a number of stimuli, $i = 1, 2, \ldots, n$, at intensities x_i, the pleasure center might be activated according to a utility function

$$u(x_1, x_2, \ldots, x_n).$$

In this case, not only would the sign of $\partial u/\partial x_1$ be determined (positive or negative according to whether utility is increasing or decreasing), but the cross partials

$$\frac{\partial^2 u}{\partial x \; \partial x_j}$$

might have a definite meaning. For example, each x_i might yield a quantity of energy $e_i x_i$, and then total utility would be a direct function of total energy

$$u(x_1, x_2, \ldots, x_n) = u\left(\sum_i e_i x_i\right).$$

Then,

$$\frac{\partial u}{\partial x_i} = \frac{du}{de} e_i, \qquad \frac{\partial^2 u}{\partial x_i \, \partial x_j} = \frac{d^2 u}{de^2} e_i e_j, \qquad e = \sum e_i x_i .$$

Consequently, $\partial^2 u/\partial x_i \, \partial x_j$ would have a meaningful sign, dependent $\partial^2 u/\partial e^2$ and on the amount of energy imparted. To further elaborate this point, Rashevsky [1951] suggests that any stimulus causes both excitation and inhibition. If the initial level of intensity of net excitation is E, then a possible equation for the net excitation over time is a solution of the differential equations

$$\frac{d\varepsilon}{dt} = a_1 e(t) - a_0 \varepsilon, \qquad \frac{d\eta}{dt} = b_1 e(t) - b_0 \eta,$$

where $e(t)$ is the quantity of stimulus over time, ε represents excitation, η represents inhibitions, a_0, b_0, a, and b, are constants, varying according to individuals. The time solution for a constant stimulus e is

$$\varepsilon - \eta = E + \left(\frac{a_1}{a_0} e^{-a_0 t} - \frac{b_1}{b_0} e^{-b_0 t}\right) e.$$

If we set utility at time t equal to

$$u = \int_{s=0}^{t} (\varepsilon - \eta) \, ds,$$

namely, the "sum" of excitation in time t, then

$$\frac{du}{de} = \int_0^t \left(\frac{a_1}{a_0} e^{-a_0 t} - \frac{b_1}{b_0} e^{-b_0 t}\right) ds$$

and

$$\frac{d^2 u}{de^2} = 0.$$

More complicated interactions lead to the same equation

$$\frac{\partial^2 u}{\partial x_i \, \partial x_j} = 0,$$

as for example in the case where the excitations and inhibitons from the different stimuli reinforce each other and are accounted for (Problem Q) This is the result of the adoption of a simple linear system and the condition that $\partial^2 u/\partial x^2 = 0$ would be regarded as unsatisfactory by most economists.

In a more realistic system, there would be a threshold effect; namely, an upper limit to ecstasy and a lower limit to pain. The differential equations of excitation and inhitition would be forced to be nonlinear in order to allow this.

For example, the net excitation might be merely dampened by the function $f(\varepsilon - \eta)$, so that

$$u = \int_0^t f(\varepsilon - \eta)\, ds.$$

Then,

$$\frac{\partial u}{\partial x_i} = \int_0^t \frac{df}{d\varepsilon - \eta} \frac{d\varepsilon - \eta}{de} \frac{\partial e}{\partial x_i}\, ds = \int_0^t \frac{df}{d\varepsilon - \eta} \frac{d\varepsilon - \eta}{de} e_i\, ds$$

Also,

$$\frac{\partial u}{\partial x_i\, \partial x_j} = \int_0^t \frac{d^2 f}{d(\varepsilon - \eta)^2} \left(\frac{d\varepsilon - \eta}{de}\right)^2 e_i e_j\, ds + \int_0^t \frac{d^2 \varepsilon - \eta}{de^2} \frac{df}{d\varepsilon - \eta} e_i e_j\, ds.$$

Since,

$$\frac{d^2 \varepsilon - \eta}{de^2} = 0,$$

the last term is zero. Then,

$$\frac{\partial u}{\partial x_i\, \partial x_j} = \int_0^t \frac{d^2 f}{d(\varepsilon - \eta)^2} \left(\frac{d\varepsilon - \eta}{de}\right)^2 e_i e_j\, ds$$

Normally, for $\varepsilon - \eta > 0$,

$$\frac{d^2 f}{d(\varepsilon - \eta)^2} < 0,$$

as in the case for f illustrated in Figure 8. Therefore,

$$\frac{\partial^2 u}{\partial x_i\, \partial x_j} < 0.$$

In particular,

$$\frac{\partial^2 u}{\partial x_i^2} < 0,$$

which is the law of diminishing marginal utility.

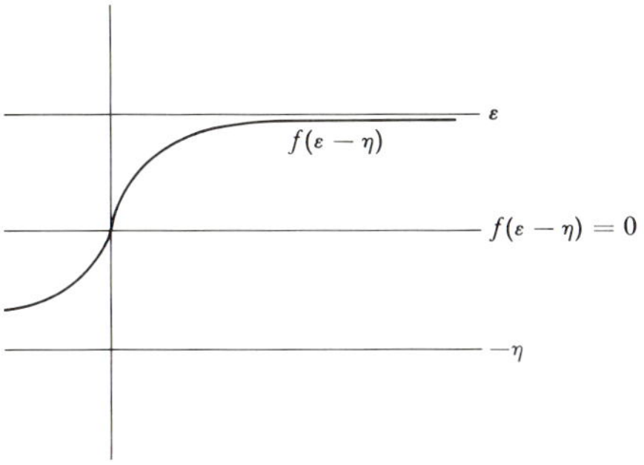

Figure 8

In Problems Q–S, various forms of utility functions are derived for multiple stimuli that are generally quasi concave and display diminishing marginal utility. We can think of each stimulus as being a different commodity, whereupon there is a utility representation with a meaningful derivative. Furthermore, under very stringent circumstances it can be shown that the matrix of partial derivatives $\partial^2 u/\partial x^2$ has positive off-diagonals, where x is the vector of the quantity of commodities. This is similar to the form of the utility function postulated by the neoclassicists. One essential point here is the dominance of excitatory effects everywhere. Otherwise,

$$\frac{\partial^2 u}{\partial x_i \, \partial x_j}, \qquad i \neq j,$$

is not positive, even as we might expect whenever commodities in general have both desirable and undesirable effects.

Several lessons can be obtained from such exercises on simple linear models of neural stimulation. By the hypothesis of a pleasure center, we can derive a utility function in an obvious manner. To state this in a different way, the neural mechanism discussed here (which is itself used in biophysics) leads to properties long assumed by economists (Dhrymes [1967]). Basic biological–psychological principles can be used to derive axioms for consumers rich in economic implications, perhaps as for physics in the case of production. (See Chapter 8, Corollary 20, or Dhrymes [1967] for analysis of the case $\partial^2 u/\partial x_i \, \partial x_j > 0$.)

PROBLEMS

P. Independent Preferences

Let utility to i be given by

$$u_i = a_{ii} v_i(x_i) + a_{ij} u_j\,, \qquad j \neq i, \quad i, j = 1, 2.$$

When are interdependent preferences solved as functions of x_1 and x_2?

This problem was suggested and solved by Theodore Bergstrom.

Q. Multiple Stimuli I

Let ε be a vector of n components representing the intensities of excitation of n stimuli, respectively. Let η be a vector of n components representing the inhibition of n stimuli. Let the stimuli be interconnected in the sense that the excitation of one stimulus leass to a repression of or inhibition of the other stimuli. Then

$$\frac{d\varepsilon}{dt} = a_{11}\varepsilon + a_{12}\eta + b_1 e(t), \qquad \frac{d\eta}{dt} = a_{21}\varepsilon + a_{22}\eta + b_2 e(t)$$

where a_{ij} are $n \times n$ matrices.

Define

$$A = \begin{bmatrix} a_{11} & a_{12} \\ a_{21} & a_{22} \end{bmatrix} \quad \text{and} \quad b(t) = \begin{bmatrix} b_1 & e(t) \\ b_2 & e(t) \end{bmatrix}.$$

The equation is

$$\frac{d}{dt}\begin{pmatrix} \varepsilon \\ \eta \end{pmatrix} = A\begin{pmatrix} \varepsilon \\ \eta \end{pmatrix} + b(t).$$

Suppose A^{-1} exists. Let

$$u(t) = \int_0^t \left[\sum_{i=1}^{n} c_i(\varepsilon_i - \eta_i)\right] ds.$$

Evaluate the second partial derivative with respect to $e_i(t)$ for the case where the b_i are positive diagonal matrices.

R. Multiple Stimuli II

Let $u(t)$ in Problem Q be altered to

$$v(t) = \int_0^t r\left[\sum_{i=1}^{n} c_i(\varepsilon_i - \eta_i)\right] ds$$

where r is a concave function. This includes the case of complementary stimuli. Suppose that A, b_1, and b_2 are nonnegative, so that all stimuli are reinforcing in both their excitation and inhibition effects.

1. Show that $\partial\varepsilon/\partial e > 0$, $\partial\eta/\partial e > 0$.
2. Show that $\partial^2\varepsilon/\partial e^2 = 0$, $\partial^2\eta/\partial e^2 = 0$.

3. Show that $\partial^2 v/\partial e^2$ is an $n \times n$ negative semidefinite matrix for concave v. (Hint: Compute $x(\partial^2 v/\partial e^2)\, x$ for arbitrary x or else show directly that v is concave in e.)

S. Multiple Stimuli III

In Problems Q and R, let $e(t)$ be a vector, $u(e(t))$ be

$$\int_0^t v(c_1(\varepsilon_1 - \eta_1), \ldots, c_n(\varepsilon_n - \eta_n))\, ds,$$

where v is concave in each variable. This allows for substitutable stimuli wherever v is strictly concave.

1. Show that v is concave in $e(t)$.
2. Consider $v(y)$, $y_i = c_i(\varepsilon_i - \eta_i)$. Let $\partial^2 v/\partial y_i\, \partial y_j$ have positive off-diagonals and suppose there are no inhibitory effects, so that v is not dependent on η. When will $\partial^2 v/\partial e^2$ have positive off-diagonals and a strictly positive vector x for which $(\partial^2 v/\partial e^2)\, x$ is nonpositive?

7

Probability

Decisions made in the face of uncertainty pervade the life of every individual and organization. — Reasoning is commonly associated with logic, but it is obvious that the implications of what is ordinarily called logic are meager indeed when uncertainty is to be faced.

Leonard Savage
in THE FOUNDATIONS OF STATISTICS, 1954, p. 6
Reprinted with permission from Wiley, New York

1. Qualitative Probabilities

Probabilities appear in Section 7 of Chapter 3 and will be used in Chapters 10 and 11. Underlying these probabilities is the belief of a consumer or firm about the likelihood of events. This chapter derives personal probability from preferences between consumptions that are contingent on uncertain events. A byproduct is a utility representation linear in probabilities.

A linear utility theory was first presented by von Neumann and Morgenstern [1944]. Personal probability was pioneered by Ramsey [1950], de Finetti [1937], and Savage [1954]. For example, under very reasonable rationality assumptions, Savage [1954] showed that sets of events can be compared by a probability measure. Contrary to the views of Knight [1921] and Shackle [1949], Savage held that in the process of decision making, there is no distinction between risk and supposedly unmeasurable uncertainty.

In this section conditions are listed under which we can say that one event is more probable than another. In Sections 2 and 3, a probability measure is derived together with von Neumann–Morgenstern utility. Section 4 presents a rule for changing probabilities after the occurrence of previously uncertain events.

A very good general approach to uncertainty is set forth by Arrow [1953] and Debreu [1960], whereby commodities are dated according to their time of occurrence.

In this context, the widely used property of convexity of preference implies risk-averting behavior. To see this, suppose there is a commodity (for example, money) that is to be given in two different quantities with probability $\frac{1}{2}$ for each of the two alternative quantities (depending perhaps on the flip of a coin). In Figure 1, a point (q_1, q_2) indicates that q_1 will be given with probability $\frac{1}{2}$, q_2 with probability $\frac{1}{2}$. Indifference curves have been drawn to show the preference ordering of the paired quantities to be offered in our coin-flipping lottery. For example, there is indifference between a lottery offering (q_1, q_2) and one offering (q_1', q_2'). The indifference curves are symmetric around the 45° line since the chance (q, q') is the same as (q', q). The slopes of the indifference curves are the marginal rates of substitution, and by their symmetry they must equal -1 at the 45° line. By weak convexity of preferences, an indifference curve bounds the perpendicular to the 45° line and curves in the direction toward higher level sets. This means that points along a perpendicular are no better (in utility) than the point at the intersection of the perpendicular with the 45° line. This is the desired proposition, since the point at the intersection gives, say, q^* with probability $\frac{1}{2}$ and q^* with probability $\frac{1}{2}$, that is, q^* with certainty, while the perpendicular has the equation $\frac{1}{2}q_1 + \frac{1}{2}q_2 = q^*$, that is, the expected value of these points is exactly q^*. Hence, the points of the same expected value as q^*, but offering uncertainty as to the possible outcome, are no better than q^* with certainty and, in fact, by the quasi concavity of utility, there is no improvement at all as we move along the line of constant expected value (that is, the perpendicular to the 45° line) away from the point giving q^* with certainty. This means that no risk-loving behavior is allowed over any range. Actually, in Figure 1 there is risk aversion with no risk neutrality.

Experiments by Ellsberg [1961] and Fellner [1961] indicate that

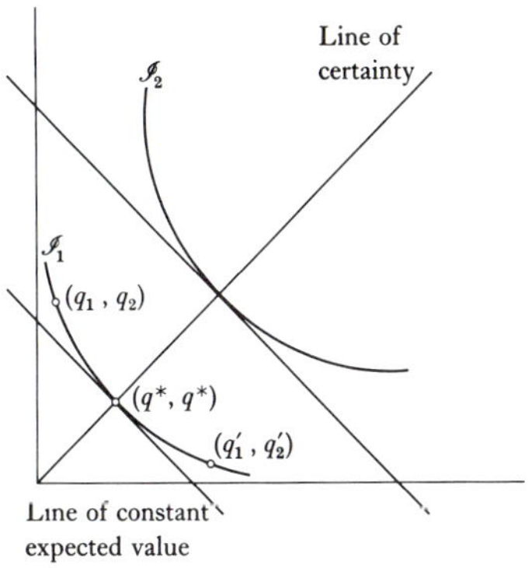

Figure 1

individuals do not always act in accordance with the law of maximizing expected utility according to a computation of objective probabilities, as in drawing black and white balls from urns. Experiments by Yaari [1965] indicate that even in these instance, preferences appear to be convex, so that classical economic theory applies. These experiments tend to support the avoidance of probability and expected utility and complete dependence on the Arrow–Debreu approach. Nevertheless, the latter approach to uncertainty has so far been insufficient for the theory of conflict and bargaining.

Choice under uncertainty leads to a topological space of *consequences* $\mathscr{C}$. Some subsets of a set $\mathscr{N}$ of *states of the world* form a Boolean algebra of *admissible events*:

$$m \subset 2^{\mathscr{N}}.$$

The space $\mathscr{F}$ of consumptions or choices contains the *simple set functions*

$$f : m \rightarrow \mathscr{C}$$

for which

$$f(\mathscr{N}_i) = c_i, \qquad c_i \in \mathscr{C},$$

where $(\mathscr{N}_i, i = 1,..., n)$ is a finite decomposition of $\mathscr{N}$ for which

$$\mathscr{N}_i \in m.$$

(If n above is countable infinity, it is said that f is a *σ-set function.*) An ordering is defined

$$\mathscr{R} \subset \mathscr{F} \times \mathscr{F}$$

which is the *preference relation*

$$(\mathscr{R}(f) = \{f' \mid (f', f) \in \mathscr{R}\}, \qquad \mathscr{R}^{-1} = \{(f, f') \mid (f', f) \in \mathscr{R}\}.)$$

The relation $\mathscr{R}$ is restricted to $\mathscr{C}$ by identifying $\mathscr{C}$ with the simple functions on the trivial decomposition $\mathscr{N}$ in the obvious way. The relation $\mathscr{R}$ is *monotone* if for a change of f to f' on $\mathscr{N}_i$ alone, from

$$f(\mathscr{N}_i) = c_i \qquad \text{to} \qquad f'(\mathscr{N}_i) = c_i' ,$$

$$c_i' \mathscr{R} c_i \qquad \text{implies} \qquad f' \mathscr{R} f.$$

Equivalantly, $\mathscr{R}$ is monotone if for f and g on the same decomposition,

$$f \mathscr{R} g \qquad \text{whenever} \qquad f(\mathscr{N}_i) \mathscr{R} g(\mathscr{N}_i) \qquad \text{for all} \quad i.$$

The relation $\mathscr{R}$ is *neutral* if for f and g defined on the same decomposition, a switching of outcomes between two events leads to an ordering of the new alternative in relation to the old, dependent only on the preference between the two outcomes charged. Formally, if

$$f(\mathscr{N}_i) = c_i , \qquad f(\mathscr{N}_j) = c_j , \qquad f(\mathscr{N}_k) = f'(\mathscr{N}_k)$$
$$f'(\mathscr{N}_i) = c_j , \qquad f'(\mathscr{N}_j) = c_i ,$$

for

$$k \neq i, j \qquad \text{and} \qquad c_i \mathscr{R} c_j ,$$

and for

$$g(\mathscr{N}_i) = \bar{c}_i , \qquad g(\mathscr{N}_j) = \bar{c}_j , \qquad g(\mathscr{N}_k) = g'(\mathscr{N}_k)$$
$$g'(\mathscr{N}_i) = \bar{c}_j , \qquad g'(\mathscr{N}_j) = \bar{c}_i ,$$

for

$$k \neq i, j \qquad \text{and} \qquad \bar{c}_i \mathscr{R} \bar{c}_j ,$$

then

$$f \mathscr{R} f' \qquad \text{iff} \qquad g \mathscr{R} g'.$$

Here $\mathscr{R}$ is *independent* if events themselves do not influence the preference relation, but only the consequences associated with them; that is, $\mathscr{R}$ is independent if

$$g(\mathscr{N}_i) = g'(\mathscr{N}_i), \qquad g(\mathscr{N}_j) = g'(\mathscr{N}_j), \qquad g(\mathscr{N}_k) = f(\mathscr{N}_k) \qquad \text{for} \quad k \neq i, j,$$
$$f(\mathscr{N}_i) = f'(\mathscr{N}_i), \qquad f(\mathscr{N}_j) = f'(\mathscr{N}_j), \qquad g'(\mathscr{N}_j) = f'(\mathscr{N}_j) \qquad \text{for} \quad k \neq i, j,$$

implies that

$$g \mathscr{R} f \qquad \text{iff} \qquad g' \mathscr{R} f'.$$

(This is the *sure thing principle* of Savage.)

Whenever $\mathscr{R}$ is neutral, it is possible to define the *probability relation* $\mathscr{Q}$ on m as

$$\text{“}(\mathscr{N}_1, \mathscr{N}_2) \in \mathscr{Q} \qquad \text{iff} \quad f \mathscr{R} g$$

whenever

$$f(\mathscr{N}_1) = g(\mathscr{N}_2) = c, \qquad f(\sim\mathscr{N}_1) = g(\sim\mathscr{N}_2) = c', \qquad c \mathscr{R} c'.\text{”}$$

In other words, $\mathscr{N}_1$ is at least as probable as $\mathscr{N}_2$ if the consumer prefers a "bet" on $\mathscr{N}_1$ to one on $\mathscr{N}_2$.

1 Remark The probability relation $\mathscr{Q}$ is reflexive and complete whenever $\mathscr{R}$ is neutral; $\mathscr{Q}$ is transitive whenever $\mathscr{R}$ is independent.

It is said that there is a *random device* if for every finite decomposition $(\mathscr{N}_i, i = 1,..., n)$ there is a split $(\bar{\mathscr{N}}_i, i = 1,..., 2n)$

$$\mathscr{N}_i = \bigcup_{k=0,1} \mathscr{N}_{i+nk}, \qquad \bar{\mathscr{N}}_i \cap \bar{\mathscr{N}}_{i+n} = \varnothing,$$

such that

$$g \mathscr{R} f \qquad \text{and} \qquad f \mathscr{R} g$$

whenever

$$\begin{aligned} f(\bar{\mathscr{N}}_j) &= c_j, & j &= 1,..., 2n, \\ g(\bar{\mathscr{N}}_j) &= c_j, & j &\neq i + nk, \quad k = 0, 1, \\ g(\bar{\mathscr{N}}_{i+nk}) &= c_{i+\pi_i(k)n}, & k &= 0, 1, \end{aligned}$$

where π_i is any permutation of $\{0, 1\}$.

In effect, it makes no difference which of the two $\bar{\mathscr{N}}_{i+nk}$'s leads to the c_i's so long as each is attached to one event. An example of a random device would be the flip of a "fair" coin, which would divide events up into two "equivalent" parts. In the context of personal probability, to postulate a random device is a restriction that will be weakened in Section 3.

An example of a preference relation $\mathscr{R}$ and a probability relation $\mathscr{Q}$ is derivable from the neoclassical utility function

$$u(f) = \sum_{i=1}^{n} f(\mathscr{N}_i) \int_{x \in \mathscr{N}_i} q(x)\, dx$$

whenever $\mathscr{N}$ is represented by the interval $(-\infty, \infty)$ and f is continuous. Formally,

$$(f, g) \in \mathscr{R} \qquad \text{iff} \qquad u(f) \geqslant ug$$

and

$$(\mathcal{N}_1, \mathcal{N}_2) \in \mathcal{Q} \qquad \text{iff} \qquad \int_{x\in\mathcal{N}_1} q(x)\,dx \geqslant \int_{x\in\mathcal{N}_2} q(x)\,dx.$$

Clearly, $\mathcal{R}$ is an ordering. It is continuous on finite decompositions since

$$u(f^m) = \sum_{i=1}^{n} f^m(\mathcal{N}_i) \int_{x\in\mathcal{N}_i} q(x)\,dx$$

tends to

$$u(f) = \sum_{i=1}^{n} f(\mathcal{N}_i) \int_{x\in\mathcal{N}_i} q(x)\,dx$$

whenever $f^m(\mathcal{N}_i)$ tends to $f(\mathcal{N}_i)$ for $m = 1, 2, \ldots.$ It is σ-continuous since $\int_{x\in\mathcal{N}} q(x)\,dx$ is σ-additive on $(-\infty, \infty)$. It is easy to verify that $\mathcal{R}$ is monotone, neutral, and independent, and there is a random device.

The independence of $\mathcal{R}$ has been especially controversial. Without it, it appears that there will be no probability measure but only a probability relation. Assume that the individual prefers c to c' and that there are two mutually exclusive events $\mathcal{A}$ and $\mathcal{B}$— either $\mathcal{A}$ happens or $\mathcal{B}$ happens, but not both. Let there be a contest with two prizes:

Prize 1 (get c if $\mathcal{A}$ occurs, and get c' if $\mathcal{B}$ occurs).

Prize 2 (get c' if $\mathcal{A}$ occurs, and get c if $\mathcal{B}$ occurs), $\qquad c\,\mathcal{P}\,c'$.

If the individual chooses prize 1 over prize 2, then it is said that he regards event $\mathcal{A}$ as more probable than event $\mathcal{B}$. It is assumed that preference of prize 1 over prize 2 is invariant to changes in the prizes c and c' as long as c is still preferred to c'.

Let $c_{\mathcal{A}}$ be a prize of c if $\mathcal{A}$ occurs, $c'_{\mathcal{B}}$ be a prize of c' if $\mathcal{B}$ occurs. Then the combined prize

$$(c_{\mathcal{A}}, c'_{\mathcal{B}})$$

can be compared to

$$(c_{\mathcal{C}}, c'_{\mathcal{D}})$$

where the world is divided into $\mathcal{A}$ and $\mathcal{B}$ and into $\mathcal{C}$ and $\mathcal{D}$. The sure thing principle says that we can change c to c' on events common to $\mathcal{A}$ and $\mathcal{C}$ without affecting the preference relations between the two prizes.

As an example, consider the Fellner–Ellsberg [1961] experiment (and consequent paradox):

Assume that there are two urns. An individual is told that one urn contains an equal number of white balls and black balls and that the other contains an uncertain number of white and black balls. Experience has shown that individuals treat the probability of drawing a black ball from either urn as $\frac{1}{2}$. Yet experience has also shown that given a choice of which urn they wish to bet on, people will pick the first urn with the known number of balls, even though they regard the probability of drawing a ball of a given color from either urn as equal. This violates the sure thing principle.

The reason is seen as follows. Let

$$\mathscr{A} - \text{black ball out of 50–50 urn}$$
$$\mathscr{B} = \text{white ball out of 50–50 urn}$$
$$\mathscr{C} = \text{black ball out of unknown urn}$$
$$\mathscr{D} = \text{white ball out of unknown urn.}$$

Next, consider the compound events

$$\mathscr{A} \text{ and } \mathscr{C},$$
$$\mathscr{A} \text{ and } \mathscr{D},$$
$$\mathscr{B} \text{ and } \mathscr{C},$$
$$\mathscr{B} \text{ and } \mathscr{D}.$$

Then by virtue of the sure thing principle,

$$(c_{\mathscr{A}\text{and}\mathscr{C}}, c_{\mathscr{A}\text{and}\mathscr{D}}, c'_{\mathscr{B}\text{and}\mathscr{C}}, c'_{\mathscr{B}\text{and}\mathscr{D}}) = (c_{\mathscr{A}}, c'_{\mathscr{B}})$$

is preferred to

$$(c'_{\mathscr{A}\text{and}\mathscr{C}}, c_{\mathscr{A}\text{and}\mathscr{D}}, c'_{\mathscr{B}\text{and}\mathscr{C}}, c_{\mathscr{B}\text{and}\mathscr{D}}) = (c_{\mathscr{C}}, c'_{\mathscr{D}})$$

if and only if

$$(c_{\mathscr{A}\text{and}\mathscr{C}}, c'_{\mathscr{A}\text{and}\mathscr{D}}, c_{\mathscr{B}\text{and}\mathscr{C}}, c_{\mathscr{B}\text{and}\mathscr{D}}) = (c_{\mathscr{A}}, c'_{\mathscr{B}}),$$

which is a contradiction, since then $(c_{\mathscr{C}}, c'_{\mathscr{D}})$ is indifferent to $(c'_{\mathscr{C}}, c_{\mathscr{D}})$ and $(c_{\mathscr{A}}, c'_{\mathscr{B}})$ is indifferent to $(c'_{\mathscr{C}}, c_{\mathscr{D}})$.

One explanation of the paradox is that the individual simply is a poor computer and does not know his own mind. For example, whatever the number of balls in the unknown urn, by flipping a coin in order to decide on choosing black or white, the individual can obtain a probability of $\frac{1}{2}$ of winning. (If x is the number of black balls and y the number of white balls, the probability of winning out of the unknown urn is

$$\begin{aligned}&\text{(probability of choosing black)} \times \text{(probability of black)}\\&\qquad + \text{(probability of choosing white)} \times \text{(probability of white)}\\&= \frac{1}{2}\frac{x}{x+y} + \frac{1}{2}\frac{y}{x+y} = \frac{1}{2}.)\end{aligned}$$

Even if the player makes a bad guess about the probabilities in the urn with unknown probability, he can use the random device, provided he thinks of doing so.

2. Derivation of Probability Measures

A *probability measure* q on $\mathcal{N}$ is a measure for which

(i) $q(\mathcal{N}_i) \geqslant 0 \quad$ for $\mathcal{N}_i \subset \mathcal{N}$,

(ii) $q(\mathcal{N}) = 1$.

Utility is *linear* in q if

$$u(x_{\mathcal{N}_i}, i = 1,\ldots, n) = \sum_{i=1}^{n} v(x_{\mathcal{N}_i})\, q(\mathcal{N}_i).$$

2 Theorem *Let $\mathcal{R}$ be a nontrivial ordering, representable by a utility function on the simple set functions from a Boolean algebra m of subsets of $\mathcal{N}$ to $\mathcal{C}$ and continuous in utility of the consequences on an event $\mathcal{N}$. If $\mathcal{R}$ is continuous on finite decompositions, σ-continuous, monotone, neutral, and independent, and there is a random device, then $\mathcal{R}$ is representable by a utility function u linear on a probability measure q on m (representing $\mathcal{Q}$). The measure q is unique and u is unique up to a linear increasing transformation. If u is quasi concave, it is concave on $\mathcal{C}$.*

The linear utility is like that derived by von Neumann and Morgenstern [1944] for objective probabilities. In effect, Theorem 2 combines subjective and objective probabilities such that the random device gives a procedure for computing objective ones. Since the same probability measure applies to objective and subjective probabilities, the utility must be linear in both. What is more, under risk aversion, von Neumann–Morgenstern utility is concave.

It is possible that bets with supposedly objective odds are not so regarded by consumers. For a small return, people will often refuse to take a fair risk. For instance, if the probability of winning a bet of \$10 is $\frac{1}{2}$, they will regard this as inferior to gaining \$5 with certainty. Alternatively, if the payoff is very large, people are often willing to accept unfair risks. Friedman and Savage [1948] explained the latter fact by presuming that the utility function of money does not display concavity over its entire range. Yaari [1965] conducted an experiment to disprove this. He showed that instead people figure their odds differently because they attribute to the probabilities subjective properties, which appear in the utility function as probabilities that the bet does not possess. In terms of Figure 1, they do not necessarily agree with an objective observer, to whom choices are symmetric. In effect, we must not jump to equate the "cardinal" linear utility with some objective phenomenon. We must preserve an ordinalist spirit. A contrary view is represented by the hypothesis of Theorem 2, which measures subjective probabilities against a random device of known probabilities. We would expect the bets of lotteries with well-known odds to evoke some general agreement with the odds makers, who themselves make only favorable bets. Therefore, they at least should not bet at unfavorable odds.

Proof Consider the simple set function

$$\bar{f}((\mathcal{N}) = c, \qquad \bar{f}(\sim\mathcal{N}) = \hat{c}.$$

Then apply Theorem 9 of Chapter 6 to $u(c)$ and $u(\hat{c})$ to obtain

$$u(\bar{f}) = u_{\mathcal{N}}(c) + u_{\sim\mathcal{N}}(\hat{c})$$

(splitting, independence, and nontriviality imply separability). Note that $u_{\mathcal{N}}$ and $u_{\sim\mathcal{N}}$ represent the same preferences (montonicity and neutrality). Of course, $u_{\mathcal{N}}$ is additive over splittings of $\mathcal{N}$, as is $u_{\sim\mathcal{N}}$ over splittings of $\sim\mathcal{N}$. Also, either one or the other or possibly both are nonconstant since u is nonconstant. Without loss of generality, assume $u_{\sim\mathcal{N}}$ nontrivial. Therefore, they are linear increasing transformations of each other,

$$u_{\mathcal{N}} = au_{\sim\mathcal{N}} + b, \qquad a \geqslant 0.$$

If $a = 0$, define

$$q(\mathcal{N}) = 0, \qquad a(\sim\mathcal{N}) = \frac{a}{1+a}.$$

(Obviously, the definition of q is invariant to increasing linear transformation on u, which proves its uniqueness for set-additive u.) Note that for $u(c) > u(\hat{c})$, and $\bar{f}(\mathcal{N}) = c, \bar{f}(\sim\mathcal{N}) = c$,

$$\begin{aligned} u(\bar{f}) &= \frac{u(c) - b}{1 + a} + a\left(\frac{u(\hat{c}) - b}{1 + a}\right) + b \\ &= \frac{u(c)}{1 + a} + \frac{a}{1 + a} u(\hat{c}) \\ &= q(\bar{\mathcal{N}})\, u(c) + q(\sim\bar{\mathcal{N}})\, u(\hat{c}). \end{aligned}$$

In particular, if $\bar{\bar{f}}$ is obtained from the definition of $\bar{f}$ by substitution of $\bar{\bar{\mathcal{N}}}$ for $\bar{\mathcal{N}}$, then $\bar{\bar{\mathcal{N}}}\ \mathcal{Q}\ \bar{\mathcal{N}}$ if and only if $u(\bar{\bar{f}}) \geqslant u(\bar{f})$ if and only if $q(\bar{\mathcal{N}}) \geqslant q(\bar{\bar{\mathcal{N}}})$. By Theorem 9 of Chapter 6, u is unique up to a linear increasing transformation and σ-additive.

For the last sentence of the theorem, apply Theorem 16 of Chapter 6 and the linearity of u in probabilities. q.e.d.

The function f is a *σ-set function* if for $\mathcal{N}_1, \mathcal{N}_2, \ldots$ disjoint,

$$\bigcup_{i=1}^{\infty} \mathcal{N}_i = \mathcal{N}, \qquad f(\mathcal{N}_i) = c_i\,.$$

3 Remark Under the conditions of Theorem 2, if $\mathcal{F}$ contains the σ-set functions, u is bounded.

A version of the corollary appears in Blackwell and Girschick [1954].

Proof Otherwise we would devise a form of the *St. Petersburg paradox* whereby

$$u(c_i) > \frac{i}{q(\mathcal{N}_i)}$$

and therefore, for $\mathcal{N}_1, \mathcal{N}_2, \ldots$ disjoint,

$$\bigcup_{i=1}^{\infty} \mathcal{N}_i = \mathcal{N},$$

f defined as

$$f(\mathcal{N}_i) = c_i\,, \qquad u(f) = \sum q(\mathcal{N}_i)\, u(c_i) > \sum i \to \infty.$$

Similarly, for negative $u(c_i)$, let

$$u(c_i) < -\frac{i}{q(\mathcal{N}_i)}\,. \qquad \text{q.e.d.}$$

If it is also true that $\mathscr{m}$ is a measure space, then utility is representable by an integral (Theorem 11 of Chapter 6).

4 Theorem *If*

(i) *$\mathscr{R}$ is continuous on utility of consequences, on simple set functions, and on finite decompositions, σ-continuous, monotone, neutral, and independent, and*

(ii) *$\mathscr{F}$ contains the σ-set functions and the simple set functions are dense in $\mathscr{F}$,*

(iii) *there is a random device,*

then there is a u unique up to a linear increasing transformation such that

$$U(f) = \int_{\mathscr{N}} u(f(x))\, d\mu(x)$$

represents preference, where μ is the probability measure.

If also

(iv) *changes in $(x_\alpha, \alpha \in \mathscr{N})$, $\mathscr{N}$ a set of measure zero, lead to no changes in rankings under $\mathscr{R}$, then*

$$U(f) = \int_{\mathscr{N}} u(f(x))(d\mu/dx)\, dx.$$

Of course, $d\mu/dx$ is a function that is the probability density function on $x \in \mathscr{N}$. The following theorem is incidentally true.

5 Theorem *If a relation $\mathscr{R}$ is representable by utility linear in the probability measure $q(\mathscr{N})$, $\mathscr{N} \in \mathscr{m}$, then $\mathscr{R}$ is neutral, monotone, and independent.*

As a last matter, we consider probability in the absence of the splitting axiom. If it is assumed that $\mathscr{m}$ has a finite number of members, $\mathscr{N}$ can be decomposed into subsets $\mathscr{N}_i \in \mathscr{m}$, $i = 1,..., n$, such that for every $\mathscr{N} \in \mathscr{m}$ there is an index set $\mathscr{I}$ such that

$$\mathscr{N} = \bigcup_{i \in \mathscr{I}} \mathscr{N}_i .$$

$(\mathscr{N}_i, i = 1,..., n)$ is called the *minimal decomposition.*

6 Theorem *If each $\mathscr{N}$ in the minimal decomposition (with three or more members) of a finite set $\mathscr{m}$ is equivalent under the probability relation $\mathscr{Q}$, $\mathscr{R}$ continuous in utility of consequences of simple set functions, neutral,* *and independent (there is no need to assume monotonocity), then there exists a utility representation of $\mathscr{R}$ linear in a (unique) probability measure $q_{\mathscr{N}}$, $\mathscr{N} \in m$. The utility is unique up to an increasing transformation. Otherwise, continuity, neutrality, and independence are consistent with preferences that allow no probability measure. Even with the $\mathscr{N}_i$ equivalent under $\mathscr{R}$, there is no necessity for a probability measure if there is not neutrality.*

The first sentence is similar to the result of Anscombe and Aumann [1963]. The examples where the probability measure does not exist differ from those of Kraft, Pratt, and Seidenberg [1959] in that for those of Theorem 6 the probability relation itself does not exist.

Proof By Debreu's theorem (Theorem 8 of Chapter 6)

$$u(f) = \sum_{i=1}^{n} v^{\mathscr{N}_i}(c_i) \qquad \text{where} \quad f(\mathscr{N}_i) = c_i .$$

If the c_i on $\mathscr{N}_i$ are interchangeable (without affecting preferences),

$$u(f) = \sum_{i=1}^{n} v(c_i)$$

$$= \sum_{i=1}^{n} \frac{1}{n} (nv(c_i)),$$

so that $1/n$ can be taken to be the probability of each $\mathscr{N}_i$. For any $\mathscr{N} \in m$,

$$\mathscr{N} = \bigcup_{i \in \mathscr{I}} \mathscr{N}_i , \qquad c_{\mathscr{N}} = \frac{k(\mathscr{I})}{n}$$

where $k(\mathscr{I})$ is defined as the number of elements in $\mathscr{I}$. This probability measure is shown to be unique in exactly the same way as is the probability measure in Theorem 2. In the same way the utility function is unique up to an increasing linear transformation.

On the other hand, if the c_i on $\mathscr{N}_i$ are not interchangeable, it is possible to obtain preferences for which $v^{\mathscr{N}_i}$ is not proportional to $v^{\mathscr{N}_j}$, $i \neq j$. Then there is no utility linear in the probabilities, since otherwise

$$\sum_{i=1}^{n} v^{\mathscr{N}_i}(c_i)$$

must be an increasing linear transformation of any

$$\sum_{i=1}^{n} q(\mathscr{N}_i)\, v(c_i),$$

which is possible only if each $v^{\mathcal{N}_i}$ is an increasing linear transformation of the u and therefore of each other.

In the case of neutrality, the $v^{\mathcal{N}_i}$ are not required to be identical and therefore can be chosen to be otherwise, which invalidates the probability measure, exactly as in the preceding paragraph. q.e.d.

PROBLEMS

A. Risk Aversion I

Consider the linear utility derived in Theorem 2, where only one commodity type varies with a possible probability distribution for the occurrence of that type. Such a commodity is an "asset."

Let the utility of the asset u be defined on x, which is distributed by a probability distribution, and $\mu = E(x)$. Then for some Π,

$$E(u(x)) = u(\mu - \Pi)$$

where E represents the expected value operator:

$$E(u(x)) = \int_{-\infty}^{\infty} u(x)\, q(x)\, dx.$$

Evidently, $\mu - \Pi$ is the certainity equivalent of x.

1. Show that

$$\Pi = \frac{1}{2}\sigma^2 \frac{u''(\mu)}{u'(\mu)} + g(\sigma^2)$$

where

$$\frac{g(\sigma^2)}{\sigma^2} \to 0 \qquad \text{as} \quad \sigma \to 0.$$

(Hint: Use the mean value theorem for both $E(u(x))$ and $u(\mu - \Pi)$.)

2. Let u be increasing in the asset. Show that Π is positive for small σ only if u is concave in consequences (with certainty). More generally, $\liminf_{\sigma\to 0} \Pi \geqslant 0$ if and only if u is concave if and only if preferences are weakly convex.

The problem was solved by Arrow [1965] and Pratt [1964].

The term

$$\frac{-u''(\mu)}{u'(\mu)}$$

is denoted $r(\mu)$.

B. Risk Aversion II

Let there be two utility functions u_1 and u_2. Let

$$r_1 = -\frac{u_1''}{u_1'}, \qquad r_2 = -\frac{u_2''}{u_2'}.$$

Let Π_1 and Π_2 be the risk premimums for the two utility functions.

1. Show that if $r_2(\mu) \geqslant r_1(\mu)$, then

$$\Pi_1 \geqslant \Pi_2 \qquad \text{for small } \sigma, \quad \text{for all } \mu.$$

2. Show that $r_2(\mu) \geqslant r_1(\mu)$ if and only if u_2 is "more concave" than u_1 in the sense that

$$\frac{u_1(\bar{\mu}) - u_1(\mu)}{u_1(\bar{\nu}) - u_1(\nu)} \leqslant \frac{u_2(\bar{\mu}) - u_2(\mu)}{u_2(\bar{\nu}) - u_2(\nu)},$$

whenever $\nu < \bar{\nu} \leqslant \mu < \bar{\mu}$.

3. Splitting and Nonatomicity

It is desirable to verify that splitting can occur even if there is no generally accepted random device.

The probability relation $\mathscr{Q}$ is *nonatomic* if for

$$\bar{\mathscr{N}}\,\mathscr{Q}\,\varnothing, \quad \text{not} \quad \varnothing\,\mathscr{Q}\,\bar{\mathscr{N}}, \quad \text{defined as} \quad \bar{\mathscr{N}}\,\mathscr{S}\,\varnothing$$

there exists an

$$\bar{\mathscr{N}}\,\mathscr{S}\,\bar{\bar{\mathscr{N}}}\,\mathscr{S}\,\varnothing, \qquad \bar{\bar{\mathscr{N}}} \subset \mathscr{N}.$$

In effect, no event ever precludes all further uncertainty. The measure m is closed under monotone limits if

$$\mathscr{N}_\alpha \subset \mathscr{N}'_\alpha, \qquad \alpha \leqslant \alpha', \quad \alpha \in \mathscr{A}$$

implies

$$\bigcup_{\alpha \in \mathscr{A}} \mathscr{N}_\alpha, \qquad \bigcap_{\alpha \in \mathscr{A}} \mathscr{N}_\alpha$$

are in m. The relation $\mathscr{R}$ is σ-*monotone continuous* on simple set functions if

$$f^i(\mathscr{N}_i) = c, \qquad \mathscr{N}_i \subset \mathscr{N}_{i+1}, \qquad i > 0,$$
$$f^i(\sim\mathscr{N}_i) = c', \qquad \bigcup \mathscr{N}_i = \mathscr{N}_0, \qquad f = f^0,$$

then

$$f^i \mathscr{R} \bar{f} \quad \text{for all } i \text{ implies} \quad f \mathscr{R} \bar{f},$$

and

$$\bar{f} \mathscr{R} f^i \quad \text{for all } i \text{ implies} \quad \bar{f} \mathscr{R} f.$$

A theorem suggested by Villegas [1964] is as follows.

7 Theorem *If $\mathscr{R}$ is σ-monotone, continuous, monotone, neutral, and independent, and if $\mathscr{Q}$ is nonatomic, then there is a random device.*

Proof Since the proof is long, we proceed by numbered steps.

1. For any

$$\bar{\bar{\mathscr{N}}} \mathscr{S} \varnothing$$

there are but a finite number of disjoint subsets

$$\mathscr{N}_i \subset \mathscr{N} \qquad \text{for which} \quad \mathscr{N}_i \mathscr{Q} \bar{\bar{\mathscr{N}}}.$$

If not, construct $\bar{f}$ as

$$\bar{f}(\bar{\bar{\mathscr{N}}}) = c', \qquad \bar{f}(\sim \bar{\bar{\mathscr{N}}}) = c,$$

and f^n as

$$f^n\left(\sim \bigcup_{i=1}^{n} \mathscr{N}_i\right) = c', \qquad f^n\left(\bigcup_{i=n+1}^{\infty} \mathscr{N}_i\right) = c, \qquad c \mathscr{P} c'.$$

Then

$$f^n \to c'.$$

However,

$$f^n \mathscr{R} \bar{f},$$

so that

$$c' \mathscr{R} \bar{f} \qquad (\sigma\text{-monotone continuity}),$$

a contradiction of

$$\bar{\bar{\mathscr{N}}} \mathscr{S} \varnothing.$$

2. For disjoint $\mathscr{N}_i$, $i = 1, 2\ldots$, and for any

$$\bar{\bar{\mathscr{N}}} \mathscr{Q} \varnothing$$

eventually

$$\bar{\bar{\mathscr{N}}} \mathscr{Q} \mathscr{N}_i.$$

3. If

$$\bar{\bar{\mathscr{N}}} \cap \bar{\mathscr{N}} = \varnothing, \qquad \varnothing \mathscr{R} \bar{\mathscr{N}},$$

then

$$\bar{\bar{\mathscr{N}}} \mathscr{Q} \bar{\mathscr{N}} \cup \bar{\bar{\mathscr{N}}}.$$

This can be seen by defining

$$f_{\mathscr{A}} = c, \qquad f_{\mathscr{A}}(\sim\mathscr{A}) = c', \qquad c \mathscr{P} c'.$$

Then

$$f_{\varnothing} \mathscr{R} f_{\bar{\mathscr{N}}}$$

and therefore apply the sure thing principle to show that if

$$f_{\bar{\mathscr{N}} \cup \bar{\bar{\mathscr{N}}}}(\bar{\mathscr{N}}) = c, \qquad f_{\bar{\mathscr{N}} \cup \bar{\bar{\mathscr{N}}}}(\bar{\bar{\mathscr{N}}}) = c, \qquad f_{\bar{\mathscr{N}} \cup \bar{\bar{\mathscr{N}}}}(\sim(\bar{\mathscr{N}} \cup \bar{\bar{\mathscr{N}}})) = c',$$

and

$$f_{\varnothing}(\bar{\bar{\mathscr{N}}}) = c, \qquad f_{\varnothing}(\sim(\bar{\bar{\mathscr{N}}} \cup \bar{\mathscr{N}})) = c',$$

then

$$f_{\bar{\mathscr{N}} \cup \bar{\bar{\mathscr{N}}}} \mathscr{R} f_{\bar{\bar{\mathscr{N}}}};$$

that is,

$$\bar{\bar{\mathscr{N}}} \mathscr{Q} \bar{\mathscr{N}} \cup \bar{\bar{\mathscr{N}}}.$$

4. For each disjoint $\bar{\mathscr{N}}_i$, $i = 1, 2, \ldots$, decompose $\bar{\mathscr{N}}$ as follows. For $\bar{\mathscr{N}}_1$, divide $\bar{\mathscr{N}}$ into as many parts as possible that are at least as probable as $\bar{\mathscr{N}}_1$. By step 1, the maximal decomposition exists. This gives $m(1)$ sets of the form

$$\mathscr{N}_j^1, \qquad j = 1, 2, \ldots, m(1).$$

Inductively, define $\mathscr{N}_j^n$ to be maximal decompositions of each

$$\mathscr{N}_j^{n-1}, \qquad j = 1, \ldots, m(n-1),$$

such that

$$\mathscr{N}_j^n \mathscr{Q} \mathscr{N}_n.$$

Consider the following-monotone sequence. Define

$$\bar{\mathscr{N}}_1 = \bigcup_{i \in \mathscr{I}_1} \mathscr{N}_i^1$$

where $\mathscr{I}_1$ is such that

$$\text{(1)} \quad \bar{\mathscr{N}} \sim \Big(\bigcup_{i \in \mathscr{I}_1} \mathscr{N}_i^1\Big) \mathscr{Q} \bigcup_{i \in \mathscr{I}_1} \mathscr{N}_i^1,$$

$$\text{(2)} \quad \bigcup_{i \in \mathscr{I}_1 \cup \{k\}} \mathscr{N}_i^1 \mathscr{S} \bar{\mathscr{N}} \sim \Big(\bigcup_{i \in \mathscr{I}_1 \cup \{k\}} \mathscr{N}_i^1\Big) \qquad \text{for any} \quad k \leqslant n, \quad k \notin \mathscr{I}_1.$$

Define

$$\mathcal{N}_n = \mathcal{N}_{n-1} \cup \Big(\bigcup_{j \in \mathcal{J}_n} \mathcal{N}_j^n \Big)$$

where $\mathcal{J}_n$ is defined such that

(1) $\mathcal{N}_j^n \cap \mathcal{N}_{n-1} = \varnothing, \quad j \in \mathcal{J}_n,$

(2) $\bar{\mathcal{N}} \sim \Big(\mathcal{N}_{n-1} \cup \Big(\bigcup_{j \in \mathcal{J}_n} \mathcal{N}_j^n \Big)\Big) \, \mathcal{Q} \, \mathcal{N}_{n-1} \cup \Big(\bigcup_{j \in \mathcal{J}_n} \mathcal{N}_j^n \Big),$

(3) $\mathcal{N}_{n-1} \cup \Big(\bigcup_{j \in \mathcal{J}_n \cup \{k\}} \mathcal{N}_j^n \Big) \, \mathcal{S} \, \mathcal{N}_{n-1} \cup \Big(\bigcup_{j \in \mathcal{J}_n} \mathcal{N}_j^n \Big)$

$$\text{for any} \quad \mathcal{N}_k^n \cap \mathcal{N}_{n-1} = \varnothing, \qquad k \leqslant m(n), \quad k \notin \mathcal{J}_n .$$

Eventually, for n large,

$$(\bar{\mathcal{N}} \sim \mathcal{N}_j^n) \, \mathcal{Q} \, \mathcal{N}_j^n \qquad \text{for all} \quad j;$$

thereafter require for one of them, $\mathcal{N}_{j_m}^m$,

$$\mathcal{N}_{j_m}^m \cap \mathcal{N}_m = \varnothing$$

for all m. (This restriction will be used in the next paragraph.) Denote the resulting limit by

$$\bar{\bar{\mathcal{N}}} = \bigcup_{n=1}^{\infty} \mathcal{N}^n.$$

Evidently,

$$\bar{\mathcal{N}} \sim \bar{\bar{\mathcal{N}}} \, \mathcal{Q} \, \bar{\mathcal{N}}$$

by σ-monotone continuity.

5.[1] On the other hand,

$$\bar{\bar{\mathcal{N}}} \cup \mathcal{N}_j^n \supset \mathcal{N}_n \cup \mathcal{N}_j^n, \qquad \varnothing = \mathcal{N}_j^n \cap \mathcal{N}^n, \qquad j \notin \mathcal{J}_n,$$

and

$$\mathcal{N}_n \cup \mathcal{N}_j^n \, \mathcal{Q} \, \mathcal{N} \sim (\mathcal{N}_n \cup \mathcal{N}_j^n) \qquad \text{for} \quad \mathcal{N}_j^n \cap \mathcal{N}_n = \varnothing, \quad j \notin \mathcal{J}_n .$$

In particular, choose $\mathcal{N}_{j_n}^n$ such that

$$\mathcal{N}^n \supset \mathcal{N}_{j_{n+1}}^{n+1} .$$

[1] Villegas [1964] seems to have omitted this part of the proof.

Evidently,

$$\bar{\bar{\mathscr{N}}} \cup \mathscr{N}_{j_n}^{n} \mathscr{Q} \mathscr{N}_n \cup \mathscr{N}_{j_n}^{n} \mathscr{Q} \bar{\mathscr{N}} \sim (\mathscr{N}_n \cup \mathscr{N}_{j_n}^{n}).$$

Therefore,

$$\bar{\bar{\mathscr{N}}} \cup \mathscr{N}_{j}^{n} \mathscr{Q} \bar{\mathscr{N}} \sim (\mathscr{N}_n \cup \mathscr{N}_{j_n}^{n})$$

Therefore, by σ-monotone continuity

$$\bar{\bar{\mathscr{N}}} \cup \bigcap_{j=1}^{\infty} \mathscr{N}_{j}^{n} \mathscr{Q} \bar{\mathscr{N}} \sim \left(\bar{\bar{\mathscr{N}}} \cup \left(\bigcap_{j=1}^{\infty} \mathscr{N}_{j}^{n}\right)\right).$$

Evidently,

$$\varnothing \mathscr{Q} \bigcap_{j=1}^{\infty} \mathscr{N}_{j}^{n} \equiv \mathscr{B}$$

(since it is the limit of ever decreasing sets). Therefore,

$$\bar{\bar{\mathscr{N}}} \mathscr{Q} \bar{\mathscr{N}} \sim (\bar{\bar{\mathscr{N}}} \cup \mathscr{B})$$

or, given step 4,

$$\bar{\bar{\mathscr{N}}} \mathscr{Q} \bar{\mathscr{N}} \sim \bar{\bar{\mathscr{N}}}. \qquad \text{q.e.d.}$$

A consequence of σ-monotonicy is that $q_{\bar{\mathscr{N}}}$ takes every value between zero and one on $\bar{\mathscr{N}} \subset \mathscr{N}$.

8 Theorem *Suppose the hypotheses of Theorems* 7 *and* 2. *Let* $\bar{\bar{\mathscr{N}}} \in \mathscr{m}$. *Then* $q_{\bar{\mathscr{N}}}$ *takes all values in the interval* $\{0, q_{\bar{\bar{\mathscr{N}}}}\}$ *on* $\bar{\mathscr{N}}$ in $\mathscr{m}$, $\bar{\mathscr{N}} \subset \bar{\bar{\mathscr{N}}}$.

Proof All values $(\frac{1}{2})^k$ are taken by splitting $\bar{\bar{\mathscr{N}}}$ k times. Let

$$m(k, t) = \max_{m}\{m \mid m = n\,(1/2)^k < t\}.$$

Then

$$m(k, t) \to t, \qquad k \to \infty.$$

Also, an increasing collection of sets can be formed from the union of $m(k, t)$ of the k splits. It is easy to verify that step functions are represented by a utility linear in probabilities with probability t assigned to the union of the members of the increasing collection. Its union is in $\mathscr{m}$ (and in $\bar{\bar{\mathscr{N}}}$), since $\mathscr{m}$ is a σ-Boolean algebra. q.e.d.

Theorem 8 allows us to define a convex topological space on the step function in $\mathscr{F}$ in the following ways. The set of the *attainable utilities*

$$\bar{\mathscr{U}} = \{\bar{u} \mid u(f) = \bar{u}, \quad f \in \mathscr{F}, \quad f \text{ a step function}, \quad u \text{ the linear utility representation}\}$$

can be shown to be convex.

9 Theorem *Under the hypotheses of Theorems 7 and 2, the set of attainable values $\mathcal{U}$ under the linear utility function u is convex.*

Proof

$$\bar{u} \in \mathcal{U} \quad \text{implies} \quad \bar{u} = \sum q_{\bar{\mathcal{N}}_i} v(\bar{c}^{\bar{\mathcal{N}}_i}) \qquad \text{for} \quad \bar{c}^{\bar{\mathcal{N}}_i} \in \mathcal{C}$$

for some decomposition ($\bar{\mathcal{N}}_i$, $i = 1, \ldots, n$). If

$$\bar{u}, \bar{\bar{u}} \in \mathcal{U},$$

consider the decomposition

$$(\bar{\mathcal{N}}_i \cap \bar{\bar{\mathcal{N}}}_j, i, j)$$

where duplicated sets appear only once. Use Theorem 8 to divide each set in the decomposition into sets of probability

$$q(\bar{\mathcal{N}}_i \cap \bar{\bar{\mathcal{N}}}_j)\, t \qquad \text{and} \qquad q(\bar{\mathcal{N}}_i \cap \bar{\bar{\mathcal{N}}}_j)(1 - t).$$

Define f as

$$f = \bar{c}^{\bar{\mathcal{N}}_i}$$

on the set with probability

$$q(\bar{\mathcal{N}}_i \cap \bar{\bar{\mathcal{N}}}_j)\, t,$$

and

$$f = \bar{\bar{c}}^{\bar{\bar{\mathcal{N}}}_j}$$

on the set with probability

$$q(\bar{\mathcal{N}}_i \cap \bar{\bar{\mathcal{N}}}_j)(1 - t).$$

Then the utility of f is

$$\begin{aligned}
&\sum_{i,j} q(\bar{\mathcal{N}}_i \cap \bar{\bar{\mathcal{N}}}_j)\, t u(\bar{c}^{\bar{\mathcal{N}}_i}) + \sum_{i,j} q(\bar{\mathcal{N}}_i \cap \bar{\bar{\mathcal{N}}}_j)(1 - t)\, u(\bar{\bar{c}}^{\bar{\bar{\mathcal{N}}}_j}) \\
&\quad = t \sum_{i,j} q(\bar{\mathcal{N}}_i \cap \bar{\bar{\mathcal{N}}}_j)\, u(\bar{c}^{\bar{\mathcal{N}}_i}) + (1 - t) \sum_{i,j} q(\bar{\mathcal{N}} \cap \bar{\bar{\mathcal{N}}}_j)\, u(\bar{\bar{c}}^{\bar{\bar{\mathcal{N}}}_j}) \\
&\quad = t\bar{u} + (1 - t)\, \bar{\bar{u}}. \qquad \text{q.e.d.}
\end{aligned}$$

4. Conditional Probability: Bayes' Rule

The idea of *conditional probability* is that the occurrence of a certain event that restricts possible states of nature to $\bar{\mathcal{N}}$ can be analyzed with essentially the same probability measure as before the event occurred.

10 Theorem

$$q(\bar{\bar{\mathcal{N}}} \mid \bar{\mathcal{N}}) = \frac{q(\bar{\bar{\mathcal{N}}} \cap \bar{\mathcal{N}})}{q(\bar{\mathcal{N}})}$$

is a probability measure for $\mathscr{Q}$ restricted to $\bar{\mathscr{N}}$, with the same linear utility representing $\mathscr{R}$.

Proof Given $\bar{\mathscr{N}}$, utility is

$$\sum u(c_i)\, q(\mathscr{N}_i), \qquad \sum q(\mathscr{N}_i) = q(\bar{\mathscr{N}}),$$
$$\bigcup_i \mathscr{N}_i = \bar{\mathscr{N}}, \qquad \mathscr{N}_i \cap \mathscr{N} = \varnothing$$

for $1 \neq j$. This is transformed to

$$\sum u(c_i)\, \frac{q(\mathscr{N}_i)}{q(\bar{\mathscr{N}})}, \qquad \sum_i \frac{q(\mathscr{N}_i)}{q(\bar{\mathscr{N}})} = 1. \qquad \text{q.e.d.}$$

11 Corollary (Bayes' Rule)

$$q(\bar{\bar{\mathscr{N}}} \mid \bar{\mathscr{N}}) = \frac{q(\bar{\mathscr{N}} \mid \bar{\bar{\mathscr{N}}})\, q(\bar{\bar{\mathscr{N}}})}{q(\bar{\mathscr{N}})}.$$

Proof

$$q(\bar{\bar{\mathscr{N}}} \cup \bar{\mathscr{N}}) \mid q(\bar{\mathscr{N}})$$

is identical with

$$q(\bar{\mathscr{N}} \mid \bar{\bar{\mathscr{N}}})\, q(\bar{\bar{\mathscr{N}}}). \qquad \text{q.e.d.}$$

Bayes' rule is the basis of the probabilistic approach to experience. (See Savage [1954, pp. 44–45].)

PROBLEMS

C. Entropy I

Let an event decomposed into subevents $\mathscr{A}_1, \mathscr{A}_2, \ldots, \mathscr{A}_n$ with respect to probabilities $q_1, q_2, \ldots, q_n$ be denoted by $\mathscr{A}$. Define *entropy* to be

$$Q(A) = \sum_{i=1}^{n} q_i \log q_i\,.$$

Show that

(i) $h(\mathscr{A}) \leqslant h(1/n, \ldots, 1/n)$,
(ii) $h(\mathscr{A} \cap \mathscr{B}) = h(\mathscr{A}) + h(\mathscr{B})$,
(iii) $h(q_1, \ldots, q_n, 0) = h(q_1, \ldots, q_n)$.

(Hint: Write $h(\mathscr{A}) = h(q_1, q_2, \ldots, q_n)$.)

The notion of entropy first arose in thermodynamics and was later applied to information theory by Shannon [1948] and Wiener.

D. Entropy II

Show that if h satisfies properties (i), (ii), and (iii) in Problem C, then

$$h(q_1, \ldots, q_2) = -\lambda \sum_{i=1}^{n} q_i \log q_i, \qquad \lambda > 0.$$

(Hint: Show that

(i) $h(1/n, 1/n, \ldots, 1/n) = \lambda \log n$ by showing that for r, s, n arbitrary integers, there is an n such that both

$$\frac{m}{n} \leqslant \frac{\log s}{\log r} < \frac{m}{n} + \frac{1}{n} \quad \text{and} \quad \frac{m}{n} \leqslant \frac{h\left(\frac{1}{s}, \frac{1}{s}, \ldots, \frac{1}{s}\right)}{h\left(\frac{1}{r}, \frac{1}{r}, \ldots, \frac{1}{r}\right)} < \frac{m}{n} + \frac{1}{n};$$

(ii) if the q_i's are rational, $h(q_1, \ldots, q_n) = -\lambda \sum q_i \log q_i$ by showing that there are integers r_i such that

$$q_i = \frac{r_i}{r}, \qquad \sum r_i = r,$$

so that $\mathscr{A}$ can be subdivided into events of equal probability, namely, $\mathscr{B}$. Then

$$\begin{aligned} \lambda = h(\mathscr{A}) + h(\mathscr{B}) &= h(\mathscr{A} \cup \mathscr{B}) = h(\mathscr{B}) + h(\mathscr{A}) = \sum q_k h(\mathscr{B}_k) + h(\mathscr{A}) \\ &= \lambda \sum q_k \log q_k + \lambda \log r + h(\mathscr{A}).) \end{aligned}$$

For a solution, see Khinchin [1957].

8

Consumer Demand

The ratio of exchange of any two commodities will be the reciprocal of the ratio of the final degrees of utility of the quantities of commodity available for consumption after the exchange is completed.

Stanley Jevons
in THE THEORY OF POLITICAL ECONOMY, 1871

1. Introduction

The theory of competitive demand was first studied by the neoclassical economists Gossen, Jevons, Walras, Menger, Marshall, and most notably Slutsky. Since then many approaches have been made to the subject, none of them comprehensive. In this section we set forth the basic framework and a few of the more important propositions of this theory. In Sections 3 and 4, a general demand theory is developed independently of the utility indicator. In Sections 2, 5, and 6, there is a study of the very special case of demand under additive utility. Homothetic preferences are considered throughout the chapter and Section 7 is devoted mainly to their study.

Perhaps the most striking result of demand theory is that there appears no necessary connection between the intuitive notions of complementarity and complementarity in the demand function. For example, in the two-good case, an increase in the price of j decreases the quantity of i if and only if it decreases the expenditure on i if and only if it increases the expenditure on j. Therefore, the complementarity of i for j depends only on the inelasticity of j's demand curve in j's own price. There is nothing in the relationship of i and j that obviously implies complementarity or substitution. In fact, in the case of an additive utility function

$$u(x_1, x_2) = u_1(x_1) + u_2(x_2)$$

with the law of diminishing marginal utility

$$\frac{d^2u_1}{dx_1^2} < 0, \qquad \frac{d^2u_2}{dx_2^2} < 0,$$

we might say that there is no intuitive complementarity whatever. Nevertheless, it will be seen in Section 5 that 1 may be a complement for 2 or 2 for 1, or both, depending on the magnitude of the second derivative, d^2u_i/dx_i^2. This paradox of demand theory is of special interest.

Throughout we assume that the consumer chooses from a consumption set $\mathscr{C}$ whose exact structure is left unspecified. We consider a consumption such as x^1 in Figure 1. The separating line $\mathscr{B}_1$ can be considered as a budget set $\mathscr{B}_1 = \{x \mid px = px^1\}$; px^1 is called *wealth*. Note that x^1 minimizes the cost of the expenditures on $\mathscr{I}(x^1)$.

1 Remark If preferences are locally saturated, necessary conditions that x optimize preferences on a budget set $\mathscr{B}$ with price vector p and wealth θ are

(i) x minimizes the value of consumption, py for $y \in \mathscr{I}(x)$, and
(ii) $px = \theta$.

2 Remark The choice by consumers at $(kp, k\theta)$ is the same as at (p, θ).

3 Remark If preferences are weakly convex, every consumption minimizes the cost of expenditure for some price vector. If the consumption is internal to $\mathscr{C}$, it optimizes preferences on the budget set.

Proof The first sentence is a restatement of Minkowski's theorem, Lemma 13 of Chapter 2. q.e.d.

Consider a fixed wealth θ, and price change from p to $\bar{p}$, which shifts demand from x^1 to x^3, as in Figure 1. Let $x^2 \in \mathscr{I}(x^1)$ and x_2 minimize cost evaluated in terms of $\bar{p}$. Then

$$x^1 - x^3 = (x^1 - x^2) + (x^2 - x^3) = (x^1 - x^2) + \frac{(x^2 - x^3)}{(\theta/k - \theta)}\left(\frac{\theta}{k} - \theta\right).$$

The term

$$x^1 - x^2 \equiv \Delta x \mid_{\mathscr{I}(x)}$$

is the *substitution effect* since it refers to the change in consumption from a change in price but with no effect on the level of preference. Remark 2 shows that given $\bar{p}$ and income θ/k, the consumer chooses just as in the case of price kp and income θ. Hence, the term $x^2 - x^3$ is the *income effect* where there is a change in income to place the consumer in his final position. Therefore, $\theta/k - \theta$ represents the *compensated income* at the new price, which if added to θ would restore the consumer to his former level of preference.

The following result is due to Marshall and Slutsky.

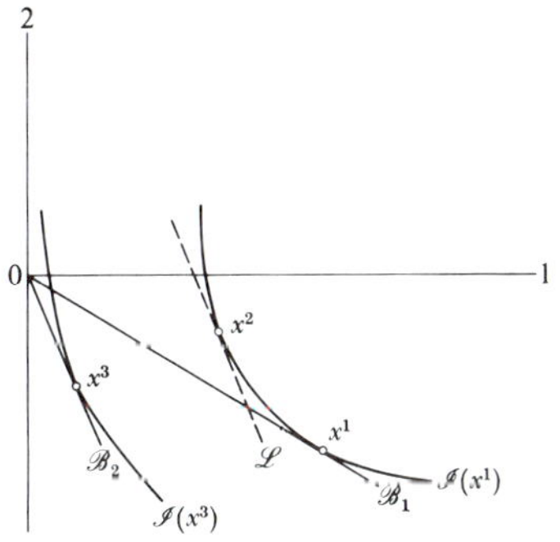

Figure 1

4 Theorem *Let preferences be locally unsaturated and weakly convex, and consider a change in price such that the compensated income choice is internal to $\mathscr{C}$. The change in consumption from a change in price is given by the formula*

$$\Delta x = \Delta x \mid_{\mathscr{I}(x)} - \frac{\Delta x}{\Delta\theta}\Delta\theta$$

where $\Delta\theta$ is the compensated income and $\Delta x/\Delta\theta$ is the rate of change of consumption that would occur if at the new price the consumer wealth were changed by $\Delta\theta$. If the change in price is small and if the substitution term $\Delta x \mid_{\mathscr{I}(x)} + x$ is chosen close to x,

$$\frac{\Delta x}{|\Delta p|} \cong \frac{\Delta x}{|\Delta p|}\Bigg|_{\mathscr{I}(x)} - \frac{\Delta x}{\Delta\theta}\frac{(\Delta p)\, x'}{|\Delta p|}. \tag{1}$$

For an increase in p_i alone

$$\frac{\Delta x_i}{\Delta p_i} \simeq \frac{\Delta x_i}{\Delta p_i}\bigg|_{\mathscr{I}(x)} - \frac{\Delta x_i}{\Delta \theta} x_i . \tag{1a}$$

Proof It remains to show that $\Delta\theta/\Delta p_i \to x_i$. Note that $\theta/k \equiv \bar{\theta} \leqslant \bar{p}x^1$ and $\theta = px^1 \leqslant px^2$ by cost minimization. Therefore,

$$\bar{p}x^2 - px^2 \leqslant \bar{\theta} - \theta \leqslant \bar{p}x^1 - px^1$$

or

$$\frac{(\bar{p} - p)\, x^2}{|\bar{p} - p|} \leqslant \frac{\bar{\theta} - \theta}{|\bar{p} - p|} \leqslant \frac{\bar{p} - p}{|\bar{p} - p|} x^1$$

as $p \to p$, $x^2 \to x^1$,

$$\frac{\theta - \theta}{|\bar{p} - p|} \to \frac{\bar{p} - p}{|\bar{p} - p|} x. \qquad \text{q.e.d.}$$

In appropriate circumstances,

$$\frac{\Delta x_j}{\Delta p_i} \to \frac{\partial x_j}{\partial p_i} = \frac{\partial x_j}{\partial p_i}\bigg|_{\mathscr{I}(x)} - \frac{\partial x_j}{\partial \theta} x_i ,$$

which is the Slutsky equation. However, it is not trivial to find such circumstances (Section 3).

If the demand for i slopes downward with respect to p_i, $\Delta x_i/\Delta p_i < 0$, i is *normal.* If $\Delta x_i/\Delta p_i > 0$, i is a *Giffen good.* A commodity j is *superior* if $\Delta x_j/\Delta\theta > 0$ and *inferior* if $\Delta x_j/\Delta\theta < 0$.

5 Corollary *Under the hypothesis of Theorem* 4, *if i is superior and $x_i > 0$, then i is normal.*

Proof With reference to Figure 1, we have

$$\bar{p}x^2 \leqslant \bar{p}x^1 \qquad \text{and} \qquad px^2 \geqslant px^1,$$

so that for a change in p_i alone

$$0 \geqslant (\bar{p} - p)(x^2 - x^1) = \Delta p_i\, \Delta x_i\, |_{\mathscr{I}(x)} .$$

Hence,

$$0 > \frac{\Delta x_i}{\Delta p_i}\bigg|_{\mathscr{I}(x)} - \frac{\Delta x_i}{\Delta\theta} x_i = \frac{\Delta x_i}{\Delta p_i}. \qquad \text{q.e.d.}$$

Exercise 1 Consider a very poor country where rice is a staple food. What would be the elasticity of demand for rice with respect to its price?

(Hint: Assume the derivative forms of (1a) hold and compute the elasticity

$$\varepsilon_{ii} = \frac{\partial x_i}{\partial p_i} \frac{p_i}{x_i}.)$$

2. Separable Preferences

An especially simple case is that where preferences are represented by additive utility; the theory thereby obtained is a good introduction to the general case. This section is concerned primarily with finding the signs of $\Delta x_i/\Delta p_j$, $i \neq j$. Also, the CES function (Chapter 3, Section 4) is shown to represent the class of homothetic and separable preferences. This utility theorem appears as an application of demand theory.

Let

$$u(x) = \sum_{i \in \mathcal{I}} u_i(x_i)$$

where x_i is the quantity consumed of the ith class of commodities. If preferences are directional dense, then u_i is continuously differentiable in x_i, where x_i is the quantity consumed of the ith class of commodities, $i = 1, \ldots, n$. The theory so developed is most appropriate for a consumer who does not produce, since if production is the consequence of joint inputs, separability of (induced) preferences would not be expected (Chapter 9).

It will be shown in Section 6 that du_i/dx_i is decreasing in x_i, $d^2u_i/dx_i^2 < 0$, if and only if all commodities are superior commodities. The proof requires a rather elaborate apparatus that will be developed for more general preferences.

6 Theorem *Let preferences be weakly convex, continuous, and separable, and suppose all commodities increase utility. If p_i increases, and if i was previously purchased, then for almost all p_i taken over the change,*

$$\frac{du_i}{dx_i} \frac{1}{p_i} = \frac{du_j}{dx_j} \frac{1}{p_j}$$

for all j. If all commodities are superior, then du_i/dx_i is nonincreasing in x_i and the consumption of i decreases.

The proof is easy with differentiability of utility. Difficulties arise solely in proving the existence of the derivative.

Proof To maximize utility at x, it is necessary that

$$u_i(x_i) + u_j(x_j) \geqslant u_i(\bar{x}_i) + u_j(\bar{x}_j)$$

for all $p_i x_i + p_j x_j = p_i \bar{x}_i + p_j \bar{x}_j$, or $\bar{x}_i = x_i + (x_j - \bar{x}_j)\, p_j/p_i$. Hence,

$$u_i(x_i) - u_i\left(x_i + (x_j - \bar{x}_j)\frac{p_j}{p_i}\right) \geqslant u_j(\bar{x}_j) - u_j(x_j),$$

or

$$\frac{p_j(u_i(x_i) - u_i(x_i + (x_j - \bar{x}_j)\, p_j/p_i)}{p_i(\bar{x}_j - x_j)\, p_j/p_i} \geqslant \frac{u_j(\bar{x}_j) - u_j(x_j)}{\bar{x}_j - x_j}.$$

Therefore,

$$\frac{p_j}{p_i} \lim_{|\bar{x}_i - x_i| \to 0} \inf_{\bar{x}_i < x_i} \frac{\Delta u_i}{\Delta x_i} \geqslant \lim_{|\bar{x}_j - x_j| \to 0} \sup_{\bar{x}_j > x_j} \frac{\Delta u_j}{\Delta x_j}$$

and

$$\frac{p_j}{p_i} \liminf_{\bar{x}_i > x_i} \frac{\Delta u_i}{\Delta x_i} \geqslant \limsup_{\bar{x}_j < x_j} \frac{\Delta u_j}{\Delta x_j}.$$

In the same way,

$$\frac{p_i}{p_j} \lim_{|\bar{x}_j - x_j| \to 0} \inf_{\bar{x}_j < x_j} \frac{\Delta u_j}{\Delta x_j} \geqslant \lim_{|\bar{x}_i - x_i| \to 0} \sup_{\bar{x}_i > x_i} \frac{\Delta u_i}{\Delta x_i}$$

and

$$\frac{p_i}{p_j} \liminf_{\bar{x}_j > x_j} \frac{\Delta u_j}{\Delta x_j} \geqslant \limsup_{\bar{x}_i < x_i} \frac{\Delta u_i}{\Delta x_i}.$$

Therefore,

$$\begin{aligned} \frac{p_j}{p_i} \liminf_{\bar{x}_i > x_i} \frac{\Delta u_j}{\Delta x_i} &\geqslant \limsup_{\bar{x}_j < x_j} \frac{\Delta u_j}{\Delta x_j} \\ &\geqslant \liminf_{\bar{x}_j < x_j} \frac{\Delta u_j}{\Delta x_{ji}} \geqslant \frac{p_j}{p_i} \limsup_{\bar{x}_i > x_i} \frac{\Delta u_i}{\Delta x_i} \\ &\geqslant \frac{p_j}{p_i} \liminf_{\bar{x}_i > x_i} \frac{\Delta u_i}{\Delta x_i}, \end{aligned}$$

so that for the one-sided derivatives, we have

$$\frac{p_j}{p_i} \frac{du_i}{dx_i^-} \equiv \frac{p_j}{p_i} \lim_{\bar{x}_i > x_i} \frac{\Delta u_i}{\Delta x_i} = \lim_{\bar{x}_j < x_j} \frac{\Delta u_j}{\Delta x_j} \equiv \frac{du_j^-}{dx_j},$$

and symmetrically,

$$\frac{p_j}{p_i} \frac{du_i}{dx_i^+} = \frac{p_j}{p_i} \lim_{\bar{x}_i < x_i} \frac{\Delta u_i}{\Delta x_i} = \lim_{\bar{x}_j > x_j} \frac{\Delta u_j}{\Delta x_j} \equiv \frac{du_j^+}{dx_j},$$

which are the first-order conditions.

Since increases in x_i lead to increases in utility u_i, u_i is almost everywhere differentiable. As p_i changes, x_i changes continuously and for almost all x_i, $du_i/dx_i = du_i/dx_i^- = du_i/dx_i^+$, so that $du_i/dx_i = du_j/dx_j^- = du_j/dx_j^+ = du_j/dx_j$.

By weak convexity, the marginal rate of substitution

$$\frac{du_i/dx_i}{du_j/dx_j}$$

is nondecreasing as x_i increases along an indifference curve. For the same reason, more general limits of lines bounding indifference curves,

$$-\frac{du_i/dx_i^+}{du_j/dx_j^-} \quad \text{and} \quad -\frac{du_i/dx_i^-}{du_j/dx_j^+}$$

are nondecreasing. Since x_j decreases as x_i increases, the foregoing (first-order) equalities are possible only if either $du_i/dx_i^{\mp}$ or $du_j/dx_j^{\pm}$ does not increase for the given increase in x_i. Since every consumption can be taken (for an appropriate price vector) and since changes in derivatives are independent of the other variables, either one or the other derivative must be nonincreasing throughout its range. Since changes in income leave the first-order equalities unchanged, all derivatives are nonincreasing in increasing quantity.

An increase in p_i must increase $du_i/dx_i^{\pm}$ or decrease $du_j/dx_j^{\pm}$. In the former case, x_i decreases; in the latter case, x_j increases, whereupon

$$\begin{aligned} 0 &= (\Delta p_i)\, x_i + (\Delta x_i)(p_i + \Delta p_i) + p_j(\Delta x_j) \\ &> (\Delta x_i)(p_i + \Delta p_i) + p_j(\Delta x_j) \end{aligned}$$

implies x_i decreases. q.e.d.

7 Theorem *Let utility be additive and let all commodities be superior. If p_i increases, then the consumption of all other commodities formerly purchased either increases, decreases, or remains the same, simultaneously.*

Proof The ratio of marginal utilities (which equals the ratio of price) is invariant for comparisons j and k, $j \neq i$, $k \neq i$. Therefore, the marginal utility for k and j must move in the same direction, as must quantities. The reasoning for x_i for which du_i/dx_i does not exist proceeds as in the second paragraph of the proof of Theorem 6. q.e.d.

In the Marshallian demand theory, it is observed that income earning and consumption processes can be separated. Changes in income are then considered separately from changes in prices of consumer goods.

A still more special case is that where preferences are not only separable, but are also homothetic, that is, an increase in income leads to no change in the proportions consumed by the consumer.

8 Theorem *If preferences are weakly convex, homothetic, and separable, then either*

(i) $u = \sum c_i(x_i)^\alpha \quad (0 \neq \alpha \leqslant 1)$

or

(ii) $u = \sum c_i \log x_i \quad (\alpha \rightarrow 0)$

where α *is a measure of the elasticity of marginal utility*

$$\alpha = \frac{du_i}{dx_i}\frac{x_i}{u_i} + 1.$$

Theorem 8 is due to Bergson [1936] (see also Samuelson [1965]). Variations in homothetic, separable preferences might occur because of

(1) different α's, indicating the flexibility of consuption to price changes, and

(2) different c_i's, indicating the emphasis on particular categories of commodities.

In Theorem 8, utility can be transformed into linear homogeneous form, for example, by using $(\sum c_i(x_i)^\alpha)^{1/\alpha}$. This is the familiar CES function (Chapter 4, Section 4) where $1 - 1/\alpha$ is the elasticity of substitution. Note that if $\alpha > 0$, more of one good is always preferred to less, whereas if $\alpha \leqslant 0$ and if there are zero quantities of a good, more of any other good leads to no improvement in preference. In contrast to the case for production, $\alpha > 0$ would seem more likely than $\alpha < 0$.

Proof Proportional increases in goods leave the marginal rates of substitution unaffected. Hence, the new combinations are chosen at higher incomes if the old ones were chosen at p. Formally,

$$\frac{du_i/dx_i}{du_j/dx_j} = \frac{u_i'}{u_j'} = \frac{p_i}{p_j} \tag{2}$$

is constant as we take positive multiples of x_i and x_j. Here u_i' is increasing whenever defined. Whenever the derivative is not defined, let $u_i'(x_i) = \liminf u_i'(\bar{x}_i)$, $\bar{x}_i \rightarrow x_i$. Then u_i' is nondecreasing and has derivatives almost everywhere, u_i'', which are also second derivatives of u_i, almost everywhere. Therefore, differentiating $u_i'(kx_i)$ and $u_j'(kx_j)$ by k, we get

$$u_i''x_i = \frac{p_i}{p_j} u_j''x_j \quad \text{(homothetic)} \qquad \text{or} \qquad \frac{u_i''x_i}{u_i'} = \frac{u_j''x_j}{u_j'}.$$

Any point on a convex indifference curve and in the interior of the consumption space can be chosen and has a marginal rate of substitution given by $p_i/p_j = u_i'/u_j'$. Therefore, the equations above remain true as x_i varies, x_j fixed. Indeed, u_i' exists since u_j' exists and therefore, u_j'' is solved as above, everywhere; that is, u_i is everywhere twice differentiable. By changing p_i, we necessarily obtain such x_i. Therefore

$$\frac{u_i''x_i}{u_i'} = \beta \qquad \text{or} \qquad \frac{\beta}{x_i} = \frac{u_i''}{u_i'},$$

or if $\beta \neq 0$,

$$\log(u_i') = \beta \log x_i + \log \bar{c}_i = \log \bar{c}_i x_i^\beta.$$

Therefore

$$u_i' = \bar{c}_i x_i$$

or if also $\beta \neq -1$, then

$$u_i = \frac{1}{1+\beta} \bar{c}_i x_i \beta.$$

Setting

$$\frac{1}{1+\beta} \bar{c}_i = c_i, \qquad 1 + \beta = \alpha,$$

gives the theorem. If $\beta = 0$, then

$$u_i'' = 0, \quad \text{or} \quad u_i' = c_i \qquad \text{or} \qquad u_i = d_i + c_i x_i \quad \text{and} \quad \alpha = 1.$$

If $\beta = -1$, then

$$u_i = \bar{c}_i \log x_i + \log d_i,$$

or, dropping the constant, we get $u_i = c_i \log x_i$, $\bar{c}_i = c_i$. q.e.d.

Let

$$q_i = \left(\frac{c_n p_i}{c_i p_n}\right)^{1/(\alpha-1)}$$

9 Theorem *Under the hypotheses of Theorem* 8, *demand is given by*

$$x = \frac{\theta q}{pq} \tag{3}$$

or

$$x_i = \left(\frac{p_i}{p_j}\frac{c_j}{c_i}\right)^{1/(\alpha-1)} x_j\,. \tag{3a}$$

10 Corollary

$$\frac{\partial x_i}{\partial p_j} = \frac{\alpha}{\alpha - 1} q_i q_j \frac{\theta}{(p'q)^2} = \frac{\alpha}{1-\alpha}\frac{x_i x_j}{\theta}, \qquad j \neq i, \tag{4}$$

which is positive for $1 \geqslant \alpha > 0$ *and negative for* $\alpha < 0$, *and*

$$\frac{\partial x_i}{\partial p_i} = \frac{x_i^2}{\theta}\frac{\alpha}{1-\alpha} - \frac{x_i}{p_i}\frac{1}{1-\alpha}\,. \tag{4a}$$

Also,

$$\varepsilon_{ii} = \frac{\partial x_i}{\partial p_i}\frac{p_i}{x_i} = \frac{p_i}{\theta} x_i \frac{\alpha}{1-\alpha} - \frac{\alpha}{1-\alpha} \tag{4b}$$

and

$$\varepsilon_{ij} = \frac{\partial x_i}{\partial p_j}\frac{p_j}{x_i} = \frac{\alpha}{1-\alpha}\frac{x_j p_j}{\theta}\,.$$

In words, for homothetic and separable consumer preferences, goods are *gross complements*, $\partial x_i/\partial p_j < 0$ for $i \neq j$, for $\alpha < 0$ and *gross substitutes*, $\partial x_i/\partial p_j > 0$ for $i \neq j$, for $\alpha > 0$; for $\alpha = 0$, $\partial x_i/\partial p_j = 0$ and goods are both weak gross substitutes, $\partial x_i/\partial p_j \geqslant 0$, and weak gross complements, $\partial x_i/\partial p_j \leqslant 0$. After we transform utility into a linear homogeneous form, corollary 10 states that there is gross substitution if the elasticity of substitution is greater than one and gross complementarity if it is less than one.

Proof The marginal conditions are

$$\left(\frac{x_i}{x_j}\right)^{\alpha-1} = \frac{p_i}{p_j}\frac{c_j}{c_i} \qquad \text{or} \qquad x_i = \left(\frac{c_n}{c_i}\frac{p_i}{p_n}\right)^{1/(\alpha-1)} x_n = \left(\frac{q_i}{q_n}\right) x_n\,.$$

Evidently,

$$\theta = \sum p_i x_i = \sum \frac{q_i}{q_n} x_n p_i = \frac{x_n}{q_n}\sum q_i p_i\,, \qquad \text{or} \qquad \frac{x_n}{q_n} = \frac{\theta}{p'q}\,.$$

Therefore,

$$x_i = \frac{\theta}{p'q} q_i\,. \qquad \text{q.e.d.}$$

PROBLEMS

A. Diminishing Marginal Utility

Let $u(x_1, x_2) = x^{1/4} + x_2 + \frac{1}{2}\cos x_2$. Show that u is quasi concave and

$$\frac{d^2u}{dx_2^2} > 0 \qquad \text{for some } x_2 .$$

B. Utility over Time IV

Let preferences on $(x^t, t = 0, 1,...)$ be homothetic. Suppose an increase in wealth θ occurs. What is the effect on savings relative to consumption, defined as

$$\frac{\theta - px^0}{\theta} = 1 - \frac{px^0}{\theta} ?$$

This problem was first solved by Modigliani and Brumberg [1954] (see also Friedman [1957]).

C. Utility over Time V

Show that if preferences are separable and identical in $\mathscr{I}_1, \mathscr{I}_2,...$, and are homothetic, then an increase in $p_{\mathscr{I}_i}$ leads to an increase in $x_{\mathscr{I}_j}, j \neq i$. (Hint: Simply treat each group as a single commodity, since goods in a group do not change their relative quantities; represent utility as in Theorem 13 of Chapter 6; then show that $\alpha > 0$ in Theorem 8, and apply Corollary 10.)

D. Utility over Time VI

Use Problem C to show that an increase in interest rates leads to an increase in savings (and in the ratio of savings to consumption).

E. Separable Preferences I

What are the only separable preferences leading to separable demand functions (defined as

$$\frac{\partial^2 x}{\partial p_i \, \partial p_j} = 0 \qquad \text{for all} \quad i = j ?$$

See Samuelson [1965].

F. Separable Preferences II

Let $x = (x_{\mathscr{I}_1}, \ldots, x_{\mathscr{I}_n})$. Goldman and Uzawa [1964] define *weak separability* to be given by

$$0 = \frac{\partial m_i / m_j}{\partial x_k} \qquad \text{for} \quad i, j \in \mathscr{I}_r, \quad k \in \sim\mathscr{I}_r .$$

Show that the income elasticities of demand for i and j are proportionate to the income elasticities for the case where expenditure on $\mathscr{I}_r$ is fixed. (See also Muth [1966].)

G. Separable Preferences III.

Consider the utility function

$$\sum_i \log(c_i y_i + b_i), \qquad y_i = f(x_1), \qquad y_i = x_i \qquad \text{for} \quad i > 1,$$

$| c_1 | \leqslant | c_j |$ for all j, $c_1 > 0$, $c_j < 0$ for $j > 1$.

Show that it is quasi concave whenever

$$\frac{df}{dx_1} > 0, \qquad \frac{d^2 f}{dx_1^2} < 0,$$

and f maps $[0, \infty]$ into $[0, 1]$. Evalutate the partial derivatives of demand with respect to prices.

H. Measurable Production Functions

Use Bergson's theorem (Theorem 8) to show that all measurable (separable) production functions are monotonic increasing transformations of CES production functions. Show that for constant returns to scale, the only measurable production functions are CES.

3. Income and Substitution Effects

The laws of consumer demand are presented here in a framework of preference maximization, without reference to utility. This approach was initiated by McKenzie [1957], who derived the Slutsky equations without using a utility index. These equations allow the statement of the standard laws of demand which give conditions for downward-sloping demand curves as in Corollary 5. However, they are insufficient for a study of complementarity and substitution. Therefore, some alternative equations will be presented in the next section.

It is assumed that an indifference surface can be given by the equation

$$x_0 = f(x), \tag{5}$$

at least in a neighborhood of (x, x_0), as it would be whenever small changes in the 0th commodity change the level of preference. Maximization of consumer preferences at x subject to a price system

$$p' = (p_1, p_2, \ldots)$$

and p_0 requires that $x'p + p_0 x_0$ be minimized at x. (A less costly expenditure could be improved by purchasing more goods or fewer undesirable commodities without violating the budget constraint.) Of course, it is assumed that preferences are locally unsaturated, that is, we can increase the preference level by arbitrarily small changes in consumption, possibly in the direction of higher cost. Weak convexity of preferences and directional density are also assumed, so that f is convex and continuously differentiable. The first-order condition is

$$\frac{\partial p'x + p_0 x_0}{\partial x} = p + p_0 \frac{\partial x_0}{\partial x} = 0,$$

or, letting

$$m \equiv -\frac{\partial x_0}{\partial x} = -\frac{\partial f}{\partial x},$$

we get

$$\frac{p}{p_0} = m. \tag{5a}$$

Equation (5a) is called Gossen's law and it holds whenever attention is restricted to those goods purchased in nonminimal quantities. The second-order condition is assumed to hold, as it does almost everywhere whenever preferences are weakly convex or more generally whenever $\partial m/\partial x$ is differentiable almost everywhere. Hence,

$$0 \leqslant \frac{d^2}{dt^2}\left(p(tx + (1-t)y) + p_0(tx_0 + (1-t)y_0)\right)\Big|_{x_0 = f(x)}$$

$$= (x - y)\left.\frac{\partial^2(px + p_0 x_0)}{\partial x^2}\right|_{x_0 = f(x)} (x - y)$$

for almost all $(x - y)$. In other words, the matrix

$$\left.\frac{\partial^2}{\partial x^2}(px + p_0 x_0)\right|_{x_0 = f(x)}$$

must be *positive semiquasi definite*; that is,

$$\frac{\partial p - p_0 m}{\partial x} = -p_0 \frac{\partial m}{\partial x} - p_0 \frac{\partial m}{\partial x_0}\left(\frac{\partial x_0}{\partial x}\right)$$

must be positive semiquasi definite. Let

$$\frac{\partial m}{\partial x} = m_x , \qquad \frac{\partial m}{\partial x_0} = m_{x_0} .$$

11 Lemma *If preferences are locally unsaturated, weakly convex, and directionally dense, and if the marginal rates of substitution are differentiable, then the matrix*

$$m_{x_0} m' - m_x$$

is positive semiquasi definite (and symmetric where the partial derivatives are continuous[2]*, which is almost everywhere).*

Whenever a matrix is positive (semi) quasi definite and symmetric, it is called *positive (semi) definite.* (We substitute "negative" for "positive" if the matrix is multiplied by minus one.)

Evidently, the marginal rate of substitution will be differentiable almost everywhere, as it is the second derivative of the convex function. Let

$$\varepsilon_{ij} = \frac{\partial x_i}{\partial p_j}\frac{p_j}{x_i}, \qquad \varepsilon_i = \frac{\partial x_i}{\partial \theta}\frac{\theta}{x_i}, \qquad \kappa_i = \frac{x_i p_i}{\theta} .$$

12 Lemma (Slutsky)

$$\frac{\partial x}{\partial p} = \frac{a}{p_0} + \frac{a m_{x_0} x'}{p_0} = \frac{a}{p_0} - \left(\frac{\partial x}{\partial \theta}\right) x', \tag{6}$$

or

$$(\varepsilon_{ij}) = \frac{1}{p_0}\left(a_{ij}\frac{p_j}{x_i}\right) - (\varepsilon_i \kappa_j). \tag{6a}$$

Lemma 12 gives the fundamental relationship. It is the Slutsky equation, where a/p_0 is the substitution effect[3] and $-(\partial x/\partial\theta)\, x'$ is the income effect.

[2] Here $m_{x_0} m' - m_x$ is positive semiquasi if the indifference surface is convex. If it is strictly convex, that is, it has no flat surfaces or subsurfaces, then $m_{x_0} m' - m_x$ is positive definite on open sets dense in the commodity space.

[3] This is seen by using Gossen's law, Equation (5a), to determine

$$\left.\frac{\partial x}{\partial p}\right|_{x_0 = f(x)},$$

The Slutsky equation was illustrated in Figure 1. Equation (6) shows that the income effect is minus the weighted sum of the substitution effect, where the weights are given by the effects of changes in x_0 on the marginal rates of substitution of x with respect to x_0. Also, the substitution effect is simply the inverse of the matrix of second-order conditions in cost. In turn, the matrix is negative quasi definite by virtue of the cost-minimization conditions.

Proof The strategy of proof is to use knowledge about changes in demand in order to obtain a view of demand theory. It is necessary to evaluate

$$\frac{\partial x}{\partial y}, \qquad \frac{\partial x_0}{\partial y}$$

for arbitrary y.

Recall that the consumer must obey the budget constraint

$$p'x + p_0 x_0 = \theta$$

where θ is income. Normally, if we are pursuing general equilibrium analysis, the summed value of trades must be zero,

$$\theta = 0.$$

But for conceptual purposes and to allow the possibility of application to restricted parts of the budget decision, the consumer is allowed to violate this Walras law by a certain specified amount.

The derivative form of (5a) is

$$m_{x_0}\left(\frac{\partial x_0}{\partial y}\right) + m_x \frac{\partial x}{\partial y} = \frac{\partial p}{\partial y}\Big/ p_0 - \frac{p}{p_0}\frac{\partial p_0}{\partial y} \tag{5b}$$

and of income

$$\frac{\partial x_0}{\partial y} = \frac{1}{p_0}\left(-\frac{\partial p_0}{\partial y} x_0 - \left(\frac{\partial x}{\partial y}\right)' p - \left(\frac{\partial p}{\partial y}\right)' x + \frac{\partial \theta}{\partial y}\right) \tag{7}$$

---

which yields the solution

$$m_x \frac{\partial x}{\partial p}\Bigg| + m_{x_0}\left(\frac{\partial x_0}{\partial x}\right)' \frac{\partial x}{\partial p}\Bigg| = I\frac{1}{p_0}$$

or

$$(m_x - m_{x_0} m')\frac{\partial x}{\partial p}\Bigg| = I\frac{1}{p_0}$$

or

$$\frac{\partial x}{\partial p}\Bigg| = \frac{a}{p_0}.$$

where y is an unspecified variable. The term $\partial x_0/\partial y$ will not be used and it is assumed to be zero. Substitution of (5b) into (7) gives

$$\left(m_x - \frac{m_{x_0}}{p_0} p'\right) \frac{\partial x}{\partial y} = \frac{1}{p_0} (I + m_{x_0} x') \frac{\partial p}{\partial y} - \frac{m_{x_0}}{p_0} \left(\frac{\partial \theta}{\partial y}\right) \tag{8}$$

where I is the identity matrix. Since

$$m_x - m_{x_0} \frac{p'}{p_0} = m - m_{x_0} m'$$

is negative quasi definite, it has an (negative quasi definite) inverse, denoted a. Then

$$\frac{\partial x}{\partial y} = a \left(\frac{1}{p_0} (I + m_{x_0} x') \frac{\partial p}{\partial y} - \frac{m_{x_0}}{p_0} \left(\frac{\partial \theta'}{\partial y}\right)\right). \tag{9}$$

Letting $y = \theta$, we have

$$\frac{\partial x}{\partial \theta} = -a \frac{m_{x_0}}{p_0}. \tag{10}$$

Letting $y = p$, we have the lemma. q.e.d.

Lemma 12 suffices for the case of three or more goods, since the components i can be interchanged with 0 to obtain all cross partials $\partial x_i/\partial p_j$. However, if there are only two goods purchased in nonminimal quantities, then we can evaluate only the derivative $\partial x_i/\partial p_i$. Therefore, it is useful to have

$$\frac{\partial x_0}{\partial \theta} = \left(1 - p' \frac{\partial x}{\partial \theta}\right) \frac{1}{p_0} \tag{10a}$$

(from (7)) and the following equations:

13 Lemma (Slutsky)

$$\frac{\partial x_0}{\partial p} = -\frac{1}{p_0} \left(\frac{\partial x}{\partial p}\right)' p - \frac{x}{p_0} = -\frac{1}{p_0^2} a' p + \frac{\partial x}{\partial p_0} \left(\frac{\partial x}{\partial \theta}\right)' p - \frac{x}{p_0} \tag{6b}$$

$$= -\frac{a' p}{p_0^2} + \left(\frac{1}{p_0} - \frac{\partial x_0}{\partial \theta}\right) x - \frac{x}{p_0}$$

$$= -\frac{a' p}{p_0^2} - \frac{\partial x_0}{\partial \theta} x$$

or

$$\varepsilon_{0j} = -\left(\frac{\sum a_{ij} p_i}{p_0 x_0}\right) \frac{p_j}{p_0} - (\varepsilon_0 \kappa_j). \tag{6c}$$

(From (7), Lemma 11, and (10a).) Like Lemma 12, Lemma 13 is the *Slutsky equation*, with the same interpretation for two terms.

If preferences are homothetic, $\partial x_i/\partial\theta = x_i/\theta$, so that Lemmata 12 and 13 give the following result.

14 Corollary (Hicks) *If preferences are homothetic,*

$$\varepsilon_i = 1,$$

$$\frac{\partial x}{\partial p} = \frac{a}{p_0} - \frac{xx'}{\theta}, \quad \textit{and} \quad \frac{\partial x_0}{\partial p} = -\frac{a'p}{p_0^2} - \frac{x_0}{\theta}x.$$

Hence, $\partial x_i/\partial p_i < 0$. *If also* $(\partial^2 px + p_0 x_0)/\partial x^2$ *is continuous, then*

$$\frac{\partial x_i}{\partial p_j} = \frac{\partial x_j}{\partial p_i}.$$

For more general preferences, we have Theorem 15.

15 Theorem (Slutsky) *If* $\partial x_i/\partial\theta > 0$, $x_i > 0$, *that is, i is a superior good, or if* $(\partial x_i/\partial\theta)\, x_i$ *is small (relative to* $(1/p_n)\, a_{ii}$*), then* $\partial x_i/\partial p_i < 0$. *If* $\partial x_i/\partial\theta < 0$, $x_i < 0$, *that is, if i is a factor that is supplied in larger quantities at higher income, then* $\partial x_i/\partial p_i < 0$.

The second sentence of Theorem 15 is the normal supply curve of a factor; that is, the higher the price, the greater the supply. Note that the assumption used, that people will provide more of the factor the richer they are, may be unrealistic, as perhaps it is in the case of labor. Theorem 15 can be rationalized in terms of Figure 1. The change from x_1 to x_2 causes a decrease in good 1, due to the convexity of the indifference curves. If also the movement from x_2 to x_3 causes a decrease in good 1 (as it does in Figure 1), then the movement from x_1 to x_3 causes a decrease in good 1.

Proof Let e_i be the column vector with one in the ith component and zero elsewhere. Note that

$$\begin{aligned}\frac{\partial x_i}{\partial p_i} &= e_i'\frac{\partial x}{\partial p}e_i \\ &= \frac{e_i'ae_i}{p_0} - e_i'\left(\frac{\partial x}{\partial\theta}\right)x'e_i \\ &= \frac{1}{p_0}(e_i'ae_i) - \frac{\partial x_i}{\partial\theta}x_i. \qquad \text{q.e.d.}\end{aligned}$$

16 Corollary *If the consumption of any one good i is a small part of the whole, then* $\partial x_i/\partial p_i < 0$.

17 Theorem *If goods are (weak) gross substitutes and all goods are superior, and consumed in positive quantities, then the substitution effect* a/p_0 *has (nonnegative) positive off-diagonals.*

Proof

$$0 < \frac{\partial x_i}{\partial p_j} = \frac{a_{ij}}{p_0} - \frac{\partial x_i}{\partial \theta} x_j \leqslant \frac{a_{ij}}{p_0}. \qquad \text{q.e.d.}$$

Whenever $a_{ij} > 0$ ($\geqslant 0$) as in Theorem 17, it is said that there is (weak) *net substitution.*

Exercise 2 For two commodities, show that the substitution matrix always has nonnegative off-diagonals.

PROBLEM

I. Aggregation

Let prices be given by $p = (p_{\sim\mathscr{I}}, kp_{\mathscr{I}})$. Evaluate

$$\frac{\partial p_{\mathscr{I}} x_{\mathscr{I}}}{\partial k}, \quad \frac{\partial p_{\mathscr{I}} x_{\mathscr{I}}}{\partial p_{\sim\mathscr{I}}}, \quad \frac{\partial x_{\sim\mathscr{I}}}{\partial k}, \quad \frac{\partial x_{\sim\mathscr{I}}}{\partial p_{\sim\mathscr{I}}}$$

to show that $p_{\mathscr{I}} x_{\mathscr{I}}$ can be treated as a single commodity.

This problem was solved by Hicks [1959].

4. Explicit Solutions

The main purpose of this section is to determine when goods are gross substitutes or gross complements. Unlike that of Hicks [1959] and McKenzie [1957], the following treatment is derived directly from the second-order conditions for maximization. Unlike the presentation of McKenzie [1957], it includes an explicit solution for demands. In particular, there is no need to rely on such notions as income effects and substitution effects. The explicit solution is similar to that derived by Barten [1964], except that no utility function appears in the equations.

We evaluate the substitution effect and state the quantitative laws of demand. To do this, we assume that m_x also has an inverse that will hold for almost all prices if m is continuously differentiable (Cronin [1964, p. 35]). Therefore,

$$m_x\left(I - \frac{m_x^{-1}m_{x_0}}{p_n}p'\right)$$

has an inverse (equal to the substitution effect)

$$a = \left(I + \frac{m_x^{-1}m_{x_0}}{p_n\left(1 - \dfrac{p'm_x^{-1}m_{x_0}}{p_0}\right)}\right)m_x^{-1}$$

$$= m_x^{-1}\left(m_x + \frac{m_{x_0}p'}{p_0(1-\mu)}\right)m_x^{-1} \tag{11}$$

provided that

$$\mu = \frac{p'm_x^{-1}m_{x_0}}{p_0} \neq 1.$$

An application occurs if u is strictly concave, whereupon

$$m_x = \frac{\partial^2 u/\partial x^2}{\partial u/\partial x_0} - \frac{\partial u/\partial x}{\partial u/\partial x_0}\,\frac{\partial^2 u/\partial x\,\partial x_0}{\partial u/\partial x_0}$$

and $\partial^2 u/\partial x^2$ is negative quasi definite on a set open and dense in the space where u is differentiable. Note that if also $\partial^2 u_i/\partial x_i^2 < 0$ and $\partial^2 u_i/\partial x_j^2 > 0$ for $i \neq j$, then $(\partial^2 u/\partial x^2)^{-1} \leqslant 0$. Hence,

$$m_x^{-1} = \frac{\partial u}{\partial x_0}\left(\frac{\partial^2 u}{\partial x^2}\right)^{-1}$$

$$\times\left(I + \frac{1}{1 - \left(\dfrac{\partial^2 u}{\partial x_0\,\partial x}\right)'\left(\dfrac{\partial^2 u}{\partial x^2}\right)^{-1}\dfrac{\partial u/\partial x}{\partial u/\partial x_0}}\;\frac{\dfrac{\partial u}{\partial x}\left(\dfrac{\partial^2 u}{\partial x_0\,\partial x}\right)'}{\dfrac{\partial u}{\partial x_0}}\left(\frac{\partial^2 u}{\partial x^2}\right)^{-1}\right)$$

and

$$m'm_x^{-1}m = \frac{\partial u}{\partial x_0}\left(\frac{\partial u}{\partial x}\right)'\left(\frac{\partial^2 u}{\partial x^2}\right)^{-1}\frac{\partial u}{\partial x}\,\frac{1}{1 - \left(\dfrac{\partial^2 u}{\partial x_0\,\partial x}\right)'\left(\dfrac{\partial^2 u}{\partial x}\right)^{-1}\dfrac{\partial u/\partial x}{\partial u/\partial x_0}}.$$

18 Lemma

$$(1-\mu)(m'(m_x^{-1})\,m) < 0,$$

that is, $1 \neq \mu$.

If $\partial^2 u_i/\partial x_i^2 < 0$, $\partial^2 u_i/\partial x_i\,\partial x_j > 0$ *for* $i \neq j$, *u concave, then* $(1-\mu) > 0$.

Proof

$$m'(m_x^{-1})\, m\mu = m'(m_x^{-1})\, m_{x_0} m'(m_x^{-1})'\, m$$

$$> m'(m_x^{-1})\, m_x (m_x^{-1})'\, m = m'(m_x^{-1})'\, m. \qquad \text{q.e.d.}$$

Equation (11) divides the substitution effect into terms, a substitution term directly determined by the dependency on various goods of the marginal rate to substitution and a term dependent on relatively complicated indirect effects. Continuing from (11), we have Theorem 19.

19 Theorem

(i)
$$\frac{\partial x}{\partial \theta} = -m_x^{-1}\left(I + \frac{m_{x_0} p' m_x^{-1}}{p_0(1-\mu)}\right)\frac{m_{x_0}}{p_0}$$
$$= -m_x^{-1}\left(I + \frac{\mu}{(1-\mu)}\right)\frac{m_{x_0}}{p_0}$$
$$= -\frac{m_{x_0}^{-1} m_{x_0}}{(1-\mu)\, p_0}$$

(ii)
$$\frac{\partial x}{\partial p} = \frac{m_x^{-1}}{p_0}\left(m_x + \frac{m_{x_0} p'}{p_0(1-\mu)}\right) m_x^{-1} - \frac{\partial x}{\partial \theta}\, x'$$
$$= \frac{m_x^{-1}}{p_0}\left(I + \frac{m_{x_0}(m' m_x^{-1} + x')}{p_0(1-\mu)}\right)$$
$$= \frac{m_x^{-1}}{p_0}\left(m_x + \frac{m_{x_0}}{(1-\mu)}\left(\frac{\partial x_0}{\partial x}\right)\right) m_x^{-1}$$
$$= \frac{m_x^{-1}}{p_0}\left(m_x + \frac{m_{x_0}}{(1-\mu)}\left(\frac{\partial \theta / p_0}{\partial x}\right)\right) m_x^{-1}$$
$$= \left(\frac{I}{p_0} - \frac{\partial x}{\partial \theta}\left(\frac{\partial \theta / p_0}{\partial x}\right)\right) m_x^{-1}$$

(iii)
$$\frac{\partial x_0}{\partial \theta} = \left(1 + \frac{p' m_x^{-1} m_{x_0}}{(1-\mu)\, p_0}\right)\frac{1}{p_0}$$
$$= \left(1 + \frac{\mu}{1-\mu}\right)\frac{1}{p_0}$$
$$= \left(\frac{\mu}{1-\mu}\right)\frac{1}{p_0}$$

or

$$\varepsilon_0 = \left(\frac{1}{1-\mu}\right) \kappa_0 \, ,$$

and

$$\text{(iv)} \quad \left(\frac{\partial x_0}{\partial p}\right)' = -\frac{p'}{p_0^2}\left(m_x^{-1} + \frac{m_x^{-1} m_{x_0} p' m_x^{-1}}{p_0(1-\mu)}\right) \frac{1}{p_0(1-\mu)\, x'}$$

$$= -\frac{p' m_x^{-1}}{p_0^2(1-\mu)} - \frac{1}{p_0(1-\mu)} x'$$

$$= -\frac{1}{(1-\mu)} \frac{1}{p_0} \frac{\partial \theta_0 / p_0}{\partial x} m_x^{-1}$$

$$= -\frac{\partial x_0}{\partial \theta} \frac{\partial \theta / p_0}{\partial x} m_x^{-1} \, .$$

20 Corollary *$\partial x / \partial \theta > 0$ whenever u is strictly concave and $\partial^2 u / \partial x_i^2 < 0$ and $\partial^2 u / \partial x_i \, \partial x_j > 0$ for $i \neq j$. Therefore, $\partial x_i / \partial p_i < 0$ whenever $x > 0$.*

Proof

$$m_x^{-1} m_{x_0} = m_x^{-1} \left(\frac{\dfrac{\partial^2 u}{\partial x_0 \, \partial x}}{\dfrac{\partial u}{\partial x_0}} - \frac{\dfrac{\partial u}{\partial x} \dfrac{\partial^2 u}{\partial x_0^2}}{\left(\dfrac{\partial u}{\partial x_0}\right)^2} \right) = \left(\frac{\partial^2 u}{\partial x^2}\right)^{-1} \frac{\partial^2 u}{\partial x_0 \, \partial x}$$

$$+ \frac{\left(\dfrac{\partial^2 u}{\partial x_0 \, \partial x}\right)' \left(\dfrac{\partial^2 u}{\partial x^2}\right)^{-1} \left(\dfrac{\partial^2 u}{\partial x_0 \, \partial x}\right)}{\dfrac{\partial u}{\partial x_0}(1-\nu)} \left(\frac{\partial^2 u}{\partial x^2}\right)^{-1} \frac{\partial u}{\partial x} - \frac{\dfrac{\partial^2 u}{\partial x_0^2}}{\dfrac{\partial u}{\partial x_0}} \left(\frac{\partial^2 u}{\partial x^2}\right)^{-1} \frac{\partial u}{\partial x} \frac{1}{1-\nu}$$

where

$$\nu = \left(\frac{\partial^2 u}{\partial x_0 \, \partial x}\right)' \left(\frac{\partial^2 u}{\partial x}\right)^{-1} \frac{\partial u / \partial x}{\partial u / \partial x_0} \, .$$

It is left as an exercise for the reader to verify that

$$\left(\frac{\partial^2 u}{\partial x_0 \, \partial x}\right)' \left(\frac{\partial^2 u}{\partial x^2}\right)^{-1} \left(\frac{\partial^2 u}{\partial x_0 \, \partial x}\right) - \frac{\partial^2 u}{\partial x_0^2} = -\det \frac{\partial^2 u}{\partial (x_0 \, , x)} \det \frac{\partial^2 u}{\partial x^2} > 0$$

(negative quasi definiteness). q.e.d.

The meaning of (i) is that the income effect is a weighted sum of the inverse of the dependency of the marginal rate of substitution between x_i and x_0 on the x_j's, $j \neq 0$, the weights being a proportion (possibly negative) of the dependency of the marginal rate of substitution between x_i and x_0 on x_0.

In (ii) the term $\partial(\theta/p_0)/\partial x$ refers to the change in the cost of the commodity bundle as the x_i change, it being assumed that prices change in order that the new x be actually purchased. This is the *cost effect*, as illustrated in Figure 2. In Figure 2a, an increase in quantity of the first good leads to an increase in cost in terms of the second good, as shown by the fact that the cost changes from *a* to *b*. In Figure 2b, the cost effect is negative. Therefore, the response of demand to price changes is seen to be in two components, the relative power and direction of each determining the total response. The first component is directly dependent on the relation between goods and their marginal rates of substitution. The second is indirectly dependent on this relationship, the dependency being determined by the income effect and the cost effect.

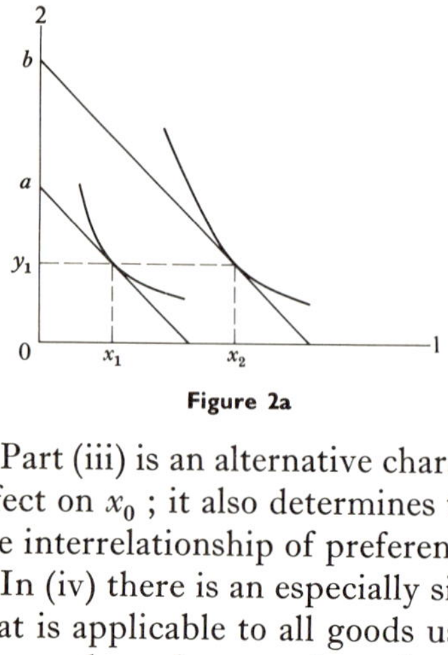

Figure 2a

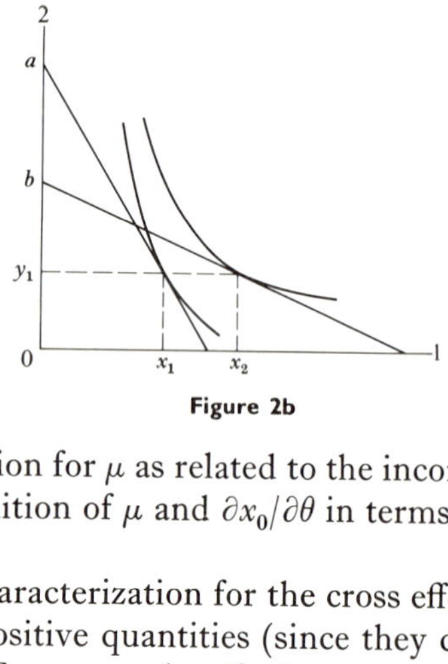

Figure 2b

Part (iii) is an alternative characterization for μ as related to the income effect on x_0; it also determines the definition of μ and $\partial x_0/\partial\theta$ in terms of the interrelationship of preferences.

In (iv) there is an especially simple characterization for the cross effect that is applicable to all goods used in positive quantities (since they can always be taken as the nth good). For example, if there are two commodities,

$$\frac{\partial x_2}{\partial p_1} = -p_2 \frac{\partial x_2}{\partial \theta} \frac{\partial \theta/p_2}{\partial x_1} \frac{1}{m_{x_1}}.$$

Letting

$$\operatorname{sign} x = \begin{cases} -1 & \text{if } x < 0 \\ 0 & \text{if } x = 0, \\ 1 & \text{if } x > 0 \end{cases}$$

we have

$$\operatorname{sign}\frac{\partial x}{\partial p_j} = \operatorname{sign}\frac{\partial x_i}{\partial \theta}\operatorname{sign}\frac{\partial \theta/p_i}{\partial x_j}, \qquad i \neq j$$

(since $m_x > 0$). For x positive, at least one $\partial x_i/\partial \theta$ is positive. Other restrictions appear in Exercise 4. Nevertheless, the sign configurations $\partial x_i/\partial p_j$, $i \neq j$, are somewhat arbitrary. For the two-commodity case, the possible sign configurations for $\partial x/\partial p$ can be derived without explicit considerations ofthe cost effect.

21 Theorem *If there are two commodities, and if the second-order conditions hold, then at least one must be a superior commodity, whereupon* $\partial x_i/\partial p_i < 0$ *for at least one commodity, and* $\partial x_i/\partial p_j > 0$ *if and only if the change in expenditure on* j *decreases as* p_j *increases, whereupon* $\partial x_j/\partial p_i < 0$. *In particular, exactly the following sign configurations of* $\partial x/\partial p$ *are consistent with strictly convex preferences.*

(i) *Two goods* ($x_1 \geqslant 0$, $x_2 \geqslant 0$):

$$\begin{bmatrix} - & + \\ + & - \end{bmatrix}, \quad \begin{bmatrix} + & + \\ - & - \end{bmatrix}, \quad \begin{bmatrix} - & - \\ + & + \end{bmatrix}.$$

(ii) *One or more factors* ($x_i \leqslant 0$):

$$\begin{bmatrix} + & - \\ - & + \end{bmatrix}, \quad \begin{bmatrix} - & - \\ + & + \end{bmatrix}$$

$$\begin{bmatrix} + & + \\ - & - \end{bmatrix}, \quad \begin{bmatrix} - & + \\ + & - \end{bmatrix}.$$

Proof For restrictions in signs, note that the budget constraint gives $\partial x_1/\partial p_i p_1 + \partial x_2/\partial p_i p_2 = 0$. By Corollary 5, at least one good is superior and hence normal. For factors the situation is more arbitrary. See Problem G. q.e.d.

For cases having the sign configurations above, the results are different from those suggested by Hicks [1959], who concludes that for two normal goods there is gross substitution. To obtain this result we must assume normality of one commodity and then use Euler's theorem applied to zero homogeneity in prices:

$$\frac{\partial x_1}{\partial p_1}p_1 + \frac{\partial x_1}{\partial p_2}p_2 = 0 \qquad \text{(Exercise 5).}$$

Alternatively, the substitution matrix for two goods has positive off-diagonals (Exercise 2).

In less technical terms, the gross substitution theorem applies only where θ is zero and the purchase of one good is contingent upon the sale of another. This Walrasean conception of demand contrasts with the more general Marshallian approach, where there is income earned from other sources that is uninfluenced by changes in the prices of consumer goods.

Exercise 3 Let a consumer hold two consumer goods in positive quantities, one a necessity, the other a luxury. Evaluate the elasticities of demand ε_{ij} , $i, j, = 1, 2$. What are their likely signs?

Exercise 4 Show that for two commodities

$$\frac{\partial\theta/p_i}{\partial x_i} + \frac{\partial\theta/p_j}{\partial x_i}\left(\frac{p_j}{p_i}\right)^2 x_j = 1 + \frac{p_j}{p_i}.$$

What are the possible sign configurations of the matrix $(\partial\theta/p_i)/\partial x_j$?

Exercise 5 Show that for $\theta = 0$ the sign pattern of $\partial x/\partial p$ is either

$$\begin{bmatrix} - & + \\ + & - \end{bmatrix} \quad \text{or} \quad \begin{bmatrix} + & - \\ - & + \end{bmatrix}.$$

What conditions on $\partial x_i/\partial\theta$ and x_i are required for the latter?

5. Independent Preferences

Here the explicit solution is used to characterize $\partial x/\partial p$ on open sets dense in the consumption space.

Preferences are *independent* provided that

$$(m_x)_{ij} = 0$$

for $j \neq i, j \neq 0$. (The case of two goods is a special one in that additive utility is not implied.) Therefore

$$\left(\frac{1}{m_i} e_i' - \frac{1}{m_j} e_j'\right)(m_x - m_{x_0} m')\left(\frac{1}{m_i} e_i - \frac{1}{m_j} e_j\right) < 0.$$

This implies that $(m_x)_{ii} < 0$ for all except possibly one i.

22 Lemma *Under independence and continuity of demand, either*

(i) m_{x_0} *is positive in all components and all but possibly one* $(m_x)_{ii}$ *is negative, or*

(ii) m_{x_0} *is nonpositive in all components and* m_x *is a negative diagonal.*

Proof According to Lemma 11, $m_i(m_{x_0})_j = m_j(m_{x_0})_i$, so that $m_{x_0} = km$ for some number k. Hence, $m_x - kmm'$ is negative definite. If k is negative, then clearly each $(m_x)_{ii}$ must be negative. If k is positive, then m_x must be negative definite on an $n - 1$ dimensional space. For m_x diagonal, this implies all but one diagonal element negative. q.e.d.

On open sets in the commodity space it is possible that

(i) $(m_x)_{ii} = 0$ for one i,
(ii) $(m_x)_{ii} < 0$ for all other i.

23 Theorem *If* $(m_x)_{ii} = 0$ *for* $\bar{x}_i < x_i < \bar{\bar{x}}_i$, *then*

$$\frac{\partial x_i}{\partial \theta} = 0, \qquad j \neq i, \qquad (\varepsilon_j = 0)$$

$$\frac{\partial x_i}{\partial \theta} = \frac{1}{p_i} \qquad \left(\varepsilon_i = \frac{1}{\kappa_i}\right)$$

$$\frac{\partial x_j}{\partial p_j} < 0 \qquad \text{for } j,$$

$$\frac{\partial x_k}{\partial p_j} = 0, \qquad k \neq j, \qquad k \neq i.$$

$$\frac{\partial x_j}{\partial p_i} > 0, \qquad j \neq i.$$

Hence, there are downward-sloping demand curves and at most there is complementarity of i with other commodities. Complementarity occurs if and only if

$$0 > \frac{\partial \theta / p_0}{\partial x_j} = \frac{\partial}{\partial x_j}(m_x + x_0)$$
$$= (m_x)_{jj}\, x_j + m_j\, .$$

The latter condition, $0 > (m_x)_{jj}\, x_j + m_j$, was first given by Wald [1936] in the form

$$\frac{\partial^2 u_j}{\partial x_j^2}\, x_j + \frac{\partial u_j}{\partial x_j} < 0.$$

Proof In case (i) $(m_x)_{ii} = 0$ for $\bar{x}_i < \bar{\bar{x}}_i < \bar{\bar{x}}_i$. At such a consumption, consider an increase in income, with prices held constant. By the continuity of demand, a small change in income will lead to a small change in demand so as to preserve the equation $(m_x)_{ii} = 0$ as income increases. Hence, we need only consider small changes in income. Since $(m_x)_{ii} = 0$, Lemma 22 gives that m_{x_0} is negative in all components. Therefore, an increase in the 0th commodity will cause m_i to rise, which is impossible if it is to be unchanged. On the other hand, for all other commodities j,

$$(m_x)_{jj} < 0,$$

so that a change in j without a change in 0 will decrease m_j, which cannot be. Therefore, so long as

$$(m_x)_{ii} = 0,$$

an increase in income increases the consumption of i alone, whereas the consumption of other commodities remains fixed. If i is a factor, the quantity provided by i falls ($|x_i|$ decreases as x_i increases).

Similarly, an increase in the price of j alone, $i \neq j$, requires a change in the jth and the ith commodities only. This follows since a change in the 0th commodity will alter m_i, whereas no small change in i can reverse the change. That the 0th commodity cannot change means that for $k \neq 0$, j, i, the kth commodity cannot change. Therefore, an increase in the price of j decreases j (so as to increase m_j) and may decrease or increase i, depending on whether the budget is exhausted or underutilized. Another way of saying this is that the demand for i increases if and only if the cost of buying of j alone (at a higher price of j) is less after the price increases.

A change in the price of the ith commodity requires that the 0th commodity increase in quantity in order that m_i rise. All other commodities j increase in quantity in order to compensate for the increase in m_j. Therefore, the demand for i decreases.

In the case of two goods, an increase in the price p_0 must force $m_i = p_i/p_0$ down and therefore x_0 must decrease. What happens to x_i again depends on what happens to the cost of the budget, exactly as before. q.e.d.

Next, consider the case where $(m_x)_{ii} \neq 0$ for all i. The inequality permits the use of the equations in the previous section.

24 Theorem *Under independence, with $(m_x)_{ii} \neq 0$ for all i, either all but one (superior) commodities are inferior commodities or else all but one* *(inferior) commodities are superior or else all commodities are superior. In the last case, m_x is a negative diagonal matrix and m_{x_0} is positive.*

There is no necessity of superior goods, even under the separability assumption. This is different from the approach of Stigler [1950], who presumes diminishing marginal utility for the utility function representing preference. Evidently, the assumption of diminishing marginal utility is more restrictive than the assumption of convexity of preference (Problem H).

Proof Evaluating (10a) gives

$$\frac{\partial x_i}{\partial \theta} = -\frac{(m_{x_0})_i}{(m_x)_{ii}\, p_0(1-\mu)} \tag{10b}$$

and

$$\frac{\partial x_0}{\partial \theta} = \frac{1}{(1-\mu)\, p_0}. \tag{10c}$$

Therefore,

$$\frac{\partial x_i}{\partial p_i} = \frac{1}{p_0 (m_x)_{ii}} = \frac{(m_{x_0})_i \dfrac{\partial \theta / p_0}{\partial x_j}}{(m_x)_{ii}\, p_0(1-\mu)},$$

$$\frac{\partial x_i}{\partial p_j} = -\frac{\partial x_i}{\partial \theta}\frac{1}{p_0}\frac{\partial \theta / p_0}{\partial x_j}\frac{1}{(m_x)_{jj}} \tag{6d}$$

$$= \frac{(m_{x_0})_i \dfrac{\partial \theta / p_0}{\partial x_j}}{(m_x)_{jj}(m_x)_{ii}\, p_0(1-\mu)} \tag{6e}$$

and

$$\frac{\partial x_0}{\partial p_j} = -\frac{1}{(1-\mu)}\frac{1}{p_0}\frac{\partial \theta / p_0}{\partial x}\frac{1}{(m_x)_{jj}}$$

$$= \frac{1}{(m_x)_{jj}}\frac{\partial x_0}{\partial \theta}\frac{\partial \theta / p_0}{\partial x}. \tag{6f}$$

If $(m_x)_{ii} < 0$ for all i, by Lemma 18, $(1-\mu) > 0$. Therefore, $\partial x_i / \partial \theta < 0$; that is, all except the 0th commodity are inferior and the 0th commodity is superior. Otherwise, two subcases emerge, namely,

$$(1-\mu) > 0 \qquad \text{and} \qquad (1-\mu) < 0.$$

In the former case, the 0th commodity is superior and all other commodities except possibly one are superior. In the latter case, all commodities are inferior commodities except one (not the 0th commodity). q.e.d.

25 Theorem *Under independence for j, for which* $(m_x)_{jj} < 0$, *there is gross substitutability,* $\partial x_0/\partial p_j < 0$, *if and only if*

$$\frac{\partial x_0}{\partial \theta}\frac{\partial \theta/p_0}{\partial x_j} < 0.$$

If $(m_x)_{jj} > 0$ *(for at most one j) there is substitutability if and only if*

$$\frac{\partial x_0}{\partial \theta}\frac{\partial \theta/p_0}{\partial x_j} < 0.$$

In particular, there is substitutability of j with all other commodities or else there is complementarity of j with all other commodities. If there are at least two superior commodities (so that $(1 - \mu) > 0$*), then for any superior commodity j,* $\partial x_i/\partial p_j > 0$ *if any only if*

$$(m_x)_{ii}\, x_i + m_i = \frac{\partial \theta/p_0}{\partial x_j} > 0$$

and for the (possibly) inferior commodity k, $\partial x_i/\partial p_k > 0$ *if and only if*

$$(m_x)_{ii}\, x_i + m_i = \frac{\partial \theta/p_0}{\partial x_i} < 0.$$

In particular, Theorem 25 makes a connection between the normality or superiority of a commodity, its cost effect, and its complementarity and/or substitutability with other commodities. It does not verify the reciprocity property (Hicks [1959]), whereby $\partial x/\partial p$ is symmetric in signs. It would seem that the reciprocity theorem applies only to the homothetic case (Corollary 14).

A consequence of Theorem 25 is that it is easy to imagine situations where

$$\frac{\partial \theta/p_0}{\partial x_j} < 0,$$

so that even though preferences have the very simple form of separability, gross complementarities can result.

6. Concavity Properties of Additive Utility

Here we consider the question as to when the additive representation gives rise to diminishing marginal utility

$$\frac{du_i}{dx_i} < 0$$

(where the u_i are continuously differentiable). Then the marginal rate of substitution is given by

$$m_i = \frac{\partial u/\partial x_i}{\partial u/\partial x_0} = \frac{du_i/dx_i}{du_0/dx_0}.$$

Therefore,

$$\frac{\partial m_i}{\partial x_0} = -\left(\frac{du_i/dx_i}{(du_0/dx_0)^2}\right)\frac{d^2u_0}{dx_0^2}.$$

Of course, $du_i/dx_i > 0$ for all i.

26 Theorem *In the case of differentiable additive utility, where the second-order conditions for cost minimization hold and* $du_i/dx_i^2 \neq 0$, *for all except possibly one commodity there is the law of diminishing marginal utility, that is,* $d^2u_i/dx_i^2 < 0$. *If there are only superior commodities, then* $d^2u_i/dx_i^2 \neq 0$ *and the law of diminishing marginal utility holds for all commodities.*

If preferences are weakly convex, it is said that utility is quasi concave. In this case, for any consumption x there is a price system $(m(x), 1)$ such that x is a cost-minimizing consumption on the indifference curve containing it. Therefore, the "weak" second-order conditions hold. Also $m_x - m_{x_0}m'$ is negative semidefinite everywhere in the interior of the commodity space, and therefore, by continuity, negative semidefinite everywhere in the commodity space. Also, if preferences are strictly convex (utility is strictly quasi concave), so that x is always the unique cost minimizer, then $m_x - m_{x_0}m'$ is negative definite on open sets dense in the commodity space.

27 Theorem *In the case of a differentiable, additive, quasi-concave utility function,* $d^2u_i/dx_i^2 \leqslant 0$ *for all except possibly one commodity. If the utility function is also strictly quasi concave, then* $d^2u_i/dx_i^2 < 0$ *for all except possibly one* i *on open sets dense in the commodity space. If all commodities are superior,* $d^2u_i/dx_i^2 < 0$ *for all* i, *with strict inequality on open sets dense in the commodity space. Consequently, if all commodities are superior,* u *is strictly concave.*

7. Consumer Surplus

Consumer surplus is used widely in applied economics to ascertain the welfare loss or gain of distortions of prices due to taxes, monopoly, and tariffs. The idea of consumer surplus is due to Dupuit [1844] and was elaborated by Marshall [1890]. It takes various forms, in all of which preferences are deduced from demand behavior. It is not known if this deduction can be made for all "reasonable" cases but there are several fragmentary results relating demand and preference. First, if the Strong Axiom of Revealed Preference holds, Richter's theorem (Theorem 6 and Problem I of Chapter 6) shows that there is a utility function as if representing preferences. Second, if preferences are directional dense, $m(x)$ is defined such that an indifference surface can be generated by equations such as $\partial x_0/\partial x_i = -m_i(x)$, where as usual $m_i(x) = p_i/p_0$.

28 Theorem *If $m(x_0, x)$ satisfies a Lipschitz condition in x_0 for fixed x, at most one continuous ordering can give the behavior described by $x(p)$.*

Proof The argument is standard in the theory of ordinary differential equations. For any two preference relations giving $m(x)$, the indifference surface can be solved along a line segment $x + t(\bar{x} - x)$ by

$$\frac{dx_0}{dt} = \frac{\partial x_0}{\partial x}(\bar{x} - x) = m(x)(\bar{x} - x).$$

Clearly, two solutions are of the form

$$x_0(s) - x_0(0) = \int_0^s m(x_0(t), tx + (1-t)\,\bar{x})(\bar{x} - x)\,dt$$

and

$$\hat{x}_0(s) - x_0(0) = \int_0^s m(\hat{x}_0(t), tx + (1-t)\,\bar{x})(\bar{x} - x)\,dt.$$

Hence,

$$|x_0(s) - \hat{x}_0(s)| = \left| \int_0^s \{m(x_0(t), tx + (1-t)\,\bar{x}) - m(\hat{x}_0(t), tx + (1 - t\,\bar{x})\}\,dt \right|$$

$$\leqslant \int_0^s |m(x_0(t), tx + (1-t)\,\bar{x}) - m(\hat{x}_0(t), tx + (1-t)\,\hat{x}|\,dt$$

$$\leqslant k \int_0^s |x_0(t) - \hat{x}_0(t)|\,dt.$$

(The last step applies the Lipschitz condition and is required only for small changes, $\bar{x} - x$.)

Let

$$0 \leqslant z(s) = \int_0^s | x_0(t) - \hat{x}_0(t)| \, dt.$$

Then

$$\frac{dz}{ds} = | x_0(s) - \hat{x}_0(s)|$$

and from the previous paragraph

$$\frac{dz}{ds} \leqslant kz(s), \qquad \text{or} \qquad \frac{dz}{ds} - kz(s) \leqslant 0.$$

Or, multiplying by e^{-ks}, we get

$$\frac{d}{ds} (z(s)\, e^{-ks}) \leqslant 0.$$

In general, if $z(0)\, e^{-ks} = 0$,

$$\frac{d}{ds} (z(0)\, e^{-ks}) \leqslant 0,$$

then

$$z(s)\, e^{-ks} \leqslant 0, \qquad \text{or} \qquad z(s) \leqslant 0.$$

Also,

$$z(s) \geqslant 0,$$

so that

$$z(s) = 0 \qquad \text{or} \qquad x_0(s) = \hat{x}_0(s). \qquad \text{q.e.d.}$$

29 Corollary *If there is a commodity, numbered zero, for which* $m(x_0, x) = m(\bar{x}_0, x)$ *for all* $x_0, x \geqslant 0$, *then there is at most one preference relation that can give the behavior described by* $m(x)$.

The corollary covers the case where the marginal utility of good zero is constant. Given the relative price of x, $m(x_0, x)$ increases in income lead to a change in x_0 only. To be specific, consumer surplus purports to evaluate changes in real income with regard to some initial or reference price system. It can be done under the hypothesis of the corollary.

The measurement of changes in consumer real income is illustrated in Figure 3. In moving from x to $\bar{x}$, real income in references prices $\bar{p}$ changes from the level of y to that of $\bar{y}$. There are great difficulties in finding the change in real income whenever relative prices change. One major problem is that observations are limited. In Figure 4, a consumer facing a change in relative prices with fixed income in reference prices moves from x to x. Even if it is assumed that the preferences are fully known in the locale of experience with regard to both going and reference prices, there is ambiguity in consumer real income—the dotted lines are acceptable indifference curves and they yield a much greater loss in income than the indifference curves illustrated. Possibly $\bar{y}^1$ or $\bar{y}^2$ is the equivalent of $\bar{x}$ or possibly some other point is. The same ambiguity appears in Figure 4b with a change in prices when nominal income is fixed. Evidently, any "holes" of ignorance between the locus of demands with reference prices and the locus of demands with going prices lead to great ambiguity about changes in consumer real income. Only "global" knowledge of the consumer's preference field can provide the correct answer. For example, Marshallian consumer surplus is a measure dependent on the behavior of the consumer at going prices. Evidently, it may greatly misstate, either over or under, the true loss in real income. Only the case of homothetic preferences is nice because knowing one indifference curve, we can generate all the rest (Theorem 14 of Chapter 6).

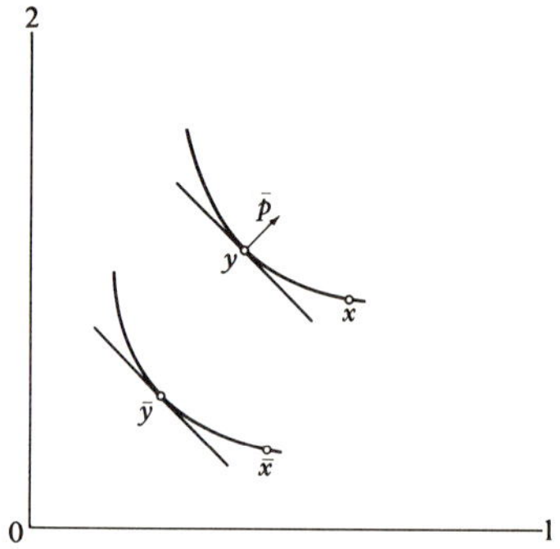

Figure 3

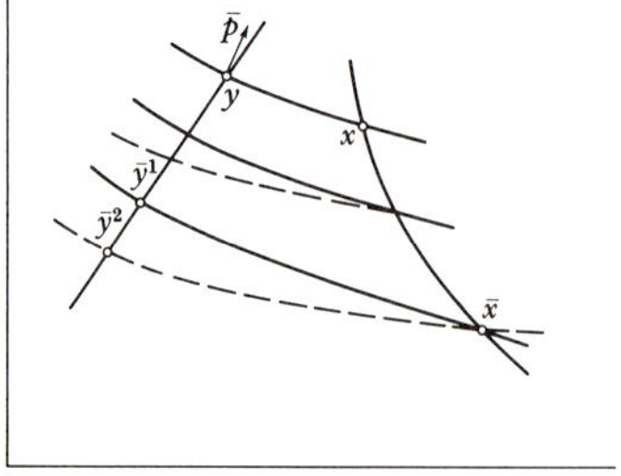

Figure 4a

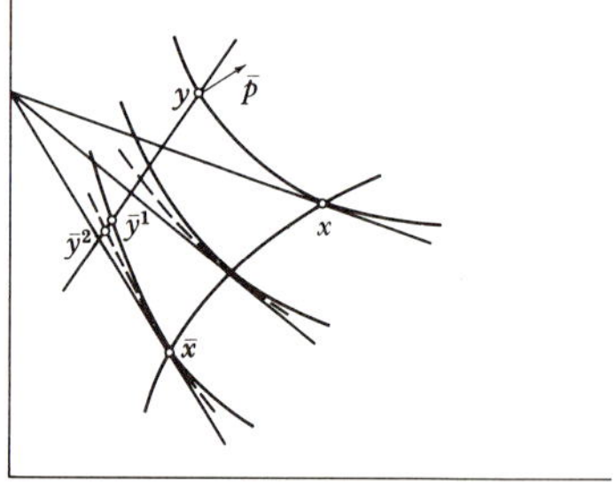

Figure 4b

30 Remark If going price ratios remain fixed and preferences are homothetic, losses in income lead to equiproportional relative losses in real consumer income. Hence, if income in the reference price system falls by 10 percent, so does real consumer income. Note that in such a state of affairs, once the change in relative prices has taken place, any further losses in income in reference prices lead to smaller losses in real consumer income. Income in reference prices is less valuable in both gain and loss whenever going price ratios are different from the reference ones.

In the general case, only for small changes in prices can the loss in real consumer income be derived from "observed" consumer behavior. Hicks [1959, Chapter XVIII] has set forth a diagrammatic presentation. A mathematical one is recorded here to cover cases of fixing income in reference prices and of fixing income in going prices. The former corresponds to the situation in which the consumer is compensated for the income losses and the latter to that in which he is not. Subsequently, we give a global theory for the homothetic case.

We define

$$(\bar{x}_0, \bar{x}) = (g^0, g)(p_0, \bar{p}, x_0, x)$$

to be the consumption giving the same preference level as (x_0, x) but a choice at the price system $(p_0, \bar{p})$. Throughout the analysis, p_0 will be fixed. The matrices or partial derivatives of (g^0, g) are

$$\frac{\partial g^0}{\partial \bar{p}} = g_2^0, \qquad \frac{\partial g}{\partial \bar{p}} = g_2,$$

$$\frac{\partial g^0}{\partial x_0} = g_3^0, \qquad \frac{\partial g}{\partial x_0} = g_3,$$

$$\frac{\partial g^0}{\partial x} = g_4^0 \qquad \frac{\partial g}{\partial x} = g_4.$$

Consumer real income is defined as

$$\begin{aligned} r(x_0, x) &= (p_0, \bar{p})(g^0, g)(p_0, \bar{p}_0, x_0, x) \\ &= \sum_i \bar{p}_i g^i(p_0, \bar{p}_0, x_0, x). \end{aligned}$$

Evidently, g_2^0 and g_2 are the Slutsky substitution effects. Also, let

$$\begin{aligned} (p_0, p) &= p_0\left(1, \frac{p_0}{p_0}\right) \\ &= p_0(1, m(x_0, x)) \end{aligned}$$

where $m(x_0, x)$ is the vector of marginal rates of substitution of other goods to good zero.

The homothetic case is of special interest.

31 Remark If preferences are homothetic, and $p = p_0 m(x)$,

$$\frac{\sum p_i g^i(p_0, p, y_0, y)}{\sum p_i x_i} = \frac{\sum \bar{p}_i g^i(p_0, \bar{p}, y_0, y)}{\sum \bar{p}_i g^i(p_0, \bar{p}, x_0, x)}.$$

Hence, if $\sum p_i x_i = \theta$

$$r(y) = \frac{r(x)}{\theta} \sum p_i g^i(p_0, p, y_0, y).$$

Proof By homotheticity,

$$(g_0, g)(p_0, p, y_0, y) = k(x_0, x)$$

Therefore,

$$(g_0, g)(p_0, \bar{p}, y_0, y) = k(g_0, g)(p_0, \bar{p}, x_0, x).$$

Premultiplying by (p_0, p) and $(p_0, \bar{p})$, respectively, gives the remark. q.e.d.

According to Remark 31, changes in r can be analyzed by knowledge of the locale of x. Evaluating $dr/d\varepsilon$ at $x = y$, we get

$$\frac{dr}{d\varepsilon} = \frac{r(x)}{\theta} \sum p_i \frac{d}{d\varepsilon} g^i(p_0, p, y_0, y).$$

Next, there is a mathematical relationship.

32 Lemma

$$\frac{\partial(g^0, g)}{\partial(x_0, x)} \equiv \begin{pmatrix} g_3^0 & g_4^0 \\ g_3 & g_4 \end{pmatrix} = I - p_0 \begin{pmatrix} g_2^0 \\ g_2 \end{pmatrix} \Bigg|_{p=m(x)} (m_{x_0}, m_x) \quad at\ g^i(p^0, p, x^0, x) = x^i.$$

Proof If

$$(x_0, x) = (g^0, g)(p_0, p_0 m(x_0, x), x_0, x),$$

then

$$I = p_0 \begin{pmatrix} g_2^0 \\ g_2 \end{pmatrix} (m_{x_0}, m_x) + \frac{\partial(g^0, g)}{\partial(x_0, x)}. \qquad \text{q.e.d.}$$

Let $\bar{\theta} = (p_0, \bar{p})(x_0, x) = \sum \bar{p}_i x_i$ be *income in reference prices.*

In measuring the change in a consumer's real income, it is convenient to think of two steps. First, there is the change in the consumer's income in reference prices, $\Delta(p_0, \bar{p})(x_0, x)$, and second, there is the change in the worth of income in consumer's terms:

$$\frac{dr}{d\varepsilon} = \left.\frac{\partial r}{\partial \theta}\right|_p \frac{d\theta}{d\varepsilon} + \left.\frac{\partial r}{\partial p}\right|_\theta \frac{dp}{d\varepsilon}. \tag{11a}$$

33 Lemma *At* $g^i(x_0, x, p_0, p) = x_i$,

$$\left.\frac{\partial r}{\partial \bar{\theta}}\right|_p = 1 - \frac{(p_0, p)}{\bar{\theta}} \begin{pmatrix} g_2^0 \\ g_2 \end{pmatrix} \frac{dp}{dk}$$

where $(\hat{x}_0, \hat{x}) = k(x_0, x)$. *For homothetic preferences where* $\bar{p} = m(x_0, x)$,

$$\left.\frac{\partial r}{\partial \theta}\right|_p = 1$$

and in general for $\bar{p} \neq m(x_0, x)$

$$\left.\frac{\partial r}{\partial \bar{\theta}}\right|_{\bar{p}} = \frac{r}{\theta}.$$

Proof

$$\left.\frac{\partial r}{\partial \bar{\theta}}\right|_p = \frac{d}{dk}\left\{\sum \bar{p}_i g^i(p_0, \bar{p}, kx_0, kx)\right\} \frac{dk}{d\theta}, \qquad \bar{\theta} = \sum \bar{p}_i \hat{x}_i = k \sum \bar{p}_i x_i .$$

Evidently,

$$\frac{dk}{d\bar{\theta}} = \frac{1}{\sum \bar{p}_i x_i}$$

and, evaluating at $k = 1$, we get

$$\left.\frac{\partial r}{\partial \bar{\theta}}\right|_p = \frac{\sum (\bar{p}_i)}{\sum \bar{p}_i x_i} \frac{\partial g^i}{\partial(x_0, x)} \frac{d(kx_0, kx)}{dk}$$

$$= \frac{1}{\bar{\theta}}(p_0, \bar{p}) \left(I - p_0 \begin{pmatrix} g_2^0 \\ g_2 \end{pmatrix} (m_{x_0}, m_x)\right) \begin{pmatrix} x_0 \\ x \end{pmatrix}$$

$$= 1 - \frac{(p_0, \bar{p})}{\bar{\theta}} \begin{pmatrix} g_2^0 \\ g_2 \end{pmatrix} \frac{dp}{dk}.$$

Apply Euler's theorem to obtain

$$\frac{\partial(g^0, g)}{\partial(x_0, x)}(x_0, x) = (g_0, g)(p_0, p, x_0, x).$$

Then apply Remark 31 and Lemma 32. q.e.d.

Consider a change in p that changes x. The exact nature of the x as a function of p is left unspecified. Let $\theta = \sum p_i x_i$.

34 Lemma *At* $g^i(x_0, x, p_0, p) = x_i$,

$$\frac{\partial r}{\partial p} = (p_0, p)\begin{pmatrix} \dfrac{\partial d_0}{\partial p} - g_2^0 \\ \dfrac{\partial d}{\partial p} - g_2 \end{pmatrix}.$$

Proof

$$\frac{\partial(g^0, g)}{\partial p} = \begin{pmatrix} g_3^0 & g_4^0 \\ g_3 & g_4 \end{pmatrix}\Bigg|_{p=m(x)} (m_{x_0}, m_x)\begin{pmatrix} \dfrac{\partial x_0}{\partial p} \\ \dfrac{\partial x}{\partial p} \end{pmatrix}$$

$$= \begin{pmatrix} \dfrac{\partial x_0}{\partial p} - g_2^0 p_0 m(x_0, x)\dfrac{\partial(x_0, x)}{\partial p} \\ \dfrac{\partial x}{\partial p} - g_2 p_0 m(x_0, x)\dfrac{\partial(x_0, x)}{\partial p} \end{pmatrix}$$

$$= \begin{pmatrix} \dfrac{\partial x_0}{\partial p} - g_2 \dfrac{\partial p}{\partial p} \\ \dfrac{\partial x}{\partial p} - g_2 \dfrac{\partial p}{\partial p} \end{pmatrix}\begin{pmatrix} \dfrac{\partial x_0}{\partial p} - g_2^0 \\ \dfrac{\partial x}{\partial p} - g_2 \end{pmatrix}$$

$$\frac{\partial r}{\partial p} = (p_0, p)\begin{pmatrix} \dfrac{\partial x_0}{\partial p} - g_2^0 \\ \dfrac{\partial x}{\partial p} - g_2 \end{pmatrix}. \qquad \text{q.e.d.}$$

35 Theorem *For the case* $\theta = \sum p_i x_i$ *fixed and* $g^i(x_0, x, p_0, p) = x_i$,

$$\frac{\partial r}{\partial p} = -x.$$

If preferences are homothetic, for $p_0 m(x) \neq p$,

$$\frac{\partial r}{\partial p} = -\left(\frac{r}{\theta}\right) x.$$

The theorem is illustrated in Figure 5. The loss is simply the consumer's surplus. To repeat, in the general case, the measure is meaningful only near the reference price system.

Proof In the case of $\sum p_i x_i$ constant, the Slutsky equation applied to Lemma 31 gives

$$\frac{\partial r}{\partial p} = (p_0, p)\frac{\partial(g^0, g)}{\partial p} = \begin{pmatrix} -\dfrac{\partial x_0}{\partial \theta} g' \\ -\dfrac{\partial x}{\partial \theta} g' \end{pmatrix}$$

$$= -\left(\sum_j \bar{p}_j \frac{\partial x_j}{\partial \theta}\right) x_i .$$

Since $\sum p_j x_j = \theta$

$$\sum \bar{p}_j \frac{\partial x}{\partial \theta} = \sum p_j \frac{\partial x_j}{\partial \theta} = 1 \qquad \text{or} \qquad \frac{\partial r}{\partial p_i} = -x_i . \qquad \text{q.e.d.}$$

36 Theorem *If $\sum \bar{p}_i x_i$ is fixed, the loss in real consumer income is the sum of the area between the demand curve and the old prices and between the quantities before and after the change in prices, weighted by r/θ in integration.*

Theorem 36 covers the case of a tax where the revenues are returned as a fixed subsidy. The traditional approach (Marshall [1890, pp. 467–470]) identifies the triangle ABC in Figure 5 as the loss and Theorems 35 and 36 give rules more in keeping with the graphical, generalized consumer surplus theory of Hicks [1959, Chapter XVIII]. Such a theory depends crucially on the homotheticity of preferences.

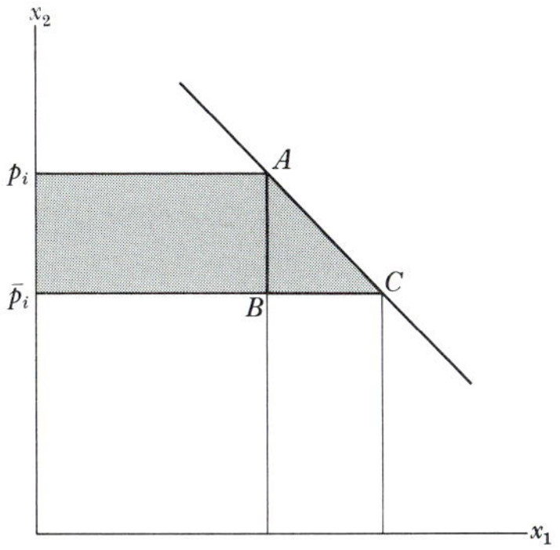

Figure 5

Proof Let $\theta = \sum p_i x_i$, $\sum \hat{p}_i x_i = \bar{\theta}$ fixed, $\bar{p}_i - \hat{p}_i = \Delta p_i$. Then

$$\frac{\partial\theta}{\partial p} = x + (p_0, p)\frac{\partial(x_0, x)}{\partial p}$$

$$= x + (p_0, \hat{p})\frac{\partial(x_0, x)}{\partial p} + \Delta(p_0, p)\frac{\partial(x_0, x)}{\partial p}$$

$$= x + \Delta(p_0, p)\frac{\partial(x_0, x)}{\partial p}$$

The Slutsky equation applies:

$$\frac{\partial(x_0, x)}{\partial p} = \frac{\partial(x_0, x)}{\partial p}\bigg| + \frac{\partial(x_0, x)}{\partial\theta}\bigg|_p \frac{\partial\theta}{\partial p}$$

$$= \frac{\partial(x_0, x)}{\partial p}\bigg| + \frac{\partial(x_0, x)}{\partial\theta}\bigg|_p \left(x + \left(\frac{\partial(x_0, x)}{\partial p}\right)' \Delta(p_0, p)'\right)$$

$$= \begin{pmatrix} g_2^0 \\ g_2 \end{pmatrix} + \frac{\partial(x_0, x)}{\partial\theta}\bigg|_p \left(\frac{\partial(x_0, x)}{\partial p}\right)' \Delta(p_0, p)'.$$

Applying Lemma 32 to $p = p_0 m(x)$, we get

$$\frac{\partial r}{\partial p} = (p_0, \bar{p})\begin{pmatrix} g_3^0 & g_4^0 \\ g_3 & g_4 \end{pmatrix}\frac{\partial(x_0, x)}{\partial p}$$

$$= (p_0, \bar{p})\left(I - p_0\begin{pmatrix} g_2^0 \\ g_2 \end{pmatrix}(m_{x_0}, m_x)\right)\frac{\partial(x_0, x)}{\partial p}$$

$$= (p_0, \bar{p})\left(\begin{pmatrix} g_2^0 \\ g_2 \end{pmatrix} + \frac{\partial(x_0, x)}{\partial\theta}\left(\frac{\partial(x_0, x)}{\partial p}\right)' \Delta(p_0, p)' - \begin{pmatrix} g_2^0 \\ g_2 \end{pmatrix}\frac{\partial p}{\partial p}\right)$$

$$= (p_0, \bar{p})\frac{\partial(x_0, x)}{\partial\theta}\left(\frac{\partial(x_0, x)}{\partial p}\right)' \Delta(p_0, p).$$

Since

$$(p_0, \bar{p})\frac{\partial(x_0, x)}{\partial\theta} = \sum \bar{p}_j \frac{\partial x_j}{\partial\theta} = 1,$$

$$\frac{\partial r}{\partial p} = \sum_j \Delta p_j \frac{\partial x_j}{\partial p}.$$

For $\hat{p} = \bar{p}$, $\Delta p_i = 0$ and $\partial r/\partial p = 0$. For homothetic preferences,

$$\frac{\partial r}{\partial p} = \frac{r}{\theta} \sum \Delta p_j \frac{\partial x_j}{\partial p}$$

or

$$r = \sum_j \int \frac{r}{\theta} \Delta p_j \frac{\partial x_j}{\partial p} dp_j = \sum_j \int \frac{r}{\theta} \Delta p_j \, dx_j . \qquad \text{q.e.d.}$$

37 Theorem *If the consumer k is homothetic,*

$$\frac{dr^k}{d\varepsilon} = \frac{r^k}{\theta^k} \frac{d\theta^k}{d\varepsilon} \qquad \textit{or} \qquad r^k = \theta^k \exp\left(\frac{1}{\theta^k}\left[\frac{d\theta^k}{d\varepsilon} + \sum \int \Delta p_j \, dx_j\right]\right)$$

where

$$\theta^k = \sum p_j x_j^k , \qquad \Delta p_j = p_j - \bar{p}_j .$$

If r^k/θ^k is the same for all k,

$$\frac{dr}{d\varepsilon} = \frac{r}{\theta} \frac{d\bar{\theta}}{d\varepsilon} + \sum \Delta p_j \, dx_j \qquad \text{or} \qquad r = \theta \exp\left(\frac{1}{\theta}\left[\frac{d\bar{\theta}}{de} + \sum \int \Delta p_j \, dx_j\right]\right)$$

where

$$r = \sum r^k, \qquad \theta = \sum \theta^k = \textit{nominal gnp},$$

$$\bar{\theta} = \sum \bar{\theta}^k = \textit{gnp} \quad \textit{in terms of reference princes},$$

$$x = \sum_k x^k \quad \textit{is the demand for j}.$$

If r^k/θ^k is the same for different k, it is said that the *burden is distributed uniformly*. Theorem 37 gives rules for evaluating the changes in real income whenever a tax, tariff, or monopoly is imposed and the burden is distributed uniformly.

UNSOLVED PROBLEM

J. Integrability of Demand

Generalize the conditions presented in this section for determinate preferences. (Hint: A counterexample due to Shapley is as follows. Draw two indifference curves as in Figure 6a, making sure that they have sufficient variability in slope for two utility-maximizing individuals with the same demand behavior.

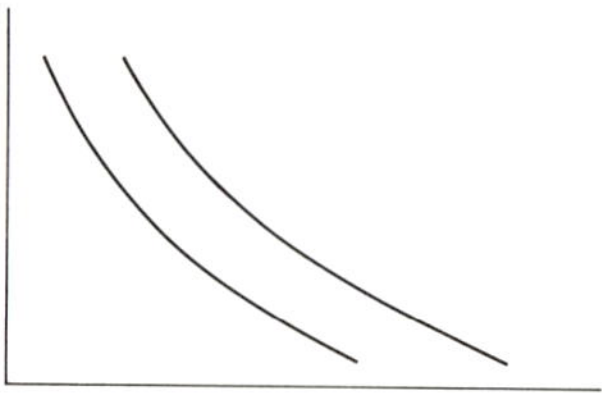
Figure 6a

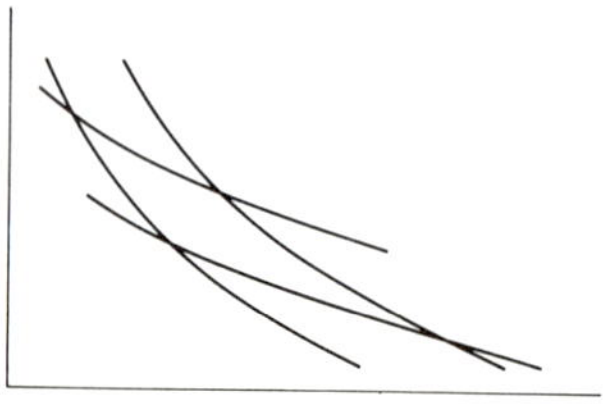
Figure 6b

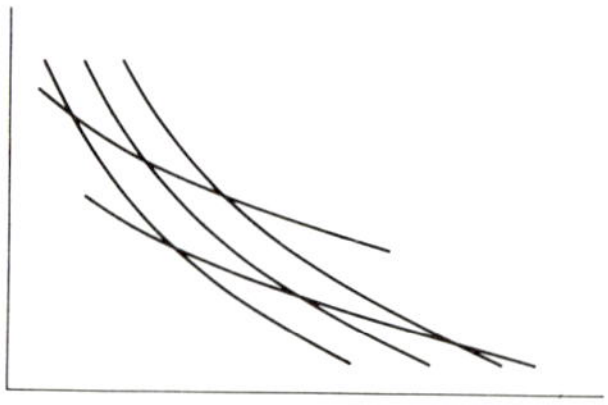
Figure 6c

As in Figure 6b, draw two curves crossing each of the first two but with tangencies at the points of crossing. Now pass a third through one tangent to the two new ones but not crossing the two old ones, as in Figure 6c. Repeat the construction, always making sure that the crossing indifference curves are tangent. In the limit, this gives two preference fields with the same slopes everywhere.)

IV

Trade

9

Exchange

Price or exchange value is determined in the same way as economic equilibrium, and the latter results from the conflict between preferences and constraints.

> Vilfredo Pareto
> Translated from Section 225 of Chapter III of
> MANUELE DI ECONOMIA POLITICA
> (translated into French by Roger Dehem as
> MANUEL D'ÉCONOMIE POLITIQUE, Librairie Droz, Geneva, 1906)

1. Production and Preferences

Normally, individuals not only have preferences, but also have some notion of ways of fulfilling them. The nature of this knowledge has already been discussed in Chapter 4.

Given a certain stock of goods, the consumer produces an output which leads to a preference-optimizing position. To apply the preference relation, we must know all future capital stocks before production; to optimize, plans must be made for the future as well as the present.

We can even allow negative initial stocks of capital and other commodities, provided these commodities can be increased to nonnegative levels after production. In this way trades and anticipated trades are subjected to consideration by the consumer.

Even in the absence of what would be regarded as production, there may well be utility-producing processes that are essentially production (Lancaster (1966]). Utility would be attached to goods that were never traded in the marketplace and that were produced from combinations of marketable goods, goods that had no utility in and of themselves (Rader [1963b, 1964]).

In the modern spirit, reference to utility is avoided. Hence everything that follows applies to partial orderings as well as orderings. This is especially relevant for economic analysis, since the preference for intertemporal efficient paths is not a complete ordering, even though the preference partial ordering satisfies certain regularity conditions; that is, it is convex, locally unsaturated (indeed, monotonic), and for it there are maximal elements on certain kinds of sets. (This is treated in Chapter 1 of the companion volume.)

Consideration is restricted to a set of trades $\mathscr{X}_i$ that is assumed closed and excludes any commodities that by their nature are not tradable.

The commodity labor presents some difficulties. Labor is produced with inputs such as food, clothing, and shelter. But in producing labor, there may be some utility or disutility. On the other hand, the *use* of labor, such as occurs when an individual hires someone else, incurs no disutility to the user. This is the opposite of the case for other commodities. It is necessary to provide for an extra commodity, "pain of labor," which is produced whenever labor services are produced and in the same quantity. This commodity should be unique to each labor-producing individual, should be differentiated according to the different kinds of labor services produced by that individual, and should not be traded. It can be prevented from being traded by fiat (that is, simply require that its component in the trade set $\mathscr{X}_i$ be zero for each individual i). The utility is unaffected by the amounts of labor goods held and is influenced only by the amount of pain-of-labor goods held.

Costs of exchange can be included simply by allowing only trades of goods that have no utility. There is a production process in ${}_t\mathscr{Y}^i_{t+1}$ that transforms desirable (or undesirable) goods into transfer goods and back again and that requires certain goods as factors, giving the "costs" of exchange. Exchanges may be instantaneous (such that the exchange–production process is reversible, transforming consumer goods into exchange goods and back again into the same goods, at the same point of time) or may take time (forbidding reversibility). For example, suppose we wish to allow for the fact that exchange takes time and, hence, involves the cost of waiting. We simply stipulate that the process turn exchange goods into consumer goods in the following period, assuming that exchange requires time.

Given a certain stream of commodity outflows from individual i

$$(x^i(t), t = 0, 1, 2, \ldots),$$

individual i performs certain production activities to obtain

$$y^i(t+1) \in {}_t\mathscr{Y}_{t+1}(y_i(t)) - \{x_i(t)\}.$$

The *trade set* or the set of possible outflows is denoted by

$$\mathscr{X}_i = \{x^i(t), t = 0, 1, 2, \ldots \mid \text{there exists} \quad y_i(t+1) \in {}_t\mathscr{Y}_{t+1}(y_i(t)) - \{x_i(t\})\}$$

and the set of possible inflows by $-\mathscr{X}_i$.

For example, there is a nonnegativity constraint imposed on $y^i(t)$. The constraint is incorporated directly into the ${}_t\mathscr{Y}^i_{t+1}(y^i(t))$ whose domain is constrained to Ω, thus forcing $x^i_j(t) \leqslant 0$ whenever $y^i_j(t) = 0$.

Additional constraints can be imposed in the same way. For example, there may be an upper limit on the amount of labor provided per unit of time. This simply means that the projection of ${}_t\mathscr{Y}^i_{t+1}(y^i(t))$ on the labor axis is bounded from above. Therefore, restrictions on the domain of consumer preferences can (and should) be incorporated directly into the production set ${}_t\mathscr{Y}^i_{t+1}(y^i(t))$.

Now consider the flow $(x^i(t),\ t = 0, 1, 2, \ldots)$. In general, several capital "paths" $y^i(t)$ can be chosen that will ensure that

$$y^i(t+1) \in {}_t\mathscr{Y}^i_{t+1}(y^i(t)) - \{x^i(t)\}.$$

For example, if $x^i(t) = 0$, then possibly inaction, $y^i(t) = 0$, $t = 0, 1, \ldots$, will do; also, if there is any free production, $y(t) > 0$, $t = 0, 1, \ldots$, is a possible stock of capital.

In Figure 1, the derivation of optimizing capital stocks is illustrated for the one-good, two-period case. It is assumed that the consumer has initial wealth equal to $y^i(1)$, which normally would deteriorate (or grow) to $y^i(2)$. Then this wealth with the transfers $x^i = (x^i(1), x^i(2))$ can be used to obtain at least $y^i(2) + z^i(2)$, where $z^i(2)$ is the change in capital that could not have been attained without transfers. In addition, production activities can be carried out to substitute the first commodity for the second or vice versa. It is required that $y^i(t+1)$ in ${}_t\mathscr{Y}_{t+1}(y^i)$ be nonnegative. Only in Figure 1 there is no free disposal, as that would seem unreasonable, since the quantity of capital in period two should depend on the quantity of capital in period one. (It is assumed that more is preferred to less in each period.) Indifference curves $\mathscr{I}_0, \mathscr{I}_1, \mathscr{I}_2, \mathscr{I}_3$ are drawn between capital in the two periods, and the optimal choice is $\bar{y}^i$, which incidentally is different from $w^i + x^i$. Note that the production set is compact (closed and bounded) and the upper contour sets $\mathscr{R}_i(y^i)$ are closed.

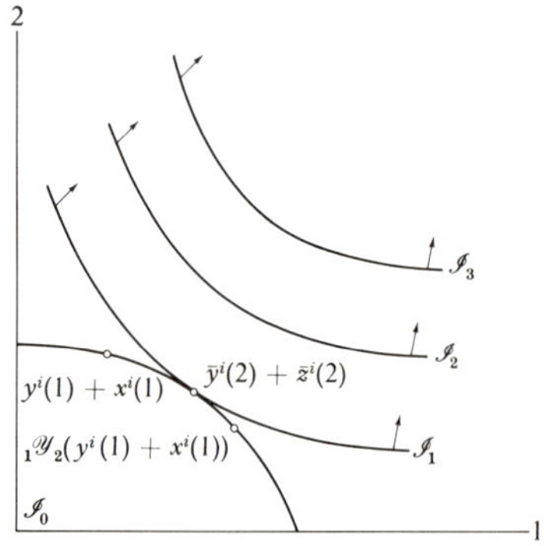

Figure 1

Let $\xi_i(x^i)$ be the set of *preference-optimizing* or *preference maximal productions* given x^i.

1 Theorem *Consider* $(x(t), t = 0, 1, 2,\ldots)$ *in the trade set* $\mathscr{X}_i$. *Suppose* $\mathscr{R}_i$ *is regular or* $\mathscr{P}_i(x)$ *is open and* ${}_t\mathscr{Y}_{t+1}(y^i)$ *is compact. Then there is an optimizing* y, *where*

$$\mathscr{X}_i = {}_0\mathscr{Y}_\infty(y_i(0) - x(0)) - \{(x^i(t), \quad t = 0, 1, 2,\ldots)\}.$$

As a matter of interpretation, note the construction of ${}_0\mathscr{Y}^i_\infty(t, y)$ to account for the outflow $x^i(t)$. As a second matter, the requirement that $\mathscr{R}_i$ be regular does not appear to be a very serious one. An interpretation of this requirement will be found in Section 1 of Chapter 6.

Proof Apply Theorem 4 of Chapter 5. q.e.d.

Theorem 1 is the fundamental result giving conditions under which $\xi^i(x^i)$ is nonempty. In the next section, further properties of this process will be considered under the name of *induced preferences*. It is said that

$$x^i \mathscr{R}^*_i \bar{x}^i, \qquad \bar{x}^i, x^i \in \mathscr{X}_i$$

if and only if for any $\bar{y}^1 \in \xi^i(\bar{x}^i)$, there is a y^i in $\xi^i(x^i)$ for which $y^i \mathscr{R}_i \bar{y}^i$; the trade x_i is not (induced) inferior to $\bar{x}^i$.

From Theorem 1, in the case of an ordering, the relation $\mathscr{R}^*$, induced by optimization, is well defined.

In the next section these ideas will be generalized in order to take account of interrelationships between consumers.

It is often interesting to know when the optimizing $\xi_j(x^j)$ is a single point:

2 Theorem *There is at most one point in $\xi_i(x^1)$ whenever $\mathscr{R}_i$ is a strictly convex complete ordering and ${}_t\mathscr{Y}^i_{t+1}$ is convex in $y(t)$.*

Proof If $\mathscr{R}_i$ is strictly convex and $y^i, \bar{y}^i \in \xi_i(x^i)$,

$$y^i \in {}_t\mathscr{Y}^i_{t+1}(y^i(t)) - \{x^i\}, \qquad \bar{y}^i \in {}_t\mathscr{Y}^i_{t+1}(y^i(t)) - \{x^i\},$$

then

$$sy^i + (1-s)\,\bar{y}^i\,\mathscr{P}_i\,y^i$$

whenever $y^i \neq \bar{y}^i$, $0 < t < 1$. But also

$$sy^i + (1-s)\,\bar{y}^i \in {}_t\mathscr{Y}_{t+1}(y^i(t)) - \{x^i\}$$

whenever ${}_t\mathscr{Y}_{t+1}(y^i(t))$ is convex in y^i. Therefore, $sy^i + (1-s)\,\bar{y}^i$ is possible with x^i. This is impossible by the definition of ξ_i, whereupon $y^i - \bar{y}^i$. q.e.d.

Exercise 1 Suppose there are three traded goods, used to produce two nontraded consumer services. Let production be Cobb–Douglas with at most two goods going into any one (Chapter 4, Section 4). Let the original utility also be Cobb–Douglas. What is the induced utility?

2. Properties of Preferences on Trades

With some effort, the properties of the original preference relation will be imputed to the induced relation. First, however, the definition of induced preferences will be extended to consumer interdependency of preferences. Then we will show the various continuity, convexity, and unsaturation properties.

Normally, consumer i has little control over the choices of the others. Nevertheless, he is still influenced by their choices. The set of consumer preferences dependent on the consumption of others, $\mathscr{R}_i$, is defined on the product of capital stock possibility sets,

$$\mathop{\mathsf{X}}_{j=1}^{n} \mathscr{C}_j .$$

There is an *induced* preference relation $\mathscr{R}_1^*$ that is defined on the product of trade sets

$$\mathop{\mathsf{X}}_{j=1}^{n} \mathscr{X}_j$$

as follows.

$$x \, \mathscr{R}_i^* \, \bar{x} \qquad \text{for} \quad x, \bar{x} \in \mathop{\mathsf{X}}_{j=1}^{n} \mathscr{X}_j$$

provided that for every $\bar{y}$ in the product of optimizing capital stocks

$$\mathop{\mathsf{X}}_{j=1}^{n} \xi_j(\bar{x}^j) \quad \text{there is a} \quad y \in \mathop{\mathsf{X}}_{j=1}^{n} \xi_j(x^j)$$

such that

$$y \, \mathscr{R}_i^* \, \bar{y}.$$

The rationale of this definition is that given a trade combination x^j, i can count on j choosing i's most desired alternative from $\xi_j(x^j)$. Otherwise, the fact that i is concerned only with the general set $\xi_j(x^j)$ indicates that he is indifferent to j's capital stock so long as j is. In effect, i only considers the preference level obtained by j, possibly because $\mathscr{R}_j$ is strictly convex and therefore $\xi_j(x^j)$ is a unique point (Theorem 2). In the absence of strict convexity, this method of consumer interdependencies may be a misrepresentation insofar as preference is related not to j's level of preference, but rather to the Veblen effect, whereby one person's holdings per se influence other individuals, especially with respect to attempts by i and j to comptete for prestige among their fellows. Nevertheless, the definition of $\mathscr{R}^*$ may capture some aspects of consumer interrelationships, especially those related to concern for the state of one's fellows.

A summary of results for this section appears in Table 1.

3 Theorem *$\mathscr{R}_1^*$ is defined on $\mathsf{X}_{j=1}^{n} \mathscr{X}_j$ provided that each $\xi_j(x^j)$ is compact and $\mathscr{R}_i$ is regular or $\mathscr{P}_i^{-1}(x)$ is open. If also ${}_t\mathscr{Y}_{t+1}(y)$ is upper semicontinuous, then $\mathscr{R}_i^*$ is regular or $(\mathscr{P}^*)^{-1}(y)$ is open, respectively. $\mathscr{R}_i^*$ is an ordering whenever $\mathscr{R}_i$ is.*

TABLE 1[a]

Induced preferences are/have	Whenever induced preferences are	And the production possibility set is	And consumer preferences are/have
Defined		Closed and there is no free production in the limit	Regular or $\mathscr{P}^{-1}(y)$ is open
Regular	Defined		Regular
$(\mathscr{P}^*)^{-1}(y)$ open	Defined	Closed	Unions of finite intersections of continuous orderings
$\mathscr{P}^*(x)$ open on the interiors of $\mathscr{X}$	Defined	Convex	$\mathscr{P}(y) \geqslant$ -open
Continuous on line segments	Defined and regular or such that $(\mathscr{P}^*)^{-1}(x)$ is open	Closed on line segments	Finite unions of intersections of orders continuous and complete on line segments
$\geqslant$-Continuous on internal points in the trade set	Defined and regular	Closed, $\geqslant$-convex, and convex	Finite unions of intersections of $\geqslant$-continuous orders
Weakly convex	Defined	Convex	Weakly convex
Convex	Defined	Convex	Convex
Strictly convex	Defined	Strictly convex	Strictly convex
Locally unsaturated (in pointwise convergence)	Defined		Locally unsaturated in goods that can be traded and can leave outputs of other goods unchanged
Monotonic increasing	Defined	Such that factors are not unproductive	Monotonic increasing

[a] To read, choose a row other than the first. Read the first phrase in the first column before the first phrase in the chosen row, then the first phrase of the second column before the second phrase in the chosen row, and so on.

Proof The finite product of compact sets is easily seen to be compact, and therefore Theorem 1 applies. For $x^n \to \bar{x}$, $y^n \mathscr{R} y$, y^n bounded, there is a convergent subsequence of $y^nk \to \bar{y}$. Therefore,

$$\bar{y} \in \xi_i(x)$$

and if $\mathscr{R}_i(y)$ is closed, $x \in \mathscr{R}_i^*(x)$. Therefore, $\mathscr{R}_i^*(x)$ is closed. The proof for $(\mathscr{P}^*)^{-1}(y)$ open follows in like manner. q.e.d.

4 Corollary *If $\mathscr{R}_i$ is the union of finite intersections of regular orderings, then $(\mathscr{P}_i^*)^{-1}(x)$ is open.*

Proof $\mathscr{P}_i^*$ is the union of finite intersections of the appropriate induced orders. q.e.d.

Cases of consumer preferences to which Theorem 3 applies are given in Chapter 5, Section 4.

The continuity of $\mathscr{R}_i^*$ is more difficult to derive. In fact, it cannot be shown that $\mathscr{R}_i^*$ is continuous whenever $\mathscr{R}_i$ is continuous, even if regularity conditions are imposed upon the production possibilities.

Example 1 If the production set ${}_t\mathscr{Y}_{t+1}(y)$ is discontinuous in y, as is the nonconvex production set in Figure 2, then the possibility for a discontinuity in utility arises. Simply let

$$(x^n(t+1) = x(t+1) + \delta t^n,\ t = 0, 1,\ldots),$$

δ a fixed vector, t^n tending to zero. This represents an input–output sequence for which the optimizing y in $\xi(x)$ may not be approximated by y^n producible from x^n. Hence, the situation may arise that the limit points of $\xi(x^n)$ are inferior to y by some given margin.

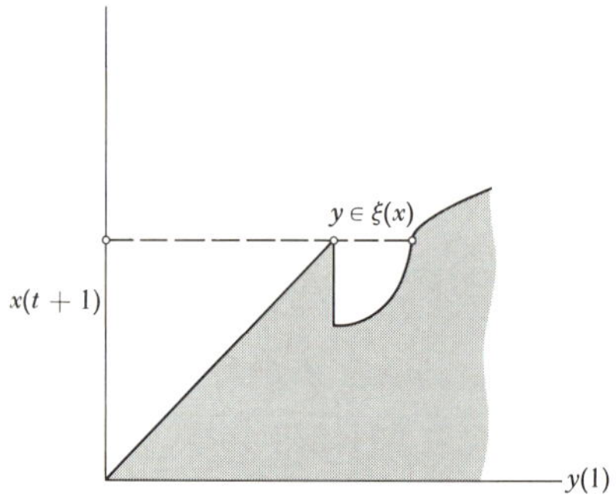

Figure 2

Example 2 It is clear from Example 1 that some restriction on the production set is necessary to obtain full continuity of ξ, but even this is not enough. Consider a two-commodity, two-period case in which one of the commodities x_1 is perishable and disappears after one period. Let there be a positive stock of each good at the beginning of the period, with a negative outflow required of the second commodity at the end of the period. Given $\bar{x}_1(1)$ and $\bar{x}_2(1)$, suppose $\bar{x}_2(2)$ is the maximum amount of $\bar{x}_2$ that can be provided in period two. Then the outflow

$$(\bar{x}_1(1), \bar{x}_2(1), 0, x(2))$$

leads to capital stock

$$(\bar{y}_1(1), \bar{y}_2(1), 0, 0).$$

Now decrease the requirement $-\bar{x}_2(0)$. Normally, this allows resources to be devoted to output of commodities for the consumer's own use. However, if $\bar{x}_2(1)$ is also reduced accordingly, then the requirements in period two will entirely "eat up" the initial capital stock. The reduction may be made in the following way. Fix the amount of the first commodity in period one and reduce the second such that after the requirement in the second commodity is met, nothing is left in period two. On the other hand, in the limit, with zero requirements the consumer can enjoy some of commodity 1 in the second period.

Example 3 A case of diminishing returns would be the requirement

$$\bar{y}_1(1) = (\bar{y}_2(1))^{\alpha}(\bar{y}_2(2))^{\beta}, \qquad \frac{1}{\beta} + \frac{\beta}{\alpha} \leqslant 1.$$

(This is merely a form of the Cobb–Douglas production function: $\bar{y}_2(2) = \bar{y}_1(1)^{1/\beta}\, \bar{y}_2(1)^{\beta/\alpha}$). Let $\bar{x}_2(2)$ tend to zero simultaneously with $\bar{y}_2(2) = -\bar{x}_2(2)$ because $\bar{y}_2(1) \to 0$. Then, the choice is always forced to be $(\bar{y}_1(1), \bar{y}_2(1), 0, 0)$. After zero is reached, however, there is no longer any requirement to produce for period 1, and therefore, the consumer can simply enjoy his commodity as it deteriorates (or grows) at its natural rate; that is, instead of $(\bar{y}_1(1), 0, 0, 0)$, which is the limiting value of his consumption, chosen from the converging input–output vectors $(\bar{y}_1(1), \bar{y}_2(1), 0, \bar{y}_2(2))$, he can obtain the strictly better consumption $(\bar{y}_1(1), 0, \delta\bar{y}_1(2), 0)$, where δ is the proportion of the first good surviving whenever it is not changed by a production process. Again, there is a sudden jump in the level of preference. Note that the production system need not display nonconvexities and indeed it corresponds closely to traditional views of production.

It can be shown that $\mathscr{R}_i^*$ is continuous on line segments in $\mathscr{X}_i$, but no continuity properties are derived on $\mathscr{X}$, since ξ_j, $j \neq i$, is not generally continuous. If $\mathscr{R}_j$ were strictly convex, then ξ_j would be a continuous function and continuity along straight lines could be deduced for $\mathscr{R}_j^*$ on $\mathscr{X}$, but in general, such a strong property is not necessary.

5 Theorem *Suppose ${}_t\mathscr{Y}_{t+1}(y(t), t)$ is convex, $\mathscr{P}_i(y)$ is open on line segments, and $\xi_i(x^i)$ is compact for all i. Then, $\mathscr{P}_i^*(x)$ is open on line segments in $\mathscr{X}_i$ if $x^j, j \neq i$ is held fixed.*

Proof Let

$$x^n \in \langle \bar{x}, \bar{\bar{x}} \rangle,$$

that is,

$$x^n = s^n\bar{x} + (1 - s^n)\,\bar{\bar{x}}, \qquad x^n \to x.$$

Then, if $s^n \to s$,

$$x^n \to s\bar{x} + (1 - s)\,\bar{\bar{x}}.$$

Without loss of generality, take $x = \bar{x}$. If $\bar{y} \in \xi_i(\bar{x})$, $\bar{\bar{y}} \in \xi_i(\bar{\bar{x}})$, then $s^n\bar{y} + (1 - s^n)\,\bar{\bar{y}}$ is possible for x^n, so that there exists

$$\bar{y}^n \in \xi^i(x^n), \qquad \bar{y}^n\, \mathscr{R}_i\, y^n \equiv s^n\bar{y} - (1 - s^n)\,\bar{\bar{y}}.$$

Of course, the preference level of y^n tends to that of y. Therefore, x^n has at least almost as high a level of preference as x; that is if $y\, \mathscr{P}_i\, y$, for large n, $\bar{y}^n\, \mathscr{P}_i\, y$.

Therefore, $\mathscr{P}_i^*(y)$ is open. q.e.d.

6 Corollary *If $\mathscr{R}$ is an ordering continuous on line segments, ${}_t\mathscr{Y}^i_{t+1}(y(t))$ is convex, and $\xi_i(x^i)$ is compact for all i, then $\mathscr{R}_i^*$ is continuous on line segments.*

7 Corollary *If $\mathscr{R}_i$ is the intersection of finite unions of orderings, with closed lower contour sets on line segments, ${}_t\mathscr{Y}_{t+1}(y)$ is convex, and $\xi_i(t)$ is compact for all i, then $(\mathscr{R}_i^*)^{-1}(x)$ is closed on line segments.*

Proof For an ordering,

$$(\mathscr{R}_i^*)^{-1}(x) = \bigcap_i (\mathscr{R}_i^*)^{-1}(x) = \bigcap_i \sim\mathscr{P}_i^*(x) = \sim\bigcup_i \mathscr{R}_i^*(x),$$

so that the induced relation has closed lower contour sets on line segments. Apply Theorems 1 and 3. q.e.d.

Actually, a modification of the foregoing proofs can be made to show that the same continuous utility representation u_i for $\mathscr{R}_i$ may be used for $\mathscr{R}_i^*$, namely, by the maximization

$$u_i^*(x^i) = \max\{u_i(y) \mid y(t+1) \in {}_t\mathscr{Y}^i_{t+1}(y^i(t)) - \{x^i(t)\}\},$$

and it could then be shown that u_i^* is continuous on line segments in $\mathscr{X}$. The reasoning above can be extended to cover regularity and continuity in terms of a rather special kind of convergence. Let y^n $\geqslant$-*converge* to y if there exist k^n, t^n such that

$$k^n y \geqslant y^n \geqslant t^n y, \qquad k^n \to 1, \quad t^n \to 1.$$

Then openness and closedness can be interpreted as $\geqslant$-openness and $\geqslant$-closedness, with $\geqslant$regularity and $\geqslant$-continuity. In cases where there are only a finite number of commodities, $\geqslant$-convergence is the same as ordinary convergence.

8 Theorem *If $\mathscr{R}_i$ is regular and ${}_t\mathscr{Y}_{t+1}$ is closed (in the $\geqslant$-convergence) and convex in y, commodities are not negatively productive, and there is $\geqslant$-convexity of production, then $\mathscr{P}_i^*(x)$ is open (in $\geqslant$-convergence) on the set of interior points of $\mathscr{X}$.*

Note that the continuity property derived is weaker than continuity under pointwise convergence. Continuity of $\mathscr{R}_i$ can be substituted for $\geqslant$-continuity, but in the framework of infinite time, $\geqslant$-continuity seems more reasonable.

Proof Let $x^n \to x$, $x \mathscr{P}_i^* \bar{x}$, $y \in \xi(x)$, $\bar{y} \in \xi(\bar{x})$. By lower semicontinuity of production (Problem B of Chapter 4), there is an output y^n feasible from x and near y (in $\geqslant$-convergence). The $\geqslant$-convergence of sums of $\geqslant$-converging sequences is easily shown. It follows that $y^n - x^n$ is near $y - x$ and preferred to $\bar{y} - \bar{x}$, provided only that x^n be in the trade set. Finally, for large n, x^n is in the trade set since x is in its interior.

9 Corollary *If $\mathscr{R}_i$ is the intersection of finite unions of orderings satisfying the hypotheses of Theorem 8, then $\mathscr{R}_i^*$ is continuous (in $\geqslant$-convergence) on the interior of $\mathscr{X}$.*

The other properties of consumer demand are more straightforward.

10 Theorem *If ${}_t\mathscr{Y}_{t+1}^i(y(t))$ is convex, and $\mathscr{R}_i$ is (strictly, weakly) convex, then so is $\mathscr{R}_i^*$.*

Proof The proof is for weak convexity only. The other cases can be obtained simply by substituting $\mathscr{P}_i$ and $\mathscr{I}_i$ for $\mathscr{R}_i$ at the appropriate places.

Suppose $x^i \mathscr{R}_i^* \bar{x}^i$. Then $\bar{y}^i \in \xi_i(\bar{x}^i)$, $y^i \in \xi_i(x^i)$, such that $y^i \mathscr{R}_i \bar{y}^i$. Therefore,

$$\bar{\bar{y}}^i \in \xi_i(tx^i + (1-t)\,\bar{x}^i), \qquad \bar{\bar{y}}^i \in \mathscr{R}_i(tx^i + (1-t)\,\bar{x}^i)$$

since the convexity of ${}_t\mathscr{Y}_{t+1}(y)$ allows $ty^i + (1-t)\,\bar{y}^i$ as a choice by i in $\xi_i(tx^i + (1-t)\,\bar{x}^i)$. Hence, by weak convexity of $\mathscr{R}_i$, for every $\bar{y}^i \in \xi_i(\bar{x}^i)$, there exists $\bar{y}^i \in \xi_i(tx^i + (1-t)\,\bar{x}^i)$ for which $\bar{y}^i \mathscr{R}_i \bar{y}^i$, or $tx^i + (1-t)\,\bar{x}^i \mathscr{R}_i^* \bar{x}^i$. q.e.d.

A very similar argument can be used to show:

11 Theorem *If u_i is (strictly) (quasi) concave and ${}_t\mathscr{Y}^i_{t+1}(y(t))$ is convex, then*

$$u_i^*(x^i) = \max\{u_i(y^i) \mid y^i(t+1) \in {}_t\mathscr{Y}^i_{t+1}(y^i(t)) - \{x^i(t)\}\}$$

is (strictly) (quasi) concave.

12 Theorem *If $\mathscr{R}_i$ is (strictly) monotonic in the commodities $\alpha \in \mathscr{A}$, then so is $\mathscr{R}_i^*$, provided that commodities can be held independently of other production decisions and allowed to deteriorate at their natural rates.*

Proof Decrease the requirements x^i in the components $\alpha \in \mathscr{A}$. The added capital stock can then lie idle to deteriorate at its natural rate. The new capital stock differs only in those components $\alpha \in \mathscr{A}$, which gives a preferred position to that before the decrease in x^i_α, $\alpha \in \mathscr{A}$. q.e.d.

13 Remark If preferences are locally unsaturated in goods that can be traded, and need not affect production of other commodities, then induced preferences are locally unsaturated.

Exercise 2 Prove Theorem 11.

3. A Characterization of Economies: The Principle of Equivalence

The trade set is critical in analysis of exchange because normally an obligation to deliver, either now or later, is incurred in return for commodities from others. Obligations minus acquisitions are termed *exchanges*, so that the trade set $\mathscr{X}_i$ is identical with the set of possible exchanges by the consumer i. For example, the Edgeworth–Bowley box in Figure 3 illustrates the two-person case, where there is no production. The point 0 represents no trade. The point $(w_{i,1}, w_{i,2})$ is the trade by which i offers to give his entire wealth to j. The point $(-w_{j,1}, -w_{j,2})$ is the trade by which i demands that j give up his entire wealth to i. The point $(w_{i,1}, -w_{j,2})$ is the trade by which i offers to exchange all of his holdings of 2 for j's holdings of 1. The graph is presented from i's point of view. Reversing the signs of all points gives j's point of view.

The economy in Figure 3 is of the so-called pure exchange type, where there is no production, and exchanges or contracts are covered by given wealth. By the theory of induced utility discussed in the previous section it is clear that we can simply regard production as the changing of the utility or level of preference attached to these trades. Of course, the set of possible community transfers will be only a convex set containing the origin and different from the rectangle in Figure 3.

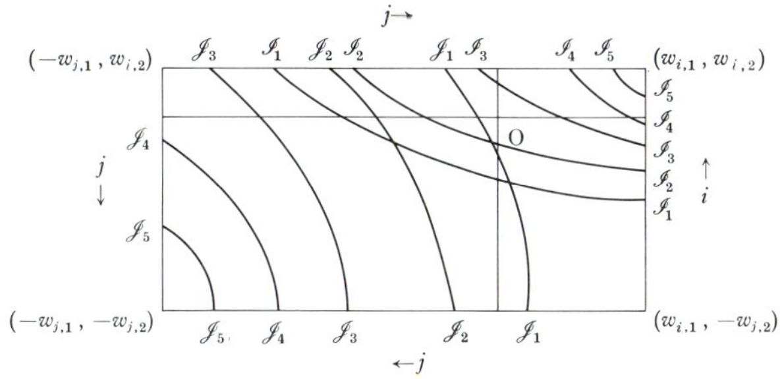

Figure 3

More generally, consider the ith consumer. His full description is given by the Cartesian product of his preferences, contained in the double product of consumption spaces of all consumers

$$\mathscr{R}_i \subset \bigtimes_{i}^{m} \mathscr{C}_j \times \mathscr{C}_j$$

and the graph

$$\mathscr{Y}_i \equiv {}_0\mathscr{Y}^i_\infty ;$$

thus

$$\bigtimes_{i=1}^{m} \mathscr{R}_i \times \mathscr{Y}_i$$

is the *general economy*. The general economy is a variant of the model of Hurwicz [1960]. It was suggested by Edgeworth [1881] and analyzed by him in detail for the two-person, one-period, two-commodity case.

In addition, there is a derived exchange or input–output set $\mathscr{X}_i$, which indicates the obligations or acquisitions that he can receive from the rest of the economy. From the point of view of exchange, this input–output set is of paramount importance.

One interesting case is where all goods are durable but not producible. Then, if x^i is an input–output vector, the capital stock is simply $x^i + w^i$.

This is the *pure exchange economy*. Here,

$$\mathscr{Y} = \{y(t) \mid y(t+1) = y(t)\}$$

is denoted by the letter $\mathscr{D}$ (for diagonal). Therefore,

$$\left(\bigtimes_{i=1}^{m} \mathscr{R}_i \right) \times \mathscr{D}$$

is the *exchange economy*, a limiting case of the general economy.

What has been shown is that every general economy can be viewed as an exchange economy, provided the exchange economy has the preference orders

$$\mathscr{R}^* \subset \mathscr{X} \times \mathscr{X}, \qquad \mathscr{X} = \bigtimes_{i=1}^{n} \mathscr{X}_i .$$

The relevant exchange economy is

$$\bigtimes_{i=1}^{m} (\mathscr{R}_i^*) \times \mathscr{D}$$

Any theorems that depend on properties described in this section can be proved for the original general economy provided appropriate assumptions are made for the general economy. In particular, it may be desirable to compute the $\xi_i(x)$ to ascertain the implications of these theorems for production. These are the general methods that will be used subsequently.

Principle of Equivalence *For every general economy*

$$\bigtimes_{i=1}^{m} (\mathscr{R}_i \times \mathscr{Y}_i)$$

there exists an exchange economy

$$\bigtimes_{i=1}^{m} (\mathscr{R}_i^*) \times \mathscr{D}$$

for which there is a one-to-one transformation from the input–output vectors $(x^i, i = 1,..., n)$, *with their preference levels as indicated by the (possibly partial) orderings*

$$\bigtimes_{i=1}^{m} \mathscr{R}_i^*$$

to the optimal capital stocks

$$\mathop{\times}_{i=1}^{m} \xi_i(x^i)$$

and the consequent preference levels indicated by the (possibly partial) orderings

$$\mathop{\times}_{i=1}^{n} \mathscr{R}_i$$

such that

(i) $x\,\mathscr{R}_i^*\,\bar{x}$, $x, \bar{x} \in X$ *if, and only if,* $y\,\mathscr{R}\,\bar{y}$ *for* $y \in \xi(x)$, $\bar{y} \in \xi(\bar{x})$, and

(ii) $\times_{i=1}^{n} (\mathscr{R}_i^*) \times \mathscr{D}$ *displays the closedness, openness, convexity, monotonicity, and unsaturation properties whenever these properties are displayed by*

$$\mathop{\times}_{i=1}^{n} (\mathscr{R}_i \times \mathscr{Y}_i),$$

as stated in Table 1.

This principle is merely a rough summary of the theorems and remarks of Section 3. Needless to say, the properties covered in the principle are not accidental and have been very fruitful in deriving theorems in economic theory. Hence, for many purposes of economic theory, the economy with exchange and production has been reduced to one with exchange alone.

4. Trade Efficiency

Here we give conditions for efficiency of trade parallel to those for producer efficiency in Chapter 4, Section 6. The induced preferences on trade are used, so that production is relegated to the background.

A trade $(x^i, i = 1, 2, \ldots, n)$ is *trade efficient* if $\bar{x}\,\mathscr{R}_i^*\,x^i$, $\sum x^i = 0$ implies $\bar{x}^i\,\mathscr{I}_i\,x^i$ for all i. Let y^0 refer to that part of production that is not attached to any particular consumers. Productions $(y^i, i = 0, 1, 2, \ldots, n)$ and consumptions $(z^i, i = 1, 2, \ldots, n)$ are *consumer efficient* (or *Pareto optimal*) if there is no $\bar{z}^i\,\mathscr{R}_i\,z^i$ for which $\sum_{i=1}^{n} \bar{z}^i = \sum_{i=0}^{n} \bar{y}^i$, y^i is feasible for all i.

14 Remark If y_0 is constant, trade efficiency and consumer efficiency are equivalent. If at least one good is desirable for consumption, consumer efficiency implies producer efficiency. If y^0 is not always constant and more than one good is involved in production, then producer efficiency and trade efficiency are not sufficient for consumer efficiency. For example, y^0 might have as one component the maximum number of possible rabbits and other components zero except for negative components for factors of production. These rabbits could be distributed in a trade-efficient manner. If y^i is identically zero for all i, then, however they were distributed, there would be no way for consumers to better themselves by trade. Since only rabbits would be available, there would be nothing to exchange for them. Trade efficiency and producer efficiency would be assured, but not consumer efficiency.

By considering the utility function as a production function, we can apply Theorems 33 and 35 of Chapter 4 to the traders. There is one simplification: no distinction need be made between "net" utilities and "gross" utilities. There is one complication: it is no longer reasonable to presume that the functions at hand are continuous. Otherwise, consumption is automatically "interindustry." However, it is more convenient to proceed directly. The presentation here is brief and the reader is invited to fill in the details on the basis of Section 6 of Chapter 4.

Preferences are *interconnected* if

(i) any good is desirable to hold in trade or has some consumer utility as a consumer good or produces a consumer good;

(ii) for every pair of consumers j and k, there are consumers i_p such that $i = j$, $i_m = k$, and every pair i_{p+1}, i_p holds a tradable good in positive amounts that both like (to assure this, consumers cannot have nonminimal preference levels without such goods),

(iii) all preferences are regular.

The following result is due to Arrow [1951b], Debreu [1959], and Koopmans and Bausch [1959]. (Even though a theorem analogous to Theorem 36 of Chapter 4 could easily be proved, the cases where marginal rates of substitution are always defined are not considered here.)

15 Theorem *If preferences are interconnected, then sufficient conditions for trade efficiency of* $(x^i, i = 1, 2, \ldots)$, *for which* $\sum x^i = x_0$ *is constant, are either of the following.*

(i) *There is a strictly positive price system* p *such that each consumer maximizes trade preferences on the budget set* $\{\bar{x}^i \mid p\bar{x}^i \leqslant px^i\}$.

(ii) *There is a strictly positive price system* p *such that each consumer minimizes* $p\bar{x}^i$ *subject to* $\bar{x}^i \in \mathscr{I}_i{}^*(x^i)$.

If also preferences are weakly convex, then the conditions are sufficient.

Proof Lemma 34 of Chapter 4 can be paraphrased to show that (i) and (ii) are equivalent. Regularity would apply to show that the limit consumptions from increases in commodities leave those receiving the commodities better off.

Sufficiency follows very simply from the fact that improvement for all involves $\bar{x}^i$ such that $p\bar{x}^i > px^i$, or $\sum p\bar{x}^i > \sum px^i = 0$. Hence, $\sum x^i = \sum \bar{x}^i = x_0$ is impossible; that is, $(\bar{x}^i, i = 1,\ldots, n)$ is not possible.

Necessity follows from the fact that $\mathscr{P}_i(x^i)$ is convex and $\sum x_i$ is in the boundary of $\sum \mathscr{P}_i(x^1)$, exactly as in the proof of Theorem 35 of Chapter 4. q.e.d.

The theorem can be improved in several directions, but this is discussed in the companion volume. There, partial orderings, infinite numbers of consumers and goods, waste products, and a budget set $\{\bar{x}^i \mid p\bar{x}^i = px^i\}$ are considered.

5. Consumer Efficiency

We consider consumer efficiency when social output y^0 is not always constant. The production set $\mathscr{Y}$ from which y^0 is chosen might be assigned arbitrarily to individuals. For example, $(1/n)\mathscr{Y}$ might be assigned to each individual. (If there are constant returns to scale, $(1/n)\mathscr{Y} = \mathscr{Y}$.) However, this assignment may not be natural in that production in $\mathscr{Y}$ can only take place if the whole of society agrees. Furthermore, production from $\mathscr{Y}$ must be distributed according to rules, and assignment of $\mathscr{Y}$ to individuals would preclude any other method of distribution. For example, *gnp* might be distributed according to factor incomes. Ordinarily this would be different from assigning each person more or less equal opportunity at social production, although in the case of constant returns to scale it turns out to be the same thing, as shown in Chapter 10, Section 3.

From the previous section, we see that if consumers use commodity bundles that are efficiently distributed, it is as if each consumer were optimizing preferences subject to a budget constraint. If the set of feasible outputs is convex, then the production sector should maximize *gnp*. In Figure 4 there are two commodities and one consumer who has indifference curve $\mathscr{I}(x)$; the set of consumptions preferred to x, $\mathscr{P}(x)$; and the budget line $\mathscr{L}$. Hence, output is consumer efficient if and only if consumer choice is competitive and *gnp* is at a maximum.

16 Remark Price equal to marginal cost and competitive consumer choice are not sufficient for consumer efficiency.

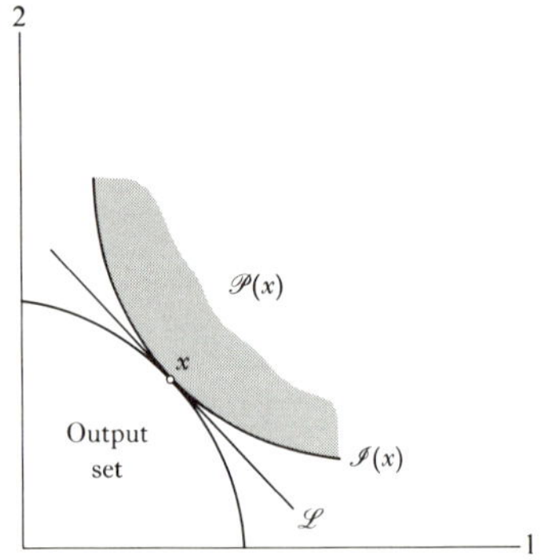

Figure 4

Proof In many cases, under increasing returns in several of the industries, the production set is not convex, as illustrated in Figure 5, where industry 2 displays increasing returns. The consumer still chooses according to a budget constraint, but *gnp* is no longer maximized. Nevertheless, the line $\mathscr{L}$ is tangent to the output set. The line $\mathscr{L}'$ is also tangent to the output set and has the same relative prices as $\mathscr{L}$. Evidently, $\bar{x}$ is not consumer efficient, even though, as will be seen, price equals marginal cost. q.e.d.

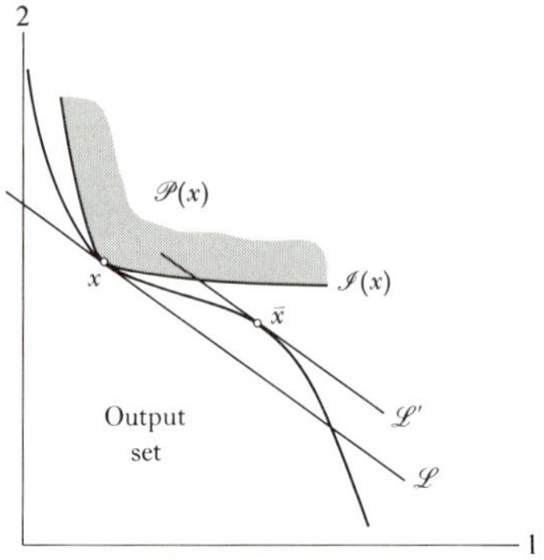

Figure 5

The distribution of output to $(x^i,\ i = 1, \ldots, n)$ is consumer efficient if and only if the output set is disjoint from the set $\sum \mathscr{P}_i(x^i)$. To establish the rule that price equals marginal cost, it is necessary to have uniqueness of the consumer price system at x given budget hyperplanes bounding each $\mathscr{P}_i(x^i)$ at x^i. In words, in the direction of production with greater *gnp*, there is a small change that can be distributed so as to improve the position of all consumers.

Production is *continuously differentiable* if industry inputs x^j are continuously differentiable in outputs of i, x_j^i, and inputs y^j.

17 Theorem *If $\sum \mathscr{P}_i(x^i)$ is directional dense, the competitive consumer price system is p, and production is interindustry, factor connected, quasi concave, and continuously differentiable, then for a consumer-efficient production and distribution with all products produced, there is a strictly positive wage system w such that*

(i) *industries minimize costs subject to the constant output constraint,*
(ii) $p(dx^j/dx_j^j)(\partial f^j/\partial y_k^j) \leqslant w_k$ *with equality whenever y^k is used in positive quantities in industry j, and*
(iii) $p_j = -\sum_{i \neq j} p_j \, dx_j^i/dx_i^i + dwy^j/dq^j$.

Note that (ii) and full employment of factors are sufficient for producer efficiency. Condition (ii) can be interpreted as paying factors the value of their marginal products.

As indicated in the preceding chapter, monopoly may be compatible with producer efficiency. But as will be shown in Chapter 10, by violating price equals marginal cost, condition (iii), monopoly is incompatible with consumer efficiency. Consumer efficiency requires that commodities be produced in desired quantities as well as efficiently.

Proof To use the wage system of Theorem 35 of Chapter 4, let

$$p \frac{dx^i}{dx_i^i} \frac{\partial f^i}{\partial y_k^i} = p \frac{\partial x^i}{\partial x_k^i} = w_k$$

whenever $y_k^i > 0$. It is easy to see that this multiplies w by a positive constant. It is also easy to see that in the limit, small changes in output must have values that tend to nonpositive numbers. For industries i and j with continuously differentiable f^i, f^j, for $y_k^i > 0$, $y_k^i > 0$, it is possible to transfer factor k from either i to j or j to i, so that the curve of change in net outputs must be tangent to the separating hyperplane. Hence,

$$p \frac{\partial x^i}{\partial y_k^i} - p \frac{\partial x^j}{\partial y_k^j} = 0 \qquad \text{or} \qquad p \frac{\partial q^i}{\partial y_k^i} = w_k .$$

For $y_k^i \neq 0$ and $y_k^i = 0$,

$$w_k = p \frac{\partial x^i}{\partial y_j^i} \geqslant p \frac{\partial x^j}{\partial y_j^j} .$$

Also,

$$p \frac{dx^i}{dx_i} = \sum_k p \frac{\partial x^i}{\partial y_k} \frac{dy_k}{dq_i} = \sum_k w_k \frac{dy_k^i}{dq_i}$$

gives value added equal to marginal cost. Transferring raw materials costs to the other side of the equation, we have the price equals marginal cost rule, (iii). q.e.d.

18 Remark In Theorem 17,

$$p\frac{\partial x^i}{\partial y_k} \leqslant aw_k \qquad \text{and} \qquad p_j - \sum_{j\neq i} p\frac{d_j x_j^i}{dx^i} = a\frac{dwy^j}{dx_j^j}$$

can be substituted in (ii) and (iii), $a > 0$. Hence, factors of production need not be paid the value of their marginal products. It is necessary only that industries act as if they were paying the factors their marginal products.

Proof If

$$p_j - \sum_{j\neq i} p_j \frac{dx_j^i}{dx_i^i} = a\frac{dwy^j}{dx_j^j},$$

we can simply increase wage to aw and apply Theorem 17. q.e.d.

Remark 18 establishes the conjecture of Lerner [1946, Chapter 9]. It suggests the possibility of attaining optimality by equalizing the "degree" of monopoly over the economy by assuring everywhere the equaltity of average value added with marginal factor costs. Simply tax competitive industries and subsidize monopolistic ones. Adjust the rates so that

(1) value added bears the same proportion to marginal costs in all industries. The proportion may be any positive number, chosen so that
(2) total government revenues equal total government subsidies.

If desired, another tax-subsidy scheme on factor incomes can be used to attain the distribution of income under pure competition. Incidentally, there are good welfare reasons for desiring the competitive distribution of benefits, which are discussed in Chapter 2 of the companion volume.

One case considered by Marshall is that in which an industry has nonconstant returns to scale but they are external to the firm. The firms can be pure competitors, and price equals industry marginal cost can be attained by an appropriate tax-subsidy scheme. The case of Cobb–Douglas production functions has been treated by Chipman [1970]. In general, let there be n identical firms with marginal factor costs equal to average industry factor costs ac. Let industry marginal factor costs be mc. Then the firms set average value added (1 + subsidy rate) = ac, which, if average value added = mc, gives

$$\frac{ac}{1 + \text{subsidy rate}} = mc, \qquad \text{or} \qquad \text{subsidy rate} = \frac{ac}{mc} - 1.$$

If output is homogeneous of degree n, $n\,mc = ac$ or subsidy rate = $n - 1$, which is the classical result.

19 Remark Larger gnp is necessary, but not sufficient, for consumer superiority.

Proof The remark is almost trivial to prove. A consumption of greater or equal preference is at least as valuable as the going one. One actually better has higher value. Hence, the sum of consumption values is greater than current gnp. The reasons for insufficiency have been considered in Figure 5. q.e.d.

PROBLEMS

A. Monopoly and Optimality

Suppose a monopoly is in a decreasing-cost industry. (See Chapter 10 for a definition of monopoly.) How much subsidy per unit of output would be necessary to place the firm at a Pareto optimal point? How much would be needed in a constant- or increasing-cost industry?

This problem is due to E.A.G. Robinson [1935].

B. Optimality and State Enterprise I

Suppose a state monopoly in a decreasing-cost industry is required to maximize output subject to the rule: losses are not in excess of subsidies. How much subsidy will be required for efficient operations?

UNSOLVED PROBLEM

C. Optimality and State Enterprise II

What conditions could assure consumer efficiency among the several points in a decreasing-cost industry, assuming price equals marginal cost and supply equals demand? When is the zero output for an industry consumer efficient?

10

Market Organization

When the number of participants becomes really great, some hope emerges that the influence of every particular participant will become negligible—and a more conventional theory become possible. These are the classical conditions of "free competition." Only after the theory for moderate numbers has been satisfactorily developed will it be possible to decide whether extremely great numbers simplify the situation. The current assertions concerning free competition appear to be very valuable surmises and inspiring anticipations of results. But they are not results and it is scientifically unsound to treat them as such as long as the conditions above are not satisfied.

John von Neumann and Oskar Morgenstern
in THEORY OF GAMES AND ECONOMIC BEHAVIOR, 1944

1. The Degree of Monopoly Power

A market situation is one of cooperation between buyer and seller and conflict between seller and seller or buyer and buyer. Therefore it should be considered from the viewpoints of both cooperative and noncooperative games. The noncooperative theory was developed in

Chapter 3, Section 7, and is applied in this section to the Cournot [1838] theory of oligopoly. In Section 2, Nash cooperative game theory is presented and in Section 3, income distributional aspects of both cooperative and noncooperative market organization are considered. The balance of the chapter is concerned with the implication of Cournot theory for the factor demands of an industry and commodity supply as a function of other prices.

If market power is assumed to be one directional, namely, pressure from one group (say, sellers) on another (say, buyers), the Cournot theory applies. More complicated interrelationships are presented in Section 2; the theory is not nearly so comprehensive as that in the simpler cases presented here.

Suppose a firm purchases its factors from a relatively large market and sells in a relatively small one. Let the commodity sold be a small part of the budget of the firm's owners, so that the firm seeks to maximize profits from production and sales in order to buy other goods and services. This tends to be a typical case of divergence from competitive behavior. In such cases, the profit-maximizing activities are referred to as the *firm*.

The totality of firms selling in the same market is called an *industry*. An industry's organization usually falls within one of these categories:

(1) purely competitive,
(2) monopolistic, or
(3) oligopolistic.

Of course, several closely related monopolistic industries may themselves compete, which gives a theory of "monopolistic competition" (Chamberlin [1932]), which would require coalition bargaining of some sort. Hence, no consideration of monopolistic competition appears until the development of bargaining theories in the companion volume. The aim of this section is to develop a precise definition of the degree of monopoly power and then to develop a theory of the relationship between that degree and the operation of the market. Later, computations will be made for the degree of monopoly power under various forms of market behavior.

In Figure 1, there is a market demand curve d and its associated marginal revenues curve mr. The curve mc is the marginal cost curve for the industry; if an industry is made up of several (competitive) firms, the curve is the sum of the firms' individual marginal cost curve. For competitive industry, the marginal cost curve is the supply curve, and market equilibrium requires that price be set at p_1, output at q_1.

If instead the industry is monopolistic, the price is p_2 and output q_2. The *degree of monopoly* is

$$\ell = \frac{mc - p}{p\, d/dp}.$$

In words, the difference between price and marginal cost is weighted by the value of changes in quantity with respect to changes in price. Much of the noncompetitive theory is based upon the value of ℓ. If $\ell = 0$ there is competition, whereas if $\ell = 1$ there is monopoly.

A *concentration measure* argued for by Herfindahl [1950] is $\sum t_i^2$, where t_i is the share of the ith firm in industry output.

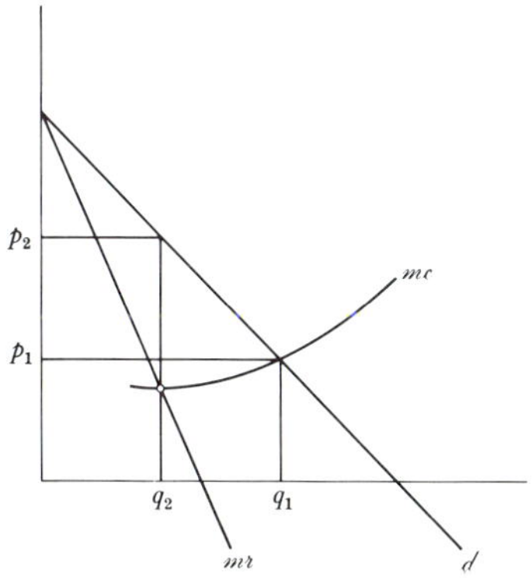

Figure 1

An intermediate case between monopoly and competition is the oligopoly theory of Cournot [1838] whereby the oligopolist maximizes profits assuming that other firms hold their output constant and cooperate in any price changes brought about by the oligopolist. The Cournot market corresponds to a game of conflict in which the strategies are outputs (Exercise 4, Chapter 2). The *Cournot solution* is the Nash solution for noncooperative games (Theorem 9 of Chapter 3). Let d denote industry demand and t_i be the share of output provided by firm i.

1 Theorem *In the Cournot solution*

$$\ell = \sum t_i^2 + \frac{1}{2} d \frac{d}{dd}\left(\sum t_i^2\right).$$

If the concentration ratio is constant at different levels of demand, the degree of monopoly equals the concentration measure.

Proof The ith oligopolist sets

$$mc_i = \left(1 - \frac{1}{|\varepsilon_i|}\right) p \tag{1}$$

where mc_i is the ith oligopolist's marginal cost, p is the price of the product, and $|\varepsilon_i|$ is the ith oligopolist's elasticity of demand, which is given by

$$\varepsilon_i = \frac{dd}{dp}\frac{p}{dt_i} = \varepsilon \frac{1}{t_i};$$

$$mc_i = \left(1 - \frac{t_i}{|\varepsilon|}\right) p; \tag{2}$$

$$\begin{aligned} mc &= \sum mc_i \frac{dt_i d}{dd} \\ &= \sum p\left(1 + \frac{t_i}{\varepsilon}\right)\frac{dt_i d}{dd} \\ &= p\sum\left(t_i + d\frac{dt_i}{dd} + \frac{t_i}{\varepsilon}\frac{dtd}{dd}\right) \\ &= p\left(1 + d\frac{d\sum t_i}{dd} + \sum\frac{t_i}{\varepsilon}\frac{dt_i d}{dd}\right) \\ &= p\left(1 + \frac{1}{\varepsilon}\sum t_i \frac{dt_i d}{dd}\right). \end{aligned} \tag{3}$$

Therefore,

$$\begin{aligned} t &= \sum t_i \frac{dt_i d}{dd} \\ &= \sum t_i^2 + \sum t_i \frac{dt_i}{dd} d. \qquad \text{q.e.d.} \end{aligned} \tag{4}$$

In particular, if there are n equal firms,

$$t = \sum t_i^2 = \sum \frac{1^2}{2} = \frac{1}{n}\sum\frac{1}{n} = \frac{1}{n},$$

and t is the inverse of the number of firms.

If t is constant, industry output and industry price will be nearly the same for an industry with two equal firms as in an industry with one firm having $\frac{2}{3}$ of the output and, say, one hundred firms with equal proportions of the remaining portion. Similarly, for

$$t_{\text{GM}} = \frac{1}{2}, \qquad t_{\text{Ford}} = \frac{1}{3}, \qquad t_{\text{Chrysler}} = \frac{1}{6},$$

$$t = \frac{7}{18}, \qquad \text{or} \qquad \frac{1}{t} = 2\frac{4}{7} = 2.6,$$

so that such a Cournot industry acts like a three-firm industry. On the other hand, were such an industry to sign a (collusive) contract, there would be Pareto optimality for the industry's owners and therefore the monopoly output. The degree of monopoly would not equal the concentration measure but would be one.

Of course, it remains to be shown that there is a solution to Equation (3) or (4). The case of (4) with constant t is easy to see and it is illustrated in Figure 2. The industry acts as though it were a single firm that was

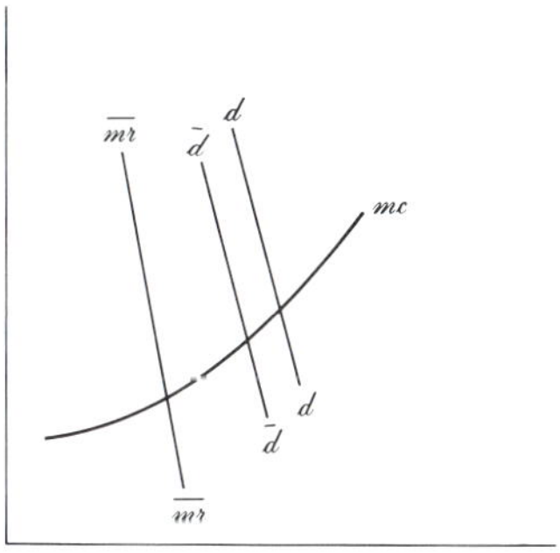

Figure 2

always assured the share $(\sum t_i^2)$ of the market and maximized profits accordingly. Therefore the "as–if" demand curve $\bar{d}\bar{d}$ is proportional to the actual demand curve dd. The relevant marginal revenue curve is $\overline{mr}$. As long as the elasticity of demand is less than or equal to 1 somewhere on dd, the "as–if" maximization is possible. In the general case we appeal to the Nash theorem, by which profit must be a concave function of outputs, which under constant costs requires that revenue be a concave function of quantity.

The case for monopoly power on the buying side, so-called *monopsony*, is similar. Profits are $pq - wi$ where i is the purchased good, w is the price, q the good produced, and p its price. In terms of the analysis, the purchased good has the negative sign and the sold good has the positive sign. We can give the purchased good the positive sign by only reversing all signs of prices, whereupon we maximize profits as before. The "demand" curve is now the supply curve of the industry from which purchases are being made, as illustrated in Figure 3. The "cost" is now the value of goods produced pq, and evidently "marginal cost" is

$$\frac{d(-pq)}{di} = -p\,\frac{dq}{di}$$

where i is the input and di/dq is the marginal product of i. As can be seen in Figure 3, this leads to the same structure as in monopoly but in the fourth quadrant instead of the first. The competitive condition is

$$w = p\,\frac{dq}{di}$$

whereas the monopoly solution is

$$p\,\frac{dq}{di} = w + i\,\frac{dw}{di}\,.$$

Evidently, the degree of monopsony power ℓ is given by the equation

$$p\,\frac{dq}{di} = w + \ell i\,\frac{dw}{di}\,, \tag{5}$$

or

$$\ell = \frac{p\;dq/di - w}{i\;dw/di} = \frac{(p/w)\;dq/di - 1}{\eta} \tag{5a}$$

where η is the elasticity of supply i with respect to changes in w.

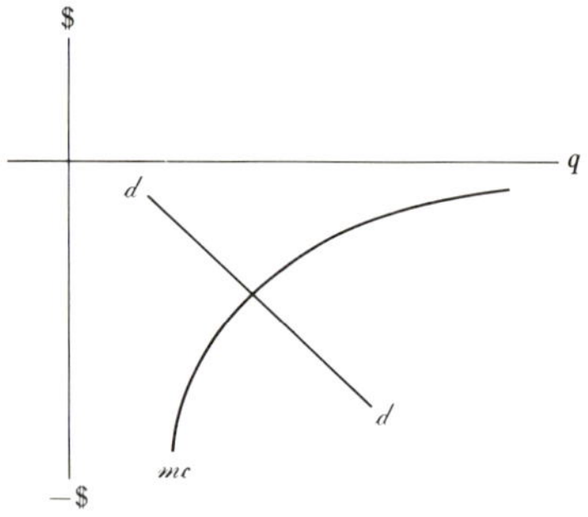

Figure 3

A theory of monopoly–monopsony can be developed along Cournot lines. The true change in cost to a monopsonist is

$$\overline{mc} = \frac{\partial tc}{\partial x_i}\frac{dx_i}{dq} + \frac{\partial tc}{\partial w_i}\frac{dw_i}{dx_i}\frac{dx_i}{dq} = \frac{w_i}{\partial f/\partial x_i} + \frac{dw_i/dx_i x_i}{\partial f/\partial x_i}$$

$$= \frac{w_i}{\partial f/\partial x_i}\left(1 + \frac{dw_i}{dx_i}\frac{x_i}{w_i}\right) = mc\left(1 - \frac{1}{\eta_i}\right) \tag{6}$$

where η_i is the supply elasticity of factor and x_i is the quantity of the factor. Of course, for the ith factor,

$$\frac{dw_i}{dx_i} = \frac{dmc}{dx_i}$$

and

$$\frac{1}{|\eta|} = \left|\frac{d^2tc}{dx_i^2}\right|\frac{x_i}{w_i}. \tag{6a}$$

If several firms regard themselves as monopsonists, each acting in the market assuming the other demand fixed, the industry is a variant of the Cournot type.

2 Theorem *Under Cournot oligopoly, buying and selling, with constant shares t_j of the product market and the factor market*

$$mc = \sum_{j=1}^{n} \frac{1 - (t_j/|\varepsilon|)}{1 - (t_j/|\eta|)}\, t_j\,.$$

Proof For the jth firm, effective marginal costs are

$$\overline{mc} = mc_j\left(1 - \frac{s_j}{|\eta|}\right) \tag{7}$$

where s_j is the jth firm's share of the purchases of i. The behavioral equations are

$$mr_j = \overline{mc}_j\,,$$

so that if p_j is the price of the good produced by j, $|\varepsilon_j|$, its elasticity of demand, is then

$$\left(1 - \frac{t_j}{|\varepsilon_j|}\right)p_j = mc_j\left(1 - \frac{s_j}{|\eta|}\right). \tag{8}$$

In the special case of a competitive industry buying the factor,

$$p_j = mc_j\left(1 - \frac{s_j}{|\eta|}\right), \tag{8a}$$

and price is greater than marginal costs, or more generally, if all buyers are in the same industry, then

$$\left(1 - \frac{t_j}{|\varepsilon|}\right) p_j = mc_j\left(1 - \frac{s_j}{|\eta|}\right), \tag{8b}$$

which leads to the theory in the proof of Theorem 1. Returning to Equation (8a), we have

$$mc = \sum_{j=1}^{n} \left(t_j + \frac{dt_j}{ddd}\right) mc_j$$

$$= p \sum_{j=1}^{n} \left(t_j + d\frac{dt_j}{dd}\right) \frac{(1 - t_j/|\varepsilon|)}{(1 - s_j/|\eta|)}. \tag{9}$$

If also the jth share of industry output equals the jth share of the factor,

$$mc = p \sum_{j=1}^{n} \left(t_j + d\frac{dt_j}{dd}\right) \frac{1 - (t_j/|\varepsilon|)}{1 - (t_j/|\eta|)} \tag{9a}$$

or for $dt_j/dd = 0$,

$$\frac{mc}{p} = \sum_{j=1}^{n} \frac{1 - (t_j/|\varepsilon|)}{(1/t_j) - (1/|\eta|)}, \tag{9b}$$

which admittedly is a bit abstruse. q.e.d.

A generalization of the Cournot approach was offered by von Stackleberg [1934], who suggested that each firm has an idea of the reaction of the other firms, given its own output policies. The Cournot case was that in which the reaction by other firms was assumed to be to hold their output fixed. Von Stackleberg offered other possibilities. In Figure 4, more complex reaction coefficients are illustrated. Given the output of q^2, 2 is expected by 1 to locate at the point indicated by his reaction function. Of course, the equilibrium occurs when both firms are satisfied that the reaction of the other firm is as expected, namely, at $(\bar{q}_1, \bar{q}_2)$.

Three questions arise:

(1) How is the reaction function computed?
(2) Does an equilibrium exist?
(3) Is it unique?

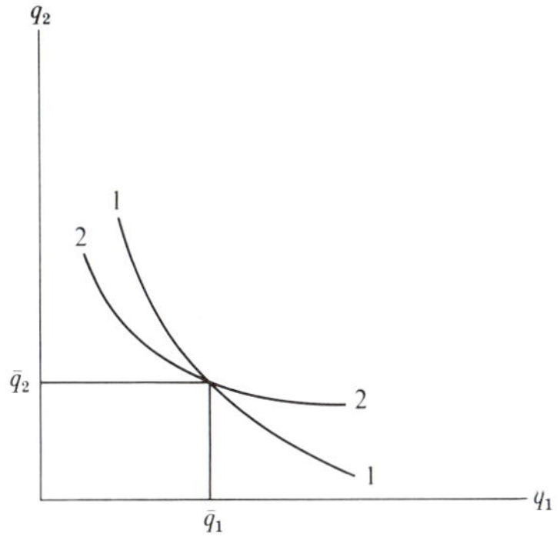

Figure 4

Some answers are offered by Fellner [1949] and Friedman [1967]. Friedman extends the analysis to n periods, so that in fact the two firms are producers of two closely competing sets of n goods of the same type but differing in the time of sales. He adopts arbitrary reaction functions. Firms maximize expected value of profits, each accounting for its influence on the future behavior of the other. Friedman shows that there is convergence of the solution as the horizon n tends to infinity.

Exercise 1 What can be said about a Cournot industry in which n firms control s percent of the industry?

PROBLEMS

A. Market Areas

Suppose n identical firms are locating in a world $\mathscr{X}$; let there be prices $p(x)$; and suppose there are transport costs as in Problems H and K of Chapter 2.

(i) Let demands at each point of x be given by a $d_i(p(x))$. If the firms are competitors, where will they locate? (Hint: What condition must prices satisfy?)

(ii) If they are Cournot duopolists insofar as they assume the other firms to fix their products and location and if $d_x = d_y$ for $x, y \in \mathscr{X}$, where do they locate? (Hint: Consider the cases of $\mathscr{X} = \mathscr{E}^2$ and $\mathscr{X} = \mathscr{S}^2$, the sphere.)

Part (ii) is related to the analysis of Hotelling [1929] (see also Mills and Lav [1964]).

The particular form here was solved by Smithies [1941].

B. Monopoly Power

(i) Let the demand curve be given by

$$p = a(t) + b(t)q.$$

Show that the degree of monopoly can be computed from an equation linear in marginal cost and price.

(ii) Let the demand curve be given by

$$p = a(t) + b(t)q + c(t)q^2.$$

Show that the degree of monopoly power is linear in price, marginal cost, and output.

C. Firm Behavior

According to Simon [1957], Baumol [1959], and others, firms do not maximize profits but only "satisfice," that is, they try to obtain a minimum profit on investment and they maximize output subject to fulfilling that profit goal.

(i) When does satisficing lead to an upper semicontinuous correspondence of supplied goods and demanded factors?

(ii) How does a satisficing firm facing a fixed price respond to changes in costs or price? How does this differ from the response of a competitive profit-maximizing firm?

(iii) How does a satisficing firm that completely dominates a market respond to changes in costs or demand? How does this differ from the response of a monopolistic profit-maximizing firm? (Hint: For the monopolist, assume constant marginal costs and use the formula $mc = p(1 - 1/|\varepsilon|)$.)

2. Two-Person Bargaining Games

Noncooperative games were considered in Section 7 of Chapter 3. The theory resulted in many possible solutions that might not be Pareto optimal. Another class of games, the *pure bargaining* games, are characterized by the fact that

(1) there is a unique, not necessarily Pareto optimal, equilibrium point that would result in the absence of collusion, and

(2) a contract can be signed between the two parties in order to obtain a Pareto optimal set of trades.

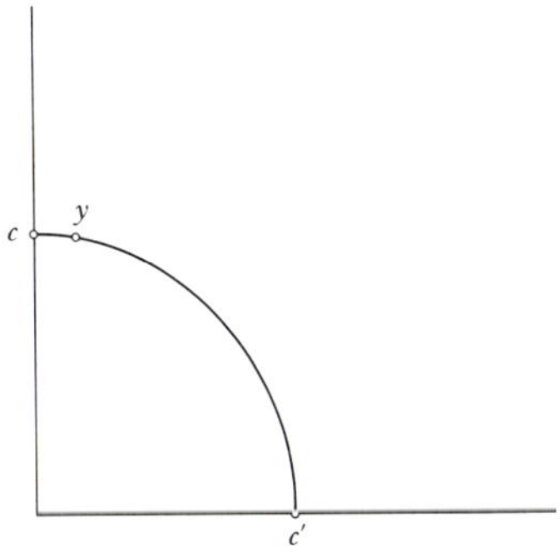

Figure 5

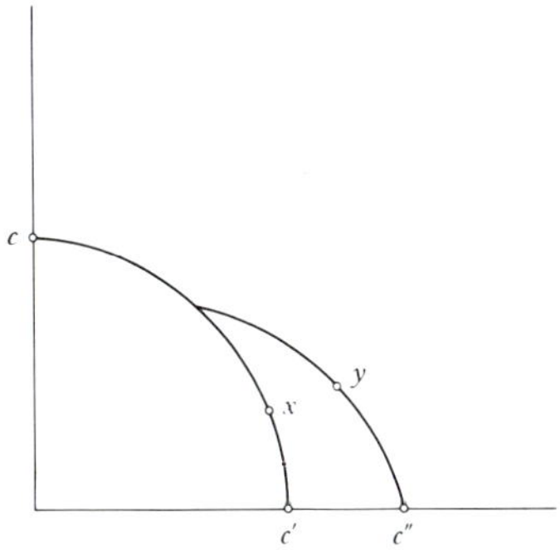

Figure 6

An example of a pure bargaining game is that of trading between two individuals when one individual can offer only positive quantities of goods to the other. The equilibrium point is simply the no-trade alternative (0, 0), since except for isolation, given that each trader has made a positive offer to the other on the presumption that the other's offer was fixed, each would do better by withdrawing his own offer.

In the rest of this section, the pure bargaining games are characterized in terms of utility linear in probabilities, as presented in Chapter 7. A dynamic process of bargaining is shown to lead to the solution.

The returns to the two traders appear in Figure 5, where cc' represents the outer frontier of utility combinations possible. Nash [1953] suggests that a solution should satisfy the following four postulates.

1. The solution should be on the curve cc' and not something less. Nash called this *Pareto optimality*, although it is not Pareto optimal with regard to the rest of the world.
2. The solution should be equal between any two parties who are identical with respect to the curve cc'. In effect, the two parties do not differ in their bargaining abilities. This is called *symmetry*.
3. If the returns in Figure 6 for an individual are all increased by a positive proportion p or changed by an additive constant c, then the solution should change accordingly. That is, if $x = (x_1, x_2)$ is a solution on cc'', and cc' is multiplied by p, then (px_1, x_2) should be the new solution. If cc' is translated by a constant amount c' then $(x_1 + c, x_2)$ should be the new solution. The idea of this is that the axes should measure von Neumann–Morgenstern utility, which is *invariant* under increasing linear transformations.
4. If x is the solution in Figure 6, and the curve changes to cc'', the equilibrium must change if at all to y on the new part of the curve

cc''. If any change in outcome is to take place as the possibilities for payoffs increase, it must be to an altogether new combination. Nash calls this *independence of irrelevant alternatives.*

The first three axioms seen very reasonable, although some doubts might exist about the third. Axiom 4 is somewhat contrived within the context here. Nevertheless, it will be seen that all four have a very reasonable rationale.

3 Theorem *Let* (u_1, u_2) *be the outcome in linear utilities of a pure bargaining game with fixed nonagreement payoffs* $\bar{u}_1, \bar{u}_2$. *Then the contract is Pareto optimal, symmetric, and invariant under increasing linear transformations and independent irrelevant alternatives if and only if it maximizes*

$$(u_1 - \bar{u}_1)(u_2 - \bar{u}_2).$$

Proof Let

$$\pi_i = (u_i - \bar{u}_i), \qquad i = 1, 2.$$

To show that only x maximizing $\pi_1\pi_2$ on cc' satisfies the Nash axioms, suppose $x = (x_1, x_2)$ maximizes $\pi_1\pi_2$ on cc' and suppose $y = (y_1, y_2)$ is chosen by another bargaining system that satisfies the Nash postulates. This is illustrated in Figure 6. Turning to Figure 7, we show the choice of y to contradict the hyposethes of the theorem. The line

$$\mathscr{L} = \overline{(0, 2x_2)(2x_1, 0)}$$

is tangent to the isopayoff curve at x (since $d\pi_1/d\pi_2 = -\pi_1/\pi_2 = -x_1/x_2$). Therefore cc'' is entirely to one side of $\mathscr{L}$, and $\mathscr{L}$ is an alternative locus of payoffs that also allows x.

To see that x is the solution of the linear case, simply change the utility of 1 by the proportion $1/x_1$ and that of 2 by the proportion $1/x_2$. Then the two have the same payoff possibilities, and by symmetry and Pareto optimality, (1, 1) is the solution. Returning to the line between $(0, 2x_2)$ and $(0, 1x_1)$, by multiplying 1's payoff by x_1 and 2's payoff by x_2, we find that by invariance the solution is (x_1, x_2).

Now if cc' is changed to the line $\mathscr{L}$, equilibrium must be x. But this would be possible only if x were the original solution for the other bargaining system. Otherwise the outcome would be changed to a point that was originally on cc': this is forbidden by the independence of irrelevant alternatives. Therefore, the solutions satisfying the Nash postulates are uniquely determined as those maximizing the product of the payoffs.

It is easy to verify that the maximization of $u = \pi_1\pi_2$ satisfies the axioms (Luce and Raiffa [1957]). This procedure represents a solution system. Since the solution is unique, given the foregoing axioms, the solution must be exactly that which maximizes the product of utility differences. q.e.d.

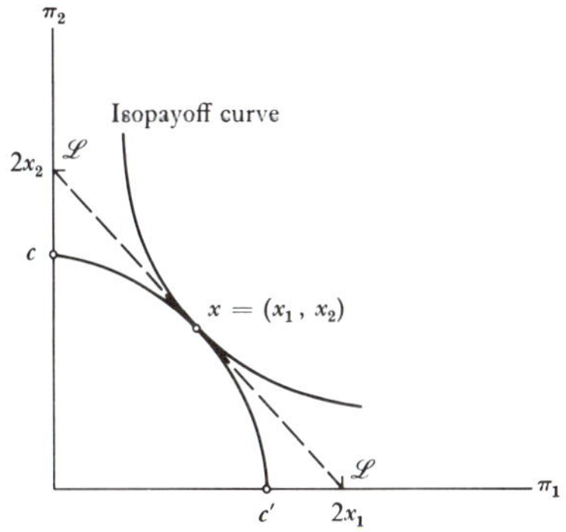

Figure 7

A bargaining process that would lead to the Nash solution is due to Zeuthen and is explained by Harsanyi [1956]. Suppose that the party that forces a concession from the other is the one who can bear the larger probability of nonagreement. This probability p_i can be computed as that for which the utility i of holding out is just equal to the utility of capitulating,

$$0 + (1 - p_i)u_i^i = u_i^j, \qquad j \neq i$$

where u_j^i is the utility to i of the proposal of individual j. Therefore,

$$p_i = 1 - \frac{u_i^j}{u_i^i}$$

is the largest probability of no agreement that i can bear without capitulating. If $p_i = p_j$, or

$$u_i^j u_j^j = u_j^i u_i^i,$$

it is assumed that both make concessions when necessary. If $p_i > p_j$,

$$u_i^j u_j^j < u_j^i u_i^i$$

and i makes the concession. Said differently, the party i whose product $u_j u_i$ is least is forced to compromise. In Figure 8, the rectangular hyperbola, the $u_1 u_2$ is less than the product $u_2^1 u_1^1$, $p_1 < p_2$, and party 1 makes concessions until

$$u_2^2 u_1^2 = u_1^1 u_2^1 ,$$

as illustrated. Then both make concessions. Therefore, the process continues until they agree on the same offer. This offer must be the product maximizer, if it exists, since otherwise the bargainer who is better off at the product-maximizing point can change his offer to the maximum and thereby force the other to make concessions. This bargaining system is the *Zeuthen process.*

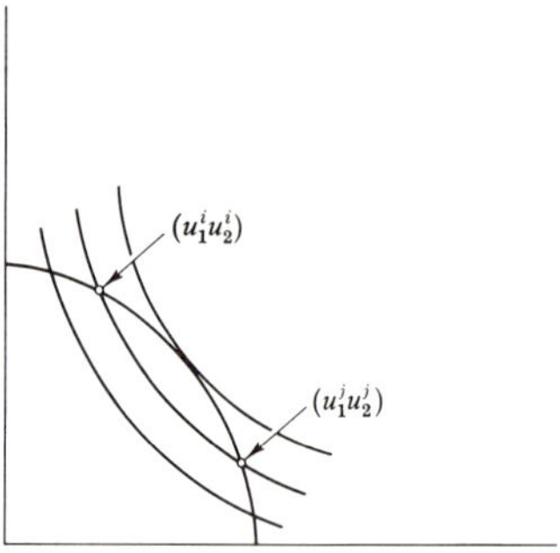

Figure 8

4 Theorem *The Zeuthen process leads to the Nash solution, provided that for any* $(u_1 u_2)$ *there is a maximal* $(\bar{u}_1 , \bar{u}_2) \geqslant (u_1 , u_2)$.

Is the Zeuthen process or some similar process a good description of bargaining? The main bone of contention would be that bargaining is determined solely by the comparison of the risk of no agreement and capitulation. This view is a bit simple, but it has some degree of attractiveness. In particular, the conclusion of maximization of the product means that the Zeuthen process satisfies the four postulates of Nash. It is especially surprising that in this view, bargaining is independent of irrelevant alternatives, since the dynamic process will change as it passes through new alternatives.

An important property of the Nash solution is expressed in the following remark.

5 Remark An increase in $\bar{u}_i$ increases u_i. The slope of the isopayoff curve is

$$\frac{du_2}{du_1} = -\frac{\dfrac{d\pi_1\pi_2}{du_1}}{\dfrac{d\pi_2\pi_1}{du_2}}$$

$$= -\frac{\dfrac{d\pi_1}{du_1}\pi_2 + \dfrac{d\pi_2}{du_1}\pi_1}{\dfrac{d\pi_2}{du_2}\pi_1 + \dfrac{d\pi_1}{du_2}\pi_2}$$

$$= -\frac{\pi_2}{\pi_1},$$

which decreases whenever π_1 decreases. Therefore, increases in $\bar{u}_1$ decrease (increase in absolute value) the slope of the isoprofit curves. A reflection on the geometry of Figure 7 should convince the reader the new solution must lie to the right of the old one.

Proof The new isoprofit curve has only one intersection with the old one and since it has a steeper slope, its values with smaller u_1 must have larger u_2. Hence, these represent higher levels of π in the old solution. Formally, let $\bar{u}_2$, u_1, v_1, and v_2 be fixed and consider

$$(u_1 - \bar{u}_1)(u_2 - u_2) = (u_1 - u_1)\frac{du_2}{d\bar{u}_1}$$

$$= -(v_2 - \bar{u}_2)$$

or

$$(u_1 - \bar{u}_1)\frac{du_2}{d\bar{u}_1} = u_2 - v_2$$

or

$$\frac{du_2}{d\bar{u}_1} = \frac{u_2 - v_2}{u_1 - \bar{u}_1} \gtrless 0$$

according as $u_2 - v_2 \gtrless 0$. q.e.d.

Bishop's [1964] version of the Nash cooperative game postulates the determining factor to be the time until agreement in case of an offer rather than a probability of rejection. Formally, these amount to the same thing. Bishop further considers the case in which profit itself does not represent utility whenever profit comes in the future, but he assumes that the two parties discount gain at the rates r_1, r_2, respectively.

Therefore, the utility of disagreement for T "years" after which the other party capitulates is

$$\pi_i^i \exp(-r_i t),$$

whereas the alternative is to accept the other party's offer of

$$\pi_j^i .$$

The maximum disagreement time is the one at which the two utilities are equal,

$$\pi_i^i e^{-r_i T_i} = \pi_j^i \qquad \text{or} \qquad T_i = \frac{\log(\pi_i^i/\pi_i^j)}{r_i} .$$

The party that can bear the smallest maximum disagreement time is forced to make concessions, so that the bargaining goes on until the following equations are fulfilled.

(a) $(\pi_i^i)^{1/r_i}\,(\pi_j^i)^{1/r_j} = (\pi_i^j)^{1/r_i}\,(\pi_j^i)^{1/r_j}$,

(b) $\pi_i^i = \pi_j^i$,

(c) $\pi_i^j = \pi_j^j$.

Therefore, the quantity

$$(\pi_i)^{1/r_i}\,(\pi_j)^{1/r_j}$$

is maximized. If the time discount rates are equal, then the product is maximized.

As an application, consider labor–management bargaining. The cost of a strike to management is the loss in profit from nonoperation. Let w be the negotiated wage rate and let $\bar{w}$ be the wage rate that workers receive during the strike (not from union funds). Let L be the total work force. Let $\bar{q}$ be the output and p the price of the output if the firm operates. In the simplest circumstances profits are

$$\pi_j = pq - w_l - c$$

where c are other costs. The return to labor is

$$\pi_i = (w - \bar{w})_l .$$

The negotiated alternative sets

$$\frac{1}{r_j}\,(\pi_i)^{1/r_i}\,\pi_j^{(1/r_j)-1}\,\frac{d\pi_j}{dw} = -\frac{1}{r_i}\,\pi_j^{1/r_i}\pi_i^{(1/r_j)-1}\,\frac{d\pi_i}{dw}$$

or

$$r_i \pi_i = r_j \pi_j$$

or

$$\pi_i = \pi_i \frac{r_j}{r_i}.$$

Evidently, the least impatient party will do the best. If both are equally impatient, they will split profits. For example, one union would normally improve its position by forcing the firms to share profits equally. However, if all industries are unionized and if all unions try to do this, no one could work in a competitive labor market. The alternative wage would be zero and then the labor share would be one half of the net increase in value. In view of the average of 80 percent labor share usually characteristic of economic systems, this would lead to a drastic reduction in labor share. The corporate state with nationwide bargaining would greatly favor management. If provisions were made for the fact that capital can be substituted for labor, bargaining would be even more unfavorable to labor (see Problem F). Without independent sources of funds, that is, opportunity to work elsewhere, the laborer appears to be at a disadvantage relative to the competitive solution.

The bargaining procedure can be generalized in two ways. First, there can be allowed games in which there are more than one threat point, and second, there can be allowed more than two players. The second extension is put off until the companion volume, even though it is the more important. The first is itself of some significance.

If at the beginning of the game the two parties announce "threat" strategies, then the Nash bargaining solution applies (Harsanyi [1956]). We simply apply the Nash solution to each choice. This gives utility outcomes to all threats. It is the two-person *bargaining-conflict game*. Each point in this game is Pareto optimal, by assumption.

6 Theorem (Nash) *If the $\mathscr{X}_i$ are compact, the bargaining-conflict game has a unique equilibrium (if any). If $\mathscr{X}_i$ is compact and $\mathscr{R}_i$ is continuous and weakly convex, the equilibrium exists.*

Proof The outcomes $\max(\pi_1 \pi_2)$ are defined for $(x, y) \in \mathscr{X}_1 \times \mathscr{X}_2$ since the $\mathscr{X}_i$, $i = 1, 2$ are compact. Therefore, it is a pure conflict game, which has a unique equilibrium.

The existence of equilibrium is assured by Theorem 3 and the fact that the maximum of a concave function $(\pi_1 \pi_2)$ compared with a quasi-concave function (u_1, u_2) is quasi concave. q.e.d.

Theorem 6 gives a complete solution to the game theory problem for two persons, provided binding contracts are allowed. In particular, if traders are allowed to make offers in addition to the nonnegative offers, there is the possibility of equilibrium at points other than zero. By adding a bargaining process to each of these processes and then considering the game consisting of all these combined outcomes, we can reach a unique solution:

7 Corollary *If the nonmixed threats are a finite set, and if mixed threats are allowed, then bargaining-conflict equilibrium exists and is unique.*

The instance of contract is only one case of bargaining. There is the possibility of noncontractual bargaining, whereby the parties abide by certain principles of cooperation out of fear of future retaliations. This is a relatively impure version of bargaining, since deviation from agreed-upon behavior leads to something less than complete retaliation. The first to violate the agreement will normally enjoy certain short-term rewards. Evidently, the time preference of individuals will determine to some degree the extent to which agreements are kept. The method by which "agreement" is reached is simply the usual bargaining game. Only the dynamic setting distinguishes it from other games. Consider the strategies

$$y^i = (y^i(t), t- = 0, 1, \ldots), \qquad i = 1, 2, \ldots, n.$$

To each y^i there are replies. Suppose

$$(x^i, y^j, j \neq i) \mathscr{R}_i (y^i, y^j, j \neq i).$$

If preferences are independent of time, then consider

$$\bar{y}^i = (y^i(t), t \in \mathscr{T}, \quad \bar{y}^i(t), t \in {\sim}\mathscr{T})$$

and

$$\bar{x}^i = (x^i(t), t \in \mathscr{T}, \quad \bar{x}^i(t), t \in {\sim}\mathscr{T}).$$

Evidently,

$$(\bar{x}^i, \bar{y}^j, j \neq i) \mathscr{R}_i (\bar{y}^i, \bar{y}^j, j \neq i).$$

This means that equilibrium strategies can be chosen independently in each time period. Therefore, an agreement would consist of producing at an output better for all.

Evidently, separate decisions would be made for each time period, so that the same agreement need not prevail at all times. On the other hand, even though the agreement could always be violated, the cost of violation would be the quick retaliation of the opponent, which would in no way depend on his previous actions. In this way, the agreement would be communicated and enforced. Since the game is never done, the agreement is never violated. This gives a loose rationale for the cooperative solution in noncontractual arrangements. The Zeuthen process might then be seen as a series of moves in which the least-favored party displays "leadership" and carries the pair to the Nash solution.

Empirical and theoretical support to this position appears in Friedman [1967, 1968].

PROBLEMS

D. The Greed Process

Let two players begin with 1 offering any trades in the compact set $\mathscr{X}_{11} \subset \mathscr{X}_1$, $0 \in \mathscr{X}_{11}$. Let 2 reply with the offer

$$\mathscr{X}_{21} = \mathscr{R}(x),$$

x is the best for 2 in $-\mathscr{X}_{11}$. Thereafter each player offers $\mathscr{R}(x)$, x the best of the previous player's offer.

(i) When does the greed process reach equilibrium on the third offer?

(ii) When does the greed process reach equilibrium on the fourth offer?

(iii) Show that equilibrium is Pareto optimal.

This problem was first solved by Hurwicz [1960].

E. Union Power I

In collective bargaining, is a monopolistic firm or a competitive market likely to be the more formidable opponent to the union? (Hint: Separate the cases of constant and increasing costs and the cases of an alternative supply of labor and no alternative supply.) How does the answer compare with the case of a make-work program that restricts the supply of labor and finances the made work by taxes on labor income?

F. Union Power II

In collective bargaining, assume that the union seeks to maximize the expected wages of its current members and the management seeks to maximize the expected profit. What would be the outcome of bargaining?

3. The Division of Profits

Under competitive conditions, as Clark [1890] first pointed out, a factor is paid its marginal product:

$$p \frac{\partial q}{\partial x_i} = w_i \tag{10}$$

where p is the price of the good, q the output, x_i the quantity of ith factor, and w_i the wage of the ith factors. If there are returns to scale such that

$$q = q(kx_1, \ldots, kx_n) = k^n q(x_1, \ldots, x_n),$$

from Euler's theorem we have that the sum of factor shares of output equals n.

8 Theorem *Under competition*

$$tc = \sum_i w_i x_i = \sum_i p \frac{\partial q}{\partial x_i} x_i = p \left(\sum_i \frac{\partial q}{\partial x_i} \right) = nq. \tag{11}$$

If there are decreasing returns to scale, $n < 1$, $tc < pq$, so that there is a surplus profit. If there are increasing returns to scale, $n > 1$, $tc > pq$, so that there is a net loss. If there are constant returns to scale, $tc = pq$, so that there is zero profit. This is the Clark–Wicksteed distribution theory.

Two deductions can be made. First, competitive pricing principles are incompatible with the competitive distribution of revenues whenever there are increasing returns to scale. For example, a government firm operating a power plant by the competitive principle of setting the marginal product of capital equal to the interest rate must necessarily be subsidized. Second, under constant returns to scale, each production unit and therefore the whose economy yields zero profits. Distribution is entirely determined by the principles of marginal productivity.

Under monopolistic conditions, Equation (11) becomes

$$mr \frac{\partial q}{\partial x_i} = w_i\,, \tag{11a}$$

and under conditions of Cournot oligopoly,

$$p + \ell \frac{dp}{dq} q = p(1 - \ell) + mr\,\ell = mc = \frac{wt_i}{\partial q/\partial x_i}$$

or

$$\frac{\partial q}{\partial x_i}(p(1 - \ell) + \ell\, mr) = w_i \tag{11b}$$

where mr is the industry marginal revenue.

9 Theorem *For a Cournot industry*

$$\sum w_i x_i = (p(1 - \ell) + \ell\, mr) \sum x_i \frac{\partial q}{\partial x_i}$$
$$= n(p(1 - \ell) + \ell\, mr)q.$$

We have

$$\frac{w_i}{\partial q/\partial x_i} = \frac{dpq_j}{dq_j} = p + \frac{dp}{dq_j} q_j$$
$$= p + \frac{d\ell}{dq} q_j \frac{dq}{dq_j}$$
$$= p + \frac{dp}{dq} qt_j,$$

where t_j is equal to the share of the j firm in the industry output q. Therefore ℓ in (11b) can be interpreted as the firm's share as well as the coefficient of concentration, depending on whether we are considering the firm or the industry. Since

$$mr < p,$$

there is a surplus profit, even under constant returns, which is called the "monopolistic exploitation of factors" (Robinson [1933]). Furthermore, under monopoly or oligopoly, increasing returns are not incompatible with laws of economic distribution.

In Cournot oligopoly, the division of profits is clear enough. The firm i shares output at price p according to $t_i\ell$. The profits can be computed by subtracting costs of $t_i\ell$ from $pt_i\ell$. On the other hand, for a Nash–Zeuthen-type contract, as presented in the preceding section, the division of profits is not so easy to find, especially when costs are different between different firms.

To consider the case of two firms with expected utility linear in profits, let π_i be the excess of profit over that in a Cournot industry. In Figure 5 the curve cc' represents the highest return that can be obtained by the two firms simultaneously. Presumably, this curve is derived from the underlying production and demand relationships. For example, the profits of two colluding firms dominating an industry with price p, demand d, and costs tc_i, $i = 1, 2$, are given by

$$\pi_1 = pt_1d - tc_1(t_1d), \qquad \pi_2 = pt_2d - tc_2(t_2d), \qquad t_1 + t_2 = 1,$$

and cc' is traced out as t_i varies from zero to one. If the firms have linear cost curves, then cc' is a straight line. Otherwise, if the marginal cost curves are increasing, cc' is a convex curve, as in Figure 5. Or, if transfer payments are allowed between the two firms, then they will simply maximize total industry profits, thereby acting as monopolists toward the outside. In that case, cc' is also a straight line and the Nash result would be relevant only to the division of the spoils. In any case, the Nash solution consists of choosing a point on cc'. Without agreement between the firms, it is assumed that zero will result, so the origin represents the profits if firms do not collude. These may possibly be the average profits resulting from fluctuating and cut-throat competition, or alternatively, the profits from the Cournot solution, which would apply in noncollusion.

10 Theorem *For two oligopolists with utility linear in profits but without side payments, the contracted solution is given by the two equations*

(i)
$$\frac{\pi_2}{\pi_1} = \frac{p - mc_2}{p - mc_1}, \tag{12}$$

and

(ii)
$$|\varepsilon| = \frac{t_1}{1 - (mc_1/p)} + \frac{t_2}{1 - (mc_2/p)}. \tag{13}$$

If the two firms have identical and constant marginal costs

$$mc_1 = mc_2 = mc,$$

then

$$|\varepsilon| = \frac{1}{(mc/p) - 1}, \tag{13a}$$

there is the monopoly output, and

$$\frac{\pi_2}{\pi_1} = \frac{p - mc}{p - mc} + 1,$$

or there is equal division of profits. Otherwise the firms operate with different marginal costs. (It is possible that the alternative to agreement is the Cournot solution or possibly the Cournot solution minus some losses due to the time of adjustment.)

Proof The condition for maximization is

$$\frac{\partial \pi_1}{\partial d}\pi_2 + \frac{\partial \pi_2}{\partial d}\pi_1 = 0,$$

and

$$\frac{\partial \pi_i}{\partial t_i}\pi_j + \frac{\partial \pi_j}{\partial t_i}\pi_i = 0, \qquad i \neq j,$$

or

$$\frac{\partial \pi_i}{\partial t_1}\pi_2 - \frac{\partial \pi_2}{\partial t_2}\pi_1 = 0. \tag{14}$$

This is evaluated as

$$\left(t_1 \frac{dp}{dd} d - mc_1 t_1 + pt_1\right)\pi_2 + \left(t_2 \frac{dp}{dd} d - mc_2 t_2 + pt_2\right)\pi_1 = 0$$

and

$$(pd - mc_1 d)\pi_2 - (pd - mc_2 d)\pi_1 = 0,$$

or

$$\frac{\pi_2}{\pi_1} = \frac{p - mc_2}{p - mc_1},$$

which is the law of division of profits. Therefore,

$$0 = t_1\left(\frac{p}{\varepsilon} - mc_1 + p\right)(p - mc_2) + t_2\left(\frac{p}{\varepsilon} - mc_2\right)(p - mc_1)$$

$$= -\frac{p}{|\varepsilon|}(t_1(p - mc_2) + t_2(p - mc_1)) + (p - mc_1)(p - mc_2)$$

or

$$|\varepsilon| = p\left(\frac{t_1}{p - mc_1} + \frac{t_2}{p - mc_2}\right)$$

$$= \frac{t_1}{1 - (mc_1/p)} + \frac{t_2}{1 - (mc_2/p)}. \qquad \text{q.e.d.}$$

The case of a monopsonist buying from a monopolist might be analyzed with the Cournot-type analysis. However, the question would then appear how one party would guess what the other's true reactions would be to the first party's strategy. In effect, the elasticities of supply of the seller would no longer be relevant and we would have to use some kind of reaction curve, as in the von Stackleberg approach. An alternative is to apply the Nash solution. In effect, the buyer and seller are regarded as subsequent producers in a single industry, since the revenues of the selling industry are also the wages of the first industry. Under the Nash solution, the selling industry would tend to maximize profits exceeding the alternative return of the monopsonized factor. Then the profits would be shared according to the maximization of the product of the profit from final sales minus the income the buyer or seller would obtain without the other's collaboration. For the seller, the alternative income might well be the going wage of that factor, whereas for the buyer, it would be the profits accruing whenever a substitute factor was used. If there were no substitute, then the alternative income for the buyer would be zero. Let π_1 be the income to the seller and π_2 be the income to the buyer. Let w_i be the alternative incomes per unit of resource x_i. The monopsonist and monopolist seek to maximize jointly the quantity

$$(\pi_1 - w_1x_1)(\pi_2 - w_2x_2).$$

Let $\bar{x}_1$ be the total resources available to the seller and $\bar{x}_2$ be the total resources available to the buyer. Then

$$\pi_1 + \pi_2 = pd - c(d, x_1, x_2) + w_1(\bar{x}_1 - x_1) + w_2(\bar{x}_2 - x_2),$$

where p is the price of the product of the monopolist and $c(d, x_1, x_2)$ is the cost of output d whenever resources x_1 and x_2 are devoted to the production of the good. Therefore, the pair seeks to optimize:

$$(\pi_1 - w_1x_1)(pd - c(d, x_1, x_2) + w_1(\bar{x}_1 - x_1) + w_2(\bar{x}_2 - x_2) - \pi_1).$$

PROBLEM

G. Cartels

In a cartel in an industry where there is learning by doing, why will total output be less than monopoly output?

This problem is due to Fellner [1949].

4. Factor Demands of the Industry

This section and the next two develop the theory of factor demands on the assumption that the market for commodities produced is a Cournot industry with constant degree of monopoly power. The most striking result obtained is that factors are normally gross complements. The analysis is due to Bear [1965], Ferguson [1966], and Rader [1968], and of course, it is in the neoclassical tradition, especially as presented by Hicks in *Value and Capital* [1938] and the *Theory of Wages* [1933]. Aside from the output decision, the main decision of the firm is to hire factors. Aggregating over firms, in an industry with monopoly power, t firms hire factors x_i, so that

$$\frac{\partial q}{\partial x_i}\,(p(1-t)+t\,mr)=w_i \tag{15}$$

where p is price, mr is marginal revenue, and w_i is the price of the ith factor. If there are decreasing returns to scale, possibly because one factor supply is held fixed, the x_i's will be uniquely determined; otherwise they will not. The approach here is to consider both cases.

If after an increase in costs, profits could be increased by increasing output, then they could be so increased before the change in costs.

11 Remark Output does not increase for Cournot oligopolists whenever factor prices increase. Hence, at least one factor input must not increase (if factors are not negatively productive).

12 Remark If output changes due to a change in demand, at least one factor must change in the same direction, provided no factors are negatively productive. If the production function is homothetic, then a change of all factor inputs in the same proportions is consistent with profit maximization.

13 Remark The second-order condition is that if x is strictly positive,

$$\frac{\partial^2 q}{\partial x^2}\,(p(1-t)+mr)+\frac{d\,mr}{dq}\,t\,\frac{\partial q}{\partial x}\left(\frac{\partial q}{\partial x}\right)$$

is negative semiquasi definite.

Under competition or linear demand $\partial^2 q/\partial x^2$ is negative semidefinite.

14 Theorem *If $t = 0$ (pure competition), then*

$$\frac{\partial x}{\partial p}=-\left(\frac{\partial^2 q}{\partial x^2}\right)^{-1}\frac{\partial q}{\partial x},$$

whenever the derivative $\partial x/\partial p$ exists and is continuous. If q is homogeneous of degree n,

$$\frac{\partial x}{\partial p} = \frac{1}{(1-n)}\, x \gg 0.$$

Proof Since $p\,\partial q/\partial x = w$,

$$p\,\frac{\partial^2 q}{\partial x^2}\frac{\partial x}{\partial p} + \frac{\partial q}{\partial x} = 0$$

or

$$\frac{\partial x}{\partial p} = -\frac{1}{p}\left(\frac{\partial^2 q}{\partial x^2}\right)^{-1}\frac{\partial q}{\partial x}.$$

By continuity, if $\det \partial^2 q/\partial x^2 = 0$, the derivative is infinite, that is, it does not exist. Since $\det \partial^2 q/\partial x^2 \neq 0$ on points dense in factor space, $\partial x/\partial p$ is continuous only if it is evaluated as above. q.e.d.

For monopoly, we cannot speak unambiguously of price changes and must analyze the change in demand involved. Let demand be

$$q = d(p) + \delta\,\Delta d.$$

Increases in demand normally raise quantity and increase demand for factors because marginal revenue increases (Figure 9). Incidentally, for a monopolist an increase in demand may *not* increase price, although it normally increases quantity.

The exact quantity increase can be deduced from Equations (15).

15 Theorem *If the degree of monopoly power is fixed, then*

$$\frac{dx}{d\delta} = \nu\,\frac{\left(\dfrac{\Delta d}{dq/dp} - \dfrac{d\,\Delta d}{dp}\right)}{\left(\dfrac{dq}{dp}\right)^2}\,\frac{\left(\dfrac{\partial^2 q}{\partial x^2}\right)^{-1}\dfrac{\partial q}{\partial x}}{p(1-t) + t\,mr + \mu\,\dfrac{dmr}{dq}} \tag{16}$$

where

$$\nu = \frac{t}{p(1-t) + t\,mr}, \qquad \mu = \left(\frac{\partial q}{\partial x}\right)'\left(\frac{\partial^2 q}{\partial x^2}\right)^{-1}\frac{\partial q}{\partial x}.$$

If production is homogeneous of degree n,

$$\frac{dx}{d\delta} = \nu\,\frac{\left(\dfrac{\Delta d}{dq/dp} - \dfrac{d\,\Delta d}{dp}\right)x\,(n-1)}{\left(\dfrac{dq}{dp}\right)^2\left(\dfrac{t}{\nu} + qn\,(n-1)\,\dfrac{dmr}{dq}\right)} = \frac{dq}{d\delta}\,\frac{x}{n}. \tag{16a}$$

Proof We have the following information.

$$\frac{\partial q}{\partial x}\left(p+t\frac{dp}{dq}q\right)=w, \qquad d+\delta\,\Delta d=q,$$

$$\frac{dp}{dq}=\frac{1}{\dfrac{dq}{dp}}, \qquad \frac{\partial\dfrac{dp}{dq}}{\partial\delta}=-\frac{\dfrac{d\,\Delta d}{dp}}{\left(\dfrac{dq}{dp}\right)^2}, \qquad \frac{\partial p}{\partial\delta}=-\frac{\Delta d}{\left(\dfrac{dq}{dp}\right)}.$$

The firm varies q by varying x. Therefore,

$$0=\frac{\partial^2 q}{\partial x^2}\frac{dx}{d\delta}\left(p+t\frac{dp}{dq}q\right)+\frac{\partial q}{\partial x}\left(\frac{dp}{dq}\frac{\partial q}{\partial x}\frac{dx}{d\delta}+t\frac{dp}{dq}\frac{\partial q}{\partial x}\frac{dx}{d\delta}+t\frac{d^2p}{dq^2}q\frac{\partial q}{\partial x}\frac{dx}{d\delta}\right)$$
$$+\frac{\partial q}{\partial x}\left(t\frac{\partial q}{\partial\delta}\left(\frac{dp}{dq}\right)+\frac{\partial p}{\partial\delta}\right),$$

or

$$\left\{\frac{\partial^2 q}{\partial x^2}\left(p+t\frac{dp}{dq}q\right)+\frac{\partial q}{\partial x}\left(\frac{\partial q}{\partial x}\right)'\left(\frac{dp}{dq}\left(1+t+t\frac{d^2p}{dq^2}q\right)\right)\right\}\frac{dx}{d\delta}$$
$$=\frac{\partial q}{\partial x}q\frac{\left(\dfrac{\Delta d}{dq/dp}-\dfrac{d\,\Delta d}{dp}\right)}{\left(\dfrac{dq}{dp}\right)^2}.$$

This solves as

$$\frac{dx}{d\delta}=\frac{(1-t)}{p(1-t)+t\,mr}$$
$$\times\left(1-\frac{\dfrac{t}{p(1-t)+t\,mr}\dfrac{dmr}{dp}\left(\dfrac{\partial^2 q}{\partial x^2}\right)^{-1}\dfrac{\partial q}{\partial x}\left(\dfrac{\partial q}{\partial x}\right)'\left(\dfrac{\partial^2 q}{\partial x^2}\right)^{-1}}{1+\dfrac{t(dmr/dp)}{p(1-t)+t\,mr+t}\left(\dfrac{\partial q}{\partial x}\right)'\left(\dfrac{\partial^2 q}{\partial x^2}\right)^{-1}\dfrac{\partial q}{\partial x}}\right)$$
$$\times\frac{\left(\dfrac{\partial^2 q}{\partial x^2}\right)^{-1}\dfrac{\partial q}{\partial x}t\left(\dfrac{dd}{dp}\right)}{\left(\dfrac{dq}{dp}\right)^2}$$
$$=\frac{\left(\dfrac{\Delta d}{dq/dp}-\dfrac{d\,\Delta d}{dp}\right)}{\left(\dfrac{dq}{dp}\right)^2}\frac{(1-t)}{p(1-t)+t\,mr}$$
$$\times\frac{\left(\dfrac{\partial^2 q}{\partial x^2}\right)^{-1}\dfrac{\partial q}{\partial x}}{p(1-t)+t\,mr+t\dfrac{dmr}{dq}\left(\dfrac{\partial q}{\partial x}\right)'\left(\dfrac{\partial^2 q}{\partial x^2}\right)^{-1}\dfrac{\partial q}{\partial x}}.$$

q.e.d.

16 Theorem *If the degree of monopoly power is fixed, then*

$$\frac{\partial x}{\partial w} = \frac{\nu}{t}\left(I - \frac{\left(\frac{\partial^2 q}{\partial x^2}\right)^{-1}\frac{\partial q}{\partial x}\left(\frac{\partial q}{\partial x}\right)'}{1 + \frac{dmr}{dq}\nu\mu}\right)\left(\frac{\partial^2 q}{\partial x^2}\right)^{-1}. \tag{17}$$

If production is homogeneous of degree n,

$$\frac{\partial x}{\partial w} = \frac{\nu}{t}\left\{\left(\frac{\partial^2 q}{\partial x^2}\right)^{-1} - \frac{xx'(n-1)^2}{1 + \nu\, nq(dmr/dq)(n-1)}\right\}. \tag{17a}$$

The form in Theorem 17 is similar to the Slutsky equation (Lemmata 12 and 13 of Chapter 8).

Proof

$$\frac{\partial^2 q}{\partial x^2}\frac{\partial x}{\partial w}(p(1-t) + t\, mr) + \frac{\partial q}{\partial x} t \frac{dmr}{dq}\left(\frac{\partial q}{\partial x}\right)'\frac{\partial x}{\partial w} = I$$

or

$$\frac{\partial x}{\partial w} = \left(\frac{\partial^2 q}{\partial x^2}(p(1-t) + t\, mr) + \frac{\partial q}{\partial x} t \frac{dmr}{dq}\left(\frac{\partial q}{\partial x}\right)'\right)^{-1}$$

$$= \frac{1}{p(1-t) + t\, mr}$$

$$\times\left(I - \frac{\left(\frac{\partial^2 q}{\partial x^2}\right)^{-1}\frac{\partial q}{\partial x}\left(\frac{\partial q}{\partial x}\right)'}{1 + \frac{t(dmr/dq)}{p(1-t) + t\, mr}\left(\frac{\partial q}{\partial x}\right)'\left(\frac{\partial^2 q}{\partial x^2}\right)^{-1}\frac{\partial q}{\partial x}}\right)\left(\frac{\partial^2 q}{\partial x^2}\right)^{-1}.$$

q.e.d.

17 Corollary *If t is fixed, and $dmr/dq \leqslant 0$, then $\partial x_i/\partial w_i < 0$.*

Proof $\partial^2 q/\partial x^2$ is negative quasi definite by cost minimization and nonsingularity, as is $(\partial^2 q/\partial x^2)^{-1}$. Therefore,

$$\nu\mu\frac{dmr}{dq} > 0$$

and

$$\frac{\partial x_i}{\partial w_i} = e_i\frac{\nu}{t}\left(I - \frac{\left(\frac{\partial^2 q}{\partial x^2}\right)^{-1}\frac{\partial q}{\partial x}\left(\frac{\partial q}{\partial x}\right)'}{1 + \frac{dmr}{dq}\nu\mu}\right)\left(\frac{\partial^2 q}{\partial x^2}\right)^{-1} e_i$$

$$< -e_i\left(\frac{\partial^2 q}{\partial x^2}\right)^{-1}\frac{\partial q}{\partial x}\left(\frac{\partial q}{\partial x}\right)'\left(\frac{\partial^2 q}{\partial x^2}\right)^{-1} e_i\frac{\nu}{t}\Big/1 + \nu\mu\frac{dmr}{dq}.$$

18 Corollary *If $\ell = 0$ (pure competition), then*

$$\frac{\partial x}{\partial w} = \frac{1}{p}\left(\frac{\partial^2 q}{\partial x^2}\right)^{-1}. \tag{17b}$$

Production is said to be *normal* if

$$\frac{\partial^2 q}{\partial x_i\, \partial x_j} \geqslant 0, \qquad i \neq j,$$

which is Wicksell's law.

For linear homogeneous production functions, with two factors, production is normal (Chapter 4, Section 4). Under decreasing returns to scale, it is possible that increasing one factor input leads to diminishing returns sufficiently rapidly to offset the normal positive effect on the productivity of other factors. In the case of constant returns to scale, where there are three or more factors, the same effect might occur for two of the factors with respect to which production displayed decreasing returns, with a normal effect on the third. However, an example of Wicksell's law under constant returns is that where $f(x_1, x_2, \ldots)$ is built up by application of g_{ijkl} to $g_{ij}(x_i, x_j)$, $g_{kl}(x_k, x_l)$, and $g_{ijklmnop}$ to g_{ijkl} and g_{mnop}, etc., where (a) $g_{ij\ldots mn}$ satisfies constant returns to scale, (b) there are diminishing returns in any one of the arguments, and (c) the elasticities of substitution do not increase as we move into the various functions $g_{ij}, \ldots, mn$. In effect, production is always from pairs of inputs satisfying Wicksell's law (Exercise 3).

If the production function is strictly concave, then on open sets dense in the space of differentiability of production with respect to factors, $\partial^2 q/\partial x^2$ is negative quasi definite and $y\, \partial^2 q/\partial x^2 y' < 0$ for $y \neq 0$. The theory developed for Leontief systems in Chapter 4 applies:

19 Lemma *If A is negative quasi definite and $a_{ij} \geqslant 0$, then A^{-1} is nonpositive with negative diagonals; if A is indecomposable, A^{-1} is strictly negative.*

Proof Since $A = D(B - I)$, D a positive diagonal, nonnegative, apply Problem K (at the end of this section) and the fact that A^{-1} is quasi definite. q.e.d.

20 Theorem *If the degree of monopoly is fixed and output is strictly concave and normal in inputs, then increases in product price lead to decreases in factor use by firms. Also, the firm's demand for the jth factor is nonincreasing as the ith price increases, as is the demand for the ith factor.*

That is, in the normal case, factors demanded by the firm are never gross substitutes. If

$$\frac{\partial^2 g}{\partial x_i \, \partial x_j} > 0, \qquad i \neq j,$$

they are gross complements.

The increase in factor price forces the firm to increase marginal costs. This is accomplished by decreasing all factors, given that their relative prices have not changed. A more striking result is that even though there is a substitution effect in favor of other factors whose prices have not increased (as will be seen), this is more than offset by the decrease in output, and hence in all inputs, due to increased marginal cost. This was anticipated by Hicks [1938, 1954] and Morishima [1954] for the case of nearly constant returns. An economic rationale would be as follows.

A rise in the price of one factor increases marginal cost and forces a reduction in output. Consequently, in the new profit-maximizing vector of factor inputs at least one factor must have been reduced in quantity. This reduction decreased the marginal products of other factors in the absence of readjustment of their quantities. Since none of the factor prices have been decreased, the equation of the value of the marginal product with the price of the factor requires adjustment to increase their marginal products and thereby continue the violation of Equations (15). Hence, in the final adjustment the other factors must be decreased in quantity as well.

Proof On open sets dense in space, $\partial q/\partial x$ is negative definite; elsewhere, it is negative semidefinite. Apply Lemma 20 and the fact that

$$\nu\mu \frac{d\mathscr{m}\imath}{dq} > 0$$

to Theorem 16. q.e.d.

The case under constant returns to scale is fairly straightforward, provided there is a unique cost-minimizing input mix, which is assured for

$$\frac{\partial^2 g}{\partial x_i \, \partial x_j} > 0, \qquad i \neq j$$

(as demonstrated in Section 5).

At an equilibrium price, where profit per unit of output is zero and output is equal to demand, an increase in the factor prices can be expected to force profits to negative levels and decrease output and inputs to zero. A decrease in factor prices will lead to an infinite expansion of output and inputs, at positive profits. Therefore, there is again a complementarity.

Prices do not equilibrate the product market if profits are not zero. Therefore small changes in prices do not change the sign of per unit profit, and therefore output remains at the same level as before (zero if profits are negative and infinite if they are positive).

21 Theorem *If*

$$\frac{\partial^2 q}{\partial x_i \, \partial x_j} > 0, \qquad i \neq j,$$

under constant returns and with a p that equilibrates the competitive product market, a change in a factor price leads to the opposite direction of change in the demand for other factors. Furthermore, at prices that do not equilibrate the product market, small changes in factor prices do not change factor demands.

Exercise 2 Suppose there are barriers to entry of workers into the skilled labor market. How would these influence the relative returns of capital, unskilled labor, skilled labor, and resources?

Exercise 3 Show that the production function built up from pairs of linear homogeneous production functions satisfies Wicksell's law.

PROBLEMS

H. Factor Demands

A factor is *inferior* in production if an increase in the product price leads to a reduction in the use of the factor. Show that a factor is inferior in production if and only if output increases with an increase in factor price if and only if an increase in its price reduces marginal costs.

The problem is due to Bear [1965].

I. Factor Incomes I

Let $f(x_1, x_2)$ give output in a competitive industry, x_1 fixed, with demand $d(p)$; let x_1 increase in quantity (or in productivity). What happens to the income of the first factor, assuming that the second gives the going wage to the quantity hired of the other factor? (Hint: The answer depends on the elasticities of substitution and demand.)

This problem was solved by Hicks [1961].

J. Nonnegative Matrices

Let $\mathscr{X} = \{x \mid x \geqslant 0, \mid x \mid = 1\}$.

(i) Show that A strictly positive maps $\mathscr{X}$ into the interior of $\mathscr{X}$.

(ii) Maximize $\lambda(x) = \{\lambda \mid \lambda x \geqslant xA\}$ on $\mathscr{X}$.

(iii) Show that the maximand in (ii) is a characteristic vector (Hint: Observe that if $xA \geqslant \lambda x$, then $xA^2 \gg \lambda xA$.)

(iv) Show that max λ in (ii) is the root with largest real part. (Hint: Define $x^+ = (\mid x_i \mid)$.)

The problem was solved by Frobenius (Gantmacher [1959, II, 53–66]). See also Debreu and Herstein [1953].

K. Infinite Nonnegative Matrices

Let A be an infinite nonnegative matrix. Show that

(i) xA is continuous in *monotone convergence, that is,*

$$x^n \geqslant x^{n+1}, \qquad x_i^n \to x_i \qquad \text{for all } i \text{ imply } x^n A \to xA$$

and

$$x^n \leqslant x^{n+1}, \qquad x_i^n \to x_i \qquad \text{for all } i \text{ imply } x^n A \to xA.$$

(ii) There is an $x \gg 0$ for which xA is finite. (Hint: Define a sequence x^n converging monotone to x and for which Ax^n is bounded from above.)

(iii) If there is an $x \geqslant 0$ for which $x \gg xA$, then

$$I + A + A^2 + \cdots + A^n$$

tends to a matrix B. (Hint: Note that $xA^n \to \bar{x}$, $A\bar{x} = 0$, and therefore for $y = (x - \bar{x})(I - A)$, $y(I + A + A + \cdots + A^n) \to (x - \bar{x})$.)

5. Factor Proportions

If there are constant returns to scale, Equations (15) of the preceding section are not independent, since profit-maximizing inputs are not unique and in fact any positive multiple of a profit-maximizing vector of inputs is profit maximizing. Therefore the mathematics of Section 4 cannot be carried through. At best we consider the case where the quantity of a particular factor is fixed, this factor being listed as the nth for convenience.

Let the firm maximize profit, so that the first $n - 1$ equations of (15) hold:

$$\frac{\partial q}{\partial x_{\sim n}}(p(1-t) + t\,mr) = w_{\sim n}\,. \tag{15a}$$

It is assumed that

$$\frac{\partial^2 q}{\partial x^2} = \left(\frac{\partial^2 q}{\partial x_i\,\partial x_j}\right)$$

is negative semiquasi definite, as would be so far concave production function. It is further assumed that

$$\frac{\partial^2 q}{\partial x_j\,\partial x_i} > 0 \qquad \text{for all} \quad i \neq j.$$

Let the nth factor be held constant.

22 Lemma *If q is concave and normal in x, then $\partial^2 q/\partial x^2_{\sim n}$ is negative semiquasi definite. If $\partial^2 q/\partial x^2_{\sim n}$ is indecomposable and $\partial^2 q/\partial x^2_{\sim n} \gg 0$, then* $(\partial^2 q/\partial x^2_{\sim n})^{-1} \ll 0$.

Proof The matrix $\partial^2 q/\partial x_{\sim n \sim n}$ has positive off-diagonals and is negative semiquasi definite, so that

$$0 \geqslant (y_{\sim n}\,, 0)\frac{\partial^2 q}{\partial x^2}(y_{\sim 0n}) - y_{\sim n}\frac{\partial^2 q}{\partial x^2_n}y_{\sim n}\,.$$

Hence, $\partial^2 q/\partial x^2_{\sim n}$ is negative semiquasi definite:

$$\frac{\partial^2 q}{\partial x^2_{\sim n}} = D(A - I).$$

Let $y^+ = (|\,y_1\,|, \ldots, |\,y_n\,|)$. Then

$$yD(A-I)\,y \leqslant y^+DAy^+ - yDy = y^+DAy^+ - y^+Dy^+$$

with equality only if $y = y^+$. Hence, if

$$y_{\sim n}\frac{\partial^2 q}{\partial x^2_{\sim n}}y_{\sim n} = 0, \qquad y_{\sim n} \neq 0,$$

$$y_{\sim n} = y^+_{\sim n} \qquad \text{for} \quad y^+_{\sim n}\frac{\partial^2 q}{\partial x^2_{\sim n}}y^2_{\sim n} > 0$$

contradicts negative semiquasi definiteness. Then

$$(y_{\sim n}\, y_n)\,\frac{\partial^2 q}{\partial x^2}\begin{pmatrix} y_{\sim n} \\ y_n \end{pmatrix} = y_n^2\,\frac{\partial^2 q}{\partial x_n^2} + y_n\, y_{\sim n}\,\frac{\partial^2 q}{\partial x_n\,\partial x_{\sim n}} > 0$$

for small $y_n > 0$ (since $\partial^2 q/\partial x_n^2\, \partial y_{\sim n} \gg 0$, $y_{\sim n} \geqslant 0$).

This is a contradiction of negative semidefiniteness of $\partial^2 q/\partial x^2$. The inverse of $\partial^2 q/\partial x^2$ is $(I + A + A^2 + \cdots)\, D^{-1}$ (Problem K). q.e.d.

That $\partial^2 q/\partial x_{\sim n}^2$ is negative definite ensures that there is a unique profit-maximizing output–factor input combination, given the quantity of one factor.

23 Theorem *In the normal case, holding one factor fixed leads to a decrease in the demand by nonmonopsonist firms for the other factors in response to an increase in their prices. In particular, an increase in the price of the* i*th factor leads to a decrease in its use relative to the fixed factor.*

An application would be to the case where one factor was fixed in the short run (Viner [1931]).

Proof Because oligopolists minimize costs at given outputs, it suffices to consider the competitive case only. Since

$$\frac{\partial^2 q}{\partial x_{\sim n}^2}$$

is a Metzler–Mosak matrix, it in fact has a strictly negative inverse as computed in the proof of Lemma 19, and in Problem K. Therefore, differentiating (15) with the nth equation deleted leads to the result

$$p\left(\frac{\partial^2 q}{\partial x_{\sim n}^2}\right)\frac{\partial x}{\partial w_0} = I;$$

or solving, we get

$$\frac{\partial x}{\partial w} = \frac{1}{p}\left[\left(\frac{\partial^2 q}{\partial x_{\sim n}^2}\right)\right]^{-1}. \tag{18}$$

Hence,

$$\frac{\partial x_i}{\partial w_k} < 0$$

whatever i or k.

Even monopoly firms minimize costs, given a fixed output. q.e.d.

The most interesting aspect of the preceding theorem is a corollary. For production functions homothetic in the factor inputs, the efficient relative factor uses are independent of the level of output chosen. It is sufficient to hold one factor fixed and find the profit-maximizing ratios at whatever level of output that may imply. In particular, the cost-minimizing ratios will be unique whenever the profit-maximizing ratios are unique. Also, the change in the cost-minimizing ratios with a change in factor prices will be exactly the change in the profit-maximizing ratios.

24 Corollary *For a homothetic production function, which is also normal,*

$$\frac{\partial^2 q}{\partial x_i \, \partial x_j} > 0, \qquad i \neq j,$$

an increase in the price of one factor leads to a decrease in its use relative to the others.

Proof Holding one factor fixed leads to an increase in the use of the other factors. q.e.d.

This theorem is a law of factor substitution that is analogous to the Hicksian laws of comparative statics for general equilibrium systems.

Another way of analyzing the case of constant returns to scale is to hold output fixed and vary factor inputs. In this case

$$q(x) = q_0$$

can be used to solve implicitly for

$$x_n = g(x_n)$$

where

$$\frac{\partial g}{\partial g_{\sim n}} = -\frac{\partial q / \partial x_{\sim n}}{\partial q / \partial x_n}.$$

Cost minimization leads to

$$w_{\sim n} = -\frac{\partial g}{\partial x_{\sim n}} x_n = w_n \frac{\partial q / \partial x_{\sim n}}{\partial q / \partial x_n}, \tag{19}$$

as in Equation (5a) of Chapter 8.

25 Theorem *At a fixed output, on open sets dense in the space where the concave production function is differentiable,*

$$\frac{\partial x_{\sim n}}{\partial w_{\sim n}}$$

is negative quasi definite.

Proof By Equation (19),

$$w_{\sim n}\frac{\partial q}{\partial x_n} = w_n\frac{\partial q}{\partial x_{\sim n}};$$

or differentiating, we get

$$\begin{aligned}
&\frac{\partial q}{\partial x_n} I + w_{\sim n}\left(\frac{\partial^2 q}{\partial x_n\,\partial x_{\sim n}}\right)'\frac{\partial x_n}{\partial w_{\sim n}} \\
&= \frac{\partial^2 q}{\partial x_{\sim n}\,\partial x_{\sim n}} w_n \frac{\partial x_{\sim n}}{\partial w_{\sim n}} + \frac{\partial^2 q}{\partial x_{\sim n}\,\partial x_n} w_n \left(\frac{\partial x_n}{\partial x_{\sim n}}\right)' \\
&= \frac{\partial^2 q}{\partial x_{\sim n}\,\partial x_{\sim n}} w_n \frac{\partial x_{\sim n}}{\partial w_{\sim n}} - \frac{\partial^2 q}{\partial x_{\sim n}\,\partial x_n} w_n \frac{\partial q/\partial x_{\sim n}}{\partial q/\partial x_n} \\
&= \frac{\partial^2 q}{\partial x_{\sim n}\,\partial x_{\sim n}} w_n \frac{\partial x_{\sim n}}{\partial w_{\sim n}} - \frac{\partial^2 q}{\partial x_{\sim n}\,\partial x_n} w_{\sim n}'.
\end{aligned}$$

Therefore,

$$\frac{\partial q}{\partial x_n} I = \left\{-\left(w_{\sim n}\left(\frac{\partial^2 q}{\partial x_n\,\partial x_{n\sim}}\right)' + \frac{\partial^2 q}{\partial x_n\,\partial x_{\sim n}} w_{\sim n}'\right) + \frac{\partial^2 q}{\partial x_{\sim n}\,\partial x_{\sim n}} w_n\right)\right\}\frac{\partial x_{\sim n}}{\partial w_{\sim n}}$$

and

$$\frac{\partial x_{\sim n}}{\partial w_{\sim n}}$$

is negative quasi definite. q.e.d.

PROBLEM

L. Linear Programming IV

Suppose output of a multiproduct firm is given by the linear programming system; maximize $\sum p_i q_i$ subject to $A(q_i) \leqslant x$. Let constraints with indices in $\mathscr{J}$ apply with equality.

(i) When is $\partial pq/\partial x_j$ given by the solution w of the equation $w_{\mathscr{J}} = (A_{\mathscr{J}})^{-1} p$, $w_i = 0$ for $j \in \mathscr{J}$?

(ii) In (i) evaluate $\partial(x_j/x_n)/\partial w_i$.

The problem was solved by Koopmans [1951].

6. Elasticities of Demand for Factors

As will be seen in Section 7, the elasticity of demand for a factor is a determinant of market behavior and the influence of monopoly power.

The *elasticity of demand* of the *i*th factor with regard to the *j*th price is

$$\varepsilon_{ij} = \frac{\partial x_i}{\partial w_j} \frac{w_j}{x_i}.$$

This elasticity can be conditional in the sense that the *n*th factor may be held fixed. Let

$$\lambda_i = \frac{\dfrac{\partial q_i}{\partial x_i} x_i}{q}$$

be the *i*th *competitive factor share* in output (it may or may not be the actual share of the *i*th factor, depending on whether or not the firm in consideration has monopoly power). Define

$$\eta_{ij} = \frac{\dfrac{\partial q}{\partial x_i} \dfrac{\partial q}{\partial x_j}}{\dfrac{\partial^2 q}{\partial x_i \, \partial x_j} q}$$

as the i–j elasticity of substitution.

26 Remark Under constant returns to scale,

$$\eta_{ii}^{-1} = \sum_{j \neq i} \eta_{ij}^{-1} \frac{\lambda_j}{\lambda_i}.$$

Proof

$$\eta_{ii}^{-1} = \frac{\dfrac{\partial^2 q}{\partial x_i^2} q}{\dfrac{\partial q}{\partial x_i} \dfrac{\partial q}{\partial x_i}} = -\frac{\sum_{j \neq i} \dfrac{\partial^2 q}{\partial x_i \, \partial x_j} \dfrac{x_j}{x_i} q}{\left(\dfrac{\partial q}{\partial x_i}\right)^2}$$

$$= -\sum_{j \neq i} \eta_{ij}^{-1} \frac{x_j \dfrac{\partial q}{\partial x_j}}{x_i \dfrac{\partial q}{\partial x_i}}. \qquad \text{q.e.d.}$$

27 Theorem *Under competition,*

$$(\varepsilon_{ij}) = \left(\frac{\lambda_i}{\eta_{ij}}\right)^{-1},$$

and if production is normal,

$$|\varepsilon_{ii}| \geqslant \frac{|\eta_{ii}|}{\lambda_i}.$$

In the case of constant returns to scale, holding one factor fixed,

$$|\varepsilon_{ii}| = \frac{|\eta_{ii}|}{\lambda_i} = \frac{1}{\sum_{j \neq i} \eta_{ij}^{-1} \lambda_j}.$$

28 Corollary *Under constant returns to scale with two factors of production,*

$$|\varepsilon_{ii}| = \frac{\eta_{ij}}{\lambda_j}.$$

Normally, factor demand is elastic for small λ_j and inelastic for large λ_j. The corollary says that under competition, a factor with most of the output is not likely to benefit by restricting its supply. If

$$\eta_{ij} = 1,$$

as in the Cobb–Douglas production function,

$$|\varepsilon_{ii}| > 1.$$

Here, monopsonistic restrictions in factor supplies in a competitive industry lead to no change in a factor's share of output. Since output falls, there is a decrease in the factor's total income (even though the wage per hour worked will rise). In other words, under Cobb–Douglas production functions, factor shares of output are constant, so that a factor is best advised to maximize output.

Proof (of Theorem 27) Let X be the diagonal matrix with elements x_i and W the diagonal matrix with elements w_i:

$$\left(\frac{\partial x_i}{\partial w_j}\frac{w_j}{x_i}\right) = X^{-1}\frac{\partial x}{\partial w}W = \left(\frac{\partial^2 q}{\partial x_i\,\partial x_j}\frac{x_j^{-1}}{\dfrac{\partial q}{\partial x_i}}\right)$$

$$= \left(\frac{\dfrac{\partial^2 q}{\partial x_i\,\partial x_j}q}{\dfrac{\partial q}{\partial x_i}\dfrac{\partial q}{\partial x_j}}\lambda_j\right)^{-1} = \left(\frac{\lambda_j}{\eta_{ij}}\right)^{-1}.$$

Now (λ_j/η_{ij}) has nonnegative off-diagonals and has a nonpositive inverse, so that the diagonal of the inverse of

$$-\left(\frac{\lambda_j}{\eta_{ij}}\right)^{-1} = c(I - A)^{-1} = \frac{1}{c}(I + A + A^2 + \cdots)$$

is no less that

$$\frac{1}{c}(1 + a_{ii} + a_{ii}^2 + \cdots) = \frac{1}{(1 - a_{ii})c} \leqslant \frac{\eta_{ii}}{\lambda_i}.$$

Therefore,

$$|\,\varepsilon_{ii}\,| \geqslant \frac{|\,\eta_{ii}\,|}{\lambda_i}. \qquad \text{q.e.d.}$$

29 Theorem *If the degree of monopoly power is fixed, then*

$$(\varepsilon_{ij}) = \frac{\nu}{t}\left(I - \frac{\left(\frac{\lambda_i}{\eta_{ij}}\right)^{-1} x \begin{pmatrix}1\\ \vdots \\ 1\end{pmatrix} q(\lambda_i)'}{1 + \nu\mu \dfrac{d\,mr}{dq}}\right)\left(\frac{\lambda_i}{\eta_{ij}}\right)^{-1}.$$

When production is normal,

$$|\,\varepsilon_{ii}\,| \geqslant \frac{|\,\eta_{ii}\,|}{\lambda_i}\,\frac{mr}{(1 - t)p + t\,mr}.$$

Theorem 29 shows that if production is normal, since $(mr\,v)/t < 1$, we can no longer deduce $|\,\varepsilon_{ii}\,| \geqslant \eta_{ii}/\lambda_i$.

Proof From Theorem 16, we have

$$X^{-1}\frac{\partial x}{\partial w}W = \frac{\nu}{t}X^{-1}\left(I - \frac{\left(\frac{\partial^2 q}{\partial x^2}\right)^{-1} WW^{-1}\frac{\partial q}{\partial x}XX^{-1}\left(\frac{\partial q}{\partial x}\right)' XX^{-1}}{1 + \nu\mu\dfrac{d\,mr}{dq}}\right)\left(\frac{\partial^2 q}{\partial x^2}\right)^{-1} W$$

$$= \frac{\nu}{t}\left(I - \frac{\left(\frac{\lambda_i}{\eta_{ij}}\right)^{-1} W^{-1}\frac{\partial q}{\partial x}\left(\frac{\partial q}{\partial x}\right)' X}{1 + \dfrac{d\,mr}{dq}\nu\mu}\right)\left(\frac{\lambda_i}{\eta_{ij}}\right)^{-1}.$$

The second sentence follows as in the previous theorem. q.e.d.

An important computational result is Theorem 30.

30 Theorem

$$\frac{\partial \lambda_i}{\partial x_j} = \frac{\lambda_i \lambda_j}{x_j}(\eta_{ii}^{-1} - 1), \qquad i \neq j$$

$$\frac{\partial \lambda_i}{\partial x_i} = \frac{\lambda_i \lambda_i}{x_i}(\eta_{ii}^{-1} - 1) + \frac{\lambda_i}{x_i} = \frac{\lambda_i}{x_i}[\lambda_i \eta_{ii}^{-1} + (1 - \lambda_i)].$$

Proof By definition of λ_i and the rules of differentiation,

$$\frac{\partial \lambda_i}{\partial x_j} = \frac{\partial^2 q}{\partial x_i\, \partial x_j}\frac{x_i}{q} - \frac{\partial q}{\partial x_i}\frac{x_i}{q^2}\frac{\partial q}{\partial x_j}$$

$$= \frac{\dfrac{\partial q}{\partial x_i}\dfrac{\partial q}{\partial x_j}x_i}{q^2}\left(\frac{\partial^2 q}{\partial x_i\, \partial x_j}\frac{q}{\dfrac{\partial q}{\partial x_i}\dfrac{\partial q}{\partial x_j}} - 1\right). \qquad \text{q.e.d.}$$

The theorem shows that if $\eta_{ij} < 1$, then $\partial \lambda_i / \partial x > 0$. Otherwise, $\partial \lambda_i / \partial x_j \leqslant 0$ $(i \neq j)$.

PROBLEMS

M. Constant Elasticity of Substitution III

(i) For the production function in Problem C of Chapter 4, compute λ_i and ε_{ii}.

(ii) Do the same for the production function in Problem D of Chapter 4.

(iii) In (i) and (ii), how do factor shares respond to changes in factor quantities?

This problem was solved by Arrow *et al.* [1961].

N. Factor Incomes II

Let there be two goods, one of which is used solely to produce the other, and let there be one (other) factor of production. Let both goods be produced under constant returns, subject to a constraint in the quantity of the first.

(i) What are the efficient productions?

(ii) Let the constrained good increase in supply. What happens to the proportions of the factor used in the two industries? To output per unit input of factor input in each industry? To the share of the second good going to the first good?

(iii) Let the constrained good become more efficient in the production of the second good. What happens to the share of output of the second good going to the first? To the proportion of the factor used in each industry? To output per unit of factor input in each industry?

(iv) Suppose a combination of the events in (ii) and (iii). Answer the same questions in such a case.

7. Comparative Statics with Imperfect Competition

In this section we study changes in equilibrium prices and quantities in response to changes in the demand of the own good or the price of other goods. By considering ℓ constant, the competitive, monopoly, and Cournot oligopoly cases are taken together.

In certain aspects, market operation under imperfect competition is like pure competition. A monopolist–monopsonist (or a Cournot industry with fixed degree of monopoly power) can be thought of as a firm participating in no production but simply having exclusive right of purchase and sales of certain competitive markets. For example, a monopolist in an increasing-cost or constant-cost industry can be thought to be dealing with the exclusive buyer from a competitive firm (itself) and the exclusive seller in its market. Of course, the monopolist tries to maximize total firm profits, given the possibility of price changes, picking up both the difference between the artificial purchase price and the sale price as well as the surplus profit due to the firm. Nevertheless, it is analytically convenient to view the production side of a monopolistic setting as if $p = mr = mc$.

31 Remark Monopolists increase output in response to increased marginal revenues (possibly from increases in demand). The remark is illustrated in Figures 9a and 9b.

Any increase in demand normally causes the monopolist to demand more by "offering" a higher "price" to the producing firm. The monopolist also offers more to take advantage of the market. Whether or not the monopolist seeks to decrease price remains a question. Consider changes in a demand to the level

$$d(\varepsilon) = d + \varepsilon\delta, \qquad \varepsilon > 0,$$

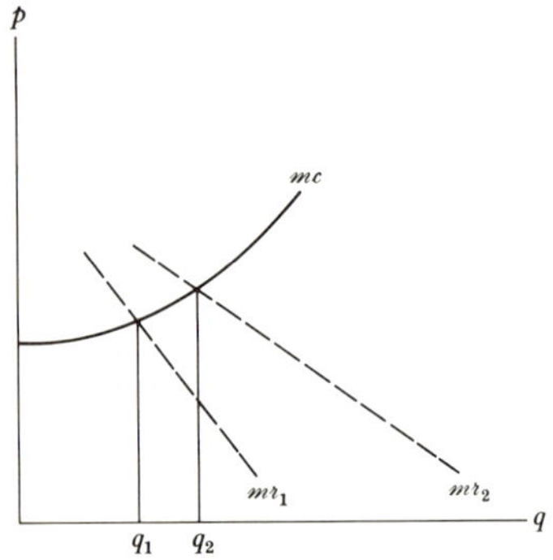

Figure 9a

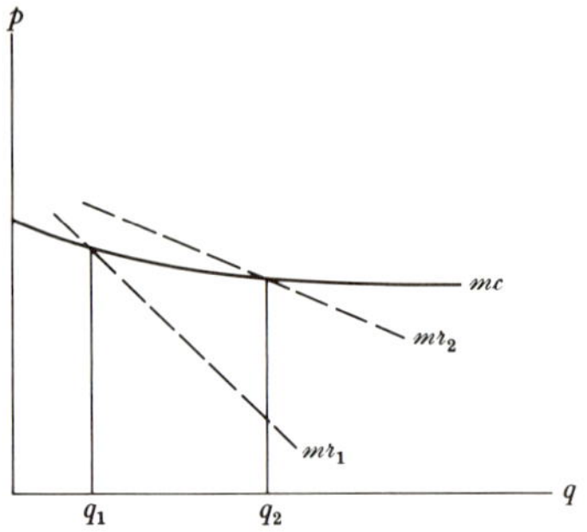

Figure 9b

where $\varepsilon\delta$ is the new demand for the monopolist. Let

$$\varepsilon_d = \frac{dd}{dp}\frac{p}{d} \qquad \text{and} \qquad \varepsilon_\delta = \frac{d\delta}{dp}\frac{p}{\delta}.$$

Differentiating the equation

$$p + td\frac{dd}{dp} = mc$$

with respect to ε, we get

$$\left(1 + t - t\frac{d}{(dd/dp)^2}\frac{d^2d}{dp^2}\right)\frac{dp}{d\varepsilon} = -t\frac{\delta}{\dfrac{dd}{dp}} + t\frac{d}{(dd/dp)^2}\frac{d\delta}{dp} + \frac{dmc}{dq}$$
$$\times\left(\frac{dd(\varepsilon)}{dp}\frac{dp}{d\varepsilon} + \delta\right).$$

32 Theorem *If the degree of monopoly power is fixed,*

$$\frac{dp}{d\varepsilon} = \frac{\left(\dfrac{t}{dd/dp}\left(1 - \dfrac{\varepsilon_\delta}{\varepsilon_d}\right) + \dfrac{dmc}{dq}\right)\delta}{1 + t - t\dfrac{dd^2d/dp^2}{(dd/dp)^2} - \dfrac{dmc}{dq}\dfrac{dd}{dp}}.$$

33 Corollary *If* $\varepsilon_\delta \leqslant \varepsilon_d$, $dmc/dd \geqslant 0$, *and* d^2d/dp^2 *small, then* $dp/d\varepsilon > 0$.

34 Corollary *If* $t = 0$, *as in pure competition, or if* t *is small,* $dmc/dq \geqslant 0$, *and* d^2d/dp^2 *small, an increase in demand leads to an increase in price.*

35 Corollary *If $dmc/dq \leqslant 0$ and $\varepsilon_\delta > \varepsilon_d$, or in general, if ε_δ is sufficiently larger than ε_d and d^2d/dp^2 small, then $dp/d\varepsilon < 0$.*

Corollaries 33 and 35 show that an increase in price will follow an increase in demand only if the elasticity of demand of the new customer is less than that for the old ones. For example, a foreign market might be highly sensitive to home price changes because competition is strong from other countries. Therefore, the development of better transportation, which allows a product to be sold at a cheaper price abroad than at home, will lead to a lower home price since the elasticity of demand will be relatively high abroad. Pricc and output arc positively related. These results will tend to be weakened as the number of firms increase, price decreases, and ε_d increases.

For the monopolist, increases in prices of substitutable products, say, other consumer goods, increase demand. Increases in prices of complementary products, say, other factors used in conjunction with the monopolized factor, tend to reduce demand. How does a monopolist respond to changes in prices other than his own? In particular, do the changes in demand due to changes in prices lead the monopolist to increase or decrease his price? In view of Theorem 32, the answer depends on the elasticity of the new demand. If the new demand is relatively inelastic, the monopolist will not supply enough to counterbalance the increase in demand.

It would seem that the higher the price of one good, the more inelastic the demand for other goods. This is because the dominant effect would be to force people into a less flexible position as they reduced their dependence on the good whose price rose. This reasoning seems valid in many cases.

36 Theorem *Under any of the conditions following, increases in the price of one good lead to a more inelastic demand of the other good.*

(i) *Both goods are consumer goods and the latter good is a sufficiently small item of the budget relative to*

$$\frac{\partial x_i}{\partial p_j}\,\frac{\partial x_i}{\partial p_j}\Big/\frac{\partial^2 x_i}{\partial p_i\,\partial p_j}$$

and the two goods are either gross substitutes and normal, or gross complements and the latter is a Giffen good, or

(ii) *both goods are consumer goods and consumer preferences are separable and homothetic, with monotonic preference even from zero quantities of other goods, or*

(iii) *the latter good is used primarily as a factor of production in a competitive industry producing the former good, or*

(iv) *the latter good is used primarily as a factor of production in the monopolized industry producing the first good with constant returns to scale and* $d\mathit{mr}/dx = 0$.

Proof

(i) $$\frac{\partial \varepsilon_{ii}}{\partial p_j} = \frac{\partial}{\partial p_j}\left(\frac{\partial x_i}{\partial p_i}\frac{p_i}{x_i}\right) = \frac{\partial^2 x_i}{\partial p_i\,\partial p_j}\frac{p_i}{x_i} - \frac{\partial x_i}{\partial p_i}\frac{p_i}{x_i^2}\frac{\partial x_i}{\partial p_j}$$

$$= \frac{p_i}{x_i}\left(\frac{\partial^2 x_i}{\partial p_i\,\partial p_j} - \frac{\partial x_i}{\partial p_i}\frac{\partial x_i}{\partial p_j}\frac{1}{x_i}\right) > 0.$$

Therefore, $|\varepsilon_{ii}|$ decreases.

(ii) In the formula for ε_{ii} in Corollary 10 of Chapter 8, ε_{ii} increases as x_i increases due to the increase in p_j, $j \neq i$.

(iii) Under homogeneous production with decreasing returns to scale, according to Theorem 27, increased prices increase outputs but also increase the portion of output going to surplus profits. Therefore, the x_i's fall, whereas the term η_{ij} remains fixed (since $\partial q/\partial x_i$ is homogeneous of degree $k - 1$, and $\partial^2 q/\partial x_i\,\partial x_j$ is homogeneous of degree $k - 2$, the total degree of homogeneity is given by

$$k + k - 2 - (k + k - 2) = 0).$$

Therefore, ε_{ii} falls in absolute value.

(iv) For monopoly, $d\mathit{mr}/dq = dp/dq + d^2p/dq^2 = q$. Under constant returns to scale, with no change in relative prices and with an increase in output, only mr and ν change in the formula of Theorem 29. Evidently, mr increases whenever elasticity of demand increases ($\mathit{mc} = (1 - \varepsilon^{-1})\,\mathit{mr}$). Therefore, $\mathit{mr}\,\nu = 1/(1 + p(1 - t)/\mathit{mr}\,t)$ increases. If $(d\mathit{mr}/dq) \simeq 0$, ε_{ii} decreases in absolute value. q.e.d.

If the price of a monopolized factor is increased, the demand for other factors used concurrently with it in normal production is reduced.

37 Theorem *If the elasticities of substitution are constant and are less than one, then there is a decrease in demand and an increase in elasticity of demand for j as the price for factor i rises, i used concurrently with j in normal production. If the elasticities of substitution are constant and greater than one, there is a decrease in the elasticity of demand for the other factor.*

Proof Reference to Theorem 30 shows that increase in the price of one factor, the price of j fixed, gives

$$\frac{\partial \lambda_j}{\partial x_i} > (<) \, 0 \qquad \text{for} \quad j \neq i, \qquad \text{for} \quad \eta_{ij} < (>) \, 1.$$

Now,

$$(\varepsilon_{ij}) = \lambda^{-1} \left(\frac{1}{\eta_{ij}} \right)^{-1},$$

where λ^{-1} is a diagonal matrix with elements λ_i and $(1/\eta_{ij})^{-1} \leqslant 0$ (Theorem 27). Therefore, $| \, \varepsilon_{ij} \, |$ increases (decreases) if and only if λ_j increases (decreases), whenever η_{ij} is constant. q.e.d.

Evidently, the case for nonconstant elasticities of substitution would be very complicated.

PROBLEM

O. Discriminating Monopoly

Suppose a monopoly operates in two entirely separate markets. What are the conditions for profit maximization? How will price markups over marginal costs depend on demand elasticities?

A solution appears in Robinson [1933].

11

Money and Assets

Capital is saved-up labor and saved-up land. Interest is the difference between the marginal productivity of saved-up labor and land and of current labor and land.

Knut Wicksell
in LECTURES IN POLITICAL ECONOMY
as translated by E. Classen, 1934

1. The Future and Futures Markets

This chapter is concerned with capital goods that survive one or more periods and whose value results from services rendered rather than the goods themselves. Financial assets such as stocks and bonds will be seen to be related to capital goods.

In Chapter 7, commodities were considered to be uncertain in their future occurrence or future use. In Chapter 9, consumer efficiency was seen to imply values for commodities over various time periods. In this section we will show conditions under which markets reflect these prices. In the next section the demand for money will be shown to depend on the demand for other goods in the future. In Sections 3–5, we present methods for evaluating capital goods from their prospective services.

Trades for future goods will themselves be uncertain in occurrence. In this case, the possible trades will be rather complicated. After specifying these possibilities, we will discuss the induced preferences with trade. Competitive behavior as discussed in Section 4 of Chapter 9 will take a different form; we will show that in some circumstances it is equivalent to the definition in Chapter 9. Consequently, any theorems about the optimality or existence of competitive equilibrium apply even when trades are uncertain.

Arrow [1953] and Debreu [1960] have proposed that the economic analysis of future transactions should be based on the futures market. Whereas there is no denying the empirical importance of futures markets, especially as insurance for users of unmanufactured commodities, the futures market is not necessarily the instrument by which purchases for the future are made. To see this, consider the individual who plans to make future use of commodities. It is clear to him that he will be able to make transactions for these commodities at some future date although the terms of the transactions are uncertain. On the other hand, the position a buyer takes in the futures market is only to contract to make some particular transactions in the future, which may be, and usually are, supplemented by other transactions at the later time. For example, a purchaser of December wheat in January often plans on selling the wheat before December. He expects to gain by the erroneous majority opinion of the future of wheat. This decision is little influenced by his own demand for bread. He expects to be a net purchaser of wheat in December (via his bread purchases) but he takes up a selling position in the futures market. This fact is in conflict with the Arrow–Debreu model of the futures market as representing a market for future use. The conflict is due to two factors:

(1) The Arrow–Debreu futures market model is designed to obtain necessary and sufficient conditions for consumer efficiency. In this it succeeds admirably.

(2) The Arrow–Debreu model allows only one set of transactions and therefore does not accurately reflect the actual process of economic decision making.

The Arrow–Debreu model must be extended to include the expectations of consumers about future prices.

There must be a distinction between *future prices*, which are to occur subsequently, and *futures prices*, which relate to current transactions for future goods. It will be seen that the futures market is a method by which the properties of Arrow–Debreu equilibrium can be attained, but only in conditions where no futures transactions need take place (Remark 8). In effect, futures transactions reflect an adjustment process rather than an equilibrium state. Furthermore, futures prices and future prices will be shown to be interrelated (Remark 6).

There is a spectrum of future prices, each of which may or may not occur but can be expected with a certain probability. The values of the probability distribution depend on the underlying assumptions that people make about the world in which they live. For example, a history-minded individual would project the past into the future. He might do this at several levels of sophistication. He might view the future as identical with the past and assume that prices tomorrow are equal to prices today. He might view the future as an extrapolation of the past and expect prices tomorrow that are equal to prices today weighted according to the difference between prices today and prices yesterday. He might take prices of the day before yesterday, or some earlier day, to determine the weighting. If we assume a discrete time frame, we obtain a distributed lag model of expectation as enunciated by Hicks [1950]. Let ψ be expected prices, p actual price. Then

$$\psi(t+1) = \phi(p(t), p(t-1), \ldots).$$

In the context of a continuum of time, price is expected to change at the rate

$$\psi = \phi\left(p(t), \frac{dp}{dt}, \frac{d^2p}{dt}, \ldots\right).$$

In addition to the expectation, there may be allowed a distribution of outcomes for unanticipated disturbances of which the expected value is only the central tendency.

To complicate matters further, commodities in the futures market are distinguished not only by the occurrence of different natural events but also by the various possible future prices. Let p^t be the vector of all prices at time t, including prices quoted in the futures market. Evidently each price vector p^t has a very large number of components. Letting p_s^t be the vector of prices at time t of commodities appearing in time s, we have $p^t = (p_t^t, p_{t+1}^t, \ldots)$. The vector p_s^t, $s > t$, refers to the futures market in time t. Only p_t^t refers to prices of goods for current delivery. For $t > 0$, p^t is the *prospective* price vector.

At each time period the trade x^t is possible only if $p^t(x^t) = 0$ for $t > 0$. The p^t are randomly distributed. Therefore, it is not known with certainty which x^t will actually be possible. We call choice according to these many and uncertain constraints the *sequential decision-making process.*

It is important that goods be distinguished according to market uncertainty as well as by other natural contingencies, since otherwise the futures market will be insufficient as an instrument of economic efficiency. As time increases, the number of contingencies increases, as does the number of commodities. Hence it is sometimes convenient to adopt a notation for prices and trades that emphasizes the events over time.

There will be a set of events n that form a Boolean algebra with events $\mathcal{N}$. It is required that

$$p^t_{\mathcal{I}(\mathcal{N})} x^t_{\mathcal{I}(\mathcal{N})} = 0$$

for $\mathcal{N} \in n$ for all t, where the commodities remaining after the occurrence of $\mathcal{N}$ are $\mathcal{I}(\mathcal{N})$. Evidently, $\mathcal{I}(\mathcal{N}) \subset \mathcal{I}(\bar{\mathcal{N}})$ whenever $\mathcal{N} \subset \bar{\mathcal{N}}$. In words, given a restriction to the set of possible occurrences in $\mathcal{N}$, there is in each period a constraint to transactions with zero value. What is more, if $\mathcal{N}$ occurs at a time in which all events not intersected with $\bar{\mathcal{N}}$ will be of no further concern, then $\bar{\mathcal{N}} \supset \mathcal{N}$ (whence for $\mathcal{N}$ occurring at time t, $\bar{\mathcal{N}}$ occurring at time s, $s \leqslant t$, $\bar{\mathcal{N}} \supset \mathcal{N}$). Without ambiguity, we identify $p^t_{\mathcal{I}(\mathcal{N})}$ with $p^t_{\mathcal{N}}$ and $x^t_{\mathcal{I}(\mathcal{N})}$ with $x^t_{\mathcal{N}}$. Evidently $x^t_{\mathcal{N}}$ results only if $\mathcal{N}$ occurs but no other more specific event occurs.

Consider preferences on $\sum_{t=0}^{\infty} x^t$. The trader chooses that x^0 which leads to the maximum expected utility of x^0 as related to the expected utility of x^1, given x^0 and p^1. We would expect an infinite regress, since x^t cannot be determined without x^{t+1}, $t = 0, 1, \ldots$. There is, however, a way to solve the problem which depends on the fact that at time t, $\sum x^t$ is already determined for those components less than t. If the other bundles are of little consequence, as when the remote future is of little consequence as compared with the present, the process can be cut off and an approximate solution can be obtained by first computing all optimal x^t as a function of $(x^s, s < t)$ and p^t. We then work backward to a solution. In fact, this is the method of *dynamic programming* first suggested by Bellman [1957].

1 Theorem *Let preferences be orderings regular in pointwise convergence and σ-continuous (in time). Then the induced preference (utility) of x^0 can be computed as that of the limit of the solution of dynamic programs terminating in year t, $t \to \infty$.*

An example would be utility continuous and time separable (Section 5 of Chapter 5).

Proof Let $(x^t(s),\ s = 1,\ldots, t)$ be chosen so as to optimize $\mathscr{R}_t$, given x^0 and $x(s) = \bar{x}(s)$ for $s > t$. Since for a subsequence of t's, $\sum_{s=0}^{t} x^t(s) \to \sum_{s=0}^{t} x(s)$ for each T, $\sum_{s=0}^{\infty} x^t(s) \to \sum_{s=0}^{\infty} x(s)$. Now suppose there is an $(\hat{x}(s),\ s = 0, 1,\ldots)$ preferred to (inferior to) $(x(s),\ s = 0, 1,\ldots)$. Then for sufficiently large t, $\sum_{s=0}^{t} \hat{x}(s) + \sum_{s>t} x(s)$ is preferred to (inferior to) $\sum_{s=0}^{\infty} x(s)$ (σ-continuity). q.e.d.

When $\mathscr{R}$ is an ordering, the twice-*induced* preferences on x^0 are defined to be

$$x^0\ \mathscr{R}^*\ \bar{x}^0$$

if the computed utility of x^0 is no less than that of $\bar{x}^0$. When $\mathscr{R}$ is a partial ordering that is the intersection and/or union of orderings, observe that if $x^0\ \mathscr{R}_i^* \bar{x}^0$ for some i in the sets united for all sets intersected, then the trader is in a superior position. Also, $x^0\ \mathscr{P}_i^* \bar{x}^0$ in similar circumstances. Therefore the induced composed relation is found when the underlying induced relations are computed.

2 Corollary *The intersection of unions of regular σ-continuous orderings can be computed as the intersections of unions of orderings computed from the dynamic programs represented by $u^i(\sum_{T^i>s>0} x)$ (T^i possibly tending to infinity as $i \to \infty$).*

The method of computation of the induced utility allows all the usual properties of preference to be applied.

3 Theorem *Let preferences be the intersection of finite unions of σ-continuous orderings. Then (induced) preferences on x^0 are*

(i) *regular (or $(\mathscr{P}^*)^{-1}(x)$ is open), continuous on straight lines continuous in the interior of the trade set, or continuous whenever original preferences have these respective properties;*

(ii) *locally unsaturated or monotonic whenever original preferences have these respective properties,*[1] *and*

(iii) *weakly convex, convex, or strictly convex whenever original preferences have these respective properties.*

The proof is left as an exercise for the reader.

As a first application we observe that equilibrium will exist in the current market if conditions on preferences are sufficient for the

[1] As defined in Chapter 2 of the companion volume, the similarity and quasi transferability of induced preferences follows from the same properties on underlying preferences.

existence of Arrow–Debreu competitive equilibrium. A competitive equilibrium with respect to induced preferences and p^0 is called a *current competitive equilibrium.*

4 Corollary *A current competitive equilibrium exists provided preferences (on trades) satisfy conditions among those listed in Theorem* 3 *that are sufficient for the existence of competitive equilibrium.*

For example, see Chapter 4 of the companion volume. A version of Corollary 4 was given by Drandakis [1966], whereby only tomorrow's goods were permitted to be traded in the future market.

Current general equilibrium can be defined as the sequential analogue of general equilibrium where, in addition to competition, monopoly and voluntary transactions are allowed (Chapter 4 of the companion volume).

5 Corollary *A current general equilibrium exists if preferences (on trades) satisfy conditions among those listed in Theorem* 3 *that are sufficient for the existence of general equilibrium.*

As a further point, it should be noted that if contigencies of different future prices are accounted in the futures market then, in equilibrium, future prices for a contingency equal future prices after the contingency has occurred.

6 Remark If there is an unsaturated competitive trader, then in general equilibrium

$$p^s_{\mathcal{N}} = p^t_{\mathcal{N}}\, k_{s,t,\mathcal{N}}\,, \qquad s \leqslant t,$$

with

$$k_{s,t,\mathcal{N}} = k_{s,u,\mathcal{N}} k_{u,t,\mathcal{N}}\,, \qquad s \leqslant u \leqslant t.$$

Proof If not, any degree of benefit can be obtained. Let trader i benefit from a trade δ. Evidently, $p^s_{\mathcal{N}}\,\delta \neq 0$. Then it can be obtained by another trade, such that γ is traded in time s, $-\gamma$ after $\mathcal{N}$ occurs, evaluated so that

$$p^s_{\mathcal{N}}\gamma = p^s_{\mathcal{N}}\,\delta,$$

not proportional to $p^s_{\mathcal{N}}$. Hence

$$p^s_{\mathcal{N}}(\gamma - \delta) = 0 \qquad \text{and} \qquad p^t_{\mathcal{N}}\gamma = 0,$$

so that the trades are admissible. Obviously, they lead to a preferred situation since the transaction in no way changed $\sum x^t$ other than by the addition of δ. q.e.d.

If $p_{\mathcal{N}} x_{\mathcal{N}}^0 > 0$, the trader is buying insurance of $x_{\mathcal{N}}^0$ in the time at which $\mathcal{N}$ may occur, whereas if $p_{\mathcal{N}}^0 x_{\mathcal{N}}^0 < 0$, the trader is selling insurance. If $p_{\mathcal{N}}^0 x_{\mathcal{N}}^0 = 0$, the trader is indifferent between buying $x_{\mathcal{N}}^0$ today and buying it when $\mathcal{N}$ occurs.

We turn next to the question of optimality of equilibrium. It may be suspected that introducing expectational differences between individuals along with sequential decision making would lead to inefficiencies. First, inefficiency can arise from insufficient coordination of decisions. Consumers with different price expectations necessarily optimize with regard to different price systems (future prices as well as futures prices appear in the constraints). The only way the existence of a futures market could lead to efficiency is to bring about an agreement on prospective future prices. Otherwise, prospective utility would be lost. To see that agreement does not necessarily occur, suppose consumer i believes with probability $\frac{1}{2}$ that the price of apples is going to rise tomorrow, whereas consumer j believes with probability $\frac{1}{2}$ that it is going to fall. Otherwise, they both expect it to remain constant. If both were risk neutral, j would simply sell i tomorrow's apples at a low price until the changes in supply convince both that tomorrow's prices will be those of today's futures markets. However, if they are both risk averters, whatever sales take place will be constrained by the possibility that the price may not change at all. Hence, there is no necessity of convergence of opinion in this case.

An example of loss of utility from competitive equilibrium is as follows. Let individual 1 own all of good A and individual 2 own all of good B. Let each of 1 and 2 assume that any addition of wealth to individual 3 will be spent on his commodity. It might then pay 1 and 2 to give equal sums of money to 3 provided the gifts were simultaneous. For instance, 1 would expect to get both his and 3's gift back in return for good A. Likewise, 2 would expect to double his money by selling B. In most instances, trader 3 would regard himself as better off. Hence, optimality would require wealth transfers, and the current competitive equilibrium would not be optimal. (The source of the nonoptimality would be a nonindividual benevolence relationship.)

Second, there may be a loss in actual future utility even if there is efficiency with regard to prospective utilities. A trader acquiring an asset in anticipation of a future profit that does not materialize would be acting inefficiently. Suppose A actually predicts the course of future prices, whereas B incorrectly predicts the outcome of the activities of A when A optimizes with regard to the current price system. This leads to optimization on a different overall price system with reference to various future contingencies, even though the initial price systems are identical. A suboptimal set of trades results, unless it should happen by accident that B can make good his loss by a different decision in the next period. Evidently, an optimal trade occurs only if B's expectations did not adversely affect his trade of current goods, since these trades cannot be improved later; time is irreversible.

At least conceptually, the inefficiency described above is correctable, since a computation can be made now to obtain a correct forecast. Presumably the rightist for whom the national debt is a threat of national bankruptcy can be persuaded by reason. Furthermore, if price expectations were correct in the sense that they reflected only those uncertainties traceable to natural phenomena, there would be no social disadvantage from individual trade, even with differing appraisals of probabilities, since there would be no way of improving any one individual's forecast. This would be the case of *perfect foresight* by consumers who would correctly appraise all contingencies and the effect they would have upon excess demands and prices. Expectations would not have to be identical, since one individual might attach personal probabilities to natural events different from those of others, provided there were no generally accepted means of computing the objective probabilities.

Equilibrium current trades account for any transactions between i and j that shift risks to, say, i, because j is more risk averting. The equilibrium trades cannot be an optimum from the viewpoint of the consumers at time t, looking backward, when some of j's distaste for risk has been abated by good experiences. In trading, the relatively risk-averse individual is at a disadvantage with others, and there is no way the market can compensate for this, even if the risk aversion is temporary. It is hard to see how changes in taste in any system could be anticipated. If future utilities cannot be appraised accurately by the trader himself, who will make a better judgment?

In the absence of perfect foresight about market operations, by simply taking prospects as given and using the competitive system to optimize with regard to actual preferences, we obtain efficiency with regard to prospective utility. Formally, it is sufficient that the contingent events be evaluated by futures markets that cover price uncertainties.

Recall that the prospective trades $x^{t,i}$, time t, consumer i, are physically possible only in the case of perfect foresight. In that case,

$$\sum_{t,i} x^{t,i} = 0,$$

which is characterized as *no euphoria*.

7 Remark Suppose there is no euphoria. Then a current (and prospective) competitive equilibrium is Pareto optimal whenever a competitive equilibrium is Pareto optimal.

This is the paradox of future markets. The way in which they effect efficiency is by enforcing common price expectations, in which case they are not actually of any use to traders, since traders might as well wait.

Proof Suppose $(\bar{x}^{0,i}, i = 1, 2,\ldots)$ is preferred to $(x^{0,i}, i = 1, 2,\ldots)$ for all i. Then prospective trades result,

$$\left(\sum_t \bar{x}^{t,i}, \quad i = 1, 2,\ldots\right)$$

such that

$$\sum (\bar{x}^{t,i}, \quad i = 1, 2,\ldots) = 0.$$

If $\sum_t \bar{x}^{t,i}$ is preferred to $\sum x^{t,i}, p^0(\sum_t x^{t,i} - \sum_t x^{t,i}) + p^0 \sum_t x^{t,i} = p^0 \sum_t x^{t,i} > 0$ for all i and hence there is a competitive equilibrium in the sense of Arrow and Debreu. q.e.d.

To take the proposition the other way, we must always be assured that there is perfect foresight, whereupon a reallocation to an optimal situation will lead to a zero trade in all periods *and* a mutual agreement that futures prices equal the prices bounding the summed upper contour sets.

8 Remark If there is perfect foresight, x is sustainable by a current competitive price system p, with wealths $y^{i,t}$ where $px^{i,t} = py^{i,t}$, provided x is sustainable by a competitive equilibrium with a possible redistribution of wealth.

A formulation of the conditions of equivalence between current competitive equilibrium and Pareto optimality can proceed by combining Remarks 7 and 8.

It does not appear that Remark 8 can be generalized to cases of nonperfect foresight.

2. The Demand for Money

In this section, fiat money is defined. It is shown that it is a kind of short-term futures that is traded whenever very short-term investments in capital goods are unprofitable. Results about the demand for this futures are discussed, and toward the end of the section, the subject of fiat money backed by gold is considered. The possibility of hyperinflation is shown to be impossible under a gold standard.

In a review of Debreu's *Theory of Value*, Saito [1961] calls for an integration of money into the general equilibrium framework. Some years ago, Hicks [1935] called for a similar integration. Perhaps the first reaction of the general equilibrium theorist is that money is already there, namely, as the *numéraire*, that is, that price which is held fixed. Certainly the *numéraire* is the unit of account. However, money is not just the *numéraire*; traders use it to cover the value of transactions. It might appear that a trader operates within a value constraint in addition to the budget constraint.

In standard theory, given the real constraints, the consumer optimizes his preferences subject to the budget constraint. Similarly, firms maximize the value of their output, net of inputs, subject to real production constraints. The "real" theory can incorporate a number of additional real constraints based upon such factors as the impossibility of negative consumption or of providing labor without food inputs, but only one value constraint appears for each consumer or firm. We might conclude, as many have (Saito [1961], Rader [1964], Tsiang [1966], Clower [1967]), that money is not in the standard system. However, as will be shown, the conclusion would be incorrect.

Fiat money is defined to be a good that is indestructible and can be exchanged without cost, but that has no inherent consumer or producer value. To represent the price of fiat money as, say, p_m is to say that for any other good priced at p_i, a unit of money is usable in the purchases of that good per unit of quantity by the ratio p_m/p_i. Of course, if p_m/p_i is zero (as with Confederate dollars), fiat money is extraneous, so that the consumer is indifferent as to whether he uses it or not. That such a good can have value is often denied on the grounds that only money backed up by a commodity can have value. As will be seen, there is no objection to an unbacked fiat money because of the structure of markets. Resistance to the concept of unbacked fiat money may be psychological in origin.

If we add a commodity fiat money, we have a new economic system, which has an equilibrium. The new equilibrium is with fiat money; the old is without fiat money. Consider the time t prices of fiat money delivered in time s under the contingency $\mathscr{N}$,

$$p^t_{s,m,\mathscr{N}}\,.$$

9 Theorem *In equilibrium without fiat money and for a trade* $x^1_{0,\mathscr{N}}$, *where* $p^0 x^0_{1,\mathscr{N}} < 0$, *a competitive trader is indifferent between that trade* *and the alternative of jointly holding fiat money in quantity* $p^1x^0_{1,\mathscr{N}}/p^1_{1,m}$ *and a futures transaction to deliver, at time* 1, $p^1x^0_{1,\mathscr{N}}/p^1_{1,m}$, *is the case of* $\sim\mathscr{N}$, *if and only if*

(i) $\sum_{\mathscr{N}\text{ occurring in time 1}} k_{0,1,\mathscr{N}}p^1_{1,m,\mathscr{N}} = p^0_{1,m}$ *and*

(ii) $p^0_{1,m} = p^0_{0,m}$.

Since all traders are willing to wait or to deal in the futures market under the conditions of Theorem 9, they are willing to hold wealth in the form of money balances instead of shares in real goods. In effect, money holdings are claims on future goods. Equilibrium with money is identical with equilibrium by which traders are allocated an equal value in claims on future goods in place of their money balances. The existence of money in the hands of one or more traders is a source of wealth. However, should we somehow reduce the money supply, any change in prices would result from changes in demand due to a redistribution of wealth, not from insufficiency in the demand for money.

Proof If $p^0_{1,m} \leqslant p^0_{0,m}$, (ii) is necessary, since otherwise no one would hold current money, whereas if $p^0_{1,m} > p^0_{0,m}$, no one would hold future money. Of course (i) is necessary. It remains to show that (i) with (ii) is also sufficient.

Evidently, $p^1_{1,m,\mathscr{N}}(p^1x^0_{1,\mathscr{N}}/p^1_{1,m,\mathscr{N}}) = p^1x^0_{1,\mathscr{N}}$, so that money held (costlessly) may be used to make the appropriate purchases in case of $\mathscr{N}$. Of course, the required delivery in the case of $\sim\mathscr{N}$ is appropriate since the trader intended no change in that contingency. Also, the cost of the proposed transaction is

$$\frac{p^1x^0_{1,\mathscr{N}}}{p^1_{1,m,\mathscr{N}}}\left(p^0_{0,m} - \sum_{\mathscr{M}\neq\mathscr{N}} \begin{array}{l}\text{price of a futures in money}\\ \quad\text{delivered at time 1 given } \mathscr{M}\end{array}\right)$$

$$= \frac{p^1x^0_{1,\mathscr{N}}}{p^1_{1,m,\mathscr{N}}}\left(p^0_{0,m} - \sum_{\mathscr{M}\neq\mathscr{N}} k_{0,1,\mathscr{M}}p^1_{1,m,\mathscr{M}}\right)$$

$$= \frac{p^1x^0_{1,\mathscr{N}}}{p^1_{1,m,\mathscr{N}}} k_{0,1,\mathscr{N}}\, p^1_{1,m,\mathscr{N}}$$

$$= p^1x^0_{1,\mathscr{N}}k_{0,1,\mathscr{N}}$$

$$= p^0x^0_{1,\mathscr{N}},$$

which is the negative of the cost of other transactions.

Finally, the trader could do neither better nor worse by holding fiat money, since anything he could purchase with money he could have purchased in the futures market. q.e.d.

Theorem 9 is still not a sufficient basis for a demand for money, since it might happen that the money prices quoted could lead the community traders to accept any positive quantity of money. For example, trader 0 could be persuaded to hold a very large quantity of money with an agreement to pass it on to trader 1 at time 1, to be passed on to trader 2 at time 2, etc. What is required is that eventually trader n will refuse to accept a future delivery of money at the current money prices but instead will insist upon a discount.

10 Remark If under the hypothesis of Theorem 9, for some s

$$\frac{\sum_{\mathcal{N}\,\text{occurring in time}\ s} k_{0,s,\mathcal{N}}\, p_{s,m,\mathcal{N}}}{\sum_{\mathcal{N}\ \text{occurring in time}\ s+1} k_{0,s+1,\mathcal{N}}\, p^{s+1}_{s+1,m,\mathcal{N}}} > 1,$$

then there is a maximum demand for current money.

Proof Let $\bar{s}$ be the first time for which the ratio in the remark is not 1. Evidently, it exceeds 1, since otherwise it would pay always to buy large amounts of current money on promise to deliver them in a future period. Whenever the ratio exceeds 1, no person could pass on money from time $\bar{s}$ to $\bar{s}+1$ without a loss. Hence, a trader would hold money only to make transactions in intervening periods, since money passed on to time $\bar{s}+1$ would have less value than if a purchase of futures money were made of the same value as the fiat money in time zero. q.e.d.

The class of money goods may include many commodities that have a low cost of exchange and do not readily deteriorate. For these goods, we might ask how the conditions of Theorem 9 and Remark 10 can be satisfied.

All money goods are generally acceptable for payment, mainly because they have low costs of transferral from one consumer to another. This property can be captured in general equilibrium analysis by the artifice of distinguishing between commodities and exchange goods (Chapter 9). In general preference levels are determined by the consumer's holdings of commodities, whereas *exchange goods* are those that can be exchanged; normally, money goods can be regarded as a subcategory of exchange goods. Commodities are distinguished according to geographical localities as well as to physical type, which accounts for transportation costs. In addition to transportation costs, the exchanges can be presumed to involve certain additional costs in real goods and services, for example, administrative costs. In summary, commodities to be exchanged must be transformed into exchange commodities.

An example of a nonexchange good is the pain-of-labor commodity. Although it is a commodity that determines preferences, it is not an exchangeable commodity, since buying the labor of others in no way assuages the pain of the labor a consumer produces himself.

A second example is a bond, which is a claim of future purchasing power. In order to sell the bond, certain inputs of labor and equipment may be necessary. Also, before the bond holder can use the bond to buy, say, an automobile, he must see the automobile, thereby incurring an extra cost. A bond held and a bond being sold are not the same commodity; there is a disadvantage to holding a bond in expectation of purchasing an automobile. A consequence of costs of exchange may well be that

$$\left(\sum_{\mathscr{N} \text{ occurring in time } s} k_{s,s+1,\mathscr{N}} \Big/ \sum_{\mathscr{N} \text{ occurring in time } s+1} k_{s-1,s,\mathscr{N}} \right)$$

is not independent of s. For example, the ratio may be 1 for $s = 1$ but smaller for larger time periods, since at some point there will be a return to investment in excess of the cost of exchange.

We turn now to the particular exchange good, money. The money and banking textbooks give four uses that distinguish money from other goods:

(1) money is a store of value;
(2) money is the unit of account;
(3) money is the medium of exchange; and
(4) money is the standard of deferred payment.

Only (2) relates to the role of money as the *numéraire*. The other three relate to money insofar as it is held. According to monetary theorists such as Keynes [1936] or Tobin [1956], money is demanded for no more than three motives:

(1) the transactions motive, whereby money is used in making purchases;

(2) the precautionary motive, whereby money is held as a contingency for future transactions whose occurrence is uncertain; and

(3) the speculative motive, whereby money may be held as an alternative to bonds until an expected rise in the bond rate materializes.

In order to show that money is in the system, it will be demonstrated that a money good provided by the state will have the four functions of money and will be demanded only for transactions, precautionary, and speculative motives. The position taken here is related to but different from the Walrasean view (see Samuelson [1947, pp. 117–124] and Kuenne [1963, Chapter 51]).

In the presence of substantial state participation in exchange, the state may be in a position to make fiat money the predominant money good. That money is always good for payment of taxes or debt to the government can be expected to ensure that it has the same positive price as the goods in which the government deals. For example, should the state fix the price of money in terms of the price of another commodity, let us say gold, and then oversupplies, money would surely command a very low price. That is to say, prices of goods other than gold would rise.

In summary, if money is generally acceptable, then there is an equilibrium with a positive price of money. This is the meaning of the maxim "money is what money is."

Assuming that the price of fiat money is positive, if an expenditure is contemplated in the near future, the buyer may hold the fiat money commodity instead of buying an income-yielding asset whose yield would not cover the cost of transforming it out of and into an exchangeable good. Whenever futures prices are not equal to future prices, there will sometimes be a definite desire on the part of individuals to hold purchasing power. This is the transactions demand for the holding of money, exactly as set forth by Tobin [1956] and Baumol [1952]. The precautionary demand enters in when the future expenditure is not expected with certainty, but nevertheless the buyer wishes to prepare for its contingency (Tobin [1957]).

Tobin and Baumol assumed that financial markets are subject to increasing returns to scale, that is, there is a cost of transaction per se. The assumption is not valid within a competitive market, since there is no assurance that competitive equilibrium exists in such a market (Chapter 4 of the companion volume). Furthermore, it would be asymmetric to exploit indivisibilities in the relatively perfect financial market while neglecting them in the relatively imperfect goods market. It is seen, however, that increasing returns are unnecessary to account for a demand for money. The only requirements are costs of transferring nonmoney goods and ample opportunity in the future. The analysis of sequential decisions of traders provides a place for money that has long been lacking in equilibrium theories.

The speculative demand would result if there were no income-yielding asset of sufficiently short term to allow the buyer to take advantage of some expected fall in the product price of other income-yielding assets (that is, a rise in their rates of return). In all these cases, the demand for money results from no inherent quality of money except that it is infinite in life and costless (in real terms) to exchange, which is not true of other commodities.[1]

Any good that has a low exchange cost could be demanded for the same reason. The important point is that fiat money is demanded for no other reason since it has no other use.

Any good whose price is nonzero may be used as the unit of account. This is true for fiat money in particular. Simply adjust $p^t_{t,m,\mathcal{N}}$ to equal 1. In addition, its use as a commodity is predicated on the fact that it is a store of value. When the demand for money is great, presumably it is the medium of exchange. Money is used only if the time for purchase of other goods and services is different from the time at which purchasing power is obtained, whereupon it is used in the receipt of income and the purchase of goods and services. In the purchase of goods, money is the medium of exchange; in the receipt of income, it becomes the method of payment and hence of deferred payment. To conclude, fiat money (as well as money goods in general) can be integrated into the general equilibrium model with sequential decisions, although there must first be (real) costs of exchange.

Of course, it is required that all the properties of consumption and production used in general equilibrium analysis, such as in Chapters 4, 5, and 9, can be imposed upon exchange commodities, which are naturally valued only insofar as they can be transformed into commodities that can be "enjoyed." This is the essence of the so-called Principle of Equivalence between the actual economy and an economy with only exchange commodities, valued according to the utility induced by an underlying optimization procedure.

11 Remark For a competitive trader, fiat money satisfies the quantity theory, so that an equiproportional increase in everyone's money balances can be absorbed by the same proportional increase in other prices. A less than equiproportional change in prices would be insufficient in equilibrium.

Proof It can be stated that if there is an equilibrium with positive money prices, then there is one at every positive quantity of money supplied by the state, provided the money is distributed proportionately to former money holdings. Suppose money holdings are increased

[1] This point is characterized by Clower [1967] in the extreme contention that only money is used in exchange for other goods, never goods for goods. Empirical observations will verify contradictions to this rule.

proportionately to each individual's former holdings. In order to preserve equilibrium, it is necessary only that the price of money decrease to overcome the increased supply. Furthermore, each person has the same quantity of money in terms of purchasing value as before. Alternatively, equilibrium can be preserved, where the price of money is held fixed, if the price of all other goods increases proportionately. The last sentence follows from the fact that increased wealth leads to preferred choices. Hence, the efficiency of competitive equilibrium requires that real wealth be the same after the change in money holdings. q.e.d.

Oddly enough, the classical dichotomy as taught by Cassel [1932], that real prices are determined independently of money prices, does not apply here in its strictest sense. Unlike an increase in money supply originating outside the system, a reduction in fiat money supply compensated by futures claims equal in value does not lead to any forces reducing equilibrium prices, so that it cannot be said strictly that the supply of money determines the level of prices. On the other hand, in equilibrium, increases in the quantity of money as a substitute for futures claims will eventually force prices upward, as the total quantity of futures claims becomes incompatible with the community's ability to absorb them. Hence, the price level is influenced by the supply of money.

The role of money is to substitute for value insurance. If supplies of money over time relative to the money supply in period zero are insufficient to exhaust demand for short-term futures, then commodity insurance will be purchased instead. The restrictions in Theorem 9 on the relative prices of money in turn imply restrictions on the relative quantities of money. For example, if the quantity of money increases precipitously over time (perhaps by a factorial expansion), there can be no equilibrium with money. To see this, adjust the price of money so that it is 1 in time zero. Let the maximal demand for money in each time period t be denoted $d_{t,m}^{t}$. Then any vector of money supply in

$$\mathscr{S} = \{x = (x_0, x_1, \ldots) \mid x \leqslant k(d_{0m}^{0}, d_{1m}^{1}, \ldots) = kd \quad \text{for some} \quad k > 0\}$$

will do as well, provided money supplies are simply substituted for futures claims. Since the set of equilibrium maximal demands will normally be compact in the pointwise convergence, $\mathscr{S}$ does not contain all nonnegative vectors. For vectors not in $\mathscr{S}$ there will be no equilibrium.

In the absence of increasing returns to scale in distribution, there is no reason why the distribution of output should necessarily be done by firms. Hence, payment in kind to factors of production involves no real costs. Nevertheless, people may prefer to hold, say, gold over time, and it might be argued that gold has alternative uses that are restricted whenever its use as a money good bids up its price beyond its "real" value. Hence fiat money might release gold for other uses.

Also it might be argued that different quantities of fiat money supplied would lead to different equilibria and hence widen the range of social choice.

Because any equilibrium with fiat money is one without, and vice versa (Theorem 9), neither of the foregoing arguments is valid. At the very best, equilibrium with money exists and is efficient, just like equilibrium without money. Like the sequential decision-making process, the existence of fiat money does not improve the efficiency of the competitive system, at least in the world of perfect foresight, no decision costs, convex production and preferences, etc. In this world, fiat money is a veil, as Pigou [1920] had it.

A bank (or the United States government) might announce that deposits with it were redeemable in money (or gold) and people might be willing to give up money in order to utilize the bank account. Under competition, such activities would be expanded until the return from investments by banks just equaled the cost of maintenance of the facilities for exchange plus the rate paid on deposits. The use of bank accounts would then be a reflection of an especially cheap way of carrying out transactions.

As a matter of fact, the banking sector is usually monopolized by restriction of entry and by government price fixing (on rates paid on deposits). Obviously, this tends to increase the income of bankers, which could be countered with a government subsidy to nonbankers. Since the rate on investment in longer-term ventures minus the rate on deposits represents the cost of exchange, the cost of exchange is increased by the bank market imperfection. Therefore, some traders make investments rather than hold low-yielding money even though an efficient system would allow them to hold money yielding a relatively high return. A fiat money system so managed is no longer a veil and certainly not an instrument of economic efficiency.

Should the state try to spend fiat money in excess of receipts from taxes or new government borrowings, the total value of demand of the state would exceed the value of the state's receipts. Even with higher prices the total value of demand includes the value of real assets plus the printed money. Therefore, demand exceeds supply. This would cause inflation until the state withdrew its printed money. Historically, printing money has often led to hyperinflation, where prices increase at an ever increasing rate until the currency ceases to be accepted as money.

It is interesting to see that inflation is checked whenever the state backs its currency with gold. Suppose the government agrees to buy or sell gold at a price fixed in money. (Whether or not citizens are allowed to keep gold for nonproductive speculative purposes is of no importance here.) In effect, gold is the *numéraire* and, assuming that it is a normal good, the demand for gold changes directly with the general price level. Therefore, if the government spends money in excess of its receipts, inflation drives the price level up, increases the demand for gold for productive uses, and causes a continuous outflow of gold. If the government persists in its policy, the government gold supply will be exhausted and the government will be forced to cease its spending or leave the gold standard. In particular, unlimited inflation is not compatible with the gold standard.

PROBLEMS

A. Transactions Demand for Money

Suppose an individual receives a constant income, which he plans to invest in bonds with an interest rate ρ and with brokerage fee a per transaction.

Show that the average cash holdings are $(\frac{1}{2}\text{ income } a/\rho)^{1/2}$.

This problem was solved by Baumol [1952] and Tobin [1956].

B. Inventory Theory

Let the demand for a good be distributed by $\phi(x)$ for n periods. Let $k(x)$ be holding costs, $c(x)$ ordering costs, and $p(x)$ shortage costs.

(i) Compute the costs charged to a given period for different stocks of goods y, including prospective (current-period) shortage and holding costs. Denote them $L(y)$.

Let ρ be the interest rate and define $C_n(x)$ to be the n-period costs due to an order of y,

$$C_n(x) = c(y - x) + L(y) + \alpha \int_0^{\infty} C_{n-1}(y - \xi)\,\phi(\xi)\,d\xi.$$

(ii) Show that if in the 1-period case, with $c_0 = 0$ and ordering cost linear, $c(y) = cy$, then the optimal policy is such that there exists an $\bar{x}$ for which we adopt the rule "If $x < \bar{x}$, buy $\bar{x} - x$, and if $x > \bar{x}$, do not buy."

(iii) Let

$$c(x) = \begin{cases} 0 & \text{if} \quad x = 0 \\ K + cz & \text{if} \quad x > 0 \end{cases}$$

and let both holding and shortage costs be linear and homogeneous. Show that in the single-period case there exist numbers (S, s) such that "if $x < s$, one orders $S - x$, and if $x > s$, one does not order." (This is referred to as an (S, s) *policy*.)

(iv) Prove (iii) whenever holding and shortage costs are nonlinear but $L(x)$ is convex,

(v) In an n-period analysis, show that an S^n, s^n policy results for the case

$$K + C_n(a + x) - C_n(x) - aC_n(x) \geqslant 0 \qquad \text{for} \quad a > 0.$$

This is the property of *K-convexity*. (Hint: Let $y = S_n$ minimize $C_n(y)$ and let s_n be defined by

$$C_n(S_n) + K.)$$

(vi) Show that C_n are K-convex. (Hint: Use induction and (v) and evaluate $c_n(x)$ for the cases $x < s_n$ and $x > s_n$.)

(vii) Under what conditions would the demand for money be characterized by an (S, s) policy?

For a solution of (ii), (iii), and (iv) see Karlin [1959]. The solutions to (v) and (vi) are due to Scarf [1960].

3. Evaluation of Assets under Certainty

The rest of this chapter is concerned with the conversion of future values of services of an asset into a single present value for the asset. In a situation where prospective returns are certain, the rate of interest links the various future returns and once that rate is known, asset values are easily computed. This section seeks to show conditions under which the rate of interest is defined and how present value is determined from that rate. The two following sections treat asset evaluation under conditions of uncertain return.

A commodity that fits a given physical description has a current price that is a component of p_0^0. For other periods, it is normally a composite of several commodities of that physical type but may be distinguished according to different contingencies. Let $\mathscr{I}_{t,i}$ be the set of time t commodities of physical type identical with commodity i in time zero.

Then the time t, commodity i, *rate of interest* is

$$\rho_j^t = \frac{\sum_{j\in\mathscr{I}_t} p_{t,j}^0}{\sum_{j\in\mathscr{I}_{t+1}} p_{t+1,j}^0} - 1.$$

That ρ_i^t need not equal ρ_i^s was emphasized by Malinvaud [1953, 1962]. On the other hand, there are conditions under which

$$\rho_i^t = \rho_i^s$$

and still others under which

$$\rho_i^t = \rho_k^t .$$

12 Remark Let an unsaturated trader have expectation of prices according to

$$\frac{p_{t+1,j}^{t+1}}{p_{t,j}^t} = f^t(p_{t,j}^t), \qquad j \in \mathscr{I}_{i,t}$$

for which $\sum_j f_j^t(p_{t,j}) = f$ is independent of $p_{t,j}$ and j. Then the equilibrium price system $p_t^0 = k_t p_t^t$, given $\rho^t = \rho_j^t$. In words, if proportional changes in prices are expected to sum, in all contingencies, to a constant value, then rates of interest are identical between different commodities. A particular instance is where everyone expects prices to remain the same, with certainty.

Proof Apply Remark 6, so that

$$\frac{\sum_{j\in\mathscr{I}_{t,i}} p_{t,j}^0}{\sum_{k\in\mathscr{I}_{t+1,i}} p_{t+1,k}^0} = \frac{k_t}{k_{t+1}} \frac{\sum_{j\in\mathscr{I}_{t,i}} p_{t,j}^t}{\sum_{k\in\mathscr{I}_{t+1,i}} p_{t+1,k}^{t+1}}$$

$$= \frac{k_t}{k_{t+1}} \frac{\sum_{j\in\mathscr{I}_{t,i}} p_{t,j}^t}{\sum_{j\in\mathscr{I}_{t,i}} p_{t,j}^t \sum_k f_k^t(p_{t,k})}$$

$$= \frac{k_t}{k_{t+1}} \frac{1}{f} \frac{\sum_{j\in\mathscr{I}_{t,i}} p_{t,j}^t}{\sum_{j\in\mathscr{I}_{t,i}} p_{t,j}^t} = \frac{k_t}{k_{t+1}} \frac{1}{f}. \qquad \text{q.e.d.}$$

As in so much of the preceding analysis of expectations, the remaining properties of interest rates depend on the argument that in certain circumstances, traders would have the opportunity for unlimited profits.

13 Remark If m is the money good (or any indestructible commodity with no costs of exchange and a certain future price) and for all t, ρ_j^t;

in time zero is expected to be equal to ρ_m^{t+1} in time one, then in equilibrium, $\rho_m^0 = \rho_m^t$ in time zero for all t.

Proof If $\rho_m^{t+1} > \rho_m^0$ (in time zero), then it would pay the trader to sell $t+1$ futures in m and deliver the next period when ρ_m^0, $1 \leqslant s \leqslant t+1$, equals time zero ρ_m^0 $(=\rho_m^t)$. If $\rho_m^{t+1} < \rho_m^0$ (in time zero), then it would pay the trader to buy $t+1$ futures in m and sell the next period when ρ_m^0, $1 \leqslant s \leqslant t+1$, equals period zero ρ_m^0 $(=\rho_m^t)$. q.e.d.

The reasoning in proof of Remark 13 applies equally well to the case of a commodity that is not certain in its price but has a constant rate of deterioration and is traded by an individual desirous of maximizing the market value of his transactions. Such an individual would be a competitive firm.

14 Remark If i is a good deteriorating at rate d, there is a competitive firm trading in the good, and for all t, ρ_i^t in time zero is expected to be equal to ρ_i^{t+1} in time one, then in equilibrium in time zero, $\rho_i^0 = \rho_i^t$ for all t.

Assets normally fall into two categories, namely, those that are claims on money (*financial assets*) and those that are claims on other goods (*real assets*).

Real assets include ownership of durable goods and/or capital (individual proprietorships) and shares in physical outputs of firms that own and operate durable capital (so-called partnerships).

A *bill* of maturity t is a payment of a certain amount of money at time t. A *bond* is a collection of bills with a constant per unit payment until maturity, at which time the payment is equal to the so-called par value. A *consol* is a payment of a fixed sum of money *in perpetuum*. A *stock* is a residual claim on the money income (after payment on bonds or bills) from a collection of real assets. These are all financial assets.

Under conditions of uniform interest rates over time, one stream of earnings can be transformed into a proportion of another by appropriate sales and purchases (in the futures market). In this case, assets can be given a *present value*, which is defined as the current value of an equivalent consol. For example, if the money rate of interest is ρ and a consol yields $(r, r, r, \ldots)$, then the price of the consol is r/ρ. Since a trader can sell a consol in the ith year for cash, buy a consol with the par value, and/or accumulate earnings of a bond maturing in the ith year, there is equivalence of consols and bonds, from the trader's viewpoint. Hence the definition of present value can be stated in terms of the equivalent value of a bond. It is not even necessary to assume that assets like bonds have uniform rates of interest over time.

Suppose a trader is to decide whether he should make an investment of x dollars that yields (with certainty) the following stream of future (money) earnings,

$$\begin{array}{ll} \text{time} & 1\pi_1 \\ \text{time} & 2\pi_2 \\ & \vdots \end{array}$$

where π_i is the payoff for the ith year. Since market value is linear, the present value to the investor of such a stream of earnings is exactly the sum (over i) of the present value of investments yielding π_1 in the ith period and nothing in any other period. Symbolically:

$$pv(\pi_1, \pi_2, \ldots) = \sum_{i=1}^{\infty} pv(0, 0, \ldots, 0, \pi_i, 0, \ldots),$$

where pv stands for the present value. The alternative to the investment that yields $(0, 0, \ldots, 0, \pi_i, 0, \ldots)$ is to lend y^i dollars at the rate until period i (that is, to exchange y^i now for a compounded payment each period until i), which by Remark 13 yields

$$y^i \prod_{j=1}^{i} (1 + \rho_m^j).$$

The *present value* or futures value of π_i is the amount of y^i that will yield π_i in the ith period, computed as

$$pv(\pi_i) = y^i = \prod_{j=1}^{i} (1 + \rho_m^j)^{-1} \pi_i .$$

15 Theorem *A firm makes an investment with many returns* (1, 2,...) *expected with certainty if and only if*

$$\sum^{\infty} \pi_i \prod_{j=1}^{i} (1 + \rho_m^j)^{-1} = pv(\pi_i, \pi_2, \ldots) \geqslant z,$$

where z is the price asked for the investment.

The proof follows easily from the definition of market evaluation. This depends on the proposition that equates the present value of a stream of earnings with the sum of the present value of each period's earnings. It might be supposed that there could be some penalty associated with the fact that an individual has sunk his money in a stream of earnings with a very peculiar time path. For example, there might be alternative periods of high and low earnings, or it might be necessary to wait until late periods to obtain substantial earnings. It can be seen that the present value formulation takes account of all these factors. We illustrate in the case $\rho_m^j = \rho$.

An individual can borrow x at the rate ρ for one period, with which he buys the investment yielding π_i at the end of the ith period, $i = 1, 2, \ldots$. (This investment can serve as collateral for the loan.) At the end of each period he borrows (or lends) enough of his profits so as to be just able to pay off his interest due. (When he lends, in effect, he is paying on the principal of his loan.) In the second period, for example, he borrows

$$\rho z + (\rho z - \pi_1)(1 + \rho_1)\, \pi_2\,;$$

at the end of the nth period, he has borrowed

$$\rho(1 + \rho)^{n-1} - \sum_{i=1}^{n} \pi_i(1 + \rho)^{n-i}.$$

His accumulated assets are the negative of the figure above. Provided he comes out with at least the principal z at this time, he will make the investment, since he has nothing to lose. He will come out even or better if the necessary borrowings at the $(n + 1)$st period are less than or equal to zero. This follows from the fact that if the interest payment at the $(n + 1)$st period in which no income is forthcoming is greater than zero, the original loan z has not been liquidated and the individual stands to lose. Otherwise, the interest payment is zero or negative (there is income on assets above and beyond the payment of the debt) and hence the amount of borrowing necessary to pay the interest is negative (that is, the individual actually has a surplus, which he can use to lend to others for interest).

An alternative measure used is the *internal rate of return*, defined to be the interest rate that just makes the present value equal to cost:

$$\sum_{t=1}^{\infty} \pi_t(1 + \rho)^{-t} = z.$$

Even if interest rates are uniform over time, it can be shown that the internal rate of return is not a dependable criterion for ranking investment projects (Fisher [1930], Hirschliefer [1958]). What the internal rate of return does give is the class of investments that are acceptable at the interest rate ρ. For example, in an economy with one good that is accumulated for capital or consumed, the value of the capital stock is the discounted sum of its future earnings. Any appropriate ρ will serve as the rate of interest on bonds with claims on capital income. Just which ρ is the rate of interest will depend on history. Incidentally the internal note of return is often unique.

16 Theorem *If $\sum \pi_i \alpha^i$ is bounded for some α and π_i in money terms, and all expected with certainty to be nonnegative, then there is a positive ρ for which*

$$\mathit{pv}(\pi_1, \ldots, \pi_n) = \sum_{i=1}^{\infty} \pi_i (1 + \rho)^{-i}.$$

Any positive ρ solving the foregoing equation decreases with increases in π_i.

Difficulties arise whenever some of the π_i are negative, whereupon investments profitable at low interest rates may not be profitable at higher ones.

Proof

$$\mathit{pv} = \sum_{t=1}^{\infty} \pi_t (1 + \rho)^{-t} = z.$$

Evidently,

$$\mathit{pv}_{\rho_0} = \sum_{t=1}^{\infty} \pi_t \alpha^t, \qquad \rho_0 = 1 - \frac{1}{\alpha},$$

is bounded. Also,

$$\frac{d\mathit{pv}_\rho}{d\rho} - \sum_{t=1}^{\infty} \pi_t t (1 + \rho)^{-1-t} < 0,$$

so decreasing ρ increases pv_ρ up to $\sum_{i=1}^{\infty} \pi_i$ for $\rho = 0$. Increasing ρ decreases pv_ρ to zero. Also,

$$\frac{\partial \mathit{pv}_\rho}{\partial \rho} \frac{d\rho}{d\pi_t} = (1 + \rho)^{-t}$$

gives $d\rho / d\pi_t < 0$. q.e.d.

An application of the theorem occurs whenever the current price of goods (equals the price of capital) increases. The effect on the rate of interest depends on whether prospective profits increase more or less than proportionately. An example of a stream of earnings with indefinite present value is

$$\pi_t = t!.$$

The factorial always outgrows any power of a positive number $(1 + \rho)^t$.

PROBLEMS

C. Marginal Efficiency

Define the s, t *marginal efficiency* of a commodity i as the minimum value of a transaction in time t resulting from an acquisition of a time s future of i.

Show that if the commodity has no acquisition costs, if it does not decrease preferences when held, and if it deteriorates from period t to $t + 1$ at the proportional rate $d_{t,t+1}$, then the $t - 1$, t marginal efficiency is no less than $\rho_i^t(1 - d_{t-1,t}) - d_{t-1,t}$.

The concept of marginal efficiency is due to Keynes [1936].

D. Capital Value I

Suppose all deterioration of a capital good with a time-uniform rate of interest takes place in a single year.

Show that purchase of the good is made if and only if the increased (discounted) revenue of adding the "machine" minus the (discounted) cost of other newly utilized factors must be greater than or equal to the cost of the investment.

Letting the discounted sum of rents equal the capital value, show that in the case above the firm buys the factor if and only if the rent equals the marginal productivity of capital.

E. Capital Value II

Show that under constant returns to scale and stationary prices, a firm invests in the capital good if and only if the increased revenue in the current period exceeds the rent on new capital in the current period.

F. Long-Run Value Maximization

Let output be denoted q, sales s, inventory I, production costs c, and storage costs h.

(i) What is the present value of the firm?

(ii) Show that profit maximization requires that the rate of change of discounted marginal cost equal the rate of change of discounted marginal revenue. (Hint: Use Problem I of Chapter 2.)

(iii) Show that profit maximization requires that the marginal cost of output equal the marginal cost of sales. (Hint: Show that there exists a time T such that policies at or beyond time T have little influence on value. Let $I(T) = 0$ and use (ii) and the fact that at time T, marginal cost equals marginal revenue.)

(iv) What are the determinants of inventory policy? Why would the firm hold inventories?

(v) Let p depend on $S = \int_{-\infty}^{t} s(u)\, d(u)$ and on s. What are the modifications required in the answers above?

G. Corporation Finance I

Let the present value of a portfolio be an additive transformation on retained earnings and dividends received from assets. Assume that a zero value accrues to a no-dividend retained-earnings asset (for example, shares in the Ford Foundation).

Show that present value depends only on prospective dividends.

4. Uncertainty with Small Numbers of Independent Assets

Here we consider the meaning of risk in investment decisions. The advantages of a diversified portfolio and the disadvantages of pure gambling are considered.

Investments with uncertain money returns are sums of conditional events having several possible present values given by a probability distribution.

If there are many independent causative factors at work, present values may be distributed by a

(1) *normal distribution*

$$\phi(y) = \frac{1}{\sqrt{2\sigma}} \exp \frac{(y - \mu)^2}{\sigma^2}$$

where μ is the expected value and σ is the standard deviation of y, for y varying in $(-\infty, \infty)$, or

(2) *Poisson distribution*

$$\phi(y) = \frac{e^{\mu} \mu y}{\Gamma(y)}$$

where Γ is the factorial function for y varying in $(0, \infty)$.

If there is no tendency of the manifold causes, then the present values may be distributed by a

(3) *Pareto distribution,* which is the solution ϕ of

$$\phi(y) = \int_{y}^{\infty} \phi(y) y \, dy = \left(\frac{y}{\bar{y}}\right)^{\beta}$$

for y varying in $(\bar{y}, \infty)$.

Were a trader to make investment decisions solely on the basis of expected value, he would ignore a great many possible contingencies. For example, he might ignore the possibility (albeit of small probability) of a great disaster, such as the costs of bankruptcy. For this reason, many people discount expected value for risk.

Just what is meant by risk is uncertain. Perhaps it is the possibility of great loss, but the very meaning of great loss varies between individuals. Economists have sought some reasonable measure for such a concept. Possible measures are

(1) probability of loss,
(1a) probability of present value less than $\bar{y}$,
(2) standard deviation,
(3) standard deviation of present values less than $\bar{y}$.

All are objectionable on the grounds that they are stated in money terms and hence do not reflect price level uncertainty, which might lead to a deterioration in the "true" value of money. This problem could be ameliorated by adopting an index of certainty other than money. The analysis would not be different.

Cases (1), (1a), and (2) are the easiest to compute, although (3) is by no means difficult. In cases (1), (1a), and (3), the choice of the cutoff point for "disaster" is left unresolved. The difficulties of the use of zero can be seen in Figure 1. Distributions ψ and γ are equally desirable by the probability-of-loss criterion. Yet γ definitely offers the highest probability of great loss as opposed to a small (and possibly insignificant) loss. Thus, probability of loss seems to be an inadequate criterion for risk. On the other hand, standard deviation of γ, σ_γ is greater than that of ψ, σ_ψ ; that is,

$$\sigma_\gamma > \sigma_\psi ,$$

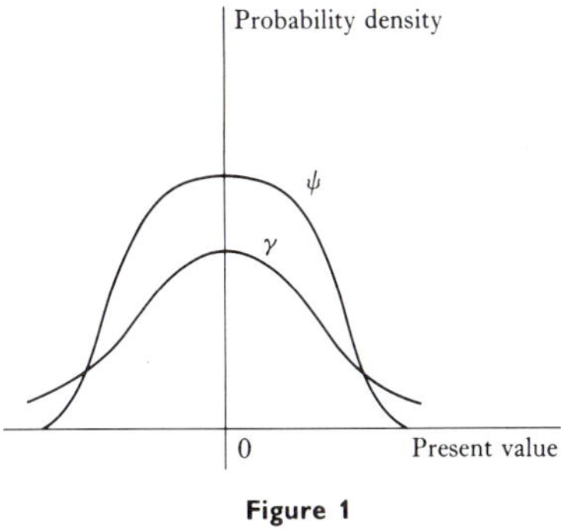

Figure 1

so that γ has the highest risk by the standard deviation criterion, which seems to be the correct result. A particular advantage of the standard deviation as a measure of risk is that for the most usual probability distributions, normal, Poisson, and Pareto, the variance and expected value together completely determine a curve among all such families of curves. Thus, two assets or investments that offer alternative normal distributions of possible return can be analyzed completely in terms of standard deviation and expected value.

The difficulties in using the standard deviation when the distributions compared are not necessarily from the same family are illustrated in Figure 2. The distributions ψ and γ have the same expected values and standard deviation. Yet γ seems to be superior in some respects in that it offers no chance of great loss, whereas it offers some chance of great benefit. To some individuals (although not, of course, to all) ψ might be preferred to γ. But this preference could not be deduced if only expected value and variance were considered. The deduction requires other indicators, such as a measure of the skewness of the distribution (this would be given by the sum of cubed deviation from the expected value multiplied by the probability of such a deviation). Note that the mean of the losses and the standard deviation of the losses as measures of risk might also give the wrong answer. These measures would denote ψ as least risky, whereas the risk-averting individual might discount great losses and judge differently. In summary, risk and expected return alone do not determine choice.

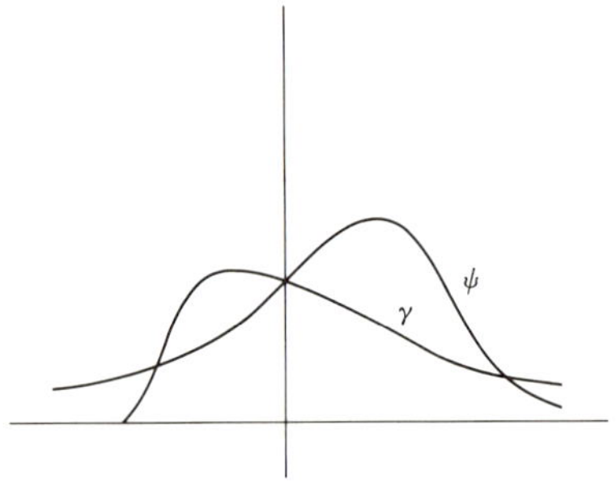

Figure 2

The internal rate of return of the expected earnings of an asset is called its *return*. Bizarre time distributions of earnings might carry special penalties if there were insufficient variety of time distributions among other uncertain assets. Hence, the results of this section apply only in the appropriate sense of approximation.

Two or more assets with returns μ_i and standard deviations σ_i can be combined in amounts t_i, which is called a *portfolio*. The return of the portfolio is $\mu = \sum \mu_i t_i$, and if the assets have independent distributions, the standard deviation $\sigma = \sqrt{\sum_i \sigma_i^2 t_i^2}$.

In Figure 3 are illustrated the combinations of a bond of return 1 and a stock of return 2 and standard deviation 2 of equal cost. The risk-averting trader whose indifference curve is denoted $\mathscr{I}_{2.5}$ chooses a return of 2.5 A result of Tobin [1965] and Markowitz [1959] is the following principle.

17 Remark In combining two risky assets differing in return, with the greater-return asset having a greater risk than the other, the lesser-risk portfolio has a higher return than the lesser-return asset. In effect, two independent assets are differentiated products, as in Figure 4 for two stocks. The combinations of y and x are a curve rather than a line. Putting eggs in separate baskets actually increases the expected survival of eggs.

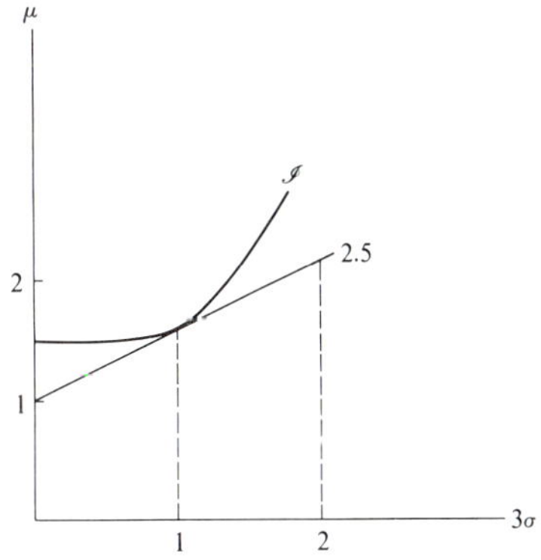

Figure 3

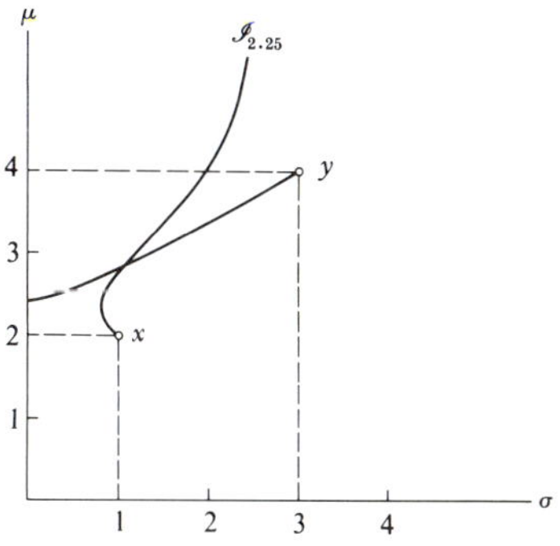

Figure 4

Proof It suffices to consider a single asset, where for a proportion s of the asset x, and $1 - s$ of y gives

$$\sigma = \sigma_{sx+(1-s)y} = \sqrt{s^2\sigma_x^2 + (1-s)^2\,\sigma_y^2}$$

or, minimizing, we get

$$\frac{d\sigma}{ds} = \frac{2s\sigma_x^2 - 2(1-s)\,\sigma_y^2}{\sigma} = 0 \qquad \text{or} \qquad s = \frac{\sigma_y^2}{\sigma_x^2 + \sigma_y^2} \neq \binom{1}{0}.$$

Since $\mu_x < \mu_y$ for μ_y maximum; $\mu_{xs+(1-s)y} > \mu_x$. q.e.d.

18 Remark The addition of a third asset can be utilized to reduce risk without reducing return even if it has a lower expected return and a higher standard deviation, provided it has a higher return than the original portfolio. If there is no riskless asset, the minimum-risk portfolio contains positive holdings of all independent assets. Consequently, risk-averting traders may be willing to purchase (risky and independent) assets with negative returns.

Proof

$$\sqrt{\sum_i \sigma_i^2 t_i^2} < \sum_i \sigma_i t_i \qquad \text{whenever} \quad \sigma_i > 0. \qquad \text{q.e.d.}$$

Remark 18 gives a justification for gambling at unfair odds, provided that there is an insufficient number of risky assets at favorable odds. Its rationale is illustrated in Figure 5, where z is the third asset and the shaded area indicates the new possibilities with its addition. The dotted line indicates the added possibilities if there is also a bond with return b. Provided the bond is held in positive quantities, the investor buys only stocks in the risk-minimizing proportions that yield point a, which is the same for all investors.

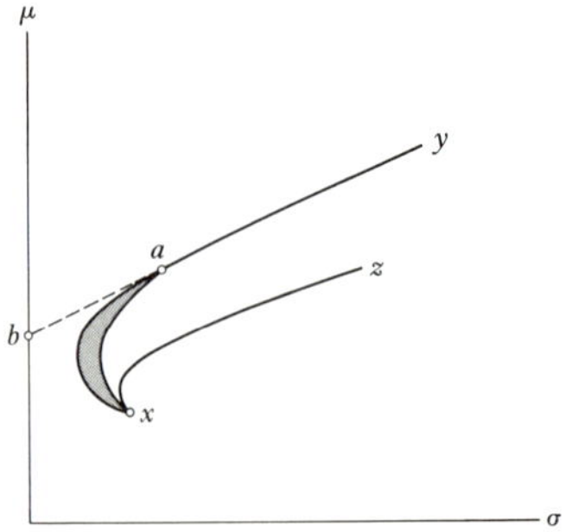

Figure 5

A risk-averting investor may rationally hold an inferior asset (or even one with negative return, provided there is no perfectly safe asset with zero return).

Proof Simply let x in the proof of Remark 17 be the original portfolio and y be the new asset. q.e.d.

19 Remark A risk-averting investor who bears any risk at all but who evaluates only expected return and standard deviation will hold some of the highest-return asset if it is independent of others.

It should be noted that betting for its own sake cannot improve a consumer position. This follows from a convexity argument due to Arrow [1953] and Debreu [1959, Chapter 6] and applied to the case at hand by Bergstrom.

First, consider a bet with one-half probability of winning and one-half probability of losing. With a win, a competitive trader will have a given trade x, whose value will be minus the amount of the bet, whereas with a loss, his trade y must be plus the amount of the bet. Consider that in the contingency of winning he instead traded y and in the contingency of losing he traded x; the new trade is as good as the former. Hence the trades (x, y) and (y, x) can be combined as $\frac{1}{2}(x, y) + \frac{1}{2}(y, x)$, which is at least as good as (x, y). The resulting consumption is $(\frac{1}{2}x + \frac{1}{2}y, \frac{1}{2}y + \frac{1}{2}x)$, namely, $\frac{1}{2}x + \frac{1}{2}y$ regardless of win or loss. Evidently, the consumer can afford $\frac{1}{2}x + \frac{1}{2}y$ if he refrains from betting $(px/2 + py/2 = 0$ since $-px = py)$. If there is strict convexity of preferences, he will actually prefer to do so.

In the case of other fair *bets* with rational fractional chances of win m/n, the consumer will also have a superior certain alternative, namely

$$\frac{m}{n}x + \frac{n-m}{n}y$$

(divide the events of winning or losing into n parts and combine alternatives on the basis of the smaller bets, one by one). Irrational bets can be shown to be inferior if they are considered as the limits of inferior rational bets (continuity of preferences in probability).

20 Remark Let a bet not affect prices of commodities. If preferences are weakly convex and continuous in probabilities, a fair bet is not superior to no bet and an unfair bet is inferior to no bet. If preferences are strictly convex and continuous in probabilities, a fair or unfair bet is inferior to no bet.

Betting will take place only upon contingencies that affect market prices.

PROBLEMS

H. Corporation Finance III

Suppose a firm borrows at the money rate of interest to make an investment. Compare this with the case where the firm sells stock to liquidate the debt and show that no new asset alternatives appear for investors.

This problem is due to Modigliani and Miller [1958]. See also Morgan [1967].

I. Quadratic Utility

Suppose utility of wealth is quadratic. Show that utility of a probability distribution of wealth is dependent only on expected wealth and its standard deviation.

This problem is presented by Tobin [1957].

J. Income Tax and Risk

Let there be a proportional income tax t, with state subsidy in the case of loss. Let w denote wealth, a the proportion held in an asset with uncertain return x, and $1 - a$ the proportion held in an asset with certain return r.

(i) What are the first- and second-order conditions for maximization of expected utility?

(ii) Show that

$$\frac{da}{dt} = \frac{ua}{1-t} - rw^2(1-t)\frac{E[U''(x-r)]}{d^2E/da^2}\,.$$

(iii) Prove:

Lemma *If $g(y) > 0$, $E(k(y)) = 0$, then $E(g(y)\,k(y)) > 0$ whenever $g'(y) > 0$ for all y, and $E(g(y)\,k(y)) < 0$ whenever $g'(y) < 0$.* (Hint: Use the mean value theorem.)

Use the lemma to show that the second term on the right in (ii) is positive for u''/u' increasing in x and negative for u''/u' decreasing in x.

(iv) What is the interpretation of (iii) with regard to risk taking under taxation? (Hint: See Problems A and B of Chapter 7.)

This problem was solved by Penner [1964] and Mossin [1968]. Early versions are due to Domar and Musgrave [1944] and Tobin [1957].

5. Uncertainty with Large Numbers of Independent Assets

The approximate results of the last section can be utilized to show that for many independent assets market value is exactly equal to discounted expected value, which is the same as expected present value.

In many circumstances, for assets x_i, $i = 1, 2, \ldots, (1/n^2) \sum \sigma_i^2 \to 0$. For example, if

$$\sigma_i \leqslant \sigma, \qquad 0 \leqslant \frac{1}{n^2} \sum \sigma_i^2 < \sigma^2 \frac{n}{n^2} = \frac{\sigma^2}{n} \to 0.$$

$(1/n) \sum x_i$ is called the *equiproportional portfolio*. In such cases, where risk on the average portfolio tends to zero, Bernoulli's law of large numbers applies.

21 Lemma *For independent assets x_i, $(1/n^2) \sum \sigma_i^2 \to 0$, and for $\varepsilon > 0$, there is an n sufficiently large that the probability of deviation of more than ε from $(1/n) \sum \mu_i$ of returns from the equiproportional portfolio tends to zero* (Halmos [1950, p. 202]). Hence there is a very broad sense in which risk averters may depend on a combination of assets to reduce risk.

22 Theorem *If there are a large number of independent assets with returns in excess of μ, $(1/n^2) \sum \sigma_i^2 \to 0$, then partial (but not total) risk-averting traders maximizing expected utility, continuous in expected returns, will hold at most small proportions of assets with return less than μ.*

Proof According to Lemma 21, we can obtain almost μ, expected for cases of arbitrarily small probability. Since expected utility is bounded (Remark 3 of Chapter 7), the exception is of arbitrarily small utility. Hence we can obtain almost the utility of almost μ. This is superior to the return with other than an arbitrarily small holding of assets with return less than μ, since no degree of certainty can compensate for the lower return (continuity of the trader's utility in expected return). q.e.d.

Theorem 22 makes it unlikely that an asset will sell at less than its expected present value, whenever there are a large number of independent assets that sell at their expected present value.

PROBLEM

K. Corporation Finance II

Let an asset yield a dividend minus personal tax equal to one dollar with certainty *in perpetuum*, which sells at $1/r$, r the money rate of interest. Let a second asset of equal value yield a dividend minus personal tax equal to q from time n on *in perpetuum*.

1. In the absence of a tax on capital gains, compute the capital gains per year in the second asset. How do the capital gains compare with the return from invested income from the first asset?

2. How is the foregoing answer modified if there is no personal income tax on retained earnings? (Hint: Compute the difference between income retained and income paid out but reinvested.) Show that the capital gains tax s needed to capture the extra income is

$$s = \frac{(k-1)r}{1+kr},$$

where $(k-1)$ is the personal income tax rate. (If $k-1 = 50$ percent, $r = 3$ percent after taxes ($r = 3$ percent on tax-exempt state and local bonds), s is about 0.03 as compared with the United States tax of about 0.25.)

This problem was first considered by Hicks [1940].

CITY OF LONDON LIBRARIES

References

Afriat, S.
[1967] "The Construction of Utility Function from Expenditure Data," *International Economic Review* **8**, 67–77.

Anscombe, F. J., and Auman, R.
[1963] "A Definition of Subjective Probability," *Annals of Mathematical Statistics* **34**, 199–205.

Armstrong, W. E.
[1939] "The Determinantness of the Utility Function," *Economic Journal* **49**, 453–467.

Arrow, K.
[1951a] *Social Choice and Individual Value.* Wiley, New York.
[1951b] "An Extension of the Basic Theorems of Classical Welfare Economics," in *Proceedings of the Second Berkeley Symposium on Mathematical Statistics and Probability* (J. Neyman, ed.), pp. 507–532. University of California Press, Berkeley, California.
[1953] "Le rôle des valeurs boursières pour la répartition la meilleure des risques," *Économétrie*, Paris, Centre National de la Recherche Scientifique, 41–48.
[1959] "Rational Choice Functions and Orderings," *Economica* (N. S.) **26**, 121–127.
[1965] *Aspects of the Theory of Risk Bearing* (Yrjo Johnson Lecture Series). Helsinki.

Arrow, K. and Debreu, G.
[1954] "Existence of an Equilibrium for a Competitive Economy," *Econometrica* **22**, 265–290.

Arrow, K. and Enthoven, A.
[1961] "Quasi-Concave Programming," *Econometrica* **29**, 779–800.

Arrow, K., Chenery, H., Minhas, B., and Solow, R.
[1961] "Capital Labor Substitution and Economic Efficiency," *Review of Economic Statistics* **43**, 225–50.

Ayer, A. J.
[1936] *Language, Truth and Logic.* Gallanez, London.

Barten, A. P.
[1964] "Consumer Demand Functions under Conditions of Almost Additive Preference," *Econometrica* **32**, 1–38.

Baumol, W.

[1952] "The Transactions Demand for Cash: Inventory Theoretic Approach," *Quarterly Journal of Economics* **66**, 545–556.

[1959] *Business Behavior, Value and Growth.* Harcourt, New York.

Bear, D. V. T.

[1965] "Inferior Inputs and the Theory of the Firm," *Journal of Political Economy* **73**, 287–289.

Bellman, R.

[1957] *Dynamic Programming.* Princeton University Press, Princeton, New Jersey.

Bentham, J.

[1789] *Principles of Morals and Legislation.*

Bergson, A.

[1936] "Real Income Expenditure Proportionality and 'Frisch's' New Methods of Measuring Marginal Utility," *Review of Economic Studies* **4**, 33–52.

Berkeley, G.

[1710] *Principles of Human Knowledge.*

Beth, E. W.

[1953] *The Foundations of Mathematics.* North-Holland, Amsterdam.

Birkhoff, G.

[1948] *Lattice Theory*, 2nd ed. American Mathematical Society, Providence, Rhode Island.

Birkhoff, G. and Rota, G.-C.

[1962] *Ordinary Differential Equations.* Ginn, Boston.

Bishop, E.

[1967] *Foundations of Constructive Analysis.* McGraw-Hill, New York.

Bishop, R. L.

[1964] "A Zeuthen–Hicks Theory of Bargaining," *Econometrica* **32**, 410–417.

Blackwell, D., and Girschick, M. A.

[1954] *Theory of Games and Statistical Decisions.* Wiley, New York.

Bliss, G. A.

[1945] *Lectures on the Calculus of Variations.* University of Chicago Press, Chicago, Illinois.

Cassel, G.

[1932] *Theory of Social Economy.* Harcourt, New York.

Chamberlin, E. H.

[1932] *The Theory of Monopolistic Competition*, Harvard University Press, Cambridge, Massachusetts.

Chipman, J.

[1960] "The Foundations of Utility," *Econometrica* **28**, 193–224.

[1965] "On the Existence of Real Valued Functions Which Consumers May Be Regarded as Acting as if They Are Maximizing," Mimeographed, University of Minnesota, Minneapolis.

[1970] "External Economies of Scale and Competitive Equilibrium," *Quarterly Journal of Economics* **84**, 347–385.

Clark, J. B.

[1890] *The Philosophy of Wealth.*

Clower, R.

[1967] "A Reconstruction of the Microfoundations of Monetary Theory," *Western Economic Journal* **6**, 1–8.

Coddington, E. A., and Levinson, N.
[1955] *Theory of Ordinary Differential Equations.* McGraw-Hill, New York.

Cook, S.
[1960] "The Obsolete 'Anti-Market' Mentality: A Critique of the Substantive Approach to Economic Anthropology," *American Anthropologist* **68**, 323–349.

Cournot, A.
[1838] *Recherches sur les principes mathématiques de la théorie des richesses.* Hachette, Paris. Translated as *Researches into the Mathematical Principles of the Theory of Wealth.* Macmillan, New York, 1929.

Cronin, J.
[1964] *Fixed Points and Topological Degree in Non-Linear Analysis.* American Mathematical Society, Providence, Rhose Island.

Debreu, G.
[1954] "Representation of a Preference Ordering by a Numerical Function," in *Decision Processes* (R. M. Thrall, C. H. Coombs, and R. L. Davis, eds.). Wiley, New York.
[1959] *Theory of Value.* Wiley, New York.
[1960] "Topological Methods in Cardinal Utility," in *Mathematical Methods in the Social Sciences* (K. Arrow, S. Karlin, and P. Suppes, eds.), pp. 16–26. Stanford University Press, Stanford, California.
[1964] "Continuity Properties of Paretian Utility," *International Economic Review* **5**, 285–93.

Debreu, G., and Herstein, I. N.
[1953] "Non-negative Square Matrices," *Econometrica* **21**, 597–607.

de Finetti, B.
[1937] "Foresight: Its Logical Laws, Its Subjective Sources," in *Studies in Subjective Probability* (H. Kyburg and H. Smokler, eds.), pp. 93–158. Wiley, New York, 1964. Translated from *Annales de l'Institut Henri Poincaré* **7**.

Dhrymes, P.
[1967] "On a Class of Utility and Production Functions Yielding Everywhere Differentiable Demand Functions," *Review of Economic Studies* **34**, 399–408.

Diamond, P. A.
[1965] "The Evaluation of Infinite Utility Streams," *Econometrica* **33**, 170–77.

Domar, E. P., and Musgrave, R. A.
[1944] "Proportional Income Taxation and Risk-Taking," *Quarterly Journal of Economics* **58**. Reprinted in *Readings in the Economics of Taxation* (R. A. Musgrave and C. Shoup, eds.), pp. 493–524. Irwin, Homewood, Illinois, 1959.

Drandakis, E. M.
[1966] "On the Competitive Equilibrium in a Monetary Economy," *International Economic Review* **7**, 304–28.

Dupuit, J.
[1844] "De la Mesure de l'Utilité des Travaux Publics," *Annales des Ponts et Chaussées* [2] **8**. Translation published in *Readings in Welfare Economics* (K. J. Arrow and T. Scitovsky, eds.), pp. 225–283. Irwin, Homewood, Illinois, 1969.

Edgeworth, F. Y.
[1881] *Mathematical Psychics.* Routledge and Kegan Paul, London.

Eilenberg, S.
[1941] "Ordered Topological Spaces," *American Journal of Mathematics* **83**, 39–45.

Ellsberg, D.

[1961] "Risk, Ambiguity, and the Savage Axiom," *Quarterly Journal of Economics* **75**, 643–669.

Ezekial, M.

[1938] "The Cobweb Theorem," *Quarterly Journal of Economics* **52**, 255–80.

Fellner, W.

[1949] *Competition among the Few*. Knopf, New York.

[1961] "Distortions of Subjective Probabilities as a Reaction to Uncertainty," *Quarterly Journal of Economics* **75**, 670–889.

Ferguson, C. E.

[1966] "Production, Prices, and the Theory of Jointly Derived Input Demand Functions," *Economica* (N.S.) **33**, 454–461.

Fisher, I.

[1930] *Theory of Interest*. Macmillan, New York.

Friedman, J.

[1967] "An Experimental Study of Cooperative Duopoly," *Econometrica* **35**, 379–397.

[1968] "Reaction Functions and the Theory of Duopoly," *Review of Economic Studies* **35**, 257–272.

Friedman, M.

[1953] *Essays in Positive Economics*. University of Chicago Press, Chicago, Illinois.

[1957] *A Theory of the Consumption Function*. Princeton University Press, Princeton, New Jersey.

Friedman, M., and Savage, L.

[1948] "The Utility Analysis of Choices Involving Risk," *Journal of Political Economy* **56**, 279–304. Reprinted in *Readings in Price Theory* (G. Stigler and K. E. Boulding, eds.), pp. 27–56. Irwin, Homewood, Illinois, 1952.

Gale, D.

[1960] *Theory of Linear Economic Models*. McGraw-Hill, New York.

Gantmacher, F. R.

[1959] *The Theory of Matrices*, Vol. 1. Chelsea, New York.

Gödel, K.

[1931] "Über formal unentscheibare Satz der Principia Mathematica und verwandter Systeme, 1," *Monathefte für Mathematik und Physik* **38**, 173–98.

Goldman, S. M., and Uzawa, H.

[1964] "A Note on Separability Analysis," *Econometrica* **32**, 387–398.

Gorman, W. M.

[1953] "Community Preference Fields," *Econometrica* **21**, 63–80.

Gossen, H.

[1854] *Entwicklung der Gesetze des Menschlichen Verkehrs und der darusfliesenden Regeln für Menschliches Handeln*. Braunschweig.

Hadley, G.

[1961] *Linear Algebra*. Addison-Wesley, Reading, Massachusetts.

Halmos, P.

[1950] *Measure Theory*. Van Nostrand-Reinhold, Princeton, New Jersey.

Harsanyi, J.

[1956] "Approaches to the Bargaining Problem," *Econometrica* **124**, 144–157.

Hartley, H. O., and Hocking, R. R.

[1963] "Convex Programming by Tangential Approximation," *Management Science* **9**, 600–612.

Hegel, G.
[1821] *Philosophy of Right and Law.*
Heisenberg, W.
[1958] *Physics and Philosophy.* Haynes, New York.
Herfindahl, O. C.
[1950] *Concentration in the Steel Industry,* unpublished doctoral dissertation, Columbia University, New York.
Hicks, J. R.
[1933] *The Theory of Wages.* Oxford University Press, London and New York.
[1935] "A Suggestion for Simplifying the Theory of Money," *Economica* (N.S.) **2**, 1–19. Reprinted in *Readings in Monetary Theory* (F. A. Lutz and L. W. Mints, eds.), pp. 13–32. Irwin, Homewood, Illinois, 1951.
[1938] *Value and Capital.* Oxford University Press, London and New York.
[1940] "The Valuation of Social Income," *Economica* (N.S.) **7**, 105–124.
[1950] *A Theory of the Trade Cycle.* Oxford University Press, London and New York.
[1954] "A Reply," *Review of Economic Studies* **21**, 218–221.
[1959] *A Revision of the Theory of Demand.* Oxford University Press, London and New York.
[1961] "Marshall's Third Rule: A Further Comment," *Oxford Economic Papers* (N.S.) **13**, 262–265.
Hicks, J. R., and Allen, R. D. G.
[1934] "A Reconsideration of the Theory of Value," *Economica* (N.S.) **1**, 52–76.
Hilbert, D.
[1899] *Grundlagen der Geometrie.*
Hirschliefer, J.
[1958] "On the Theory of Optimal Investments Decision," *Journal of Political Economy* **66**, 329–352.
Hochwald, W.
[1968] "An Economist's Image of History," *Southern Economic Journal* **35**, 3–16.
Hotelling, H.
[1929] "Stability in Competition," *Economic Journal* **39**, 41–57.
Houthakker, H.
[1950] "Revealed Preference and the Utility Function," *Economica* (N.S.) **17**, 159–174.
Hurwicz, L.
[1960] "Optimality and Informational Efficiency in Resource Allocation Processes," in *Mathematical Methods in the Social Sciences* (K. Arrow, S. Karlin, and P. Suppes, eds.), pp. 27–46. Stanford University Press, Stanford, California.
Jevons, W. S.
[1871] *The Theory of Political Economy.* Macmillan, New York.
Jorgenson, D. W.
[1961] "The Structure of Multi-Sector Dynamic Models," *International Economic Review* **2**, 276–293.
Kant, I.
[1788] *Critique of Practical Reason.*
[1791] *The Metaphysics of Morals.*
Karlin, S.
[1959] *Mathematical Methods and Theory in Games, Programming and Economics,* Vol. I. Addison-Wesley, Reading, Massachusetts.

Kelley, J. G.
[1960] "The Cutting Plane Method for Solving Convex Programs," *SIAM Journal* **8**, 703–712.
Kelly, J.
[1955] *General Topology*. Van Nostrand-Reinhold, Princeton, New Jersey.
Kelly, J., and Namioka, I.
[1963] *Linear Topological Spaces*. Van Nostrand-Reinhold, Princeton, New Jersey.
Keynes, J. M.
[1936] *General Theory of Employment, Interest and Money*. Harcourt, New York.
Khinchin, A. I.
[1957] *Mathematical Foundations of Information Theory*. Dover, New York.
Kleene, S. C.
[1952] *Introduction to Meta-Mathematics*. Van Nostrand-Reinhold, Princeton, New Jersey.
Knaster, B., Kuratowski, C., and Mazukiewicz, S.
[1931] "Ein Beweis des Fixpunktsatzes für *n*-dimensionale simplex," *Fundamenta Mathematicae* **14**, 132–137.
Knight, F. H.
[1921] *Risk, Uncertainty and Profit*. Houghton-Mifflin, New York.
Koopmans, T. C.
[1947] "Measurement without Theory," *Review of Economic Statistics* **29**, 161–172.
[1949] "A Reply" (To Rutledge Vining), *Review of Economic Statistics* **31**, 77–94.
[1951] "Analysis of Production as an Efficient Allocation of Resources," in *Activity Analysis of Production and Allocation* (T. C. Koopmans, ed.), pp. 33–97. Wiley, New York.
[1966] "Structure of Preference over Time," Cowles Foundation, Discussion Paper, No. 206.
[1957] *Three Essays on the State of Economic Science*, McGraw-Hill, New York.
Koopmans, T. C., and Bausch, A.
[1959] "Selected Topics in Economics involving Mathematical Reasoning," *SIAM Review* **1**.
Kraft, C. H., Pratt, J. W., and Seidenberg, A.
[1959] "Intuitive Probability on Finite Sets," *Annals of Mathematical Statistics* **30**, 408–19.
Kuenne, R. E.
[1963] *The Theory of General Economics Equilibrium*. Princeton University Press, Princeton, New Jersey.
Kuhn, H. W., and Tucker, A. W.
[1951] "Nonlinear Programming," *Proceedings of the Second Berkeley Symposium on Mathematical Statistics and Probability* (J. Neyman, ed.), pp. 481–492. University of California Press, Berkeley, California.
Lagrange
[1787] *Mécanique Analytique*.
Lancaster, K.
[1966] "A New Approach to Consumer Theory," *Journal of Political Economy* **74**, 132–157.
Leontief, W.
[1941] *The Structure of the American Economy, 1919–1939*. Oxford University Press, London and New York.

Leontief, W.
[1947] "Introduction to a Theory of the Internal Structure of Functional Relationship," *Econometrica* **15**, 361–373.
Lerner, A.
[1946] *The Economics of Control.* Macmillan, New York.
Lindsay, R. B., and Margenau, H.
[1936] *Foundations of Physics.* Dover, New York.
Luce, R. D., and Raiffa, H.
[1957] *Games and Decisions.* Wiley, New York.
Mach, E.
[1902] *The Science of Mechanics.* Translated from German by T. J. McCormack, K. Paul, Trench, Trübner & Co., London.
McKenzie, L.
[1957] "Demand Theory without a Utility Index," *Review of Economic Studies* **24**, 185–189.
Malinvaud, E.
[1953] "Capital Accumulation and Efficient Allocation of Resources," *Econometrica* **21**, 233–262.
[1962] "Efficient Capital Accumulation: A Corrigendum," *Econometrica* **30**, 570–573.
Markowitz, H.
[1959] *Portfolio Selection.* Wiley, New York.
Marshall, A.
[1890] *Principles of Economics.* Macmillan, London and New York.
Menger, C.
[1871] *Grundsatze der Volkswirtschaftslehre*, Vienna.
Menger, K.
[1936] "Bemerkung zu den Ertragsgesetzen," *Zeitschrift für Nationalökonomie* 325–326, 388–397. Translated as "The Logic and the Laws of Returns, A Study of Meta-Economics," in *Economic Activity Analysis* (O. Morgenstern, ed.), pp. 419–482. Wiley, New York, 1954.
Metzler, L.
[1941] "The Nature and Stability of Inventory Cycles," *Review of Economic Statistics* **23**, 113–129.
Milgram, A. N.
[1939] "Partially Ordered Sets, Separating Systems, and Inductiveness," *Reports of a Mathematical Colloquium* **1**, 18–30. University of Notre Dame, Notre Dame, Indiana.
Mills, E., and Lav, M. A.
[1964] "A Model of Market Areas with Free Entry," *Journal of Political Economy* **72**, 278–288.
Modigliani, F., and Brumberg, R.
[1954] "Utility Analysis and the Consumption Function," in *Post-Keynesian Economics* (K. Kurihara, ed.), pp. 388–436. Rutgers University Press, New Brunswick, New Jersey.
Modigliani, F., and Miller, M. H.
[1958] "The Cost of Capital, Corporation Finance and the Theory of Investment," *American Economic Review* **48**, 261–297.
Montias, J.
[1962] *Planning in Poland.* Yale University Press, New Haven, Connecticut.

Morgan, B. W.
[1967] "Corporate Debt and Stockholder Portfolio Selection," *Yale Economic Essays* **7**, 198–259.

Morishima, M.
[1954] "A Note on a Point in 'Value and Capital,'" *Review of Economic Studies* **21** 214–217.

Mossin, J.
[1968] "Taxation and Risk Taking: An Expected Utility Approach," *Economica* (N.S.) **35**, 74–82.

Muth, R.
[1966] "Household Production and Consumer Demand Functions," *Econometrica* **34**, 699–708.

Nash, J.
[1950] "Equilibrium Points in *n*-Person Games," *Proceedings of the National Academy of Sciences of the USA* **36**, 48–49.
[1953] "Two Person Cooperative Games," *Econometrica* **21**, 128–140.

Noble, S. B.
[1958] "Measures of the Structure of Some Static Linear Economic Models," Serial T-90, the George Washington University Logistics Research Project.

Pareto, V.
[1906] *Manuela di economia politica*. Societa Editrice Libraries, Milan.

Paroush, L.
[1964] "A Note on the C.E.S. Production Function," *Econometrica* **32**, 213–214.

Penner, R. G.
[1964] "A Note on Portfolio Selection and Taxation," *Review of Economic Studies* **31**, 83–86.

Pigou, A. C.
[1920] *The Economics of Welfare*. Macmillan, New York.

Polanyi, K.
[1947] "Our Obsolete Market Mentality," *Commentary* **3**, 109–117.
[1957] "Aristotle Discovers the Economy," in *Trade and Market in the Early Empires* (K. Polanyi, C. M. Arensberg, and H. W. Pearson, eds.), pp. 64–69. Macmillan (Free Press), New York.

Popper, K.
[1959] *The Logic of Scientific Discovery*. Basic Books, New York.

Pratt, J. W.
[1964] "Risk Aversion in the Small and in the Large," *Econometrica* **32**, 122–137.

Rader, T.
[1963a] "On the Existence of a Utility Function to Represent Preferences," *Review of Economic Studies* **30**, 229–232.
[1963b] "Edgeworth Exchange and General Economic Equilibrium," unpublished dissertation, Yale University, New Haven, Connecticut.
[1964] "Edgeworth Exchange and General Economic Equilibrium," *Yale Economic Essays* **4**, 133–180.
[1968] "Normally, Factor Inputs Are Never Gross Substitutes," *Journal of Political Economy* **76**, 38–43.
[]970] "Resource Allocation under Increasing Returns to Scale," *American Economic Review,* **60**, 814–825.

Ramsey, F.
[1950] *The Foundations of Mathematics*. Routledge and Keegan Paul, London.

Rashevsky, N.
[1951] *Mathematical Biology of Social Behavior.* University of Chicago Press, Chicago, Illinois.

Richter, M.
[1966] "Revealed Preference Theory," *Econometrica* **34**, 635–645.

Riesz, F., and Sz-Nagy, B.
[1955] *Functional Analysis.* Ungar, New York.

Robbins, L.
[1935] *An Essay on the Nature and Significance of Economic Science.* Macmillan, New York.

Robinson, E. A. G.
[1935] *Structure of Competitive Industry.* Cambridge University Press, London and New York.

Robinson, J.
[1933] *Economics of Imperfect Competition.* Macmillan, New York.
[1962] *Economic Philosophy.* Doubleday, Garden City, New York.

Saito, M.
[1961] "Professor Debreu on 'Theory of Value': A Review Article," *International Economic Review* **2**, 231–237.

Saks, S.
[1937] *Theory of the Integral.* Hafner, New York.

Samuelson, P.
[1938] "A Note on the Pure Theory of Consumer's Behavior," *Economica* (N.S.) **5**, 61–71, 352–354.
[1939] "Interactions between the Multiplier Analysis and the Principle of Acceleration," *Review of Economic Statistics* **21**, 75–78.
[1947] *Foundations of Economic Analysis.* Harvard University Press, Cambridge, Massachusetts.
[1950] "The Problem of Integrability in Utility Theory," *Economica* (N.S.) **17**, 355–385.
[1965] "Using Full Duality to Show that Simultaneously Additive Direct and Indirect Utilities Implies Unitary Elasticity of Demand," *Econometrica* **4**, 781–796.

Savage, L.
[1954] *The Foundation of Statistics.* Wiley, New York.

Scarf, H.
[1960] "The Optimality of (S, s) Policies, in the Dynamic Inventory Problem," in *Mathematical Methods in the Social Sciences* (K. J. Arrow, S. Karlin, and P. Suppes, eds.), pp. 196–204. Stanford University Press, Stanford, California.

Shackle, G. L. S.
[1949] *Expectations in Economics.* Cambridge University Press, London and New York.

Shannon, C. E.
[1948] "The Mathematical Theory of Communications," *Bell System Technical Journal* **27**, 279–423, 623–656.

Simon, H.
[1957] *Models of Man.* Wiley, New York.

Smithies, A.
[1941] "Optimum Location in Special Competition," *Journal of Political Economy* **49**, 423–439.

Sonnenschein, H.
[1965] "A Study of the Relation between Transitive Preference and the Structure of Choice," *Econometrica* **33**, 642–735.
[1967a] "Demand Theory without the Transitivity Axiom," Mimeographed.
[1967b] "On the Continuity of Demand Functions which Satisfy the Axiom of Revealed Preferences," Mimeographed, University of Minnesota, Minneapolis.

Sono, M.
[1961] "The Effect of Price Changes on the Demand and Supply of Separable Goods," *International Economic Review* **3**, 239–271.

Stigler, G.
[1950] "The Development of Utility Theory," *Journal of Political Economy* **57**, 307–327, 373–396.

Tobin, J.
[1956] "The Interest-Elasticity of Transactions Demand for Cash," *Review of Economics and Statistics* **38**, 241–247.
[1957] "Liquidity Preferences as Behavior toward Risk," *Review of Economic Studies* **40**, 65–86.
[1965] "Theory of Portfolio Selection," in *The Theory of Interest Rates* (F. Hahn and F. Brechling, eds.), pp. 3–51. Macmillan, New York.

Tsiang, S. C.
[1966] "Walras' Law, Say's Law and Liquidity Preferences in General Equilibrium Analysis," *International Economic Review* **7**, 329–345.

Uzawa, H.
[1962] "Production Functions with Constant Elasticities of Substitution," *Review of Economic Studies* **29**, 291–299.

van Moeseke, P.
[1964] "A Duality Theorem of Convex Homogeneous Programming," *Metroeconomica* **16**, 32–40.

Vickrey, W.
[1960] "Utility, Strategy, and Social Decision Rules," *Quarterly Journal of Economics* **79**, 507–535.

Villegas, C.
[1964] "On Qualitative σ Algebras," *Annals of Mathematical Statistics* **35**, 1787–1796.

Viner, J.
[1931] "Cost Curves and Supply Curves," *Zeitschrift für Nationalökonomie* **3**, 23–46.

Vinning, R.
[1949] "Koopmans on the Choice of Variable to be Studied and Methods of Measurement," *Review of Economic Statistics* **31**, 77–94.

von Mises, L.
[1949] *Human Action.* Yale University Press, New Haven, Connecticut.
[1962] *The Ultimate Foundations of Economic Science.* Van Nostrand-Reinhold, Princeton, New Jersey.

von Neumann, J.
[1928] "Zur Theorie der Gesellschaftsspiele," *Mathematische Annalen* **100**, 295–320.
[1937] Über ein Ökonomisches Gleichungs-Systeme und eine Verallgemeinerung der Browershen Fixpunktsatzes," in *Ergebnisse eines Mathematisches Kolloquiums* (K. Menger, ed.), English transl.: "A Model of General Economics Equilibrium," *Review of Economic Studies* **13**, 1–9.

von Neumann, J., and Morgenstern, O.
[1944] *Theory of Games and Economic Behavior*. Princeton University Press, Princeton, New Jersey.

von Stackelberg, H.
[1934] *Marktform und Gleichgewicht*. Springer-Verlag, Berlin.

Wald, A.
[1936] "Über einige Gleichungssysteme der Mathematische Okonomie," *Zeitschrift für Nationalökonomie* **7**, 637–670. Translated as "On Some Systems of Equations of Mathematical Economics," *Econometrica* **19**, 368–403 (1951).

Walras, L.
[1874] *Éléments d'économie politique pure*. Corbaz, Lausanne. Translated as *Elements of Pure Economics*. Irwin, Homewood, Illinois, 1954.

Wicksell, K.
[1934] *Lectures on Political Economy*. Macmillan, New York.

Wilder, R. L.
[1949] *Theory of Manifolds* (Coll. Publ. **32**). American Mathematical Society, Providence, Rhode Island.

Wold, H.
[1943] "A Synthesis of Pure Demand Analysis," *Scandinavisk Aktuarietidskrift* **26**, 85–118, 200–263.
[1944] "A Synthesis of Pure Demand Analysis," *Scandinavisk Aktuarietidskrift* **27**, 69–120.

Yaari, M.
[1965] "Convexity in the Theory of Choice under Risk," *Quarterly Journal of Economics* **79**, 278–290.

Author Index

Numbers in italics refer to the pages on which the complete references are listed.

Subject Index